THE HOLOCAUST AND AUSTRALIA

T0320451

PERSPECTIVES ON THE HOLOCAUST

A series of books designed to help students further their understanding of key topics within the field of Holocaust studies.

Published:

HOLOCAUST REPRESENTATIONS IN HISTORY (2ND EDITION),
Daniel H. Magilow and Lisa Silverman

POSTWAR GERMANY AND THE HOLOCAUST,
Caroline Sharples

ANTI-SEMITISM AND THE HOLOCAUST,
Beth A. Griech-Polelle

THE HOLOCAUST IN EASTERN EUROPE,
Waitman Wade Beorn

THE UNITED STATES AND THE NAZI HOLOCAUST,
Barry Trachtenberg

WITNESSING THE HOLOCAUST,
Judith M. Hughes

HITLER'S 'MEIN KAMPF' AND THE HOLOCAUST: A PRELUDE TO GENOCIDE,
John J. Michalczyk, Michael S. Bryant and Susan A. Michalczyk (eds.)

THE HOLOCAUST AND AUSTRALIA: REFUGEES, REJECTION, AND MEMORY,
Paul R. Bartrop

Forthcoming:

SITES OF HOLOCAUST MEMORY,
Janet Ward

THE PERPETRATORS OF THE HOLOCAUST: THE FOLLY OF THE THIRD REICH,
Nathan Stoltzfus

THE HOLOCAUST AND AUSTRALIA

REFUGEES, REJECTION, AND MEMORY

Paul R. Bartrop

BLOOMSBURY ACADEMIC
LONDON · NEW YORK · OXFORD · NEW DELHI · SYDNEY

BLOOMSBURY ACADEMIC
Bloomsbury Publishing Plc
50 Bedford Square, London, WC1B 3DP, UK
1385 Broadway, New York, NY 10018, USA
29 Earlsfort Terrace, Dublin 2, Ireland

BLOOMSBURY, BLOOMSBURY ACADEMIC and the Diana logo are
trademarks of Bloomsbury Publishing Plc

First published in Great Britain 2022

Series design by Jesse Holborn/Design Holborn
Cover image: AU 4362. Holocaust memorial. Jewish sectors, Melbourne General Cemetery.
Melbourne, Victoria, Australia © Jono David/Chayim HaYehudim Jewish Photo Library

A catalogue record for this book is available from the British Library.

A catalog record for this book is available from the Library of Congress.

ISBN: HB: 978-1-3501-8514-2
         PB: 978-1-3501-8513-5
         ePDF: 978-1-3501-8515-9
         eBook: 978-1-3501-8516-6

Typeset by Integra Software Services Pvt. Ltd.

To find out more about our authors and books visit www.bloomsbury.com
and sign up for our newsletters.

For Eve, again

You must remember this…

CONTENTS

ACKNOWLEDGEMENTS

This book, in one form or another, has been worked on for the better part of three decades. Over the course of this time, I received invaluable assistance from a wide range of people and institutions, to whom I should like to express my gratitude.

Within Australia, I wish to acknowledge the unerring assistance of the Reference and Guidance staff at the National Archives of Australia in Canberra and Melbourne. Across many years and countless visits, they helped to develop my familiarity with the intricacies of archive storage and retrieval, and their many suggestions frequently enabled me to strike out in new directions at times when other options were drying up. Archivists at the Australian Jewish Historical Society in Sydney; the staff of the Manuscripts Library; National Library of Australia, Canberra; and officers of the Australian Jewish Welfare Society, Sydney, all provided me with help and, where necessary, permission to research archival materials held by their respective organizations.

In the UK, I was the grateful recipient of assistance from the then Executive Director of the Board of Deputies of British Jews, David Massel, who authorized me to view Board papers covering the 1930s. The staff of the Search Department of The National Archives in Kew took me through the subtleties of the system with patience and good humour, as did the reference staff at the Imperial War Museum.

As this project has developed, I have been fortunate in receiving encouragement and support from several people at what was my home institution for many years, Florida Gulf Coast University (FGCU). The opportunities presented for me to develop and extend my thoughts about a broad range of issues germane to this book have been many, and as Director of the Center for Holocaust and Genocide Research I received ongoing support from President Michael V. Martin throughout the difficult years of the COVID-19 pandemic. The Library staff at FGCU, in particular the History subject librarian, Rachel Tait, assisted in numerous ways throughout the project and deserve my deep respect and gratitude. And in New Jersey, my dear friend from Stockton University, Mike Dickerman, was steadfast in his encouragement. There is not a word in this book he did not read, often at my urgent insistence, and it is immensely richer for his input.

Finally, I must – as always – give an appropriate salute to Eve, my muse, sounding board, critic and advocate. Without her belief in the merits of the project, it would never have seen the light of day, and it is to Eve I dedicate this book. Truly it has been written, 'She brings him good, not harm, all the days of her life' (Proverbs, 31:12).

ABBREVIATIONS

AJHS	*Australian Jewish Historical Society, Sydney*
AJWS	*Australian Jewish Welfare Society, Sydney*
CPD	*Commonwealth Parliamentary Debates (Hansard)*
H. of R.	*House of Representatives*
IWM	*Imperial War Museum, London*
NAA	*National Archives of Australia, Canberra and Melbourne*
NLA	*National Library of Australia, Canberra*
TNA	*The National Archives, London*
TSA	*Tasmanian State Archives, Hobart*
VIREC	*Victorian International Refugee Emergency Council*
VRIAC	*Victorian Refugee Immigrational Appeals Committee*

DRAMATIS PERSONAE

Stanley Melbourne Bruce was the Nationalist Prime Minister of Australia from 1923 to 1929. Born in Melbourne on 15 April 1883, he studied at Cambridge University. During the First World War he served at Gallipoli and France and returned to Australia after having been wounded in 1917. He was elected to Parliament in 1918 and appointed Treasurer in 1921 before becoming Prime Minister in 1923, in which position he remained until 1929. As Prime Minister, Bruce upheld the White Australia policy and preferred migrants from Britain and the Dominions, restricting immigration from other countries. In September 1933 he was appointed as Australia's High Commissioner to the UK by Prime Minister Joseph Lyons. He served with distinction as Australia's senior overseas representative, often taking considerable initiative without awaiting instructions from Canberra. He retained his position during the subsequent governments of Robert Menzies, John Curtin and Ben Chifley before retiring as High Commissioner in 1945. Bruce later became chairman of the Food and Agriculture Organization, a position he held between 1946 and 1951. He was elevated to the peerage as Viscount Bruce of Melbourne in 1947 by British Prime Minister Clement Attlee. He died on 25 August 1967, aged eighty-four.

Arthur Augustus Calwell was an Australian politician who served as the leader of the Labor Party from 1960 to 1967. He was born in Melbourne on 28 August 1896 and after leaving school began his working life as a clerk with the Victorian government. He entered Federal politics in 1940 and in 1943 was promoted to Cabinet as Minister for Information in the government of John Curtin. In 1945 he became Australia's first Minister for Immigration. He designed and oversaw Australia's post-war immigration scheme, promoted under the heading 'populate or perish'. This benefited large numbers of European refugees. In July 1947 he signed an agreement with the International Refugee Organisation to accept displaced persons from Europe, even while remaining a staunch advocate of the White Australia Policy. In 1951 Calwell was elected deputy leader of the Labor Party, and then leader in 1960. In 1966 he survived an assassination attempt, but after the 1972 general election, won by Calwell's successor as Labor leader, Gough Whitlam, he retired from Parliament. On 8 July 1973 he died in Melbourne.

Joseph Aloysius Carrodus was the Permanent Head of the Department of the Interior between 1935 and 1949. Born in Melbourne in 1885, he attended St. Patrick's College, East Melbourne, where he matriculated into the University of Melbourne with honours. He entered the Commonwealth public service in 1904. During the First World War he served with the Australian Army, rising from private to captain by April 1917. He represented Australia's New Guinea territory before the Permanent Mandates Commission in Geneva in 1926 and was later Acting Administrator of the Northern

Territory in 1934 before appointment as Secretary to the Department of the Interior on 25 November 1935. He was appointed Commander of the British Empire (CBE) in 1939. He retired as Secretary of the Department of the Interior on 1 May 1949. At the age of sixty-four he was then appointed Director of Civil Defence for the Commonwealth, where he stayed through to 1950. He died on 8 April 1961 in Canberra.

Joseph Silver (Joe) Collings was an Australian Labor Party politician. He was born in Brighton, England, on 11 May 1865. When aged eighteen he and his parents migrated to Brisbane, where he became a trade union organizer. In 1910 he was elected to local council, and in 1913 was elected to the Queensland central executive of the Labor Party. He served in this role until 1928. He was appointed to Queensland's upper house, the Legislative Council, in 1920 and took part in the successful vote to abolish it in 1922. Collings was elected to Australian Senate in 1931 and became Leader of the Opposition in 1935. In October 1941 he became Senate Leader of the Government in the Senate with the coming to power of the Curtin government in October 1941. At the same time, he became Minister for the Interior, a position he held until July 1945. He retired from the Senate in June 1950 at the age of eighty-five – the oldest person to have served in the Senate. Joe Collings died at home in Brisbane on 20 June 1955.

John Curtin was an Australian Labor Party politician who was Prime Minister of Australia between 1941 and his death in office in 1945. He was the leader of the Party between 1935 and 1945, and Prime Minister through most of the Second World War. Born in Creswick, Victoria on 8 January 1885, he left school aged thirteen and became involved in the trade union movement in Melbourne. He joined the Labor Party and became heavily involved with the Timberworkers' Union. He was opposed to overseas conscription during the First World War and was briefly jailed for his views. Moving to Perth, he became a journalist. He was elected to Federal Parliament in 1928, lost his seat in 1931, and won it back in 1934. In 1935 he was elected Party leader. By October 1941 he was Prime Minister. During the Second World War Curtin turned Australia away from reliance on Britain for its defence in favour of the United States. In home affairs during the war, Curtin proposed several measures founded on social justice grounds; these were implemented after his death by his successor, Joseph Benedict (Ben) Chifley. John Curtin died in office at The Lodge, the Prime Minister's residence in Canberra, on 5 July 1945.

Thomas Hugh (Tom) Garrett was Assistant Secretary of the Department of the Interior from 1938. A Tasmanian born in Dalton-in-Furness, Lancashire, England, in 1890, he joined the Commonwealth public service in 1905 and worked with the Department of Trade and Customs, the Development and Migration Commission, and the Department of Markets and Transport before joining Interior in 1932. In 1936 he was promoted to Chief Clerk; in 1938, to Assistant Secretary. As immediate superior to Albert Peters, and as the Acting Head of the Department whenever Joseph Carrodus was absent, Garrett often found himself delegating authority and suggesting ideas in both directions. He died on 23 June 1943 in Canberra.

Hattil Spencer (Harry) Foll was a United Australia Party politician who served as a Senator for Queensland between 1917 and 1947. He was born in London on 30 May 1890 and moved to Australia in 1909, settling in Queensland. Upon the outbreak of the

First World War in 1914, he enlisted in Australian Army and was among those who landed at Gallipoli on 25 April 1915. Wounded twice, he received a medical discharge in February 1916 and returned to Australia. In May 1917 he was elected to the Senate at the age of twenty-seven. He would remain a Senator for the next thirty years before standing down in 1947. As a member of Cabinet, Foll's portfolios included Repatriation (1937–1939), Health (1938–1939) and Interior (1939–1941). During the latter period he was a member of the War Cabinet (1939–1941) and in 1940 he became Minister for Information until the government changed hands in 1941. In 1942 he enlisted as a captain in the Volunteer Defence Corps. In 1957 he retired to Port Macquarie (NSW) and died there on 7 July 1977 at the age of eighty-seven.

Julian Layton (*ne* Loewenstein) was born in London in 1904 to German Jewish parents who had migrated to England from Frankfurt in 1893. In the early 1930s he worked as a stockbroker, but in 1934 helped in the migration process for German and Austrian Jews seeking to move to the British colonies. During the 1930s he visited Australia trying to persuade the Australian government to accept more German Jewish refugees. With the outbreak of war, he worked assisting German Jewish refugees staying at the Kitchener transmigration camp. When many were interned in 1940 on the Isle of Man, Layton continued his help. After the journey of the transport ship *Dunera* to Australia in 1940, Layton was sent to Australia as a Home Office Liaison Officer to oversee the process of compensation and repatriation. He arrived in early 1941 and was successful in obtaining the release of hundreds of men. To assist those who did not obtain release, Layton remained in Australia until January 1945. Awarded an OBE for services to the Jewish community, he died in London in July 1989.

Joseph Aloysius Lyons was an Australian politician who served as United Australia Party Prime Minister between 1932 and his death in office in 1939. He was born on 15 September 1879 in Stanley, Tasmania, and became a schoolteacher. Initially a member of the Australian Labor Party, he was Premier of Tasmania from 1923 to 1928 before entering Federal politics and immediately becoming a Cabinet Minister in the government of Prime Minister James Scullin in 1929. In 1931 he defected from the Labor Party before being instrumental in the formation of the United Australia Party, which he led into government. As Prime Minister, Lyons showed interest in foreign relations. Prior to the Second World War his government pursued twin policies of appeasement and rearmament, liaising closely with the UK government throughout the 1930s. On 7 April 1939 Lyons died a heart attack. He was the first Australian Prime Minister to die in office. Several years after his death, his widow, Enid (later Dame Enid) Lyons, became the first woman elected to the Federal House of Representatives.

John McEwen was an Australian Country Party politician who served as Prime Minister between 19 December 1967 and 10 January 1968 in a caretaker capacity after the disappearance of his Liberal Party colleague, Harold Holt. He was the leader of the Country Party from 1958 to 1971. McEwen was born in Chiltern, Victoria on 29 March 1900. At the age of eighteen he joined the Australian Army, but the First World War ended prior to his deployment. He was elected to Federal Parliament in 1934 and was appointed Minister for the Interior in 1937, where he remained until the coalition government broke down in April 1939. He later served as Minister for External Affairs, Minister for Air and Minister for Civil Aviation. He became deputy leader of the Country Party in 1940, and leader in 1958. From 1949 onwards he oversaw Australia's economic development, becoming Minister for Commerce and Agriculture and then Minister for Trade. In December 1967, after Prime Minister Harold Holt disappeared, presumed dead, McEwen was appointed caretaker Prime Minister for twenty-three days. McEwen was awarded the Companion of Honour in 1969. He retired from politics in 1971 and was knighted the same year, prior to returning to farming. John McEwen died on 20 November 1980.

Robert Gordon Menzies was a United Australia Party politician (and later, founder of the Liberal Party of Australia), who served as Prime Minister for two terms (1939–1941 and 1949–1966). Born in Jeparit, Victoria on 20 December 1894, he studied law at the University of Melbourne and was Deputy Premier of Victoria (1932–1934) before switching to Federal politics where he became Attorney-General and Minister for Industry in the Lyons ministry. As early as 1933 he condemned Nazi antisemitism and in August 1938 spent several weeks on an official visit to Nazi Germany. He was lukewarm in his opposition to the Hitler regime and was a strong supporter of Britain's appeasement policy. In April 1939 he became Prime Minister upon Lyons's death, serving in that role until August 1941. He reformed conservative politics into the Liberal Party and was re-elected to office in 1949. He retained the Prime Ministership until retiring in 1966 as the longest-serving politician in that role. Among many achievements, his second term in office upheld and extended the post-war immigration scheme that had been initiated by Labor's Arthur Calwell. He was knighted by Queen Elizabeth II in 1963, The father of Australian conservative politics, Menzies died from a heart attack at his home in Melbourne on 15 May 1978.

Albert George Ogilvie was the Australian Labor Party Premier of the Australian state of Tasmania between 1934 and 1939, and a rescuer of Jews from Nazi Germany prior to the Second World War. Born in Hobart on 16 March 1890, he was educated at one of Australia's prestigious Catholic colleges, St. Patrick's (Ballarat, Victoria), and the University of Tasmania, where he graduated in law. Ogilvie was elected to the Tasmanian Parliament in 1919; in 1928 he became leader of the Labor Party, and Premier in 1934. In 1935 he took a trip to Europe and upon his return to Australia was driven to help Jews who applied to his state for refuge – even though, as a state Premier, he had no say over immigration policy. All his government was able to do was forward requests to the Department of the Interior in Canberra. Given this, there were times when Ogilvie found himself affronted by the Federal government's dismissive attitude. He often interceded regarding the progress of refugee applications, requesting that Jewish refugees be allowed entry to his island home. On 10 June 1939, while still in office, Ogilvie collapsed and died of a heart attack in Melbourne.

Thomas Paterson was an Australian Country Party politician who served as deputy leader of the Party between 1929 and 1937. He was born on 20 November 1882 in Aston, near Birmingham, England. In November 1908 he left for Australia with his wife and extended family, settling on a farm in central Victoria. He joined the Victorian Farmers'

Union in 1916, became its president in March 1922, and was instrumental in the process leading to the establishment of its political arm, the Country Party, in November 1922. At the 1922 elections he won the Federal seat of Gippsland. In the government of Stanley Bruce, he was Minister for Markets and Migration (1926–1928), Minister for Markets (1928) and Minister for Markets and Transport (1928–1929). He was deputy leader of the Country Party from 1929 to 1937 and acting leader for several months in 1933 when the leader, Sir Earle Page, stood aside following the death of his son. He served as Minister for the Interior between 1934 and 1937. Thomas Paterson died in Melbourne on 24 January 1952.

Albert Robert Peters, for most of the 1920s and through to 1945, was the officer in charge of the Immigration Branch within the Department of the Interior. Born into a large family of eighteen children to German immigrant parents on 23 October 1882 in Toowoomba, Queensland, he joined the Queensland public service in 1899 starting his working life with the Customs Department. While there he began working on immigration matters, during which he contributed to Queensland's draft of what became the White Australia policy after Federation. He remained with the State Service until he transferred to the Commonwealth in 1912. He joined the Department of External Affairs, which then had responsibility for immigration; he soon rose to become head of the Immigration Branch and moved to Canberra in 1927 when Australia's capital shifted there from Melbourne. He became Assistant Secretary of the new Department of Immigration in 1945, and then its acting Secretary until his retirement in 1946. He then moved back to Melbourne until, late in life after the death of his wife, he moved to Sydney to be with his daughter and her family. He died in 1969.

Alfred Stirling was an Australian diplomat. Born on 8 September 1902, he graduated from the University of Melbourne and won a scholarship to undertake a second degree at Oxford University. Sent to London by the Department of External Affairs in 1937, he was appointed as Australia's liaison officer to the UK, based at Australia House. Returning to Australia, Stirling worked in Canberra at the Department of External Affairs through the war years. In 1941 he was honoured with the award of Officer of the Order of the British Empire (OBE). In 1945–1946 he was Australian High Commissioner to Canada, before becoming Minister resident in Washington, DC (1947–1948). In 1948 he was High Commissioner to South Africa, before serving as Australian Ambassador to the Netherlands (1950–1955). In 1953 he received a second honour as Commander of the Order of the British Empire (CBE). He was Ambassador to France (1955–1959), the Philippines (1959–1962), Italy (1962–1967) and Greece (1964–1965). He retired in 1967 and died on 3 July 1981 in East Melbourne.

Victor Thompson (born Charles Victor Thompson) was an Australian Country Party politician. Born on 10 September 1885 in Sydney, he was educated in local schools before becoming a journalist. Instrumental in the Northern New State secessionist movement in New South Wales from 1919, focusing on the New England region, Thompson worked closely with Dr Earle Page, founder of the Country Party, and was rewarded in December 1922 by election to Parliament as the Member for New England. Serving on several Parliamentary committees, between 1934 and 1937 he was Country Party

Whip and Parliamentary Secretary. From 1937 to 1940 he was Assistant Minister to the Treasurer and the Ministers for Repatriation, Commerce and the Interior; in this latter capacity he was responsible for much of the work relating to Jewish refugee migration. In the September 1940 election he lost his seat to another member of the Country Party, Joseph Palmer (Joe) Abbott. Thompson died at Ashfield, Sydney, on 11 May 1968.

Thomas Walter White was a United Australia Party politician and Cabinet Minister. Born on 26 April 1888 in Melbourne, during the First World War he saw service as a founding member of the Australian Flying Corps (AFC), was captured by the Turks in November 1915 and escaped in July 1918. In 1920 he married Vera Deakin, the daughter of Australia's second Prime Minister, Alfred Deakin. He entered politics in 1929 as the Member for Balaclava in Victoria. In January 1933 he was appointed Minister for Trade and Customs by Prime Minister Joseph Lyons, a position he held until 1938. In July of that year, he represented Australia at the Evian Conference in France. Soon after the outbreak of the Second World War White took leave from Parliament and joined the Royal Australian Air Force, seeing service in Australia and Britain. In October 1944 he was instrumental in helping to form the Liberal Party with Robert Menzies, and between 1949 and 1951 served as Minister for Air and Minister for Civil Aviation. On 21 June 1951, he resigned from Parliament to become Australian High Commissioner to the UK, a position he held until 1956. White was knighted in January 1952. On 13 October 1957 he died of a heart attack at his home in Melbourne.

INTRODUCTION

In 1973 the Labor government of Australian Prime Minister Gough Whitlam initiated and adopted a non-discriminatory immigration policy that ended the White Australia policy which, across the century, had given preference to western and northern Europeans over peoples from elsewhere. This new approach was enhanced further between 1975 and 1983 under Malcolm Fraser's conservative Liberal-National coalition government, where the plight of refugees – in particular, the so-called boat people from Vietnam – saw Australia responding sympathetically to what was a major humanitarian crisis. The government introduced a refugee policy with quality resettlement programmes and services, such that by the time Fraser left office in 1983 the Australian Department of Immigration's budget was four times larger than it had been in 1975–1976. Nearly 80,000 Indochinese refugees were resettled, with another 80,000 arriving later via orderly immigration channels established by Fraser's government.

Malcolm Fraser, born in 1930, was certainly a socially aware young man by the time the Second World War ended. In government, there were rumours that as an adult he was so touched by revelations about the Holocaust and the world's relative failure to stop it that once in a position of high authority he sought to open Australia's refugee channels to all who needed sanctuary. Fraser's thinking about the impact of the Holocaust has never been verified. Well over twenty years ago I wrote to his office seeking to discuss the matter with him, in the hope that I could put the rumour to rest. As at the time of his death in March 2015, I was still awaiting a reply.

These rumours suggest that the Holocaust played a part in shaping at least this aspect of Australian history. Although Australia was neither a European combatant nor a country occupied by Germany during the period of the Third Reich, it nonetheless shared with other countries a role in the destruction of the European Jews, almost exclusively in its response to the pleas of those seeking desperately to leave during the period prior to the outbreak of war.

Before the Second World War Australia's policy towards refugees was, to all intents and purposes, haphazard and made up as circumstances dictated. The study of refugee migration to Australia has almost always commenced with the post–Second World War period. If Australia did not have an established refugee policy operating prior to the Second World War, why not? After all, the first third of the twentieth century had seen events in Europe and elsewhere which forced a refugee problem on the world the likes of which had never been seen before. Inescapable questions emerge: were the Australians attuned to developments overseas? Did they only wish to take in selected nationalities? Did preservation of the British character of Australian society matter so much that there were fears of racial or ethnic contamination if other peoples were allowed into the country?

Once it seemed as if Jews from Germany might seek to escape Nazi persecution the nucleus of a refugee immigration policy was developed hurriedly by the conservative United Australia Party government and the officials of the Department of the Interior controlling immigration. They were convinced that care would have to be taken to ensure that no significant number of Jews arrived in Australia. From June 1933, when that position became policy, until the end of the struggle against Nazism twelve years later, the responsible authorities held fast to that goal. It seemed always to be in the back of the bureaucrats' minds, guiding their every step as tens of thousands of refugee Jews in Germany, Austria, Czechoslovakia and other parts of Europe pleaded for admission to the Commonwealth. This book is an examination of why the government of Australia adopted such a stance, how the officials in the Department of the Interior put it into practice and what the response of the Australian public was to that policy.

It will be argued that the government and the popular will coalesced to produce an unsympathetic and anti-refugee Australia. The government was certainly informed as to the issues involved, and yet it consistently searched for ways to ensure that refugees could be kept out. The policy was one which almost always sought to fall on the side of exclusion rather than acceptance. Why should this have been so? Australia was a liberal-democratic nation founded on immigration, which prided itself on its high level of perceived tolerance and carried a strong image as a progressive, humanitarian and caring community.

Earlier work on this topic has generated many questions still requiring answers. Why did the Australians see the issues only in racial terms? Why did the officials in the Department of the Interior seem to wield so much authority in the development and execution of government policy? Where were the political leaders in all this, and should they be exonerated of responsibility? If Australia was an environment in which Jews could feel safe, why did the Anglo-Jewish establishment so fear the prospect of antisemitism? Did the post-war immigration boom – in which Jewish survivors of the Holocaust featured in the calculations of policy-makers – have any relationship to the policies of the previous twelve years? And what of the decades that followed? Why did Australian governments decide in the late 1980s to pursue Nazi war criminals in the country's very midst, and did that have any relationship to earlier events? Finally, could it be argued that Australia was somehow involved in the fate of the Jews?

Clearly, Australia was not responsible for the Nazi genocide of the Jews. Absolutely not. The Holocaust was from first to last a German project, with mass murder conducted by the National Socialist government of Germany assisted in the enterprise by its collaborators in occupied and allied countries.

Australia was not murderous, but it had a role to play. Of course, no-one before the war could anticipate what would happen during it, but Australians were kept informed of developments in Germany. Despite possessing this knowledge, they instituted policies that deliberately sought to exclude Germany's Jewish victims from entering, in violation of existing standards and criteria for admission. Why did the Australians adopt such a position? This work probes four main ideas, which can be listed under the broad headings of traditional prejudices, economic concern, anti-foreign xenophobia and antisemitism.

First, Australia at the outset of the period carried prejudices towards foreigners that had been formed according to racial criteria. In the nineteenth century, Chinese, Pacific Islanders and Indians had all been the subject of special legislation or anti-foreign agitation, and this antipathy was projected onto selected European nationalities, particularly southern Europeans, after the Great War. The second reason for rejection of Jewish refugees related to the economy. During the Depression decade of the 1930s, there was opposition from both the labour movement and middle-class Australia to the migration of immigrants from non-British backgrounds – the labour movement on the ground that refugees would allow themselves to be exploited, lowering living and industrial standards; middle-class opposition relating to a fear that wherever employment possibilities existed, ordinary Australians would be crowded out of the workplace if immigrants arrived and began competing with those already in the country.

Interwoven with these fears was the third motif running through the Australian rejection of refugees: an intolerance of 'foreign' (i.e. non-British) immigrants. It is probably in the nature of immigrant reception and integration that recent arrivals are those most likely to bear the brunt of local animosities and prejudices. Australians, with a relatively short history of foreign migration by the 1930s, saw every new arrival as an object of suspicion, and the fears which usually emerge from this were often quick to surface. An anti-foreigner stance played a huge role in the rejection of Jews from Germany, Austria and Czechoslovakia before, and indeed, during, the Second World War.

Finally, the question of antisemitism must be examined: it is an issue which should not be considered lightly. The ironic aspect of this, however, is that in the 1930s Australia did not have an antisemitic tradition in the same sense as did the countries of Europe or the Americas. There are those who have seen any manifestation of antisemitism in Australia as pointing to the existence of an antisemitic society, but Australia had not been such a society up to this time. That the Nazi period saw an anti-alien and anti-immigrant stance adopted, moreover, should not automatically imply that the Australian people had become antisemites overnight. That the foreigners of the 1930s and early 1940s were Jewish as well as foreign placed them in double jeopardy, but the overwhelming conclusion to be drawn from the evidence is that the Australians rejected them in the first instance because they were foreign: their Jewishness, at least until late 1938, was employed to reinforce the rejection, not to establish it. After then the issue became clouded by fears of Jewish migration on a much larger scale, and activities were directed towards denying Jews any possibility of entry because of their Jewishness alone.

If we are to approach an understanding of the motives behind the policymakers, it is important that we identify the nature and impact of several key relationships. These include the interrelationship between public opinion and the government; connections between the immigration authorities and other government agencies; interaction between Ministers and the bureaucracy and between the bureaucrats and the public. It is necessary to look at the relationship between the Jews and everyone else, and between Australia and the outside world. What were these relationships? How extensive were they, and how far did they influence policy formation or execution? How far can it be said that these relationships acted to the detriment or benefit of the Jewish refugees? None of these questions is easy to answer, and for that reason this book is broad in its scope: it aims to clarify the social, political and international pressures acting upon and within the Australian government in establishing and executing its refugee policy.

Two main themes stand out. For Australia, the whole refugee issue in the 1930s and 1940s was a major inconvenience imposing upon the nation a jolting period of reassessment regarding its place in the world and its responsibilities towards other human beings in need of help. The second theme springs from the first: a large measure of indifference to the fate of persecuted people in Europe characterized both government policy and majority perceptions for most of the period in question. Refugees were always looked upon as alien immigrants and judged on that basis rather than on the urgency of their situation. The government's policy fluctuated throughout the period 1933–1945 and was certainly far from consistent when deciding who was desirable and who was not: but on the whole Australian governments exhibited an ongoing opposition to the entry of Jewish refugees. The conservative governments of Joseph Lyons and Robert Menzies had an ideological commitment to favouring the immigration of British settlers; the bureaucrats objected to an immigration policy being thrust onto them by circumstances over which they had no control; large sections of the Australian public had concerns surrounding labour displacement and racial blending. There were few in Australia in the 1930s and 1940s who thought positively about refugee immigration. Moreover, while there were many who felt that the Nazi persecution of the Jews was abhorrent and evil, an oft-repeated opinion was that it should be the responsibility of other countries to find a solution.

The twin motifs of indifference and inconvenience combined to make the practical realization of any alternatives unimaginable. To suggest that Australia could have done more because the Nazis' plans to murder all Jews were obvious is fallacious. They were *not* obvious, at least, not in the final form they took. The Australian record must be judged in its time-and-place context, and according to the standards of the day. This approach is not only correct historical method but is also common sense.

While the events of the war years could not be foreseen, this book dispels several misunderstandings about the Australian position, and brings to light additional aspects exposing hostility towards Jews during the period between 1933 and 1945. These include, but are not restricted to, the following: that in August 1938 it was determined that 90 per cent of all applications coming from German Jews without guarantors in Australia, but who met every standard for admission, were rejected by the authorities on 'racial' grounds; that the bureaucracy adopted a threefold categorization, taken directly from the Nazis, of Aryan, non-Aryan and 'non-Aryan Christian'; that existing schemes by which Jews could enter before 1 December 1938 allowed for a potential yearly maximum of 5,100, but that this was reduced by a political sleight of hand authorizing the admission of 15,000 refugees – Jews and non-Jews – over the next three years, divided into 4,000 for Jews and 1,000 for non-Jews per annum; that the figure of 1,000 non-Jews was dispensed with early in 1939 and declared open-ended, while the quota for Jews remained fixed; that Sir Thomas White, at the Evian Conference in July 1938, most definitely did not declare that Australia would accept 15,000 Jewish refugees; that despite assertions to the contrary, Australia accepted immigrants from European countries during the war years, provided they were not Jewish; that a clause was introduced into Australian immigration application forms in 1939 demanding all aspiring immigrants to declare whether they were 'of the Jewish race'; and that restrictive policies regarding Jews from Germany and Austria mutated incrementally into policies covering all Jews from everywhere – with the acceptance of Jews from Britain left at the discretion of the Minister for the Interior.

The Australian record was more welcoming of Jews than some other countries at the same time, but arguments suggesting that this should count positively in the Commonwealth's favour should be weighed against both the standards of the day and the assumptions upon which those standards were based. In this sense, relativity must not enter the equation, if only because the Australians knew what they were doing, knew why they were doing it, and were not measuring themselves against any other countries. How Australia stacked up against the rest of the world is to some extent a red herring; as this book shows, it is only by examining the Australian record within its own context that we may truly gauge its worth. The material contained in this volume demonstrates how that record leaves a great deal to be desired – not for what the Australians failed to do, but for what they said they were doing and how this did not match up with their actual behaviour.

Several years ago, working in the National Archives of Australian in Canberra researching letters sent to the Australian government from Jews threatened by the Nazis, the files disclosed a letter dated 24 November 1938, written soon after *Kristallnacht*. This was one of the saddest – even most pathetic – I ever encountered in the files. It was written by a Jewish widow then living in Danzig and addressed to Australian Prime Minister Joseph Lyons. Frau Henriette Tzarlinsky had earlier seen Lyons's name in Danzig's Jewish newspaper after he, along with many other world leaders, had sent out greetings in advance of the Jewish High Holy Days. Reading this, Frau Tzarlinsky wrote that 'the mention of your honourable name attracted my attention'. She informed the Prime Minister that 'I myself was born a "Lyon"', which was the family name of her late father, David. She continued that 'we had a relative in our family whose name was Joseph Lyon who is said to have gone abroad many years ago. Is it perhaps possible that we are related?' If this was the case, she begged the Prime Minister to 'claim my son'.

The heartrending aspect of the letter lay in the desperation that would lead this woman to 'offer' her only son to the Australian Prime Minister in the pitiable hope that he might claim some sort of family connection that could save the young man's life. It is a clear indication of how desperate this woman was for her son to be safe. Unfortunately for Frau Tzarlinsky, there was to be no happy ending in Australia. The last item in the file, after her letter, was marked simply 'No action'.

CHAPTER 1
AUSTRALIANS, JEWS AND A HOSTILE WORLD

An insular Australia

The month of July 1931 found the noted Australian artist and writer Norman Lindsay in a state of exasperation. Despite his fame as an acclaimed author-illustrator of classic children's books such as the *The Magic Pudding* and the creator of key recruiting posters during the First World War, his most recent novel, *Redheap*, had been banned as an affront to Australian values. Based in a small country town in Victoria, it was a critique of the social restrictions of the day, exposing narrow-mindedness then characteristic in much of Australian society. *Redheap*, the first locally written novel to be banned by the Australian censors, would remain proscribed for the next twenty-eight years.

In response, Lindsay decided to turn his back on the stifling culture that allowed this to happen, abandoning temporarily the country of his birth and which he loved. Prior to his departure for New Zealand, he said that 'minor officials' were making 'an organized effort to stamp out culture' and that 'the Australian mind could not make the effort necessary to fight them, nor could it make the effort to care'.[1] His parting shot was that 'the inertia of the Australian mind was such that it did not care' what would happen in the future.[2] Lindsay's departure was a lucid and damning indictment of Australian intolerance.

Australians in the 1930s were largely complacent and insular people, proud of their British heritage, disdainful of other cultures, rejoicing in their status equality, 'a strong sense of egalitarianism, and, on the whole, anti-intellectual'. It was a 'lucky, unsophisticated, [and] backward'.[3]

This attitude was exemplified in the Australian passion for physical pursuits, from construction to farming, to football, racing and cricket. Public education lagged in relation to other countries, with compulsory schooling only required to primary level. State secondary schools were few, and student numbers were small: 'In 1938, out of every hundred children in Australia who were aged from 15 to 16, only twenty-five attended school, and of every hundred 17-year-olds, only seven still received full time education.'[4] Public libraries did not provide much by way of compensation. Indeed, 'the free public library was almost non-existent', with, for example, 'only two municipal libraries in the whole of New South Wales'.[5]

One reality prevailed, however: the country was a long, long way from its cultural roots. This was a world in which the five (or more) weeks it took to travel from Australia to Britain by ship meant that nation-building of necessity had to take place within Australia and according to local values and priorities. Communications were slow; it was only in 1907 that a telephone service opened between Melbourne (then the capital city) and Sydney, and when Prime Minister James Scullin spoke on the telephone to British Prime Minister Ramsay MacDonald in London on 30 April 1930 the event was hailed around the world for the modern-day marvel it was. Journeys between Australia's major cities took place by train rather than air, though passengers travelling from Melbourne to Sydney had to change at Albury owing to different rail gauges. Personal communications took place via letters that could take up to a week to reach their destination – but this could be mitigated by two daily mail deliveries and one on Saturday morning in the cities.

Awareness of events was for the most part disseminated through the newspaper press, and papers proliferated in cities and towns. Wireless radio allowed homes to hear latest developments, plays and music. In March 1932 the conservative United Australia Party government of Joseph Lyons established the Australian Broadcasting Commission as a Federal operation, while commercial stations also grew throughout the decade.

Above all, Australia was complacent, satisfied with social continuities, and wary of both change and alien intrusion. This was played out in Australian attitudes towards the outside world no less than domestically. As one historian has noted, 'Apathy towards, and ignorance about, foreign events, prevented Australians from understanding the full significance of many of the crises between 1935 and 1939',[6] and that 'few Australians would have any detailed information on the background to the European situation'. Nor, he suggests, 'would they have had any incentive to learn of it'.[7]

Jews in Australia

Australian Jews in the 1930s were not generally regarded as aliens or foreigners. In large part this can be traced to the history of Australian Jewish settlement dating back to the nation's foundation in 1788, when between eight and fourteen Jewish convicts arrived aboard the First Fleet. Convict settlement in New South Wales, Tasmania, Queensland and Western Australia was solely responsible for an initial Jewish presence, while in the free colonies of Victoria and South Australia Jews were present almost from the beginning.

Although small, the various Jewish communities found life in the Australian colonies congenial enough to take up permanent residence and establish solid congregations. The first of these was established in Sydney in 1832 and was followed by Melbourne in 1841 and the other major cities over the next sixty years. Other synagogues were also established in the regional centres as well as in city suburbs.[8]

Apart from religion, Jews passed in colonial society indistinguishable from the general population, playing a full and important role in Australian development unimpeded by discriminatory legislation or social restrictions. They set up their own charity organizations, while at the same time contributing generously to public welfare. Many underwent military training to defend the British Empire of which Australia was part. In every major sphere of enterprise and activity, Australian Jews showed themselves to be just as loyal as Australian non-Jews. Up to the end of the nineteenth century Jews were a thoroughly integrated and committed element in Australian society.[9]

Jews arriving from non-English speaking backgrounds in the final years of the century, however, presented a problem. The arrival of even a few Russian and Polish Jews – Yiddish-speaking, distinctively dressed, and less attuned to British or western European customs – was sufficient to upset the thoroughly Anglicized character of the existing Jewish community, which sought to assimilate foreigners quickly into the mainstream of Australian life.

Anglo-Jewish society, already assimilated into the majority culture, saw a rising rate of intermarriage between Jews and non-Jews, frequent (and flagrant) disregard of Sabbath observance and adherence to Jewish dietary laws, and a reduction in the level of participation in the Jewish festivals and holy days. By the time of the pogroms against Jews in Russia in the early 1880s, this trend was apparent.[10]

Despite this, and in keeping with the European trend, antisemites in Australia were active throughout the last years of the nineteenth century. Popular journals such as *Punch* and *The Bulletin*, for instance, published stories and cartoons highlighting antisemitic images of the non-productive parasite living off the sweat of the workers, who sought to control the lives of others through chicanery, bribery, double-dealing or outright theft.[11] Perhaps, under such a shadow, it is not surprising that the Australian Jewish community should seek to submerge itself into the mass of the population.

This attempt at conformity to avoid criticism did not, however, work. Its main result was the creation of a community of Jews who sought to be seen as anything but Jewish. Writing of the assimilationist nature of Melbourne Jewish life in the 1920s, noted sociologist P. Y. Medding has noted:

The community was small [and] intermarriage was widespread. … The synagogues were poorly attended. Hebrew – the language of prayer – was known to few, and comprehensible to even fewer, facilities for Jewish education were abysmal, the spiritual leadership was pedestrian, the performance of the Jewish rituals was minimal, Jewish cultural life was non-existent, and Zionism was in its earliest infancy. … For Melbourne Jewry in those days, the chances of survival were very dim indeed.[12]

Some non-Jewish Australians noticed what was happening. In 1927 an academic at the University of Melbourne, Jens Lyng, observed that 'Judaism in Australia hitherto has held its ground – owing, probably, to the steady infusion of fresh blood from overseas – [but] the possibility of eventually being absorbed is by no means an imaginary one'.[13] His view was that the trend would continue if existing rates of intermarriage were maintained.

Jewish assimilation was motivated by the misconception that antisemitism would break out the moment Jews were seen to be anything other than loyal Australians true to the British Empire.[14] Given this, expressions of antisemitism sprang from two main sources. The first lay in the rich history of political populism which had for decades helped to shape Australian attitudes towards complex issues. Antisemitic jokes, cartoons and satires poked fun but rarely intended to affront 'real' Australian (or British) Jews. In his narrative of the rise and decline of *Smith's Weekly*, George Blaikie noted that the newspaper 'loved … good Jews,' and 'hated … bad Jews,'[15] the latter always being depicted with big noses, ugly faces, strange-sounding accents and an unscrupulous attitude towards money.

Increasingly, the second source of antisemitism was the political far right. This ranged from crusading organizations such as the far-right New Guard movement[16] to the Australia First Movement, whose leadership was interned in 1942 as a danger to national security.[17] National Socialism was also a factor. Germany financed and arranged for the distribution of Nazi propaganda among Germans living in Australia,[18] and through a local publication entitled *Die Brücke*, the German consul in Sydney, Dr. Rudolf Asmis, was able to rally support among German Australians for Nazi principles.[19] This included the expression of antisemitic speeches emanating from Berlin, with Asmis pushing the German government's position to the Australian public while supporting German and Nazi organizations in Sydney and Melbourne.[20] Antisemitic noise came from a variety of sources at one time or another, but few Australians took sufficient notice of them to themselves become active antisemites.

Jewish racial stereotypes could not persist, however, without the ongoing arrival of immigrants who were different in appearance, language and culture from British Australians. Thus, the migration of Jews from Poland became the subject of special government restrictions in 1925, on the grounds that they were of 'poor physique', spoke only Polish and Yiddish, and were neither farmers or skilled labourers.[21] They were considered to be 'a peculiarly backward class, living as their ancestors lived about 2,000 years ago, and not assimilating with the general community'.[22] British passport control officers in Poland were given discretionary power regarding applicants' suitability, and could reject them there before the applications were seen by any Australian official. A leading official involved in regulating immigrant arrivals identified that a protest might be raised when it was learned that Australia was discriminating against Jews as immigrants but suggested that 'as many of these Polish Jews – particularly the illiterate and poorer types – are known to be anything but desirable, the Department will be prepared to meet any such protests that may be made'.[23]

The prevailing view in the 1920s, as expressed by *Smith's Weekly*, was that 'good Jews' were those who were Australian or British, conformed with the norms of the Anglicized Australian community, spoke English without an accent, engaged in 'respectable' business practices and in no way stood out from the mass of other Australians. 'Bad Jews' were the opposite: they were foreign, exhibited different customs and modes of behaviour, spoke accented and jumbled English, and had business conventions derived from the eastern European village or market town.

That radical antisemitism did not emerge into the mainstream must be seen as due to the relatively high esteem in which Australian Jews were held prior to and throughout the period. This should not be underestimated. A Jewish general of the calibre of Sir John Monash, who commanding an entire allied army in the First World War, was recognized as Australia's greatest soldier; an Australian-born Jew, Sir Isaac Isaacs, was the monarch's representative as Governor-General (and thus Head of State), over the protestations of Buckingham Palace; and a rabbi, David Freedman, represent Australia as its delegate at no less a forum than the League of Nations.[24] Despite these achievements, Australia was very much an anti-foreign society. Almost invariably as the 1920s gave way to the 1930s, animosity was directed towards foreign Jews; rarely if ever were negative comments meant to apply to those who were native-born or British.

Prior to 1933, how did Australians perceive Jews? Responses were diverse; while there were some antisemites, as in any society, there were also philosemites who sought to perpetuate good relations between Australian Jews and non-Jews. Support for foreign Jews was expressed only rarely. Native-born and British Jews were admired and accepted by most citizens; foreign Jews were not.

At the 1921 census, Jews in Australian society numbered just 21,615.[25] Despite this small number, there was an ongoing fear across many sectors of society that foreign Jews might choose Australia as a desirable place of abode. For those trying to escape persecution by the 1930s – whether it be Germany, Austria, Poland or elsewhere – the development of this attitude was to have far-reaching implications which would increasingly mean life or death.

Foreign immigration and the bureaucracy

How was Australian immigration managed? Given the general apathy and ignorance characterizing general Australian attitudes towards the implementation of government activities, the Australian public 'knew little of the intricacies of government departments'.[26] While government policies underwent various changes between the two World Wars, their execution remained largely static owing to what seems to have been unwillingness on the part of successive governments to commit themselves to significant improvement of resources or personnel. It was the administrators who bore the full brunt of pressure from overseas to expand immigration.[27]

Australia's immigration policy throughout most of the 1920s was administered by the Department of Home and Territories. An Immigration Branch inside the Department handled day-to-day routine, keeping the Secretary informed on migration matters and providing initiatives which could be passed on to the Minister. The Immigration Branch was transferred to the new Department of Home Affairs in 1928; this, in turn, was replaced by the Department of the Interior in 1932. The officer in charge of the Immigration Branch throughout the period was Albert Robert Peters, who remained in this position until 1945.

Peters was a specialist in the field of immigration management, with knowledge based on years of experience. Nothing concerning his Branch took place without his being aware of it; nothing was devoid of his signature or initials. His knowledge and, more significantly, his awareness, made him perhaps the most crucial figure in immigration in the interwar period.

But the early years of Interior's existence suffered from a succession of Ministers who lacked interest in the immigration aspects of the Department's many responsibilities. Only Thomas Paterson, who was Minister between 1934 and 1937, brought some measure of stability to the Department. When he resigned owing to ill-health, his place was taken by John McEwen. Then, with the intensification of the Jewish refugee problem during the 1930s, Victor Thompson was appointed as Assistant Minister in 1938. In April 1939, Interior was taken over by Senator Hattil Spencer (Harry) Foll, who remained in this role until the United Australia Party lost office in October 1941.

Joseph Aloysius Carrodus served as the permanent head of the Department of the Interior from 1935. His tenure as Secretary transcended the milder period of the early 1930s, the gradual reintroduction of immigration in the middle of the decade, and the frantic months prior to the outbreak of war in 1939 when tens of thousands of applications for entry from Jewish refugees were received by the Department. The official with whom Peters had the most dealings, it was Carrodus who forwarded or rejected policy recommendations for the Minister.

Although he was the main link in the Department between Peters and the Minister, there was a further key office in the chain: the office of Assistant Secretary. From 1938 this was Thomas Hugh (Tom) Garrett, a man who understood migration issues and could support Peters's endeavours to run a tight ship. As Acting Secretary whenever Carrodus was absent, he often found himself delegating authority and suggesting ideas in both directions. Owing to his role as sometime Acting Secretary and his knowledge of immigration matters, he was sent to London representing the Department in 1939 to investigate the refugee crisis at first hand and brief the Australian High Commissioner of current developments in Canberra. His subsequent report illustrated how effective his position, as the link between the head of the Immigration Branch and the Secretary of the Department, could be.

Within the Immigration Branch, Albert Peters's written recommendations and memoranda, once approved by Carrodus or Garrett, were presented to all relevant Departments as and when required. These were for the most part produced with such clarity that from the angle of administration little objection could be raised. As the expert on the scene, Peters often suggested to Carrodus what his brief should be, carrying out his tasks and attempting to ease the stress of immigration management whenever possible. The unique aspect of his position was that he could offer suggestions for approval and execute them without exceeding the limits of his authority or undermining the governmental process. He was the person most likely to read correspondence from the public; he was also the one most likely to draft replies for Carrodus and press statements for the Minister. He liaised with staff of other Departments, keeping them informed of the official stance on immigration matters. In this way he was able to exert substantial influence over Australian immigration policy throughout the 1930s.

He did not, of course, dictate policy: only the government could do that, and even then, it was constrained by outside considerations such as the Federal system, the state governments, the demands of supporting groups and parties, and awareness of public feeling. Yet anomalies could (and did) occur that allowed for unusual developments to take place.

The Immigration Branch was often required to liaise with other Commonwealth departments, notably External Affairs, with Prime Minister Stanley Bruce fearful in the 1920s that a harsh immigration policy could create resentment abroad. By 1935 External Affairs had a permanent officer located in London, where most of Australia's international representation already took place through the office of the High Commissioner. Alfred Stirling was chosen for the London-based position of External Affairs Officer in 1937. His task was largely one of liaison with the High Commissioner's Office and briefing it on foreign policy matters.

The Immigration Branch had another important relationship in the 1930s, centring on security. In this, it liaised most closely with the Commonwealth Investigation Branch of the Attorney-General's Department, operating as Australia's security intelligence service. In immigration matters it checked the bona fides of foreigners, investigated complaints about illegal practices by alien workers, and inquired into the financial status of Australian residents guaranteeing the maintenance of foreign immigrants.

By the late 1930s, the bureaucratic structure administering immigration was clearly too small to cope with the requirements of large-scale policy formation and the huge growth in applications from persons seeking relief from Nazi oppression. Big decisions often had to be made on the spot. There could therefore be only one option for the exercise of good administration: the Head of the Immigration Branch would have to provide the policy initiatives himself, as there was no other authority to perform the task. The whole issue of immigration grew too big too quickly, and the existing structure proved inadequate. Albert Peters thus had to take on a measure of responsibility to which he would probably not have aspired, and certainly not considered appropriate a decade earlier. The bureaucrats did not give the government its policy, but with a lack of any other form of leadership or guidance they carried on operations while awaiting further orders. Given that, it is a testament to the abilities of Peters, Carrodus and Garrett that Australia had a functioning immigration policy at all in the years leading up to the outbreak of the Second World War.

Legacies of the Great War

The aftermath of the Great War – known as such at the time, though not yet the First World War – saw a traumatized Australia. The shock was intensified by the realization that the peoples of the world could no longer be placed into neat categories based on racial or national stereotypes. Australians had been exposed to a greater variety of people from other countries than ever before, and the experience left them somewhat confused. As historian Bill Gammage has observed:

> The Germans, for example, were 'bad' but white, while the Japanese were 'good'
> but not white, and the Russians were white and 'good' until December 1917, but

white and 'bad' thereafter. Further, during the War Australians learnt that 'bad' Germans yet possessed at least some British virtues, and that 'bad' and non-white Turks displayed qualities regrettably lacking in many an Anglo-Saxon. Whiteness and virtue and to a lesser extent whiteness and superiority could no longer be considered inevitably synonymous, and although nothing was sufficient to shake a general Australian conviction of white supremacy, the war did make more difficult the drawing of racial distinctions within 'the white race'.[28]

Australians sought ways to rationalize these distinctions, and as a result became more ethnocentric and prejudiced than before the war. Feelings of insecurity abounded, and a need for national self-preservation became paramount. Distrust of foreigners intensified and there emerged a yearning for likeminded conformity, an attempt to stop the world – if only for a little while – to take stock after the convulsions brought by the previous four years.

This attitude was encapsulated well by wartime Prime Minister William Morris (Billy) Hughes in an address to Parliament on 10 September 1919:

> What has been won? If the fruits of victory are to be measured by national safety and liberty, and the high ideals for which these boys died, the sacrifice has not been in vain. They died for the safety of Australia. Australia is safe. They died for liberty, and liberty is now assured to us and to all men. … We turn now from war to peace. We live in a new world, a world bled white by the cruel wounds of war. Victory is ours, but the price of victory is heavy. The whole earth has been shaken to its very core. Upon the foundations of victory we would build the new temple of our choice.[29]

Here, he was building on a tradition already established from the late nineteenth century that saw White Australia dominated by anxieties over its vulnerability as a small and largely undefended British community located 12,000 miles from the Mother Country and facing an expansionist and increasingly militarized Japan.

The Great War, which had begun with such enthusiasm at its inception, had ended in bitterness, confusion and frustration. Australia, a society of little more than 5 million people, federated into a single nation for less than twenty years, had yielded up 330,000 of its fittest young men to fight overseas. Sixty thousand never returned; over 150,000 were wounded or gassed, while at home the country was torn apart by bitter debates over conscription. It was an enormous contribution to the Empire's war effort. Historian Michael McKernan has noted that the war brought to the surface the other side of patriotism – the 'mean, hating, divisive spirit which forced people to judge others on slim evidence, to lose their natural tolerance and to turn savagely on those they perceived as the enemy'.[30]

Perhaps not surprisingly, Australians in 1918 sought to find a quick way back to the spirit prevailing prior to the war, a period they remembered as having been tranquil and trouble-free. The enthusiasm with which people had embraced the war at the start gave way to class conflict, religious animosity and social dislocation.

Preferring the familiar

An early example of this took place soon after the end of the war, when a measure was introduced into the *Immigration Act 1901* prohibiting the entry of 'any person who ... is of German, Austro-German, Bulgarian or Hungarian parentage and nationality, or is a Turk of Ottoman race'.[31] By 1922, however, the government's position had modified to one of not discriminating against 'white friendly aliens' other than those from former enemy countries.[32]

How well did this align with Australia's rejection of the outside world after 1918, in which the familiar was preferred over the foreign? It provided all the customary frameworks by which Australians ordered their lives, in which what was alien was regarded as inferior, less good, to be avoided or excluded or assimilated. Foreigners were intruders who stood in the way of a return to 'ordinary' times. Order and conformity were the desired goals, and aliens, by definition, were out of the ordinary and undesirable.

In explaining Australian ethnocentrism in 1919, however, it would be wrong to look only at the war and its traumatic effects. Australians had already inherited a racist tradition from before the war and had been schooled in prejudice through active discrimination against people whose skin colour was not white.[33] Non-white peoples had been the subject of racial animosity throughout the nineteenth century, and the *Immigration Act 1901* – colloquially termed the White Australia Policy – was drafted to formalize this animosity through a policy of ethnic exclusion.[34] The Australian colonies, moreover, had themselves been founded on the premise that the continent was unoccupied by the country's Aboriginal population and was territory owned by no-one (*terra nullius*). Yet for all that, the prejudicial attitudes of the post-war period seemed to spring from a new sense of isolationism which had as its object the exclusion of all things foreign.

These attitudes, moreover, did not change overnight. Even as early as 1922, concern was expressed in the populist newspaper *Smith's Weekly* over the possibility that the future might see the Italian population of north Queensland demanding the teaching of their language in state schools.[35] The books likely to be procured for such purposes were deemed to be of dubious content, and literature from Australia was seen as far preferable to 'the nasty sex stuff we import from abroad'.[36] A similar view was expressed again two years later, when, in an article headed 'Dagoes Pour into South Australia/ Italian and Maltese Invasion', *Smith's Weekly* drew attention to the 'dago toilers [who] work harder, longer and more uncomplainingly than white [*sic*], and accept the isolation and barrenness of existence in ... desert mining camps without protest'.[37] The 'Mediterranean scum', as *Smith's* called them, were accustomed to 'breadline wages in their own countries'; because of this, they were prepared to work for 'a little above the breadline' in Australia, which meant, in reality, 'a bit below what the white man gets'.[38]

The likelihood of racial deterioration was another continuing theme among those opposed to a foreign presence. In 1925 the Australian Labor Party newspaper *Labor Call* queried whether anyone could doubt 'that Australia is destined to become a great nation inhabited by superior people', and registered concern that there were those who 'preach contempt for our desire to keep this country for posterity'.[39] In an interview with Prime Minister Stanley Bruce in 1927, a delegation from the conservative Australian Natives' Association presented the view that they 'very strongly wished to see the racial purity of Australia maintained' – not from a feeling of superiority, but rather 'from the point of view of what was most advantageous to the country'.[40] The possibility that Australia would become a 'polyglot' nation like the United States was also of concern. Sir Elliot Johnson, the Nationalist Member for Lang (NSW) in the House of Representatives, stated how he 'could not forget the lesson learned from the experience of the countries of North America'. When he contemplated the races which 'largely form the population of these countries', he said, 'I am not at all enamoured of the prospect of large numbers of Southern Europeans being brought here'.[41]

The weight of public opinion was such that some form of regulation had to be established over the entry of peoples from specific nations, and the government established a quota for immigrants from Greece, Yugoslavia and Albania. On 1 April 1925 the government instituted a new regulation under which all alien immigrants would henceforth require the sum of £35 upon arrival as a guarantee that they would not automatically become a charge upon the state.[42] This was later increased to £40. The principle of 'landing money' thus became established, and it – together with an accompanying landing permit – henceforth formed the basis of Australia's immigration management. From now on, landing money was to prove a stumbling block for many intending migrants. The worsening state of the Australian economy with the onset of the Depression saw the quotas reduced even further.[43]

The Depression was a major catastrophe. Before the end of 1931 perhaps a third of the Australian workforce was unemployed, and widespread suffering occurred as the country attempted to cope with no work, paltry government assistance, mass evictions, little or no ready cash with which to buy life's essentials, and a business sector unwilling to expand. In 1930 assisted migration from Britain was cut back, and by 1931 severe restrictions on immigration from Europe were imposed. The foreign migration policy Australia was to take into the 1930s was now fully dependent on the landing permit system, and the granting of permits was confined to an extremely narrow circle: only close dependent relatives of persons already resident in Australia, or persons with £500 landing money (increased in 1931 from £40), or experts specifically required by the Commonwealth for some special industry, would be allowed entry.

Responses to foreigners in the 1920s

On 6 January 1932 Joseph Lyons became Prime Minister of a conservative United Australia Party (UAP) government. He would be Prime Minister until his death in

April 1939: the UAP would, however, remain in office under Robert Menzies until October 1941. From the outset, immigration policy was opposed to alien entry, the UAP's 1931 election platform calling for 'rigorous limitation of alien entrance to the Commonwealth'.[44] What were the continuities in public perceptions Lyons would have to consider when tackling the issue of alien migration? It should be emphasized that while some Australians thought critically about the long-term consequences of foreign immigration, most saw the issue only in terms of its current impact. Foreigners remained unwelcome.

Thinking about immigrants only in terms of their 'race' saw calls to exclude those viewed as incompatible from the start of the decade. Calls for restriction began to increase commensurate with arrivals, though Scandinavians and others from northern Europe, despite being foreign, were nonetheless highly desirable. *The Argus*, commenting on the descendants of early Scandinavian immigrants to Australia, noted in 1927 how they had 'enriched the Commonwealth with a considerable infusion of good Nordic blood'. It informed its readers that 'The Scandinavians are home-lovers and home-builders. The women are splendid housewives, and their tastes conform to the Australian standard of good living'.[45] A blend of Scandinavians with British Australians would, it was argued, be highly beneficial for the country.

Protest over alleged displacement by aliens was prosecuted with considerable vigour by the Returned Soldiers' and Sailors' Imperial League of Australia (RSSILA). Beginning early in the 1920s, these protests concerned the affront to the memory of Australia's war dead by 'importing' foreigners to replace Australian wartime losses.[46] Further protests came from the Sailors' and Soldiers' Fathers' Association. In 1925 a series of meetings throughout its various state branches concluded that something needed to be done to call a halt to foreign immigration. The Queensland group was the first to pass a resolution on the matter, followed quickly by Tasmania, whose resolution referred, in part, to 'the insult offered to Australia's 59,300 dead soldiers by the Commonwealth Government filling their places with the mixed races now coming to Australia'.[47]

Other Australians were fearful that the time for resolutions was past. Even as early as 1922, *Labor Call* was suggesting that ex-soldiers on the Queensland cane-fields would soon have to take up arms to defend themselves and fight for those rights which had been eroded by the foreign influx. In Queensland, when a confrontation took place between striking Australian workers and non-unionized Maltese labourers in 1927, one of the strike leaders resolved that unless the government did something to stop the menace to 'good Australians', there was only one course left open: 'we shall have to take the law into our own hands and exterminate the vermin.'[48]

Attitudes to the outside world

As Prime Minister Joseph Lyons and his government took office during 1932, events overseas began to attract the Australian public's attention. Europe seemed in a state of constant tension, and a mood existed that something would soon have to give if the stability necessary for economic and social recovery was to be achieved.

Was any of this seen to be of relevance to Australia, situated such a vast distance from Europe? The country's relationship with Britain influenced all strategic, diplomatic, cultural and institutional thinking, and although by the Statute of Westminster 1931 Australia had effectively been granted the right to full independence, the Australians had shown no inclination to ratify it. The British Empire stood at its widest extent and was considered the single most important guarantor of Australia's future security, and Australians were quite happy to work with Britain in determining the broad lines of the country's external and defence policy.[49]

Consequently, whatever happened in Europe and took British attention was, directly or indirectly, of concern to Australia. The dilemma for the Australians was what to do should Britain choose to adopt 'the continental commitment', that is, to look inward to European affairs rather than outward towards the ongoing defence of the Empire. The Statute of Westminster was an implicit communication to the Dominions that in future they would have to take a greater role in providing for their own defence, but Australia continued devotedly to follow Britain's lead in the hope that by doing so Britain would in turn remain loyal to Australia.[50]

Watching European events, then, was more than just idle curiosity. Germany was of vital concern to Australia, and any events might divert Britain's eyes from its Imperial responsibilities. Simple as it may appear, it was with these misgivings that political leaders viewed developments in Germany, while at the same time assessing their impact for Australia. There were few, however, who considered Hitler's attitude towards issues of race, or of his ideas concerning Germany's Jewish population, prior to 1933.

We can best assess the Australian attitude towards the outside world between 1918 and 1933 by looking at the influence wielded by that period's major events. And, for a naïve and unworldly nation such as Australia, those events were indeed momentous. The shocks of the war and the consequent rejection of the outside world found expression in two courses of action: a restriction of those from outside who could enter Australia, and a reliance upon Britain to defend and represent Australian interests abroad. Australia's conduct reflected its concerns that it was a vulnerable country surrounded by a hostile and uncaring world. Anything foreign was a threat; any country other than Britain was considered to have ulterior motives and was not to be trusted; aliens were viewed as unassimilable, stealers of jobs and a menace to the Anglo-Australian way of life.

How effective this attitude might be in the face of a genuine challenge would have to wait until 1942, when Australia was in imminent danger.[51] Meanwhile, a different challenge was forced upon the country from 1933 onwards. Whether or not Australia had an official position regarding the racial persecution of Germany's Jews by Hitler's regime did not matter. In the years following 1933 Australians were compelled to confront its effects as refugees from Nazism sought in increasing numbers to enter. Australia might not have sought an involvement with the outside world, but Hitler ensured one. The period following would be a time of testing.

CHAPTER 2
CONFRONTING THE REFUGEE CHALLENGE

Evolving a refugee policy

Adolf Hitler was appointed Chancellor of Germany on 30 January 1933, and almost immediately his National Socialist government began applying its antisemitic racial ideologies with a view to removing the Jews from Germany. Race and race theory formed the basis of Hitler's political and social philosophy, central to which was the concept of the 'Aryan'. In the Nazi lexicon, the term applied to nobility of blood, unmixed racial lineage, strength of character and untold aesthetic beauty; in short, a superior species of human. Aryans were deemed responsible for all human progress; the betterment of humanity was believed to have occurred because of an eternal struggle between them and everyone else. The terms 'Aryan' and 'non-Aryan' were subsequently embraced by some foreign governments to address the issues presented by Nazi Germany, and Australia, from an early date, adopted them when determining its refugee policy.

At first, the Australian government treated the Nazi regime and its policies towards Jews with detachment. The minutes of the Adelaide Hebrew Congregation (AHC) for 1 June 1933 disclose one instance of the Federal government's attitude. The AHC had planned a public protest meeting against the Nazi treatment of the Jews which was to be held in the Adelaide Town Hall on 6 June 1933. The South Australian Premier, R. L. (later Sir Richard) Butler, had agreed to move the principal motion of protest, and Andrew Lacey, the Leader of the Opposition, was to second it. Other speakers were to include representatives of the Catholic and Anglican Churches, as well as civic groups and other prominent citizens. All was in readiness for the big night, but as the minutes of the AHC explain, things did not turn out as expected:

> The day after the Premier had consented, he phoned the Secretary [of the AHC] and asked him to attend at his office. On attending, the Premier advised the Secretary that he had received a telegram from the Prime Minister, Mr. Lyons, asking he or any member of his Government not to associate themselves with the Protest Meeting as it might embarrass the British Government. In view of this intimation the Protest Committee met and decided not to proceed with the meeting. It was very unfortunate that circumstances prevented the Committee from proceeding with the meeting. A wire had been forwarded to the Protest Committee, Sydney, which had advised us not to proceed with the Meeting, in view of the Government attitude.[1]

A few days later the Minister for External Affairs, J. G. (later Sir John) Latham, went one step further. When the Newcastle City Council passed a resolution condemning the German actions and requested that the Federal government forward the resolution to Germany through the British Ambassador in Berlin, Latham refused on the ground that 'it would not be correct for the Australian Government to comply [as it was] a well established principle that one country did not interfere in the internal affairs of another'. For this reason, the government would not see its way clear to forward the protest 'or make any representations on the subject unless some Australian was directly concerned'.[2] This non-committal approach was largely in keeping with the Australian outlook on foreign policy matters. Australia would not involve itself in the German-Jewish situation as it was assumed that Britain would look after Australia's overseas interests. As Britain's appeasement policy began to take shape, this meant that Australia portrayed its attitude in such a way as to pacify, rather than antagonize, Nazi Germany.[3]

From the outset, the Australian government was concerned about the possibility of the Jewish targets of Nazism seeking refuge. Community comment was also apparent early. The most frequent concern in 1933 was the 'racial' and political status of Jews. Thus, a citizen of Sydney, in a letter to the editor of the *Sydney Morning Herald*, wrote that there was 'a vast difference between the refined and well-educated type of Jew we know in Australia and those who swarmed into Germany after the war from Russia and Poland'. This 'swarm', he wrote, had the effect of increasing the population of Berlin alone 'by 500,000'. The letter concluded that 'One may wonder what would happen if the population of Sydney were to be increased at that rate by a foreign race within two years'.[4]

Such comments set the stage for what was to become an important battlefield in the years to come. The *Sydney Morning Herald* rarely missed an opportunity to offer a counter position, and throughout the 1930s it was arguably the lone Australian press voice in favour of refugee immigration (though the *West Australian*, in Perth, also showed a positive attitude from time to time). On 29 May 1933, for example, it addressed negative views with an editorial opinion stating: 'If some among the Jews are proved to have been Communists or criminals (two names which mean pretty much the same), then as Communists or criminals let them be judged – not as Jews.'[5]

In some bureaucratic circles there was no doubt that German Jews were being persecuted because they were communists. A report sent to Inspector Roland S. Browne of the Commonwealth Investigation Branch spelled this out:

> The Communist element in Germany, which is very strong, had a vast number of Jews in it, and this Hitler ban is not 100% antisemetic [*sic*]. How far the racial factor was brought to make some element the scapegoat, it is impossible for me to say. I doubt if anyone outside the inner circle of Hitler can say.[6]

The report considered that Australia should tread warily. Even Australian Jews, it stated, had 'mingled in Communistic matters', and it would be easy to make converts to communism among German Jewish refugees given the current climate. For this reason, the report recommended it would probably be best to resist any large-scale introduction of Jews to Australia. There was also an economic aspect to be considered:

> It is a known and irrefutable fact that no Jewish migrant to Australia seeks employment outside cities. He is no agriculturist and a poor manual labourer. No matter what assurances any local committee offers that these 'Emigres' will not be a charge on any Australian Government, these newcomers are bound theoretically to displace Australian labour in the cities where unemployment is great.[7]

Despite this – in one of the more cynical comments by an Australian official – the report stated that 'Politically any Minister that favoured … a scheme to absorb into Australia the figure of … 1,000 to 1,500 [refugees] would earn the undying gratitude of Jewry in Australia and judiciously worked at election time would sway a considerable amount of votes.' Not only that, but 'Financially, Jews are a national asset, both in true finance and in industry'.[8] The report concluded that it should be the place 'of local Jewry to formulate any plan of action and submit it to the Government'. Inspector Browne was cautioned, however, not to create the impression when dealing with Jewish leaders 'that any scheme propounded having the financial backing and responsibility of local Jewry would immediately meet with the approbation of the Government'.[9] The Investigation Branch was advised that it should canvass the opinions of local Jews, inform them that it was their responsibility to do something about the situation, but make no promises that would commit the government to any course of action.

Hovering over this period was the Depression, which overshadowed Australia in the 1930s more thoroughly than any other national concern. The census of 1933 listed 22.89 per cent of the workforce as unemployed; another 8.14 per cent were employed part-time.[10] For those with work, wages were being cut continually. Protests often resulted in dismissal; no hardship to employers at a time when selection from a vast body of available replacements was easy. It should be little wonder that those suffering most from the Depression were also among the first to condemn immigration – even prior to the possibility of Jews from Germany arriving. The issue was almost always seen as one in which competitors for jobs were being introduced, rather than importers of capital who could establish new industries employing Australians. The unemployment crisis gave Australians a pressing reason to exclude immigrants, as unchecked migration would lead to grave consequences for the government responsible. The logic ran that no migrant should be allowed into the country if the result saw Australian children going hungry.

Preventing a 'serious influx'

Governments often avoid addressing potentially controversial issues. The refugee issue, in 1933, was accorded such a status by the Lyons government. Indeed, the government's refugee policy at the outset was in most respects non-existent. Refugees were viewed as no different to other immigrants, and when the first applications for entry to Australia arrived from German Jews the Department of the Interior refused to acknowledge either the seriousness or the immediacy of the situation. A good illustration of this was a Cabinet memorandum prepared for the Minister on 2 June 1933. The matter for discussion concerned an application received from 'an Australian resident of good standing' for permission to introduce from Germany his brother, a medical practitioner, together with the brother's wife and child. It was observed that 'they are of Jewish race', and the reason given for the application was that 'the relatives here are anxious about them on account of the reported persecution of Jews in Germany'.[11] After deliberation, Cabinet decided that in this case, 'provided the Minister is satisfied', admission of the family in question would be granted.

The Department sought a policy guideline beyond this single case, however. It was observed:

> As a result of persecution, it is possible that large numbers of German Jews may desire to emigrate. Australia may be selected as a country having attractions for such emigrants. The question arises as to whether any special precautions should be taken to ensure that the Commonwealth does not receive an undue proportion of such migrants.

Answering its own question, the memorandum continued that 'it is not considered desirable that any special facilities should be given for Jews from Germany to migrate to Australia'. It might, furthermore, 'be felt desirable to take special precautions' against those applicants who fell outside the already-narrow criteria for admission. Cabinet's opinion was expressed by the Minister for Defence and External Affairs, Senator Sir George Pearce, who minuted on behalf of the Prime Minister that Cabinet approved the view 'as to care being exercised to prevent a serious influx' of Jews to Australia.[12]

Articles concerning 'sweating' in the clothing industry, reported in Melbourne's *Age* on 16–17 August 1933, provoked further discussion. These articles, it was noted by the Department of the Interior, pointed out 'the necessity for the strictest control of the introduction of Polish and German Jews'.[13] While Australians were concerned about *any* immigrants taking jobs, there was an even greater fear of unscrupulous Jews who would present 'a menace to the general community as well as to reputable manufacturers'.[14] The prospect that all Jews from Europe might engage in unsavoury employment practices intensified the factors working against the admission of refugees from Germany.

Immigration of any kind had reached a low ebb by 1933, and admissions were tightly controlled. White alien immigration was governed by the landing permit system, and the regulations controlling the issue of permits were extremely rigid:[15] as the criteria for the issuance of landing permits stood in 1933, few German Jews would be able to migrate to Australia. The government realized that there 'probably will not be many who come within the categories of close relatives already settled here', recognizing that the unique situation of the German Jews would militate against their being able to comply with the entrance criteria: 'with regard to those who possess capital, ... [Jews are only] able to bring a limited sum to Australia as the German Government [has] prohibited the transfer of money to foreign countries'.[16]

Two images are apparent here. First, the government still had no expectations that the refugee issue would assume the proportions it did. The second general image relates to the first. Because the government did not perceive the issue as one that would assume large proportions, it stood to reason that there would probably not be many Jews who would choose Australia as a haven, regardless of the admission requirements. It was assumed that the country's location and the landing permit system would combine to minimize refugee admissions – though it was tacitly accepted within the Department that the numbers in question would only be small in any case.[17]

By 1936, however, officers in the Department of the Interior determined that the criteria they had designed to regulate alien immigration were, in fact, too tight. The main issue centred around the amount of landing capital immigrants were required to bring with them. Up to March 1936, the Department was satisfied that it had been successful in preventing an inrush of Jews, and in a memorandum for Cabinet it reported that applications 'have been dealt with in accordance with the general rules, and there has been no serious influx'.[18] The £500 landing money requirement had a huge role to play in this.

Owing to a rethink within the Department, however, the amount of landing money was reduced for all practical purposes – yet even here, the rationale for doing so was not to alleviate the condition of refugee immigrants from Germany. True to its rule of not giving special consideration to any classes of immigrants, the Department only proposed an amendment to the existing regulations because *all* aliens, including those attractive to the Commonwealth, were required to be in possession of £500. In many cases applicants being introduced by relatives already living in Australia did not possess such a large amount, and had their applications rejected. The Department suggested that the time had, therefore, arrived when the possession of £500 could be dispensed with 'in cases where the immigrants are nominated by persons already established in Australia who guarantee that the nominees will not be allowed to become a charge on the State'.[19] Included among the questions submitted to Cabinet was 'whether the existing conditions under which Jews from Germany may be admitted into Australia are to continue, and if not, the extent to which they are to be modified'. The question was further put as to whether the possession of £500 pounds – indeed, of any amount – should still insisted upon where an alien was guaranteed by Australian residents in good financial standing. It was suggested that the Minister should continue to reserve the right to refuse those who, in his opinion, 'would not be desirable in the public interest'. It was specified that Polish Jews were to be included among those 'who as a class are not desirable'.[20] The memorandum would act as the foundation for Australia's refugee policy until the outbreak of war in 1939.

Cabinet subsequently agreed on a new procedure for the admission of white non-British aliens which it considered both realistic and fair. Under the new scheme, they could be admitted to Australia under one of two categories: (a) those nominated 'by persons or associations in Australia guaranteeing to the satisfaction of the Minister that the nominee will not become a charge upon the State', will engage in trades and occupations without detriment to Australian workers, and possess £50 pounds upon arrival; and (b) those without such guarantees, who will engage in trades and occupations without detriment to Australian workers, and possess £200 upon arrival. The Minister would retain discriminatory power to permit entry for those with less capital in special circumstances.[21] This policy served the Commonwealth's interests nicely. The amount of £50 would ensure that immigrants would not automatically become charges upon the state, a development which was in any case improbable owing to the fact of their being guaranteed by persons or organizations resident in Australia. In the case of non-guaranteed migrants, £200 was an amount which lay within the scope of middle-class applicants. Both categories, guaranteed and non-guaranteed, would only operate in individual cases, each assessed on its merits.

The new landing permit system was a liberalization of the existing immigration laws, the only such positive move to take place before 1945. Its goal was not to make it easier for Jewish refugees to enter Australia, but rather to facilitate a measure of acceptable white alien immigration from those who could afford it and were deemed to be racially attractive to the future ethnic composition of the Commonwealth. It was hoped that a rise in northern European immigration would follow. Cabinet considered that as insufficient British migrants were arriving, 'we must be prepared to accept the next best'.[22]

The new policy was announced in Parliament on 6 May 1936 by the Minister for the Interior, Thomas Paterson.[23] On 22 May, the Department of the Interior made one of the first public announcements concerning the newly liberalized policy.[24] There was, however, no organization in Australia equipped to handle immigrant reception and welfare, and the Department realized quickly that such an organization would need to be established. Even though the new system required guarantees and landing money, there were still fears that a 'serious influx' of Jews might descend from Europe. Assistant Secretary Tom Garrett was unconvinced that external organizations could protect the country from being swamped, expressing the opinion that 'Jews as a class are not desirable immigrants for the reason that they do not assimilate; speaking generally, they preserve their identity as Jews'. He considered it would be inappropriate for the government to give its blessing 'to any scheme involving block nominations of Jews for admission into the Commonwealth'.[25] Garrett feared that if organizations were created guaranteeing immigrants, 'groups of unnamed Jews' might be introduced without Departmental awareness as to their employment, character or other details. The government should be extremely careful in its next steps.

Creating the Australian Jewish Welfare Society

It was against this background that an English stockbroker, Julian David Layton, first came upon the Australian refugee scene. Layton, who was later to play a vital role in securing the release of hundreds of Jewish internees in Australia during the war years, was on a business trip to Australia in 1936 when he received a cable from Otto Schiff of the London-based German Jewish Aid Committee. As Schiff was a leading merchant banker in the City, and the broking firm of Layton's family operated from the London Stock Exchange, the two had been acquainted with each other long before this. Schiff's request was that Layton go to Canberra to try to persuade the Federal government to accept a greater number of Jewish refugees.[26]

As a result of this request Layton contacted Jewish leaders in Sydney, particularly Samuel S. Cohen, a prominent businessman who would be knighted in 1937 for his services to industry. The two travelled to Canberra to speak with the immigration authorities. Layton later recalled the upshot of this (and subsequent) meetings:

> I'm glad to say that we managed to persuade after many interviews and correspondence the Australian Government to take five hundred refugees provided they were artisans. And I had to interview each one and recommend that they be accepted to the migration office in London and this was duly carried out.[27]

The 'migration office' referred to by Layton had no official status: he was, it seems, talking about Schiff's German Jewish Aid Committee. Travelling then from Australia to Germany, Layton chose the 500 nominees, and his choices were conveyed to Schiff. The names were then forwarded to Sydney. Samuel Cohen, on behalf of the Sydney-based German Jewish Relief Fund, then gave his personal guarantee for the well-being and upkeep of the refugees.[28]

The selection criteria Layton employed were stringent. Taking some nine months to complete, and including visits to Frankfurt and Vienna to conduct interviews, Layton's activities were restricted by the following standards:

> [The nominees] had to be the very younger generation round the twenty, twenty-five mark, and skilled artisans, as skilled as a person could be at that age so that they would easily be able to be integrated into the life in Australia. But apart from that I had discretion from various Jewish families in London to bring over a considerable number of young people and elderly people who did not come into the categories which I was selecting, which I was using for selection for Australia. And this of course helped me considerably.[29]

The Australian government could not rely on the services of Julian Layton indefinitely, nor could it allow wealthy individuals like Sir Samuel Cohen to continue guaranteeing migrants on behalf of narrowly based organisations such as the German Jewish Relief Fund, which was primarily a fund-raising organization.[30] In the Department of the Interior Tom Garrett had a change of heart and saw the attractiveness of a single refugee-relief body speaking for all Australian Jews and dealing directly with the government, as it would uphold the government's policy rather than working against it. There were some in the Department, however, who feared the possibility of Jewish organizations in the United Kingdom being permitted to send out 'batches of migrants'[31] under the pretext of them having special circumstances. The Department decided, therefore, that the local

Jewish community should be mobilized to work with the government in nominating and guaranteeing refugee Jews from Germany. More formal contact could then be made with Jewish organizations in Britain, and a methodical approach to refugee applications and admissions could begin.

To establish such an organization, Interior sent a letter to the religious heads of Jewish communities in each of the Australian capital cities, asking them 'to form local committees of responsible Jewish citizens to arrange for the reception and placing' of future immigrants.[32] At a meeting of the German Jewish Relief Fund in Sydney in late November 1936, a representative from London's Council for German Jewry advised that the British-based Jewish Refugees Committee also had in mind the formation of a central Jewish refugee body for Australia 'to save the Commonwealth Government from being bombarded with applications for Permits from every Jewish organisation in Australia'.[33] The opinion was expressed that 'unless the proposed Committee took the strong line an undesirable class of immigrant would come to Australia'.[34] One member of the German Jewish Relief Fund Executive then stated that from time to time he had discussed the question of Jewish immigration 'with nearly every member of the Federal Cabinet'. The attitude of these men, he reported, was that 'although they were all willing to help they were annoyed at being approached by individuals, not only in regard to Jewish Emigration, but in regard to Permits for numerous other European Immigrants'.[35] In the ensuing discussion, a consensus was reached that it would be 'very desirable' in the future for the Cabinet to be approached by one responsible body.[36]

The next meeting was held on 3 December 1936, and the basis of the Australian Jewish Welfare Society (AJWS) was laid down. By April 1937, every aspect of its operation was established. Its task was to oversee all activities in Australia concerning applications of such Jewish refugees who came within the acceptable criteria created by the government. A body such as this was attractive both to the Jewish community and to the government, as it was a Jewish organization that would work with or on behalf of the government rather than independently of it.

The British government noticed this, too. In April 1937, the Dominions Office observed that future activity concerning refugee migration to all the Dominions and Southern Rhodesia should ideally operate along the same lines as in Australia, with the Dominions Secretary, Malcolm MacDonald, commenting on the soundness of the Australian arrangement.[37] Despite the apparent easing of immigration restrictions for Jewish refugees, however, in numerous ways the Department of the Interior would later exploit its good intentions to reduce its own workload and responsibilities.

Beyond the Department of the Interior

Within some sectors of the bureaucracy, concern emerged during 1936 and 1937 that Interior took too much upon itself in determining the future racial composition of Australia. The most specific charges came from the Commonwealth Investigation Branch. In a confidential memorandum the Branch head, Inspector D. R. B. Mitchell, declared his opinion that 'the Department of the Interior pays little attention to reports from this Branch'. He was aware of cases in which 'for good and clearly stated reasons, distinctly adverse reports [from the Branch] were submitted but the applications [for entry] were granted'. Interior's risky attitude, he wrote, was 'somewhat apparent from the very set out [*sic*] of the form issued to reporting officers. The space left for "Remarks" appears designedly small, as if the Reporting Officer's remarks were of little consideration.'[38] Where investigations were carried out as to the veracity of individuals claiming the status of guarantors, Mitchell asserted that in many cases their ability to maintain alien immigrants was disproved. Despite this, the Department of the Interior continued to grant approvals based solely on the word of those acting as guarantors. Mitchell put forth the view:

> The whole system of the administration leans towards the cunning liar. Letters are obtained to say the intending migrant will be given employment, but for what duration? The cases, if followed up, would show how palpably futile the system is, so much so, that possibly it is designedly an official camouflage, a show of discrimination and enquiry to further a policy of alien immigration.[39]

He further argued that 'the methods of getting people should be selective and discriminatory, not haphazard, and dependent upon lying statements supporting applications for unwanted migrants to join in the already hard struggle for existence in our cities'. He continued that in his view 'there is only one class of migrant, alien or otherwise, Australia should welcome and that is a primary producer or a potential one. City or town dwellers are not required.' And with most nominations coming from 'Italians, Greeks, foreign Jews (principally Polish), Jugo-slavs and Syrians', it was apparent that the Department of the Interior was allowing these nominations to be accepted without fully realizing their significance. Bringing people to Australia to take the jobs which Australian unemployed workers could be filling was, for Mitchell, foolhardy and unjust.

Indeed, there were mutterings throughout 1937 that the easing of restrictions on alien immigration might not have favourable ramifications. *Smith's Weekly*, in an editorial from 12 June, informed its readers that there was 'practically no restriction on the entrance of aliens of European blood'. It was observed that the government's new landing money policy had a significant flaw:

> The incoming foreigner invariably produces his fifty [pounds] and is passed in upon which that same fifty pounds is returned to the head man of the group to become the deposit guaranteeing another entrant. It is just the same old fifty pounds, making return trips to the Customs Department like a stage army walking round and round past the footlights.[40]

On 28 June 1937, the Minister for the Interior, Thomas Paterson, attempted to staunch such comments by highlighting the British component of Australia's migration programme. In a long speech to Parliament, he announced that the Commonwealth was again prepared to grant assisted passages to eligible British migrants.[41] And with that, the issue, so far as Interior was concerned, ended – especially as the Department had concluded that 'unemployment has practically fallen to pre-depression levels'.[42]

For all this, by 1937 the refugee issue had not yet assumed a position of priority for the Department of the Interior. The government generally took little direct interest in Germany's antisemitic policies. At the time of the 1936 Berlin Olympics, for example, when the world's attention was focused on Nazi Germany and some countries even threatened to boycott the games due to antisemitism, there was only one reference made in the Australian Parliament to the great sporting event – and that concerned the use of a government grant for the Olympic team.[43] Indeed, the Australians generally took little interest in *any* aspect of the Games prior to the first event taking place.[44]

A matter of greater interest to Australia came in late 1937, when a report showed that the German government had decided, because of overcrowding, to exile Jews then in concentration camps. *The Argus*, in Melbourne, noted that 'those who are liberated must promise to leave Germany immediately',[45] a development which might have implications for Australia. Whatever happened next would depend largely on where the Jews would seek refuge.

Interior had other immigration worries requiring attention. Closely related to the German refugee issue, though not exactly falling within it, involved the admission of Jews from Poland; scores of thousands were seeking to leave for economic reasons and because of repression then taking place in that country.

Confronting European realities

During 1937 letters from Polish Jews pleading with the Australian government for permission to enter began arriving in increasing numbers. Most were written in Polish, Yiddish or German, requiring translation by linguists either in the Department of External Affairs or in the Australian universities. Occasionally the applicant would write in English in the hope of obtaining a better hearing of his (or, far less frequently, her) case. The pathos of these letters would have softened all but the hardest of hearts, and the number that survive in the files of the Department of the Interior indicate that the letters were read and considered. Often, however, such letters were more bothersome than helpful. The case of one Sdmerek Perle illustrates the position in which the Department found itself. Addressed to 'His Excellence Mr. Premier Minister of Australia,' Perle's letter read as follows:

> Deep bowing I am standing for His High Honour I am afraid and my pen is trembling in my hands when I am writing my request letter for I as a simple labourer am unworthy that my letter would be read for H.G.E. [?] but I beg H.G.E. whom you destined to be the hearer and leader of quite a part of the world, will understand my application: I am seeking, by the bureaux where to emigrate to

honestly earn. They said that in H.G.E. land was facilitate the emigration, but only the men who have their relatives can they get a permit unfortunately.

I have not there any relatives. I hope with my diligence owing what I came to the new existence. I beg H.G.E. with tears in my eyes. Please pity on a diligent man, who will work and earn but he has not where. Please H.G.E. to give a permit for me and my wife with two children.

I can add 50 pounds as a guarantee for an emigrated man. H.G.E. knows a man who comes to a land brings also the same great uses for the land as for himself. I am 36 years old (1901 born). I am healthy physically and psychologically.

I am unparty. I am a native of the Polish land. I add to this letter a coupon (post stamp) for an answer, while I will hope to cover costs for me.

I end my request letter and beg from H.G.E. to answer me my plain request.[46]

How could Interior respond to such a letter, or to hundreds of others like it? Sdmerek Perle had everything running against him: he did not have relatives in Australia, so his £50 was inadequate; he called himself a labourer, which suggested he was an urban worker who might displace an Australian from a job; his English was of a poor standard; and he was a Polish Jew, belonging, thereby, to a class of immigrant which was already considered undesirable for settlement in Australia. His fate is unrecorded in the available government archives.

His was not an isolated case. Dawid Henenfeld, a twenty-six-year-old who wrote to the Prime Minister in German, gave further demonstration of the unacceptability of Polish Jews. After the death of Dawid's father, he wrote, 'difficult times' began. He had no financial means for continuing his education,

and so was obliged to work for my daily bread, but as a result of the economic crisis and the anti-Jewism [sic] prevailing throughout the world I lost my work. I am living in the greatest poverty and need, without any future or better prospects.

I have no means for obtaining a living. I am suffering from hunger and cannot remember the day when I have had enough to eat. In these sad circumstances I see no prospects for me in this country. I have no one to whom I could turn in my miserable situation.[47]

Henenfeld's letter drew the government's attention to the fact of his impoverishment – and of course, poverty and immigration were incompatible to a Department set only on the introduction of migrants who would not become a charge upon the state.

Polish Jews always found themselves in the 'undesirable' class, so when a Melbourne group calling itself the Polish Jewish Relief Fund applied for permission to introduce some twenty orphan boys from 'the most needy and distressed Jewish families in Poland', the Department found itself in something of a quandary.[48] The Fund intended to undertake the same functions the AJWS was performing for German Jewish refugees: it would arrange with 'a well known Jewish relief organisation in Poland' to supervise the selection of the children, who would be chosen according to their academic merit, physical development and psychological disposition; it would take care of the children upon their arrival in Australia and oversee their training in the trades or professions for which they showed aptitude, or place them in the country as agricultural workers; and it could submit the names of twenty suitable Polish Jewish families in Melbourne able to guarantee the financial welfare of the boys in accordance with the government's policy.[49]

Having played such a leading part in the formation of the AJWS, the government could now utilize the services of another organization displaying similar features. But Polish Jews had no friends in the Department of the Interior. Thomas Paterson commented that 'Polish Jews have not, on the whole, proved the most satisfactory class of immigrants'. Besides this, 'The admission of youths, selected from the poorest classes, who may deprive local youths of opportunities of employment in useful trades, is not an attractive proposition.'[50] Later, Cabinet rejected the scheme; on 7 April 1938 Prime Minister Lyons endorsed the government's disapproval.[51]

The issue did not end there, however. Two months later a strange sequel took place when mysteriously the decision was overturned, and the children were granted permission to come to Australia. On his copy of the Cabinet memorandum proposing (and rejecting) the scheme, Lyons minuted, on 9 June 1938, '20 children to be approved'.[52] Somewhere, the government had had a change of heart; possibly the inconsistency located in the policies regarding relief for Jews from Germany and Poland had been noted. The government would allow this scheme to proceed only on the condition that it was sui generis. There would not, under any circumstances, be a departure from the existing policy of single applications and acceptance based on the individual merits of each case.

Within that framework, Interior believed it was working with the AJWS in an effective and mutually beneficial relationship. The Department was content that the AJWS 'exercises special care to see that the migrants are of a satisfactory type and that there will be no difficulty in placing them in suitable employment on their arrival'.[53] Activity might typically take place in the following way: of the large number of applications forwarded directly to the Council for German Jewry in London by the corresponding refugee organization in Germany (the *Hilfsverein der Deutschen Juden*), those cases which most closely fitted Australian admission criteria would be forwarded to the AJWS in Sydney, where they would be further studied and, if approved by the Society, application made to the Department of the Interior for a landing permit to be issued. The AJWS would nominate itself as guarantor for the applicant. Upon receipt of the application, the Department would investigate the case. Once it had been approved, the landing permit would be issued (to be forwarded to the applicant upon evidence being presented of £50 landing money). Emigration would then proceed with approval from the Australian authorities.

Satisfactory though this system was for those fortunate enough to fall within it, the migration of Jewish refugees still took place on an individual basis, with no quotas or numerical limits imposed. The Department of the Interior rested its strategy on the premise that those eligible to come to Australia formed a tiny percentage of all the applications received, and that consequently a natural 'upper limit' would establish itself. As 1937 ended, the prevailing attitude was that the system was working. Although under stress, Interior held that – provided no new refugee crisis developed – the gates could remain guarded using the method in operation. The New Year of 1938 would see to it, however, that the government's refugee policy would not remain static. The Immigration Branch of the Department of the Interior was in for its greatest test.

CHAPTER 3
DEVELOPING A RESPONSE

Before and after the Anschluss

On 3 February 1938, the Secretary of the Australian Jewish Welfare Society, Paul A. Cohen, met with the Assistant Minister for the Interior, Victor Thompson, to discuss easing further refugee entry. Cohen explained that the AJWS was not looking at targeting a specific number of people. Thompson replied, 'How many are you asking for each year?' Cohen answered, 'No definite number … we have left it at the maximum for the whole of Australia of ten each week.' Thompson seized upon this: 'You are asking for admission of about 500 a year? … 500 from Germany? Will they all be from Germany?' Cohen stated that the AJWS was formed to deal with German-Jewish emigration and was not in charge of Jewish immigration from other lands. The AJWS was only seeking to introduce *no more* than 500 German Jewish refugees into Australia annually, which was what the Welfare Society considered could be reasonably absorbed.[1]

Thompson came away with a positive impression that the AJWS would take every care both to aid in the selection of suitable immigrants and to see that they did not cause problems after their arrival. His recommendation to the new Interior Minister, John McEwen, prepared five days later, was that 'I can see no valid objection to this request for the admission of not more than 500 German-Jews a year. … It is almost impossible to see how the proposal could be rejected on any rational grounds.'[2] He acknowledged that there could be 'possible political repercussions', and that 'if large numbers of these people come out in boat loads, there would be an augmentation of the newspaper outcry which usually follows' the arrival of other immigrant groups. He considered, however, that the safeguards were such that protests could quickly and easily be dismissed.

The bureaucrats in the Department of the Interior had their own thoughts, Albert Peters recommending that the Commonwealth limit the number to just 100. Five hundred, in his view, was unreasonably high, but if that figure was to be approved then at the very least Interior should have some say in the conditions under which such approval might take place.[3] He suggested the following: a reaffirmation be given about no special facilities for groups of Jewish migrants; the AJWS undertake to place all immigrants in employment, at award rates, and in such circumstances that no-one currently employed would be displaced; and that the number of landing permits be limited to no more than 500 annually, provided that not more than six Jews arrive on any one ship.[4] McEwen approved the recommendation on 7 March 1938 and it was accepted by Cabinet shortly after.[5] The only change made was that the number to be included on any one ship would not exceed twenty.

On 19 April Paul Cohen requested further that 'children under the age of 14 years accompanying their parents be not counted as separate persons'.[6] Peters took this issue up with his senior colleagues in the Department of the Interior on 3 May, pointing out that 'it is presumed that the Quota of 500 approved by Cabinet is to include children under 14'.[7] Tom Garrett prepared a memorandum pointing out that Cabinet's decision was based on the assumption that the number of permits granted to the AJWS would be limited to 500 persons overall, and that Cohen's request be refused. Joseph Carrodus endorsed this, and, on these recommendations, McEwen rejected the request on 9 May 1938.[8]

The pressure now placed on the AJWS was substantial. It could no longer find 500 of the most suitable families and recommend their admission: if children were to be counted among those for admission, the number of families who could enter would be significantly less than 500. Moreover, the Department decided that ninety-three permits, issued to people who had applied for admission through the AJWS in the first quarter of 1938, would be included in the quota of 500 for the remaining nine months of the year.[9] Thus, by the time the Society was informed of the government's decision, one-quarter of the year had gone, and one-fifth of its quota used up – before it even had a chance to commence the scheme.

The AJWS was put under even greater pressure by Germany's annexation of Austria (*Anschluss*) on 12–13 March 1938, when all the same antisemitic measures that had been introduced in Germany over the past five years were now applied to Austrian Jews in the space of some six weeks. Cabinet immediately extended the policies concerning Germany to include Austria, deciding that the new scheme involving 500 AJWS-sponsored refugees per annum 'will include Jews from Austria as well and be subject to the present policy and rules regulating migration to Australia'.[10] Carrodus included this point in his letter to Paul Cohen of 13 April.

Austrian Jews already in London were now reportedly pouring into Australia House in the hope of arranging emigration to Australia. A report in the *Sydney Morning Herald* noted that one such person had asked for ten application forms, 'but only one was available, as the supply had run out'.[11] Not long before, 200,000 forms had been distributed throughout Europe by British embassies acting on behalf of Australia, but these supplies had been quickly used up.[12] The complicating factor for the Australian authorities was that the Nazis, while not prohibiting the departure of Jews from Austria, refused to let them leave with more money than the equivalent of £1 sterling.[13] On this basis alone the Australians would have grounds to reject the refugees. For the sake of international appearances, however, the government preferred to promote an image of welcome and openness.

Indeed, it was only regarding the question of Jewish refugee immigration that the Australian public had any opinion regarding the *Anschluss* at all. There seemed to have been a lack of public interest in the *Anschluss*, and no clear reason why Australia should be involved.[14] This continued the Australian public's ongoing detachment from European affairs, which would persist, in some quarters, right through to the outbreak of war eighteen months later.

Of course, the *Anschluss* was not yet an issue when Paul Cohen and Victor Thompson spoke on 3 February. There were still some 360,000 Jews left in Germany at the beginning of 1938, and the *Anschluss* added another 180,000, making a total of 540,000 – a figure which was 40,000 higher than at the outset of the period in 1933. The annual quota of 500 German Jews, which included children as well as adults and included the newly added Jewish population of Austria, thus disadvantaged Jews seeking to come to Australia. While figures concerning the Jewish identity of immigrants were not kept during these years, the Department of the Interior always proceeded from the assumption that at least 90 per cent of all applicants from Germany and Austria were Jewish.[15] Given the increase in numbers of those who would now be applying, the Australian government's annual figure of 500 AJWS-sponsored refugees was meagre.

The AJWS scheme was not the only way for Jews from Germany and Austria to enter Australia. While the AJWS acted as a clearing house for applications made through approved refugee organizations in Europe or the United Kingdom, many people chose to apply directly to the Department in Canberra, with such applications already assuming deluge proportions even before the *Anschluss*. The *Sydney Morning Herald*, for example, reported in early February 1938 that 'About 30 Germans are referred every day to Australia House [London], where they fill in papers which are sent to Canberra'.[16] Those people, whom the *Herald* identified as 'mostly Jewish exiles', were ready and willing to provide up to £500 in landing money, unaware that only £200 was now necessary.[17] Most were not accepted.

Soon after the *Anschluss*, Interior addressed the new circumstances. In a memorandum dated 14 April 1938, Albert Peters noted that as early as 31 January 1938 the High Commissioner's Office had advised that applications for landing permits were increasing at a rapid rate; now, since the *Anschluss*, a communication had been received from Vienna asking for a further 10,000 application forms.[18] He urged caution in allowing too many of these to be circulated, especially considering that most applicants would be refused in any case. The problem could be solved through the introduction of a quota for Jewish immigrants, and it would be 'unsatisfactory to fix quotas for one country unless similar action were taken in regard to other countries',[19] such as Poland, Hungary and Romania. Arguably, this could have the effect of encouraging those countries to step up their own persecution of Jews in expectation of their unwanted Jewish population being accepted as immigrants to Australia. Peters proposed:

> If it is found that an excessive number of applications are being received from Jews in various countries, and if those who would ordinarily be eligible to receive landing permits considerably exceed 100 a month in the case of any particular nationality, it is suggested that the best applications be selected with the limit of 100 (having regard to the applicant's age, profession or trade, amount of landing capital available, ability to speak English, etc.) and other applications deferred pending further review of the general question shortly after 30th June next.[20]

Joseph Carrodus endorsed these remarks in a private memorandum to John McEwen on 19 April. He drew the Minister's attention to the fact that 'in addition to Jews sponsored by the [Australian Jewish Welfare] Society, large numbers not connected with the Society will desire to come to Australia'. He sought advice, therefore, as to whether special precautions be taken to prevent a large influx of Jews, as it could be anticipated that 'there will be large numbers of applicants who will come within the categories eligible for admission and who, *if they were not Jews*, would be granted permission to enter Australia'.[21]

It was a vexing question. If McEwen agreed to 'special precautions' being taken, he would be agreeing to the imposition of a quota for Jews. If, on the other hand, he was to agree to Peters's suggestion of a go-slow on Jewish applications with a review in a few months' time, he would be sanctioning discrimination along racial lines. Forwarding the issue to Cabinet, the response was to wait and see. The existing policy of evaluating every application according to its merits and rejecting or accepting the applicant on that basis (in reality, accepting or rejecting on the grounds of Jewishness), would continue indefinitely, though the whole issue could be reviewed at some later time.[22]

While not the best outcome, it was probably more satisfactory for the Australian bureaucrats at that time than any alternatives. The Department of the Interior was becoming overworked due to the volume of applications being received, and there was a danger that standards might drop, or a few undesirables slip through its elaborate system of checks and balances – but overall, maintenance of the status quo was the government's preferred option. On one hand, overt racial discrimination was rejected; on the other, all due care would be given to avoid a disproportionate influx of Jews.

March 1938 saw adjustments affecting other areas of European migration. Consideration regarding landing money was to be given to applications from 'Scandinavians, Finns, Danes, Dutch and Germans of non-Jewish origin', as 'they are a desirable type of immigrant who readily assimilate with the general community'. These preferred immigrants had not been arriving in adequate numbers,[23] so it was resolved to modify their landing money requirements. Although single unguaranteed migrants required £100, or £200 in the case of a man with dependent relatives, sympathetic consideration would be given to any individual case which presented 'special features'.[24]

In addition, the Australian and Netherlands governments made an agreement under which migrants guaranteed by the Netherlands Migration Office would have their landing money requirement reduced from £200 to £50 (in the case of a single man) or £100 in the case of a married man with dependent relatives. The major stipulation was that only skilled artisans or agricultural labourers would be included, and that these conditions of entry 'would not apply to persons of Jewish race'.[25] Cabinet gave assent to the scheme on 8 April 1938.[26]

With the proviso effectively barring entry to Jews from the Netherlands, the government's refugee policy, supposedly evolving from one of fear and restriction to token acceptance and admission, was proved to be hollow. In its desire to avoid an influx of Jews from Germany and Austria, Cabinet determined that henceforth all European Jews represented a singular danger to Australia's racial composition and standard of living. Maintaining the status quo in respect of central and eastern European Jews was one way of safeguarding the Commonwealth. Exclusion of Jews from any new arrangements with countries possessing attractive target populations was another. By March 1938, and regardless of the rationale, most European Jews wishing to enter Australia now had little chance of doing so.

Searching for a lead from Britain

While attitudes within the Commonwealth Departments were vital in helping to determine the government's policy, the British government and its overseas representatives also provided significant information, and this intensified during the early part of 1938. As a result, some government Departments placed an increasing reliance upon British precedents or practices in matters outside their own experience. As early as January, for example, an Interdepartmental Committee on the Migration and Control of Aliens discussed whether certificates of naturalization should be denied to aliens who were known members of Nazi and fascist organizations. It was decided that the Australian External Affairs Officer in London be asked to ascertain the British practice in such matters.[27]

Throughout 1938 British representatives in Europe began suggesting policy implementation to their Australian colleagues in Canberra. One such initiative came from the British passport control officer at Budapest, V. C. Farrell. In a letter dated 29 March 1938 to the Secretary of the Department of the Interior, he offered a few observations regarding immigrant applications from Hungary which, he believed, 'may be of interest' to the Commonwealth authorities.

In the first place, he noted, some '99% of the applications are from persons of Jewish race'. This came as no surprise to Peters and Garrett, but Farrell's next statement must surely have raised eyebrows. 'Whilst desiring to be fair-minded', he wrote, 'the present wave of anti-semitism in Central Europe may be attributed very largely to the tendency of Jews, where possible, to unite among themselves in unceasing clannish endeavour to oust Aryan enterprise whenever it appears in competition with Jewish interests.'[28] He then proceeded to outline the professions in which such immigrants usually engaged ('medicine, architecture, salesmanship, [and] shopkeeping'), drawing the conclusion that 'This type of immigrant ... does not as a rule give the impression of ever being likely to become a loyal and creditable pioneer in the Dominions.'[29] Sentiments like this had rarely been forthcoming in the past. Coming from a member of His Majesty's Foreign Service, the document gave those in the Department of the Interior something to think about. Farrell's authority could not be questioned; he was, after all, a specialist in passport matters, the man on the spot and the officer designated by the British government to represent Australia's migration interests in Budapest.

Further, he suggested that the Australian government could improve its immigration process if application forms were only issued to prospective migrants from a British passport control officer 'of the country in which the immigrant is domiciled'. This would disqualify Jews moving from country to country seeking permanent admission to British territories. Once an application form had been completed, 'it should be accompanied by a letter giving the views of this officer on the case submitted.'[30] Although Farrell's suggestion was not taken up, handwritten notations indicate that his ideas were taken into consideration by the Department of the Interior in the months and years that followed.

British policy was opposed to any direct interference in Dominion affairs. This was spelled out most clearly in London, in a letter from the Secretary of State for the Dominions, Lord Stanley, in May 1938. He stated:

> the question of Jewish migration to Australia is one entirely for the Commonwealth Government and it is for them to decide the numbers of migrants who can be admitted and the conditions with which each migrant may be required to comply. It is not a matter on which the Government here could intervene with the Commonwealth Government. Indeed, any such intervention might do more harm than good.[31]

A few days later, as if to highlight the point, an official in the Dominions Office minuted to Lord Stanley that it would be 'best for us, while helping unofficially in any way in our power, to keep out of anything which looks like intervention with the Dominion Governments'.[32] The British and Australian governments thus found themselves in a curious relationship. While the Australians sought guidance from Whitehall from time to time, the British government was conscious that assistance might be viewed in Canberra as interference.

Australia's relationship with Britain throughout this period was dominated by concern over appeasement. Should Australia align itself with the policies pursued by British Prime Minister Neville Chamberlain? Should it seek to influence Britain in concert with the other Dominions? Or should it retreat into a policy of isolation which, while leaving the country vulnerable, would nonetheless not find itself chained to Downing Street's position, the outcome of which was uncertain?[33] Where matters relating to immigration were concerned, moreover, the Australians found themselves in a further quandary. Acknowledgement of a person's status as a refugee is a statement about the nature of that person's origin. It is a judgement being passed on the regime from which the person comes. Every time Australia used the term 'refugee' to describe those fleeing Nazi Germany – whether Jewish or not – the government was commenting negatively on the conduct of another sovereign state. In this way, immigration policy and foreign affairs bisected, a situation the leery Australians would unquestionably have preferred to avoid.

At this time, however, and despite these concerns, some British representatives did seek to help Australia where they could. Certainly, the British High Commissioner in Canberra, Sir Geoffrey Whiskard, saw distinct advantages for Australia from an increase in foreign population. He expressed his views in a letter to London dated 23 June 1938:

I should regard this alien admixture as valuable to a country whose population is at present rather monotonous in its composition. My personal view is that this comparatively small admixture is likely to bring considerable benefits, not least in promoting a higher competitive standard in those professional and commercial activities in which they are most likely to be engaged.[34]

Interested British parties were one thing; concrete action in Australia as a positive response to that interest was quite another. The Australians were prepared to refer to London regarding the broader aspects of the refugee problem, notwithstanding the fact that the actual admission or rejection of immigrants was always up to the Australian government. These two approaches – consultation and autonomy – would merge in March 1938 when the United States issued an invitation to specially selected countries to attend a conference that would discuss the issue of refugees from Germany and Austria.[35] Australia would find itself faced with the dilemma of either participating in this potentially crucial gathering on its own responsibility or following an unknown, uncertain and possibly disinterested British line.

Agreement to participate did not, however, signal a shelving of Australia's own attempts at finding a solution to the refugee problem. On the contrary, the Department of the Interior, fully aware that the *Anschluss* had aggravated the number of refugees, soon sought Cabinet approval to rationalize refugee admission to manageable dimensions. The Australian Jewish Welfare Society was taking care of 500 applications annually; that presented no problem, as the administrative details and the necessary guarantees had largely been assumed by the Society. Of greater concern to the Department were those applicants who did not have guarantors but who, possessing at least £200 landing money, and fulfilling the usual health and character standards, were applying for admission independently.

After the Anschluss: Jews are a race

The volume of such applications intensified after the *Anschluss*. On 31 March 1938, a report from Vienna referred to 6,000 applications from Austrian Jews seeking visas to Australia, to which Prime Minister Lyons responded: 'as much as we sympathise with the sufferings of these people, the Ministry cannot permit a large influx of aliens into Australia.'[36] However, as the number of applications increased, Lyons stopped making statements and left the problem in the hands of the Minister of the Interior and his Department. On 5 April Melbourne's *Argus* reported that requests for immigration application forms 'have increased until at present they have reached nearly 100 a day'.[37] A few weeks later, interviewing a Polish Jew recently arrived in Perth, the paper printed his comment that 'Almost all Poland's 3,500,000 Jews would leave the country overnight if they had a chance'.[38]

This immediately set off alarm bells. The Department of the Interior came under increasing pressure to do something to ease Parliamentary concerns and responded by preparing a memorandum which John McEwen presented to Cabinet on 25 May. In this, he noted that applications from non-guaranteed Austrian and German Jews 'are now being received at the average rate of approximately 300 a week', which, with dependents, 'may cover twice this number'.[39] He identified the government's dilemma: the majority of applications made by non-guaranteed Jews possessing at least £200 landing money, 'if dealt with according to the usual rules *and not taking the racial aspect into consideration*, would be ones for approval.' To grant them would mean, however, issuing landing permits 'in favour of approximately 20,000 Jews for this year, assuming, as seems likely to be the case, that the present rate of applications will be maintained'.[40] Further, there was 'little doubt' that 'the majority of the Jewish applicants, if admitted, would be able to establish themselves in business or occupations without much difficulty'.

It seemed, therefore, that the time for a larger intake of Jewish refugee immigrants, all of whom satisfied government standards of maintenance, character, health and employment, had arrived. But the government's long-standing aversion to a more liberal policy was apparent: despite all the factors in favour of increased Jewish immigration, McEwen raised three objections to the idea of admitting what he called 'a large number of Jews'. These were '(a) their non-assimilability; (b) their disregard of Australian living and working conditions … [and] (c) that the number of alien migrants would be considerably swelled in relation to British migration'.[41] He put the proposition, therefore, that Cabinet consider whether 'to limit the number of Jews to be granted permits to enter Australia'.

Moreover, he sought a blanket ruling concerning all Jews, not simply those seeking admission as refugees. The choice came down to one of two options: whether each individual application should be considered on its merits according to the general rules (notwithstanding the fact that doing so would probably involve the annual admission of over 20,000 Jews), or whether 'some limitation of numbers should be placed on the issue of permits to Jews'.

In making its decision, Cabinet took its lead from Interior. McEwen had asked, for example, whether a quota of 300 Jews with no guarantors per month should be established. When the question was put to Cabinet for consideration, that figure was accepted.[42] Other questions, in a similar vein, were also put:

Is any preference to be given to persons of one nationality as against another, e.g. Austrians and Germans in preference to Poles?

Is any preference to be given in respect of occupations?

Is any preference to be given according to the amount of capital an applicant can introduce?

Is preference to be given to younger applicants, e.g. if a selection say of 300 is to be made from 1,000 applicants, should preference be given to those under 40 years of age, other qualifications being more or less equal?

Is discretion to be allowed as regards types (to be judged from photographs and references furnished, as well as from questions of nationality and occupation)?

The answers to all these questions, initialled by the Prime Minister, was an unconditional 'Yes'.[43]

The memorandum resulted in a reduction of overall numbers of Jews to be admitted. From an average 300 non-guaranteed *weekly* approvals (which was only ever a potential figure, and never actually reached), government policy henceforth saw that a quota should operate for the admission of not more than 300 non-guaranteed Jews *per month*. It was a decision based solely according to racial criteria; the memorandum itself admitted this when it concluded that 'the adoption of the suggestion to limit the number would mean the establishment of a quota for Jews, *who are a race as distinct from a nationality*'.[44] From now on the government would be knowingly adopting a discriminatory policy.

The following month, Lyons instructed Bruce in London to inform British representatives in Berlin, Vienna, Warsaw and Budapest that they should warn intending applicants that 'there is little prospect of further applications being granted during [the] present year except in very special circumstances'.[45] It was considered there were 'more than sufficient applications already at hand to cover [the] number likely to be approved' for the next year.

With all the talk of vast numbers of Jews applying to come to Australia, the Department of the Interior decided the time had come to reassure the nation that it still had the situation in hand. In a memorandum to the Department of External Affairs in April 1938, Interior stated there was currently a 'misapprehension' that 'the British proportion in Australia is likely to be seriously diluted by the numbers of aliens arriving in Australia'.[46] The Department pointed out that this was not the case. It noted how the 1933 census revealed that the overall proportion of people 'of British birth' was 98 per cent.[47] As a counter to fears of what large-scale alien immigration could do, the Department projected:

If the alien population increased by 10,000 annually during the next ten years and there was no gain of population by British migration, the dilution of the population of British birth at the end of that period would be only 2.3 per cent, provided the annual natural increase remained at 50,000 per annum.

It was highly unlikely that this would take place, especially as an increase in British migration was expected from 1938 onwards – an increase which, it was hoped, would turn 'the tide of British migration in favour of Australia and … lessen the degree of alien dilution'.[48] Following this, on 4 May 1938 McEwen duly informed Parliament that there was no need for alarm at the reports of increased Jewish immigration, as the government had decided 'no special facilities could be granted for the admission of Jewish migrants'.[49]

The Commonwealth Investigation Branch had its own view about the future of Jewish immigration after the *Anschluss*. Notes prepared for the assistance of Branch officers declared that it was improbable that an anti-Jewish feeling would be created by the admission of a restricted number of Jews from Germany and Austria, given than any anti-Jewish feeling 'seems largely directed against certain types of Eastern Jews and their business and sweating methods'. Further, admitting 'a few thousand' would not be felt as an undue increase of the Jewish percentage.[50]

The view was expressed that Jewish refugees fleeing Germany and Austria were generally both desirable and highly attractive. 'A great proportion of Austrian Jews,' for example, were 'of a very cultured type, completely assimilated to western civilisation'; they were '98–99% townspeople, mostly active in trade and commerce'. Those needing to emigrate included lawyers, doctors, industrialists (some of whom could establish industries 'which had up to now not existed' in Australia) and scientists.[51] German Jews were considered to be of a 'high standard' culturally – especially those from the larger cities. They, like the Austrian Jews, belonged mostly to the trade, commerce and professional classes, but 'Many of them are willing to take on other occupations'. The attitude of the Investigation Branch was:

In type, culture and economic standard these Jews form a completely different nation from the Jews who here have created some anti-Jewish feeling: the Polish and other Eastern Jews in Carlton [Melbourne] for instance. In looks and behaviour they are rather German than Jewish, [and] the same applies to their culture and their business ethics.[52]

Polish and eastern European Jews remained the bane of Australian immigration:

a great proportion of the Jews is very poor, culturally on a similar level as the people with which they live and used to different moral, cultural and ethical standards than those prevailing in Western Europe. … If … [they] may easily be assimilated in Australia remains open to doubt.[53]

Austrian and German Jewish refugees, then, were relatively more desirable as immigrants than other Jews seeking admission. Further, the Investigation Branch identified Australia as being 'second in the scale of overseas countries open to Jewish immigration' after the United States. These attitudes indicated that if the Investigation Branch had controlled immigration – as many were later to suggest it should – a different set of policies might have been adopted.

Of course, not everyone in Australia felt as welcoming of German and Austrian refugee Jews as the Commonwealth Investigation Branch would have preferred. A key issue was that of dilution of White Australia. As early as January 1938 Sydney's *Daily Telegraph* had stated that 'we cannot permit the establishment of any colony detached from the broad stream of Australian life', and that, while Australia 'will welcome Jewish immigrants who become Australian citizens,' nonetheless 'we owe much of our national content to the homogeneity of our population'. The Jewish people had, it noted, 'proved themselves admirable immigrants and settlers,' but 'Australia cannot permit the growth of any isolated foreign community, whatever its nationality'.[54] Radical right-wing weekly *The Bulletin* had similar sentiments, when in April 1938 it expressed the view that 'So long as European immigrants are personally desirable, and are ready to make Australia their country, and so long as they do not come in such numbers as to threaten to alter the racial balance, they should be welcome'.[55]

Occasionally, avowedly antisemitic letters made their way to the Department of the Interior, though these only came in significant numbers later in the year. One early example, however, came from Peter Ferrier, a citizen of Brisbane. His letter, dated 11 February 1938, circulated through the Department throughout the first few months of 1938. His first statement was that 'we have far too many' Jews in Australia already, who form 'a real menace to any white nation if allowed much latitude'. On refugees, he observed that 'scores of thousands of cunning, beastly, Communists who advocate every beastiality [sic] including drugging, abortion, and white family life have been booted out of Germany'. This was bad enough, but 'Even if Jews weren't in the main Communistically inclined, I should still object to them for themselves'. Removing the Jews had had a profound effect on Germany, which had 'never been so progressive and strong'. And what was the nature of those the Germans were expelling? The same as those in Australia – 'the hordes of clothing sweaters, rack-renting slum owners, "fences," burgulars [sic], share and other business racketeers, drug peddlers, abortionists, and contraceptive agents'. He noted that 'A flood of Jews to Australia would mean that before very long nearly every public medical and legal post would be held by a Jew as in pre-Hitler Germany, Poland, [and] Roumania'.[56] The impressions presented in this letter touched on images long advanced by acknowledged antisemites. Notably, it was one of the first of this genre received by the Department of the Interior as a direct response to the refugee issue.[57] It was certainly not the last, especially once a refugee presence in Australia was established later in 1938 and during 1939.

Admission of non-Jewish refugees

The variety of post-*Anschluss* statements and observations concerning future refugee migration seemed united in one area – the refugee issue was racial, not political, and the 'race' in question was Jewish. Midway through 1938, however, the government's attention was directed to the fact that not all refugees were in fact Jews. Representations were received, almost simultaneously, outlining two such instances; the plight of German and Austrian Catholics, and that of so-called non-Aryan Christians (i.e. professed Christians with at least one Jewish grandparent). Definite proposals concerning the latter's migration to Australia were received first.

On 1 June 1938, the Honorary Secretary of the German Emergency Fellowship Committee (GEFC), Camilla Wedgwood, approached John McEwen in Canberra to put the cause of the 'non-Aryan Christians' before the government. After stating that the GEFC was 'not a very financial body', and that consequently it could not 'give the guarantees for after-care that the Jewish Welfare Association was in a position to give', she asked McEwen the following questions for his earliest consideration:

(1)   Could the landing money be reduced in cases where the Committee was in a position to introduce a person and find him or her employment?

(2)   Could the production of a certificate from a police officer as to character be dispensed with, and a personal guarantee substituted?

(3)   Could the period of guarantee be reduced from 5 years?

(4)   Could a joint guarantee from the employer and the Committee be accepted?[58]

She then suggested that the government consider admitting a trial number of twenty families under GEFC auspices.

McEwen's response was to ask Wedgwood to submit a more definite proposal on this final point, 'setting out where they would go, [and] what arrangements would be made for placing them and for general after-care'. After this had been done, the whole scheme could be discussed with Albert Peters.[59] A few days later, Wedgwood and Peters hammered out the details of a compromise proposal which then found its way to Cabinet, where it was approved on 9 June. The proposal suggested that the Committee be granted permission to introduce up to twenty single 'non-Aryan Christians' for agricultural work or domestic service over the next six months, that they be under thirty years of age, and that males possess at least £50 and females at least £25 pounds landing money.[60]

This saw the figure of twenty families drop to twenty individuals. Still, a precedent had now been set for Interior to provide special facilities for the admission of suitably guaranteed non-Jewish refugees. Any organization offering to help in coordinating and regulating the flow of applications from such people, it seemed, was now likely to obtain a sympathetic hearing.

This logic determined the course of action taken by Interior over the second class of non-Jewish refugees, German and Austrian Catholics. Life for Catholics in Nazi Germany became steadily harsher as time went on and by 1938 thousands, often for political reasons, were fleeing Germany. Many settled temporarily in Britain with a view to future, more permanent, emigration. In 1938 a Catholic Committee was established in the United Kingdom by Cardinal Hinsley, the Archbishop of Westminster, for the purpose of assisting those who had already escaped from Germany. On 23 May he wrote to Prime Minister Lyons – himself a Catholic – to ask for Lyons's 'generous assistance in regard to the possibility of admitting German and Austrian Catholics of good character as immigrants into Australia'. His letter asked how 'well-selected cases of these Catholic refugees might be admitted to the Commonwealth'. Further, he inquired 'In what occupations or professions are there any openings?' and whether preliminary training would be required prior to applications behind made. He would be grateful to the Prime Minister for 'any guidance upon these and other such practical questions as may occur'. He would then, upon receipt of an informative reply, construct a detailed and formal proposal.[61]

On 4 July Lyons acknowledged the Cardinal's letter and stated that he would take the matter up with McEwen before advising him 'of the conditions under which these Catholic refugees from Germany and Austria can be admitted to Australia'.[62] The main thrust of Hinsley's letter had been to request information; Lyons now gave a personal and immediate undertaking that a way would be found to get Catholic refugees into Australia. Assistant Minister Victor Thompson asked Peters to prepare a memorandum as an aid in drafting a detailed positive reply to Cardinal Hinsley.

The memorandum reaffirmed the existing policy pertaining to aliens generally: that is, that those who were guaranteed possessed at least £50 landing money, and those without guarantors at least £200. Peters then outlined the work done by the AJWS (for Jews) and the GEFC (for 'non-Aryan Christians'), together with the terms under which the government had agreed to their activities. Based on the examples shown by these two organizations, the memorandum suggested that Cardinal Hinsley be advised:

> that the satisfactory settlement in Australia of the class of immigrant in question would best be achieved if some responsible organisation of the Roman Catholic Church in Australia were to undertake to be responsible for their maintenance for a period, say, of two years after arrival, and also to find employment for them at ruling rates of pay without Australian workers being displaced to make way for them; and that if such an organisation were set up, every consideration would be given to the question of authorising the admission of a limited number of nominees of the organisation, subject to 50 pounds landing money for male nominees, and 25 pounds in the case of females, provided that particulars were furnished to enable each case to be judged on its merits in accordance with the usual practice.[63]

Based on this response, an organization called the Continental Catholic Migrants Welfare Committee was set up in Sydney.

Catholics formed a significant minority of the Australian population. E. M. Andrews has estimated that between 1935 and 1939 somewhere between 20 and 22 per cent of the population were Catholics, with most living in New South Wales and Victoria.[64] Their most prominent and influential religious leader was the outspoken Archbishop Daniel Mannix of Melbourne, while another Irish-born senior cleric, Archbishop James Duhig of Brisbane, also held a great deal of authority over the Church in Australia (albeit in a more conciliatory and less vociferous manner). The Melbourne Catholic newspaper, *The Advocate*, edited by D. G. M. (Denys) Jackson, was 'outstanding in its interest in, and knowledge of, foreign events',[65] which Jackson reinforced through his contributions to the weekly *Sunday Catholic Hour* on the radio. In New South Wales, on the other hand, the *Catholic Freeman's Journal* and the *Catholic Press* were much less concerned with overseas events. Indeed:

> Catholic spokesmen seem agreed that lay Catholic opinion was largely naïve and uninformed between the wars, adopting the stand of the rest of the community unless roused specifically to do otherwise by foreign events which had an emotional impact.[66]

It has been suggested that Catholics might also act 'if roused by the united force of Catholic journals, preachers, and leaders'.[67]

These inputs contributed to an atmosphere in which the educated Catholic elites held sway and spoke on behalf of a Catholic population that was simultaneously ignorant of, and disinterested in, overseas issues. The establishment of the Continental Catholic Migrants Welfare Committee in Sydney was thus underwritten by only a small (though highly influential) segment of Catholics. How far the introduction of German and Austrian Catholics into the Australian mainstream would have been supported or even welcomed is impossible to determine. What can be concluded, however, is that Catholics in positions of authority, such as Lyons, were often well placed to achieve specific outcomes without having to consider an informed, broad-based wider Catholic population.

Taken collectively, the Australian Jewish Welfare Society, the German Emergency Fellowship Committee (later renamed the European Emergency Committee) and the Continental Catholic Migrants Welfare Committee provided an important avenue for the promotion of non-Jewish refugee immigration, and subsequent months would see an intensification of effort on the part of all three organizations.

The refugee situation up to mid-1938

At the beginning of 1938 Australia had only the rudimentary outline of a refugee policy. Government Ministers, uncertain of what to do in view of the increasing number of applications coming from Jews in Germany, decided not to act in the hope that the problem would either clear up or go away. Yet in the second quarter of the year the government, forced by pressures both in and outside the country, would develop a definite policy regarding refugees and, later, perform at a major international gathering on the refugee question. Projecting itself to the world as the model for all democratic immigrant-receiving countries, Australia nonetheless proceeded with a policy restricting, rather than relaxing, refugee admission. It remained to be seen whether the international meeting on refugees, to be held in France in July 1938 at the invitation of US President Franklin Roosevelt, would have any effect on this position.

The first steps on the road to German domination of Europe had already been taken with the forcible incorporation of Austria into the Reich in March 1938, with the antisemitic measures the Nazis had taken five years to develop in Germany applied to Austria in a space of weeks. The brutality of the *Anschluss* was reported extensively in the Australian press, and public opinion now began to play a role in the formation of government policy. But harsh though the Nazis' methods were, when considering Australian refugee policy, it is important to realize that the Australians were developing a refugee policy (where none had previously existed), not a rescue-from-the-Holocaust policy.

Therefore, the formation and execution of Australian strategies towards the Jews of Germany and Austria must, from the beginning of 1938 onwards, be judged according to the standards of the time. If Australia had a migration policy which was ostensibly non-discriminatory, it is according to that claim against which its admission of refugees needs to be measured. If Jews were being rejected despite meeting the government's own established criteria, it is on this basis that the government should be assessed. Finally, where the Australian public was deliberately deceived over certain aspects of the government's policy, this too is a fair basis for evaluating those who framed and executed the Australian position in 1938.

The first six months of 1938 provided just such an opportunity. The greater the intensification of anti-Jewish measures in Germany became, the more Australia was forced to respond to them – and these responses, as we shall see, nearly always compromised existing assumptions and criteria.

CHAPTER 4
AUSTRALIA AND THE EVIAN CONFERENCE

Initial responses

The Evian Conference of July 1938, prompted by key political advisers in Washington, DC, was the brainchild of US President Franklin D. Roosevelt, who invited selected countries to meet and discuss what had by now become a global refugee crisis. His motive in calling the conference was to deflect American public opinion and make it appear that the United States was doing something tangible to assist Germany's Jews. Inviting selected countries to participate would show that the United States was concerned to find a solution to the refugee issue, and that the problem was not to be dumped onto the United States. Invitees were advised that the gathering was not intended to compromise any country's existing policy, and none would be required to make a commitment to receive refugee Jews.[1] Yet the initiative was received cautiously in some quarters, particularly in Switzerland – the home of the League of Nations High Commission for Refugees. Roosevelt had originally hoped to locate his meeting in a Swiss city, the better to establish it as a legitimate gathering of a genuinely international nature. The Swiss refused, possibly to avoid embarrassment over their own increasingly restrictive policies.[2] A French city near the Swiss border was chosen as the next best option to retain the internationalist spirit. Invitations went out to some twenty-nine nations with an interest in the refugee issue; the final number of those attending was thirty-two.

The United States issued its invitation in hopes of convening a committee that would facilitate 'the emigration from Austria, and presumably from Germany, of political refugees'.[3] Australia, which did not possess an international diplomatic presence, found itself faced with the dilemma of either participating on its own responsibility or slavishly following an unknown, uncertain, and possibly disinterested British line.

On 24 March 1938, the US government asked Britain's Foreign Office whether 'the British Government (on its own behalf or on behalf of the self-governing Dominions) [would] be willing to cooperate with the Government of the United States in setting up such a committee. The idea was that 'whereas such representatives would be designated by the Governments concerned, any financing of the emergency emigration referred to would be undertaken by private organisations within the respective countries'. It reiterated that 'no country would be expected or asked to receive a greater number of emigrants than is permitted by its existing legislation.'[4] The invitation stated that the reason for calling the meeting was 'the urgency of the problem with which the world is faced and the necessity of speedy cooperative effort under Government supervision if widespread human suffering is to be averted'.[5]

The immediate attitude of the British Foreign Office was expressed by a senior official, Roger Makins (later Baron Sherfield), the next day. Owing to America's long post-war tradition of isolationism, Makins minuted that 'it is on general grounds desirable to encourage and support any United States proposal involving American interest in European affairs and any inclination to co-operate with foreign governments, however "half-baked" a particular proposal may in its inception appear'.[6] His major misgiving was that if it was shown that the countries of the world were prepared to open their doors wider to refugees, it could encourage the German government to intensify its anti-Jewish persecution. And not the German government alone: 'Other European countries with surplus populations, and particularly Poland and Roumania, may well intensify the persecution of Jews and others whom they do not want in the hope of getting rid of them through the good offices of the committee.'[7] Makins recommended that the British Empire 'should as far as possible present a united front in regard to this question [and] we ought to urge the Dominions to do all they can to bring this about'.[8]

Later that same day the first attempt at gaining such cooperation was made when the Foreign Office suggested to the Treasury and the Home, Colonial, and Dominions Offices that an interdepartmental meeting take place to discuss the questions raised by the American proposal.[9] This meeting took place a few days later. Makins represented the Foreign Office and W. J. Garnett, a specialist on migration matters, acted for the Dominions Office. The meeting produced a lengthy memorandum which was transmitted to the US government on 30 March. The gist was relatively simple; the US initiative was welcomed but should not be used to detract from the work of existing refugee agencies such as the League of Nations High Commission for Refugees (of which the United States was not a member). The British government would, however, 'gladly accept the proposals in the United States memorandum'.[10] Doubts as to the success of the meeting remained, Garrett suggesting that 'there is little prospect of the Dom[inion]s or Col[onie]s being able to help materially in finding homes for the refugees' and this would likely be 'the general reaction of all nations participating'.[11]

Australia first heard officially about the American proposal when R. A. Wiseman of the Dominions Office sent a letter to Stanley Bruce in London on 1 April 1938. Informing Bruce that the United States had invited Britain and other European and American countries as well as Canada, South Africa and Eire, Wiseman asked, 'what reply His Majesty's Government in the Commonwealth of Australia would wish to be returned to the invitation made to them by the United States Government?'[12] The British government stated it was disposed favourably to the idea of a gathering on German refugees, vital information in helping the Australian government to make its decision. On 5 April the Official Secretary at Australia House, V. C. Duffy, wrote to the Dominions Office requesting a copy of the British government's response to the American proposal before any Australian statement was made.[13]

In London, Bruce's instinct was that Australia should accept the invitation.[14] Writing to Prime Minister Lyons, he noted that Australia would not be going out on a limb if it agreed to participate, as France, Sweden and five Latin American countries had already agreed to join with the United States in the new committee, 'prompted by [the] urgency of [the] problem and [a] desire to avert widespread human suffering'.[15] All relevant correspondence was forwarded to Duffy at Australia House on 8 April.[16]

A cable sent from Lyons to Bruce on the same day stated that Australia was prepared to attend, but only if Britain was also there. Once Britain's participation had been confirmed – and only then – would Bruce be permitted to accept the American invitation on behalf of Australia.[17] It was a Cabinet decision,[18] influenced strongly by Lyons himself. The Prime Minister's own views were clear: once Australia's participation had been finalized, its delegate would be instructed along the following lines: 'each case will be considered on its merits on application in the usual form being submitted to the Department of the Interior,' and Australia was prepared 'to receive applications for permits from non-Jewish Austrians'.[19] Lyons's instructions were for Bruce's 'personal information only at present'.[20]

For its part, the US Embassy in London remained unsure about Australia's attendance as late as 26 May 1938.[21] By now, the date and place of the proposed meeting had been arranged: it was to take place at the Royal Hotel in the French resort town of Evian-les-Bains from 6 July onwards and was henceforth to be referred to as an 'Inter-Governmental Committee' rather than a conference or meeting.

At an interdepartmental meeting in London on 8 June the Foreign Office informed other Departments that the Dominions were not pulling their weight. Australia would be represented, but prospects for attendance by the others were not good. Discussion took place as to whether the British government should request the Dominion governments to cooperate, for 'on broad grounds of policy it is undesirable that the Dominions should not appear interested or willing to assist in this problem'.[22] R. A. Wiseman expressed the view that it was 'not possible for His Majesty's Government in the United Kingdom to influence [the Dominions'] attitude',[23] but Roger Makins commented on the external implications for Britain and the Empire:

> the United States Government probably regarded the British Empire as in a position to make an important contribution to the problem, but it seemed that not only could the Empire make no adequate contribution, but that only one or two Dominions would even be represented at the conference. It would be open to the United States to criticise very strongly this negative response to their initiative and to attribute to it any blame that may accrue from a possible failure of the meeting.[24]

The Dominions Office countered that 'it is best for us, while helping unofficially in any way in our power, to keep out of anything which looks like intervention with the Dominion governments'.[25] The view was expressed that while the Dominions sought the British lead in foreign affairs, immigration was viewed as a domestic rather than an external matter and that they would find British intervention in their domestic affairs an unwarranted intrusion.

The interdepartmental committee resolved that the respective Secretaries of State suggest to Cabinet that Britain approach the Dominions and seek their attendance at the conference. The Dominions Office remained sceptical that it would do any good but would not stand in the way of such an attempt being made.[26] In the event, something positive did come out of these representations; while South Africa did not attend, Australia, Canada, New Zealand and Eire (which had not been invited but went anyway) did – a significant improvement over Australia alone. As 6 July drew closer, Australian activity in Canberra and London intensified, until the final matter – the composition of the Australia delegation – was addressed.

The Australian team was assembled from staff serving at the High Commissioner's Office in London, but was led by Lieutenant-Colonel Thomas Walter White, the Federal Minister for Trade and Customs. His advisers were Alfred Stirling (External Affairs Officer, Department of External Affairs, based at London) and A. W. Stuart-Smith (Australia House, London); his Private Secretary was Mrs M. Grant. White arrived at Evian on the evening of 5 July, having flown that day from Berlin; the other members of the delegation left from London the day before, and had arrived at Evian in time to greet the Minister.

Colonel White was a second-choice candidate. Also present in London at the time of the conference were Sir Earle Page, leader of the Country Party and thus de facto Deputy Prime Minister, and Robert Menzies, the Commonwealth Attorney-General. The formidable team of Page, Menzies, White and Bruce had been in London to discuss imperial trade, though responses to Nazi Germany's expansionist foreign policy were also high on the agenda in their discussions with senior British political leaders.[27] When attention turned to the meeting at Evian, a more logical choice as Australia's representative could have been Stanley Bruce, but he had earlier declined to propose himself as a delegate, preferring to work from London in a liaison capacity. Besides, White was not altogether unsuitable as a delegate, as his qualifications as a civic and military leader in interwar Australia were without match. He had served as the Minister for Trade and Customs since 1933, and although the matters to be discussed at the Evian Conference did not concern his portfolio directly, he was nonetheless senior enough in the Cabinet to speak on behalf of the government.

Britain's Jewish community was confident about the success of the conference, and in this, Australia featured highly. As early as 7 April, Norman Bentwich, Professor of Law and a leading figure in London's Council for German Jewry, reported to Roger Makins that 'as regards the British Empire his main hopes were now centred on Australia and New Zealand,' and these hopes could be realized at Evian.[28] Bentwich was later to recall that Australia had become a 'blessed word' to the victims of persecution in Europe.[29]

In contrast, hopes for the success of the conference ran high among only a few in Australia. One was Colonel Harold Cohen, a leading member of Melbourne's Jewish community and Member for Caulfield in the Victorian Parliament. On 7 July 1938 *The Argus* reported him as saying that out of an overall Australian population of seven-and-a-half million 'a few thousand people of high technical knowledge, most of whom had means', would present little problem of absorption:

> people of the type described did not remain a self-contained community as did some of the European nationalities. No one had more reason to be a loyal Australian,

or to desire to serve the community in which he lived, than had a British citizen of the Jewish faith, and there were innumerable examples in Australia of effective public service rendered by such people.[30]

In Australia, such statements issued while the conference was taking place served to heighten interest. Perhaps the most thought-provoking comment, however, came from the editor of the *Sydney Morning Herald* on the opening day of the conference, 6 July. Several important issues were raised in an editorial which reinforced the *Herald's* well-known attitude to the refugee issue:

> The test of the sincerity of international sympathy with the refugees and would-be refugees will come when the conference is invited to consider what practical steps can be taken to succour them. Pious resolutions will not help the distressed or deliver the oppressed from the hands of the persecutor. They must be given sanctuary in new lands and assistance to reach those lands. How far are the nations represented at Evian prepared to go?[31]

On Australia's participation, the *Herald* was even more forthright:

> Are we in Australia, for example – to bring the question right home – ready to adopt a generous policy regarding the admission of the thousands of Austro-German refugees who are clamouring to come to these shores? ... over-nicety ... must defeat the whole purpose of the Evian Conference, and expose the delegations to the Nazi taunt that democratic commiseration with and championship of persecuted peoples stop short of giving them the only kind of sympathy and support that counts.

'Why should,' the *Herald* asked, 'the rest of the world ... burden itself with the consequences of Germany's barbaric treatment of the Jews?' The answer was simple: because the Nazi pursuit of 'these unfortunate people' was one to 'excite the indignant contempt of all liberal-minded peoples'. Germany's actions were 'entirely indefensible', and it mattered greatly that 'something should be done to relieve the sufferings of the victims of malice and misfortune'.[32] It remained to be seen, of course, whether the attitude of the *Sydney Morning Herald* would be also that of the Australian government.

Australia at Evian

On the opening morning of the conference, Thomas White sought out the representatives of Britain and the other Dominions – Lord Winterton (United Kingdom), Hume Wrong (Canada), Cyril Burdekin (New Zealand) and Frank Cremins (Eire) – and a short consultation took place between them.[33] Information was necessary, as those attending had received very little information as to the conference agenda or its specific aims.[34] A measure of uncertainty prevailed as to 'whether the Conference would take in not only the actual problem of German and Austrian refugees..., but the potential problem as it existed in Poland, Roumania, and Hungary and also of course in such other countries as Spain'.[35] There was clearly a great deal of which the delegates needed to become apprised before the conference actually got under way, and the Dominion representatives, facing the Pandora's Box of problems the conference had lain before them, sought safety in numbers from the outset.

The plenary meeting of the conference took place later that morning. The French delegate, Henry Bérenger, took the Chair as host to welcome representatives of the thirty-two states attending.[36] Speeches of welcome then followed from the American and British representatives (the former of whom, Myron C. Taylor, was elected Conference President). The formalities over, the conference then proceeded to hear statements from all the nations present. The representatives quickly got to the point, and it was not long before the gist of the Evian Conference was made clear: all countries understood the need for international cooperation, 'but in almost every instance it was pointed out that the opportunity for absorbing refugees was limited owing to economic conditions'.[37] The countries represented at Evian were unable, or unwilling, to agree to anything like mass migration. Some countries – particularly those from Latin America – indicated a willingness to accept agricultural refugees or those who could bring a degree of wealth with them; others agreed to consider plans for refugee settlement in rural colonies only. It appeared, in the words of one observer, as though all these expressions 'had been prepared for "home consumption" as well as with an eye to public opinion abroad, and that consequently delegates had refrained as far as possible from making any specific commitments'.[38] The United States, as host, did nothing more than publicly affirm its already existing annual quota of 27,370 Germans and Austrians, a figure that had to include non-refugee German immigrants and non-Jewish refugees, as well as Jews.

The British government had misgivings about the whole conference, and much preferred to utilize the already existing League of Nations High Commission for Refugees. Britain was also wary about drawing too much attention to the refugee problem in case the representatives assembled at Evian began to make disquieting noises about Palestine as a Jewish haven. Indeed, this concern led to the British government insisting that the President of the Jewish Agency for Palestine, Dr. Chaim Weizmann, not be permitted to address the delegates, even privately.[39]

On the second day of the conference Thomas White outlined Australia's refugee policy. The thrust of his speech was in line with that of the others. He asserted the special position of the Dominions regarding the policy of Britain, espousing that the Dominions were 'free partners in the British Commonwealth and arbiters of their own economies and national destinies'. He stated that 'Australia has her own particular difficulties', and that only British migration could be countenanced. Despite this, he said that Australia had over recent years given a great deal of consideration to 'the problem of foreign migration'. Recognizing 'the unhappy plight' of Jews in Germany and Austria, 'they have been included on a pro rata basis, which we venture to think is comparable with that of any other country'. White added, in what one journal has since called the most depressing speech of the conference,[40] that:

> Under the circumstances, Australia cannot do more, for it will be appreciated that in a young country man power from the source from which most of its citizens have come is preferred, while undue privileges cannot be given to one particular class of non-British subject without injustice to others. *It will no doubt be appreciated also that, as we have no real racial problems, we are not desirous of importing one by encouraging any scheme of large-scale foreign migration.*[41]

The speech continued for another few minutes, but it could easily have stopped there. White had effectively declared Australia to be a country out of bounds for Jewish refugees. It was clear that Australia would not now find cause to admit Jews under any circumstances. White had even placed Jewish refugees in the same category as other non-British immigrants, as if the same motivations for emigration (and therefore the same criteria for acceptance) should apply. Immigration might not have been within White's portfolio, but he knew that special consideration was not being provided for Jews to enter the country. His final words summed up the extent to which Australia's participation at the conference was prepared to go:

> What the United Kingdom is doing, together with our own efforts and those of others already related, will probably, we trust, encourage members of this inter-governmental committee here assembled to formulate further plans for cooperation towards the solution of a tragic world problem and thus bring hope to many unhappy people.[42]

This omitted the fact that Australia's 'efforts' were directed towards keeping Jews out, rather than letting them in; that no 'further' plans could be formulated by the committee, because no initial plans had been devised, and that no 'co-operation towards the solution' of the refugee problem had been achieved because the delegates, more concerned with stating what their countries could not do rather than what they could do, had hardly created an environment conducive to practical international co-operation.

Responses to White's comments were scattered through the Australian press in the days following. The populist *Bulletin* applauded his stance, holding fast to its belief that the 'great majority' of Australians would approve of his statement and that they would not tolerate 'any influx of foreign Jews on the scale which evidently appeals' to newspapers like the *Sydney Morning Herald*.[43] Moreover, as the link between Jews and communists was (in its view) inextricable, *The Bulletin* urged that:

> Every immigrant Jew from Europe or Palestine should be made to sign a declaration that he has never been a member of a Communist organisation, open or disguised, and realizes that he will be liable to deportation if he joins any such organisation in Australia.[44]

The *Sydney Morning Herald* did not agree. On 9 July, the editor wrote that 'there cannot but be disappointment with the negative nature of [White's] speech'. He had 'little that was constructive to offer' towards a solution of the refugee problem:

> It is a truism, of course, that the Commonwealth has no racial problem and does not desire to import one. On the other hand, it prides itself on being a democracy, with a strong tradition of tolerance, and any suggestion of racial intolerance constitutes a betrayal of our cherished traditions.[45]

There was even a response – practically the only one, it would seem – to White's comment that Australia 'cannot do more'. To the *Herald*, such a claim was not plausible, especially considering the 'undeniable' fact that the Commonwealth had a great need 'for more citizens to develop and defend this continent'.[46] There was little doubt, in the *Herald's* view, that White was wrong and that his opinions, if reflecting the true attitude of the Australian government, left a great deal to be desired.

Readers of the *Sydney Morning Herald* generally (though not always) felt the same way. A correspondent using the pen-name 'Humanitas', in a letter to the editor dated 13 July, asked 'Can we not open our doors wide to all the Jews who wish to come here?'[47] Another reader, 'Australian Scot', wrote two days later that 'we should welcome persecuted Jews to this country'; while there were difficulties in doing so, they were 'not insurmountable'.[48] In such letters there were many reasons given in support of allowing Jews into the country, and the files of the Department of the Interior indicate that letters like these were read by Albert Peters and others. The refugee issue was becoming increasingly complex, and opinions were forming and polarizing around the twin axes of exclusion or admission.

In the aftermath of the Evian Conference, the Department of the Interior was to find pressures from both sides bearing down on it, to the point where something had to give, and policy had to be seen to be undergoing some form of modification. It was quite prophetic, therefore, that Melbourne's *Argus* should state, immediately after White's speech, that 'a review of existing migration arrangements will be undertaken later in the year by the Federal Cabinet'.[49] The paper had no evidence, however, for making such a statement.

Once all the speeches had been made, the conference convened two sub-committees, designated the *Technical Sub-committee*[50] and the *Sub-committee for the Reception of Organisations Concerned with the Relief of Political Refugees coming from Germany (including Austria)*. This latter sub-committee was established to accommodate the numerous non-governmental refugee organizations that had been registered to attend the conference, but which were not permitted to take part in the general sessions. According to Norman Bentwich from the Board of Deputies of British Jews, these organizations 'had of course not been invited and really had no locus standi at the conference, [but] nevertheless, their presence and interest were regarded as natural'.[51] There were more than a hundred of these organizations present, most of which were Jewish. Their emissaries had been sent to Evian, Bentwich stated, 'to present their need or their panaceas and, if that was denied them, to waylay the delegates'.[52] Myron Taylor, as Conference President, invited the major organizations that had previously presented memoranda 'to amplify their views, if they so wished'.[53] Some thirty-nine organizations took advantage of the offer to put their case.

The members of the sub-committee were from Australia, Belgium, Costa Rica, Cuba, France, Mexico, Nicaragua, Peru, the United Kingdom, the United States and Venezuela, with Thomas White elected to the Chair. He pressured his sub-committee to hear the depositions of no fewer than twenty-five of the thirty-nine organizations on the single afternoon of 8 July, having decided that each refugee organization should be heard separately.[54] Since time was limited, speed was of the essence, and the deputations were thus processed, in the words of Alfred Stirling, 'with unprecedented despatch'.[55] Prior to the sub-committee's initial sitting, clear guidelines as to procedure were set down. Each organization would present a written memorandum, and its representative would be permitted to speak for a limited time. A synopsis would then be made of the memoranda, which would then be conveyed back to the conference.[56]

The hearing was, according to a contemporary witness, 'a humiliating procedure'. The representatives of the organizations had to

> queue up at the door of the meeting room to be called in, one after the other, and to face the eleven members of the Sub-committee to whom they were supposed to tell their tale within ten minutes at the most. There were very distinguished public figures amongst the petitioners – scientists, authors, politicians, etc. – none of them accustomed to any kind of interrogation procedure in front of a Committee, before which they felt rather as though they were on trial, without time to forward their plea, as they had soon to make room for the next invited spokesman. All left the room disheartened and disillusioned.[57]

Norman Bentwich later recalled that the process of hearing the organizations was speeded up when members of the sub-committee began to grow weary: the period of 10 minutes was compressed to five.[58] Moreover, depositions had to be translated into French if not presented in that language, leaving hardly time for a deposition to be heard before it had to make way for the next organization. Bentwich – who presented a deposition on behalf of the Council for German Jewry – remembered that the audience chamber was dubbed the 'Modern Wailing Wall' by the delegates.[59]

Unsurprisingly, White's speech at the plenary session and his chairmanship of this sub-committee did little to endear him to many of those present, with one of the Jewish representatives who had run the gauntlet of the audience chamber proudly informing Bentwich that he had stood up to White's dismissive treatment of those present:

> I told Col. White ... exactly what I thought of him and his statement that Australia had no racial problem and did not want to import any. I told them that as far as racial origin was concerned, Australians themselves had little cause for pride as to their own ancestors!!![60]

The greatest irony of them all was that White's activities at the conference received a special mention at its close.[61] Alfred Stirling reported on this back to Canberra, noting that White's speech 'was one of the earliest, our statement on migration policy was the first to be handed in, and Colonel White's chairmanship of the Committee to receive Deputations … led to a special reference' to the part played by Australia in the proceedings.[62] By the time the Australian delegation left Evian, all seemed satisfied with its accomplishments.

White's comments, and his activities both in general and as chairman of the sub-committee, did not occur in isolation. The Australian government was thoroughly apprised of what was being said and done in its name through the presence of High Commissioner Bruce. Halfway through the conference, Alfred Stirling received a telephone call from Bruce who was then conveniently attending a meeting of the League of Nations Nutrition Committee in Geneva. Bruce proposed to drive over to Evian, avoiding the main part of the town and the hotel where the Conference was sitting. He would come incognito, 'and we would meet in the Casino garden down by the lake, in the best traditions of Phillips Oppenheim novels, and exchange news'.[63] They met and had dinner at the Casino restaurant, but the attempt at arriving incognito did not work. The intention was that Bruce would not be seen in Evian lest he be 'overwhelmed by delegates and deputations',[64] but he did not count on the possibility of being recognized by political colleagues from Britain.[65] He and Stirling managed to escape to the solitude of a nearby meeting room, where they discussed the conference and how Australia was doing. Bruce was clearly keeping an eye on White's performance, so the Commonwealth government would be totally informed as to the situation. As it turned out, such surveillance was unnecessary, with Stirling's own reports indicating that Australian interests were at no stage placed in jeopardy at Evian.

After the conference

The conference broke up on 15 July 1938, its main outcome being the establishment of a permanent organization in London. When the Inter-Governmental Committee on Refugees convened there on 3 August 1938, Australia's representation was largely the same, but with one important exception: a professional administrator, rather than a politician, was appointed as Leader of Delegation. John Duncan, the Official Secretary at Australia House (and Acting High Commissioner in Bruce's absence), was the new Australian representative, with Alfred Stirling as Adviser and A. W. Stuart-Smith as Secretary.

In the long run, the existence of the Inter-Governmental Committee did not improve the outcome for the Jews of Europe. Attitudes such as those expressed by Thomas White demonstrated to Hitler that those whom he did not want were also unwanted throughout the rest of the world.[66] This was clearly apparent to perceptive observers at the time. The tragedy is that while all saw the dangers of inaction – and that, after all, was the ostensible reason for Roosevelt's calling of the meeting in the first place – no country was prepared to put its words of sympathy into practice. Australia, in this regard, was at least more honest than most, as its representative gave reasons as to why Australia was doing nothing. That exercise did little to mollify the fears of Jews seeking emigration from Germany and Austria. The Evian Conference demonstrated clearly that the nations of the world – and particularly Australia – did not yet fully understand the implications of what was happening in Germany.

Perhaps as if to assuage the consciences of those who knowingly did so little at this time, a myth very quickly sprang up in Australia that its performance at the Evian Conference was both worthwhile and humanitarian. One of the great myths of Australian immigration history is that Australia agreed to take in 15,000 Jewish refugees at Evian.[67] The Australian government, of course, made no such announcement at the conference. A later ministerial statement of 1 December 1938, that Australia would take in 15,000 refugees (not specifically *Jewish* refugees) over the next three years, quickly became merged with the Evian Conference in the popular consciousness, but there was no relationship between the two events.

Subsequently, the purported relationship between Evian and a quota of 15,000 refugees was repeated and became entrenched in popular discourse.[68] A close examination of the government archives, however, shows that this perception is based on a misleading document. On 3 March 1939 Alfred Stirling sent a draft report to the Secretary of the Department of External Affairs in Canberra, covering a meeting of the Intergovernmental Committee on Refugees held at Lancaster House, London, on 13–14 February 1939. Part of the report reproduced the first page of White's speech at Evian, but the second page came from an address to the Intergovernmental Committee from John Duncan acting as the Australian delegate to the Committee. In a pitiable example of bureaucratic filing, White's first page and Duncan's first page were placed alongside each other in the file. Duncan's referred to 15,000 refugees – a policy which was introduced in December 1938 and had no relationship to Evian back in July. Those reading the two pages, one after the other, could draw the conclusion that they were the same document – and that the policy of 15,000 was part of White's speech. The reality, of course, was far different. White did not make an offer of 15,000 refugees or any other number; moreover, as will be recalled, he basically declared Australia out of bounds for Jewish refugee admissions.[69]

Australia's record at Evian stands on par with those of the other states attending. Thomas White informed the world that Australia had neither an interest in nor a desire to help the resolution of, the refugee problem. It is not surprising that Evian saw no grand commitments to refugee acceptance: that had never been part of Roosevelt's proposal when calling the meeting back in March. The original invitation indicated that no country would be expected to receive a greater number of immigrants than was already permitted by its existing legislation. In the eyes of many of those who went there, this was an attractive reason for attending. It was optimistic, then, that any of these countries would agree to an easing of their refugee policies, as none had been asked to do so. The nations of the world did not let down the Jews of Germany; the Jews – not only of Germany but also elsewhere – put too much faith in the concept of an international conference the object of which was only to talk about the refugee crisis. Jewish hopes were misplaced, and their expectations too high.

For all that, the gathering at Evian did serve the purpose of enabling government leaders, if only for a short time, to examine their respective refugee policies. It *could* have acted as an occasion for caring administrations to announce that they would agree to an increase in their refugee quotas. None, however, chose to do so, and in this lay Evian's real tragedy.[70] Australia, which had to some extent been drifting in its approach to the problem prior to the Evian Conference, set its sails at that meeting. Few of the nations of the world can claim that in 1938 they were helpful in receiving Jews or alleviating their plight, and Australia, it must be said, typified the world's approach as it stood in middle of the year.

CHAPTER 5
HOLDING THE LINE

Rejected: Nine out of every ten

The immediate aftermath of the Evian Conference did not see a change in Australian policy. In a memorandum prepared by the Prime Minister's Department on 27 July 1938, the existing three-tiered policy was outlined and reaffirmed: applications for admission could be granted to dependent relatives of persons already settled in Australia; aliens other than dependent relatives who possessed at least £50 landing money and were nominated and guaranteed by persons in Australia; and aliens without guarantors in Australia who could introduce at least £200.

Some other groups, however, were subject to special conditions beyond these general rules. The Dutch, for example, required only £50 for a single man or £100 for a married man where a guarantee was furnished by the Netherlands Migration Office. Where no guarantee existed, £100 landing money for a single man might still be considered sufficient. Admission of northern Europeans was still seen as highly desirable, and the Minister for the Interior was granted discretionary power for the purpose of reducing the required amount of landing capital for individual cases involving non-Jewish applicants from such countries. Reductions of landing money were also granted in respect of Maltese immigrants due to their standing as British European subjects.[1]

The varying amounts of landing money demonstrated the government's discriminatory approach and were deemed sufficient to safeguard Australian living standards. Prospective immigrants might be able to meet health, character and other criteria for acceptance, but without the required landing money as well these were largely irrelevant. This was thus a vital tool for immigration management: it was one thing to have set criteria for entrance, but entirely another to be faced with large numbers of applicants, all of whom seemed to meet them. Ways had to be found to reduce eligible numbers. The question was really whether the government's policy would discriminate against Jews as Jews or classify them along with other 'unassimilable' aliens. This issue had to be addressed when considering whether British Jews would be entitled to receive assisted passages for emigration.

The assisted passage scheme, a joint Australian-British programme designed to encourage the settlement of British families in Australia through financial incentives and travel grants, had been suspended indefinitely when the worst effects of the Depression hit Australia in 1932. On 4 March 1938 it was re-established, though some states had strong reservations: the Federal government therefore agreed to apply the scheme only to those states volunteering to participate. When the question of assisted passages for British Jews was raised in August 1938, the government decided that they could not be debarred from receiving assisted passages.[2] In a memorandum for Cabinet, though, the Department of the Interior implied that approvals for British Jews should be retained, though subject to Federal oversight. It recommended three courses of action: (a) nominations in favour of British Jews approved by a state be accepted by the Commonwealth; (b) nominations in favour of Jews refused by a state be not approved by the Commonwealth; and (c) nominations in favour of Jews submitted to the Federal government by a state for consideration, or which are nominated by individuals resident in Western Australia or Tasmania, be decided by the Minister for the Interior and approved or rejected at his discretion.[3] Cabinet approved these recommendations on 16 November 1938.[4] The recommendations themselves could not be identified as discriminatory; but at the same time, the wording of paragraph (c) was sufficiently vague to give the Minister discretionary power over every individual case should he so decide.

The second half of 1938 saw extensive comment throughout Australia regarding the 'undesirable' aspects of foreign (but not British) Jews. To *The Bulletin*, Jewish refugees from Germany would form into colonies of 'brooding aliens, ulcerated with hatred' for Germany;[5] to H. T. McCrea, a citizen of Sydney who wrote to External Affairs Minister Billy Hughes, the type of Jew seeking to come to Australia was 'un-British...., unscrupulous, [and] unprincipled except towards his own kith and kin';[6] while to Albert Carlyle Willis, also of Sydney, European Jews were 'essentially parasitic' people who would 'for all time ... form a hard, indigestible core in our body politic and, in the main, choose to live on the efforts of others instead of pulling their own weight'.[7] Other opponents of Jewish migration concentrated their concerns on the economic consequences of Jewish refugees. In this way, for example, a citizen from Melbourne could write to the Minister of the Interior that 'these people, whom *NO* country has ever "wanted," [are] "financiers," first and last, and they prosper always, at the expense of their fellow citizens'.[8] A scribbled note sent to the Department of the Interior from an unemployed Sydney worker asked the Minister to explain:

When is the jewish [*sic*] migration stopped! My boss – a jew – sacked me and a German jew got me job. The city is full of unemployment and jews still get the permits [to land]. They get our jobs because the employers are mostly jews. Send your answer to the Domain.[9]

It is not possible to determine how typical or representative of Australian opinion such comments were, but their appearance in significant numbers in mid-1938 indicates the extent to which the refugee issue dominated the thinking of a vocal group of Australians.

Their anxiety was as much economic as it was racial: thousands throughout the Commonwealth at this time held ongoing unemployment concerns. Nor were these restricted to the unskilled or semi-skilled. A group of medical students at the University of Melbourne, for example, showed considerable unease at the 'influx of foreign practising doctors' coming into Australia, and organized a petition calling on the government to limit the registration of new arrivals.[10] The Dean of the Faculty of Medicine dissociated himself from the petition, but offered the comment that German-trained doctors might not be desirable due to their being 'more philosophic and attentive to science, than to the human patient'.[11] By the middle of 1938 several sectors of the community were directing the government's attention to the fact that feeling was growing very strongly against what seemed to be the wholesale arrival of undesirable people, and that 'Good Australians are growing uneasy about this Jewish question'.[12]

Against such negative statements, advocates of refugee immigration found themselves fighting a losing battle. Arrivals into Australia in mid-1938 were still relatively slight, but the potential menace of unspecified numbers of non-English-speaking foreigners pouring into Australia despite existing government regulations provoked an increasingly negative reaction. And until the government provided the public with a clear direction on how it was going to confront this issue, it seemed as though such disquiet would intensify. The task of enlightening the population fell to the Department of the Interior.

The Assistant Minister, Victor Thompson, decided it would be best to clarify the alien immigration issue, and in a memorandum dated 17 August 1938 he outlined several matters for Cabinet's information: precisely where Australia's immigration intake was heading, who was coming into the country, how they were being admitted, and what the general consequences of their presence might be. This document, purportedly dealing with alien migration generally, concentrated only on two groups: southern Europeans and Jews. Its intention was to allay any fears Cabinet members may have had about the number of 'undesirables' coming to Australia.

Indicative of the limited extent to which Interior recognized the gravity of the situation is the fact that German Jews were not viewed as refugees, but immigrants. Thompson's memorandum made no reference to their plight, other than to refer to 'many of the Jewish applicants [who] are under the necessity of leaving Austria or Germany at an early date'.[13] There was neither a sense of urgency nor an expressed desire to alleviate distress. In the entire memorandum there was not a single reference to Jews as 'refugees'. They were simply 'Jewish residents of Europe'.[14]

Thompson's memorandum recounted the various ways in which they were being permitted to enter Australia: 500 annually guaranteed by the Australian Jewish Welfare Society; approximately 1,000 annually guaranteed by individual relatives or friends already resident in Australia; and the recently approved scheme allowing entry to 300 without guarantees per month, provided they possessed at least £200 landing capital. This made for a potential yearly total of 5,100 Jews from Europe.

Of these, Thompson noted, the last category – independent non-guaranteed migrants who fitted all the government's entrance criteria – 'created a difficult position'. The rate of applications for entry was so great that it was 'necessary to defer or reject many applications which *would have been considered satisfactory if the necessity had not arisen to limit the number of approvals*'. With vast numbers of people applying for entry, 'under present conditions ... only about *one in ten* applications can be approved'.[15] The position had intensified recently with a rise in applications to over 500 per week. Considering this – a situation in which nine out of every ten Jewish applicants who had met government criteria for entry and would normally have been acceptable were now being rejected – Thompson was satisfied that the existing safeguards were holding firm. The present position would of course need to be watched 'very carefully' in the future, though for the present the percentage of Jews in Australia was only about 0.35 per cent.[16] The memorandum was received and read by the Cabinet, which accepted it without comment.

Still, the pressure being exerted upon the Department of the Interior by large numbers of applications from non-guaranteed Jews was sufficient to raise concern that the existing staff were losing the battle to deal with everybody fairly. Their task was not being made any easier, Thompson added, by the 'numerous enquiries and representations from Members of Parliament, solicitors and others who have been urged to make such enquiries and representations on behalf of the applicants'. New staffing proposals for the Department had been drawn up and approved some time ago; but when they were being considered, 'it was not contemplated that so many people in Australia would be taking up the cases of the Jews and making representations to the Department'.[17] Reassessing the situation, the Immigration Branch was expanded after August 1938 to facilitate the handling of increased refugee applications.

Visitors seek to stay

The situation facing German and Austrian Jews after the *Anschluss* became so desperate that many did not even wait for landing permits. Wealthy Jews who could afford passenger tickets as tourists on world cruises began landing in Australia during 1938 with the aim of forcing a *fait accompli* upon the authorities. Having arrived, some did not intend to leave; certainly, they argued, the Australian government would not be so heartless as to return them to Germany. In such a situation the Department of the Interior would grant temporary certificates of exemption for a period of up to three months, during which time a case would be considered in accordance with the usual rules. Ultimately, most stayed. But the Department objected to this forcing of its hand, and on 16 September 1938 Peters was directed to do something about it.

He responded by sending a cable to Bruce in London, outlining the position and at the same time requesting how it could be rectified:

> Jewish passengers have arrived by several ships recently holding return tickets and seeking admission as tourist or business visitors but real object to obtain permission remain permanently. Stop. In view Government's decision limit number and as full quota Landing Permits are being issued, and having regard also to difficulties likely arise respecting return to country of former residence if permission remain Australia not approved, Minister desires that shipping companies be advised refrain from booking passages Australia favour alien Jews unless they can produce authority enter Australia as otherwise they will be prohibited from landing.[18]

Pursuant to this, the High Commissioner's Office notified all shipping companies of Interior's request. They were warned that any passengers who failed to produce evidence of authority to land would be prohibited from entering the country.[19]

The government moved quickly to extend this decision to Australian-based shipping companies and on 6 October the *Sydney Morning Herald* reported that the Department of the Interior had advised that ships were 'not to accept as passengers for Australia any Jewish aliens who do not hold landing permits'.[20] This, it was stated, was being done for the refugees' own good, as it was feared that 'those who travel to Australia on return tickets may experience great difficulty in returning to their own country when permission to remain in Australia has been refused'.[21] Minister for the Interior John McEwen declared that this new initiative implied 'no discrimination against Jews'. for 'Tourists who were beyond doubt bona-fide and business visitors ... will experience no difficulty in securing passages'.[22] He suppressed the fact that this measure referred exclusively to 'Jewish aliens'.

The issue of 'tourist immigrants' came to a head in early October 1938, with the arrival in Brisbane of the Dutch ship *Nieuw Holland*. On board were twenty-two Austrians, three Germans and two Czechs, none of whom possessed landing permits. Nine Jews on the ship who did have valid permits were permitted to land, but the twenty-seven who did not were denied entry. Even though most of them were in possession of at least £200 (and some had letters of credit for over £800),[23] the decision to deny them permission to land held firm. Within a day, however, the government had decided to allow the tourists to land under temporary permits. Having been on the water when the new regulations were established, it was considered that to discriminate at this point would be unfair.[24] The newly arrived refugees were ultimately permitted to stay or arrange further migration elsewhere. Some were known to people in Australia; in such cases, guarantees were often forthcoming in the same manner as if they were for applications made in the normal course of events.

With the operation of what was effectively a quota regarding the number of Jews being admitted to Australia, and the isolating of Jews in respect of the shipping companies, the government's much-repeated policy of not discriminating against suitable immigrants on the grounds of nationality, race or religion was now proven to be hollow. The Department conceded that it was discriminating against Jews in a confidential cable to Bruce on 14 October 1938. Concerned about any adverse publicity, Interior suggested to the High Commissioner's Office – which was handling many hundreds of applications per week from Jewish refugees on transit permits in London – that it would be 'extremely desirable' if

> reference not be made to quota or to 'Jews' in official communications or statements where restriction of entry is mentioned. Government's declared policy is not [to] discriminate against any nationality, race or religion. Recent reference to Jews in instructions issued here regarding tourists has caused embarrassment.[25]

It was not in the Department's interest for undue publicity to be attracted towards the government's refugee policy. It might not have wanted to accept large numbers of

Jews, but neither did it want the immigration function to become the subject of public scrutiny. Provided things remained as they were, with the experts stating, framing and enacting policy, all would be well.

It was thus to the Department's consternation that reports were received in the second half of 1938 from Australian firms stating that Austrian and German Jews were writing directly to them in search of employment. If work could be guaranteed prior to arrival in Australia, an application for immigration would stand a much greater chance of favourable consideration. It is unclear from where these prospective immigrants were obtaining the addresses of the business houses. One Interior report asked the High Commissioner's Office in London whether it was providing the details of Australian firms to the 'distressed residents' of Austria and Germany.[26] If so, the practice should be stopped. The High Commissioner's Office duly complied with Interior's request.

On 21 September 1938 John McEwen again affirmed the official line: 'It is the policy of the Government that there shall be no discrimination as between nations in regard to the immigration of white aliens.'[27] At this time he found himself frequently adopting the line that there would be no 'radical change' made in the landing permit system in the foreseeable future.[28] Moreover, there would be no loosening of immigration control through the granting of permits at Australia House, as the control of landing permits 'must be retained under the immediate control of the responsible Minister, so that he could continue to give constant and careful attention to developments and review policy from time to time'.[29] It would only be during 1939 that criticism began to surface from members of the public suggesting that the government's policy was indeed discriminatory. Prior to then the suggestion that the Department of the Interior was not pursuing a discriminatory policy prevailed, due in no small part to the Department not revealing the true motives behind its activities.

The pleas of the persecuted

The second half of 1938 provided the Department of the Interior with ample opportunity to apprise itself of what was happening in Germany. The vast number of letters arriving from European Jews drew a picture of despair and an increasing sense of panic which must have touched all but the most insensitive.[30] Such letters could be divided into three types: those from German and Austrian Jews seeking admission to Australia; those from people already registered seeking further news of the progress of their applications; and letters from Jews in other countries, such as Poland and Hungary.

One of the clearest accounts of the options facing Jews in Nazi Germany was presented in a letter from Oskar Pollak, an Austrian Jew who had obtained temporary residence in Czechoslovakia but was forced to seek a more permanent home owing to the Sudetenland crisis of September 1938. Writing directly to Prime Minister Joseph Lyons in the hope of obtaining a personal nomination for entry, Pollak stated that 'for easily intelligible reasons, only a small part of what is really going on [in Europe] is to be read in the paper'. Pollak cautioned Lyons that 'in the general opinion the culminating point is not reached yet'. Possibly worse was the fact that 'a European war may break out now or within the next coming months which will absolutely lay waste the continent in every respect'. Such a war would result in the Jews of central Europe being wiped out – or, at the very least, 'we shall be doomed to flee once more'. What was happening in Germany, moreover, was not unique to Jews: 'It is the same the case with all the many hundreds of thousands of men and their families, without any difference their descent and religion, who are known, they are Democrats and not Nazis or Fascists.'[31]

Letters from Germany were not, however, always so reasoned, and appeared frequently to have been written out of sheer terror. One letter, from Hersh Zeil Wozingh of Magdeburg to the 'right Honourable, the first Minister', was dated 3 October 1938. It began, 'I allow to send a beg on you Honourable to give the permit for to land in Australia.' After presenting a description of his family and their respective occupations, he wrote, 'We like to go abroad, if possible this year, because we have no businuss [sic], and the situation to day is very disagreeable for [us].'[32] Fritz Fischer, a painter from Vienna, wrote to Australian Governor-General Lord Gowrie in the hope of obtaining admission to Australia. 'My familly [sic] and I being Jews,' he wrote, 'we cannot earn any more our living in this country, and consequently are obliged to emigrate[.] Your Excellency would save our lives by granting us the immigration to your country.' Theirs was a 'very urgent request', and Fischer pleaded with the Governor-General 'to help ous [sic] in our distress'. He implored His Excellency 'to grant us a favourable reply very soon'; such was the immediacy of the situation.[33] Also from Vienna was Oskar Rosner, who sent a letter to the Prime Minister on 13 October 1938. He sought admission to Australia because the 'circumstances prevailling [sic] at present oblige me and my family to leave this country'. It was, he stated, his 'keenest wish to emigrate to Australia', because 'Australia is a continent of hopeful future possibilities.'[34] There is no evidence in the files of the Department of the Interior that any of these applicants were successful in obtaining entry to Australia.

Other letters arrived from Jews who had already applied for admission. These letters sought the acceleration of their applications so that they could leave Germany as soon as possible, and the flow of such correspondence quickened in the aftermath of the Sudetenland crisis. As the situation was becoming more desperate than at the time of the *Anschluss*, supplicants were writing directly to the Prime Minister in the hope that his personal intervention might help to expedite their case.

One example was from Maximilian Jacobson, an electrical engineer from Vienna, who wrote on 10 October 1938 that 'We have sent already our application in April, beside photografies, and certificates to the Secretary of the Department of the Interio[r], and now Dear Sir, I beg you again to intervene as a very well known philanthropist.'[35] Jacobson had, it seems, applied originally in the days following the *Anschluss*; his despair must have become so acute in the wake of events in Austria between April and September that the idea of writing to the Prime Minister was attempted as a final hope.

Influence was also sought for the application of Arthur Andermann by his fourteen-year-old son Alfred. His poignant letter typified this form of representation:

I, Your Excellency's petitioner, am 14 years old and have finished the 4th class of a grammar-school with best results. Here I have no possibility, neither to learn a trade, nor to study on. My 45 years old father Arthur Andermann, who is diplomed insurance-mathematician and electrical engineer, and who is also well versed in the production of marmalade, juice of fruit, jam and ice, has here no possibility to earn his living.

As my parents are desperated because of the situation, now there I got the idea to address the humble petition to Your Excellency for the benevolent recommendation of our application for permission to immigrate to Australia. It is registered under the number 38/22708 at the Department of the Interior in Canberra. We are all healthy and strong and will make it to our study to be useful to the country in working industrious and loyal. Hoping for a favourable and soon reply … [36]

The available files of the Department of the Interior do not show whether the Andermann family's case was ever considered, or whether they managed to arrive in Australia.

Other letters also began arriving from refugees whose applications had already been refused but were now asking for a reconsideration of their case. One such letter, from Siegfried Posner of Berlin, informed the Prime Minister that the initial refusal from the Department of the Interior 'was such a hard blow for me that I cannot help having recourse to your Honourable personally[.] I implore you to help us out of reasons of humanity, to enter Australia that I might get into the condition of working and earning my living for me and my family'.[37] Otto Ayrt, a metallurgist from Dresden, made a similar appeal, requesting 'most urgently' that the Prime Minister 'not refuse me the favour of becoming a useful member of Australian Society'. His exhortation was underscored through the impassioned plea that 'I lay in the hands of Your Excellency the decision over the life or complete despair of a family'.[38] One thing must have become clear to the Department from such letters: the situation for Jews in Germany and Austria was worsening, and increased efforts were being made for their emigration. These developments saw the Immigration Branch called upon to display maximum objectivity if the government's policy was to be carried out effectively.

It was not aided in this by letters of application for entry coming from other countries of Jewish persecution – particularly Poland, whence many Jews had been deported from Germany during 1938. By the end of the year there was an increase in letters from Polish Jews who were becoming steadily more anxious about their future. These letters came from a broad cross-section of Polish Jewry: the professions, skilled and unskilled tradespeople, and even housewives wrote to whoever they believed to be the ruling power in Australia. Some wrote to the Prime Minister, some to 'the Government', some to the Governor-General. One was even addressed to 'His Majesty'.[39] Anxious émigrés explored every avenue to present cases that would convince the Australian authorities to consider their applications favourably, and letters from Jews in other parts of Europe such as Hungary also arrived throughout the latter half of 1938.[40]

In the immediate aftermath of the Munich crisis over Germany's demands for the annexation of Czechoslovakia's Sudetenland at the end of September, a new refugee problem confronted the Australian government. Non-Jewish refugees from a country other than Germany or Austria were beginning to apply for admission. A letter to the editor of the *Sydney Morning Herald* on 6 October alerted the public to the problem. 'It would be a right gesture,' it stated, 'if we contributed some reparation to the Czechs by opening the doors of Australia, freely, to every refugee from their occupied areas.' The plan would be for the Australian government to make an exception to its usual rule of no block settlements, by allowing the Czechs to establish a community 'somewhere inland' where it would be possible for them to live in peace.[41]

At least one sector of the government service agreed that refugees from Czechoslovakia should be encouraged to settle in Australia. Colonel Harold Jones, the Director of the Commonwealth Investigation Branch, forwarded a strongly worded memorandum to the Solicitor-General on 21 October in which he made a series of observations and suggestions. Noting that most German refugees from the Sudetenland would be socialists or communists fleeing for political reasons, Jones offered for consideration the following proposition:

> The immigration into Australia of a percentage of refugees from Sudetenland with avowed socialistic views would be of value and act as a balance of power in local German institutions, such as social clubs, some of which are fighting desperately to avoid Nazi ... domination through an organisation in Germany known as the Bund der Deutschentums.

> These refugees would be of even greater assistance in combating German propaganda among people of German descent residing in Australia, and at the same time, Australia would receive a number of settlers of Nordic race, thus counter-balancing the large proportion of southern European migrants.[42]

Given the anti-communist attitudes held in Australia since the time of the Bolshevik Revolution, a suggestion such as Jones's must have seemed outrageous. That known socialists or communists would have been allowed – indeed, *encouraged* – to emigrate to Australia on account of their political views was too much to take, especially for a conservative coalition government dedicated to the anti-communist cause. Lyons's attitude on this had in fact been spelled out earlier. In response to a question in Parliament back in April concerning the suspected presence of a Nazi club and camp in the eastern foothills area outside Melbourne, Lyons replied: 'I do not know whether such a club and camp existed, but I suggest that we should be just as much concerned about the establishment of Communist clubs as of Nazi clubs.'[43] In view of such a fixed position, Jones's proposal stood no chance from the outset. The episode was a further reinforcement of just how closed the administration was to imaginative solutions to complex issues generated by European politics.

Activities of the Australian Jewish Welfare Society

With the further intensification of the refugee situation in Europe, Australian refugee-relief organizations were at their busiest, but by now they had become more organized and had overcome the first stumbling months of the crisis. This was exemplified no better than through the activities of the Australian Jewish Welfare Society. A rationale and priority listing had now been worked out for AJWS operations, and in a long fundraising letter sent out to members of the New South Wales Jewish community these were explained. The AJWS was used:

> to welcome those people [that is, the refugees] on arrival, to cater for them on their first day in this country with meals, organising their housing and finding of accommodation; their selection for employment and various enterprises, which is handled by a large number of effective Sub-committees; the organization of sustenance and relief to those who cannot immediately be found employment; the teaching of English in classes, because no one can be a worthy citizen unless he is a fair English scholar and the teaching of citizenship, which is being carried out in regular social functions.[44]

One of the 'social functions' referred to here was attended by Rabbi L. A. Falk of Sydney's Great Synagogue in August 1938. The letter of invitation he received gave a good indication of how the Welfare Society viewed the immigrants it had sponsored, informing him that by attending he would 'have an opportunity of meeting not only the really desirable type of immigrant, brought out under the auspices of the Australian Jewish Welfare Society, but also those who came to Australia as independent settlers'.[45]

The Society's drive to ensure that only the 'really desirable type of immigrant' arrived was matched by its determination to take control of all applications for fear of an antisemitic backlash. In the Society's fundraising letter of 1938, the position was explained as follows:

> You will realise that unless all this work is carried out efficiently, unless funds are available for sustenance, for farms and for enterprise, that the danger may exist that new arrivals may become a burden to the State.
>
> We say that THIS MUST NOT HAPPEN, because the immediate outcome would be to create anti-semitism in this fair country of ours.
>
> We say that to help those unfortunate people who are coming out to Australia and to assist in the preservation and prestige of the good name of Jewry in this country, the work and the burden is YOUR RESPONSIBILITY as well as ours.[46]

Thus, the AJWS took upon itself the onus of protector and standard setter for the refugees. The activities in which the Society engaged were vitally important for the refugees' future integration into the Australian community. The Society also decided that it would make no discrimination between Jews from Germany and those from Poland brought to Australia under AJWS auspices.[47] The significance of this lay in the fact that the government had originally agreed to the Welfare Society being established on the grounds that it would function solely in assisting *German* Jewish refugees – not 'undesirable' Polish Jews. By the end of October, the executive committee was quite determined to ensure that no arriving refugees slipped through without at least having the opportunity of contacting the Welfare Society, and to this end an officer of the AJWS was despatched to meet every incoming ship known to have Jewish refugees on board.

In early September the Welfare Society felt emboldened to contact the Department of the Interior with a proposal which would, if accepted, place all Jewish immigration wholly in the Society's hands. A letter from Sir Samuel Cohen to Joseph Carrodus, dated 6 September 1938, outlined the proposal: in short, it suggested that '*all* applications (or as many as possible) from Jewish persons overseas for permits to reside in Australia be submitted to the Australian Jewish Welfare Society', and that from those applications some 250 would be selected by the Society per month.[48] Cohen listed a number of grounds by which this could be justified. He included the financial aspects of the Society's activities, its national character, the steps it took to facilitate a smooth transition to Australian life, and the fact that '90% of migrants who come out independently of the Society immediately call on the local office for advice'. Added to this was the assertion that 'The Jewish Community generally, having subscribed to the Society's funds[,] expects that the Society' will do the work of ensuring that all refugee migrants were looked after once they had arrived. The main thrust of the proposal was that 'such assistance could best be given if the Society were allowed to *select* the migrants to whom Permits are to be granted'.[49]

The Department of the Interior did not respond immediately, and in the hope of hurrying things along the Joint Secretaries of the AJWS paid a visit to Canberra on 22–23 September to make representations to Carrodus personally. In the long run, little came from it, though at the time the Department's attitude was reported as being 'very sympathetic'.[50] The Secretaries returned to Sydney believing the meeting had been 'quite satisfactory' and the matter was then left in the hands of the Minister, who promised to 'submit a scheme after the approval of the government had been obtained whereby the AJWS may assist the government in matters of Jewish migration'.[51] The affair was thus taken out of the hands of the Welfare Society, and the Department was left to make concessions at its own discretion. How far this aligned with future events, of course, remained to be seen; but provided there was no escalation of the crisis, the AJWS could hope that things might be resolved in its favour and that the selection of refugees acceptable to the Jewish community could be placed in its hands.

CHAPTER 6
PUBLIC OPINION AND POLICY OPTIONS

Views of the Australian public

There is little doubt that by late 1938 the Department of the Interior was confronted by an intensification of both the practical realities of refugee immigration and the state of public opinion. This latter took one of three forms: a limited acceptance of Jews who met the government's criteria for admission, outright opposition to a Jewish presence, and a cautious compromise between the two calling for calm and a balanced approach. The welcoming attitude was expressed in several ways. Far-left organizations such as the League for Peace and Democracy and the International Peace Campaign called on the Federal government to 'ensure that every facility is provided for Czech and German refugees who may wish to make a home in this country',[1] or to 'make the immigration laws less restrictive [in view of the] calamitous situation in Europe'.[2] A public meeting of residents of the small Victorian town of Poowong in South Gippsland expressed the opinion that 'the German and Austrian refugees, the inhuman treatment of whom offers them a special claim on our sympathies, represent a most valuable source of potential migrants to this country', who would, 'by their outstanding skill and intelligence[,] ... contribute to our own national development'.[3] Some support for refugees came backhandedly, such as in a letter to the Prime Minister from the Secretary of the Australian United Empire Party in Queensland. In this letter – essentially an anti-Italian protest – the Party noted that 'for obvious reasons, we very much prefer ... reputable Jewish Refugees with a ban on Italians altogether'.[4]

The Commonwealth Investigation Branch noted at the beginning of October that 'A marked anti-Jewish feeling is [being] observed ... in certain business circles here where Jewish business competition is making itself felt'.[5] A letter to John McEwen from the Business Brokers' Association of New South Wales on 2 November 1938 confirmed the Investigation Branch's claims. The Association's Board of Management considered it had to inform the Minister that:

small shopkeepers and manufacturers will shortly be in a serious position if any more refugees are permitted to open in opposition. Instead of observing local conditions and standards, and showing appreciation of the protection and shelter accorded to them in this country, they engage in a fierce competition, and cut prices to about non-profit point. ... [The] Board is of the opinion that a very serious position will develop if the refugees take away the living of more Australian small business people.[6]

Other expressions of protest were not so rational. One came from a citizen of Melbourne who wrote directly to John McEwen:

> The Jew does not fight in emergencies. He plays safe and gets 100% out of the nations' misery and distress. His religion is against him helping a Gentile under any circumstances.
>
> At the present time there are thousands of Catholics and Protestants being persecuted in Germany, but unlike the Jew, they are patriots and stay, risking death itself, in the hope that one day Hitler will be no more. Not so the Jew. Like the rat he leaves the sinking ship.[7]

There was, in addition, a good measure of caution. This was expressed most eloquently in Melbourne by *The Argus* and *The Age*, in two editorials of 7 and 14 October, respectively. In the first, *The Argus* spoke of the general problem of immigration to Australia, referring to it as 'essentially a problem in which a long view must be taken', as it would be wrong for the Commonwealth 'to accept all comers without discrimination'.[8] While 'Every nation has an inherent right to decide the composition and quality of its population', Australia, in exercising that right, 'cannot be conditioned by any natural sympathy which might be felt by Australians as individuals for people who have been driven out of older countries because of religious or racial antipathy'.[9] *The Age* editorial of 14 October was more specific:

> The Jewish refugee is, of course, a pity-moving type, and any attitude save that of complete acceptance of hosts of such migrants can easily be misconstrued. Judgement, however, may not be surrendered to sentiment. Australia has the utmost sympathy with any people who, simply because they are a people, are being rendered homeless and denied harborage. … The plight of these refugees arouses the Australian people's humanitarian impulses. Prudence, however, must be exercised, since it is possible that by action taken to relieve the immediate distress of refugees serious future problems might be created for Australians themselves.

The editorial continued that 'Australia reserves to herself the right to say how widely or closely she will keep her entrance gates' for reasons of 'rational self-defence'.[10]

Was this the attitude held by most Australians? Certainly, many readers of *The Age* and *The Argus* in Melbourne would have agreed with these views, but who took the *West Australian* in Perth or the *Sydney Morning Herald* may well have maintained a different stance. It seems, though, that most Australians – if ever they thought about the problem – came down on the side of sympathy for the persecuted Jews of Europe, though not necessarily *as immigrants*. By and large they retained a dual approach which had its roots as long ago as 1933, when Australians were decrying Nazi persecution and at the same time doubting that the crisis should have any impact on Australia's immigration policy.

Facing up to Kristallnacht

On the night of 9–10 November 1938, a sudden, widespread and orchestrated assault by the Nazi regime took place against Jews and their property in Germany and Austria. It soon became known as *Kristallnacht*, the 'Night of Broken Glass' or the 'November Pogrom'. The first widespread use of massive force against Jews by the Nazi regime, the attack legitimized violence against Jews.

The violence was supposedly a spontaneous anti-Jewish protest in retaliation for the assassination of the third secretary of the German Embassy in Paris, Ernst vom Rath, by a distraught Jewish seventeen-year-old Polish youth living in Paris, Herschel Grynzpan, on 7 November 1938. After learning of the news, Nazi Propaganda Minister Joseph Goebbels organized a widespread attack on Jewish businesses and synagogues, and on German Jews themselves. Nazi storm troopers led groups of 'civilians', who were mostly Nazis in plain clothes, across urban centres of Germany, where they ransacked Jewish homes, synagogues and storefronts. During the attack, German men also raped Jewish women, despite severe penalties regarding sexual relations between Jews and Aryans. The resultant pogrom was portrayed as a righteous and spontaneous outpouring of anger by ordinary Germans against all Jews.[11] The possibility that there could ever be an accommodation reached with Nazism – a hope long held by many – now vanished for Germany's Jews, and the painful truth which they had for so long tried to avoid had to be faced: they were being forced to quit the country and would have to leave Germany for other lands. Prior to *Kristallnacht* many would not confront that awful reality.

The events of 9–10 November 1938 in Germany also acted as a watershed for Australian opinion. Henceforth, views became polarized between those for or against refugee admission. An early instance of the pro-admission stance came from an unexpected source. On 18 November, the New South Wales Trades and Labour Council, on humanitarian grounds, departed from its usual policy of opposition to immigration to pass a resolution calling on the government not only to admit Jewish refugees, but to accept financial responsibility for doing so. It also urged the government to deport the German Consul-General, Rudolf Asmis, to protest Germany's antisemitic measures.[12] The Trades and Labour Council was not an isolated instance of union sympathy. In Melbourne, too, the Trades Hall Council enjoyed a good relationship with those promoting the refugee cause, principally the executive committee of the Australian Council for Civil Liberties (ACCL). This relationship was reflected in an invitation from the ACCL to the Trades Hall Council to attend a conference on the refugee question to be held in early December. The unionists' interest, it was noted, lay in the fact that the refugee problem was directly related to 'the fascist drive to smash trade unionism and the political parties of the working class', and many of the refugees were being forced to seek asylum 'because of their working class activity in the countries of their birth'.[13] There was no reference here to the refugees' Jewish origin (which overlooked a great deal), but it was nevertheless important that the labour movement was seen to be taking an active role in the refugee issue.

Some sectors of Australian opinion, even after *Kristallnacht*, maintained a noncommittal approach, preferring to say, 'it's not our problem' and leaving it to the rest of the world to do something. Thus Irene L. Couve, a resident of Maroubra (Sydney), wrote to the Prime Minister in late November to ask, 'Why should the troubles of the Old World be allowed to grow here, as grow they naturally will and become our troubles?' Her opinion was that 'our poor Australia is expected to take on what other lands cannot straighten out', and as it was 'Europe's mess' Australia should 'let Europe handle it'.[14] The editor of *The Argus* concurred. The problem, he asserted, was in reality 'not a problem for Australia, but for Europe'; unfortunately, 'Europe as a whole is unresponsive and individual European countries which might be sympathetic are helpless'.[15] *The Bulletin* held a similar opinion, though its suggestion was that the problem of the refugees should be taken over by the United States. The rationale was simple:

That country is rich enough and strong enough and sufficiently benevolent and energetic and vocal to become Jewry's patron and protector. Australia cannot be expected to imperil its existence or receive vast masses of alien refugees for the gratification of German Jews or New York politicians and editors, and it is not going to do so either.[16]

Historian E. M. Andrews has argued that 'some Australians revealed a lack of understanding of the full rigours of the refugees' plight', and that reports of German antisemitic violence 'were discounted by those who wished to appease Hitler and modified as too sensational by the press'. Further, given that Australia was so far from Europe, many 'found it difficult to believe that such inhumanity was possible'.[17]

For all this, there was an undercurrent of support for the refugee cause, unquestionably enhanced by the events of *Kristallnacht*. A secret Commonwealth Investigation Branch report dated 21 November 1938 referred explicitly to this development, remarking that 'most Australians take an extremely broad-minded attitude' towards Jewish refugee immigration, and that 'The recent press publications of the persecutions in Germany have had a soothing effect on those few who grew indignant at the growing number of immigrants who are now clearly discernible in the streets'.[18] It was an opportunity for many to state clearly what they thought of the government's stance. Mrs. Roberta Clapperton (who informed McEwen that 'I'm not a Jew I'm Scotch resident in Queensland 53 years') demanded to know why the Jews could not be allowed 'a refuge in our great empty spaces in the North where they would be a great asset and in sheer gratitude would help to fight our battles if occasion arose'. Her main point was that 'All the World is horrified at the German treatment of [the Jews] but *Deeds* are wanted more than sympathy & pity'.[19]

The *Sydney Morning Herald*, true to its previous welcoming record, stated in an editorial dated 18 November 1938 that Australia had 'abundant room for migrants of a suitable type'.[20] Again it called on the Federal government to liberalize the existing immigration machinery through the establishment of a migration bureau in London, noting that the principles for admission should not be 'grudging and niggardly in character'. With an eye to the international audience, the *Herald* remarked, 'Nothing would be more deplorable were the impression created abroad that we do not really want foreign migrants and are admitting a limited quota only in the hope of stifling criticism overseas.'[21] A call such as this served as a useful reminder to the Department of the Interior that other people were aware of the policy options and what the possible repercussions would be if certain initiatives were (or were not) taken.

Protests over German barbarity were numerous, but more telling, perhaps, was the silence emanating from Canberra. As shown by David S. Bird in his monumental account of the appeasement policies of Joseph Lyons, on 18 November the Prime Minister 'would only assure parliament ... that the government was giving "full consideration" to supporting any British communication' on the matter. Over the course of the following week 'he still declined to express any sympathy for the Jews, or even for persecuted German Catholics'. Lyons dismissed further discussion on the ground that there were 'more pressing' matters for consideration.[22] He was much more comfortable maintaining his silence on Germany until he could ascertain Britain's position 'so as not to offend the Axis and so hinder appeasement'.[23] In response, the New South Wales branch of the Australian Labor Party issued a condemnation of the Lyons government for its failure to communicate to Hitler the 'public indignation of Australia at the atrocities committed on innocent men, women and children'.[24]

On 18 November 1938, a little over a week after *Kristallnacht*, two left-wing deputations – from the Australian League for Peace and Democracy and the Spanish Relief Committee – visited the German Consulate in Melbourne to protest the Nazi antisemitic measures of the previous few days. The Spanish Relief Committee called upon the Consul, Dr R. W. Drechsler, to convey a resolution to the people of Germany 'to take a strong action to end the persecution of a defenceless people'.[25] The League's message objected to 'the frightful atrocities being perpetrated by the Nazis against the Jews', expressing its view that the 'barbarous crimes' were 'a menace to civilisation'.[26]

Other objections followed around the country. These included a petition to Lyons and External Affairs Minister Billy Hughes dated 26 November 1938, urging the government to protest direct to Germany over its persecution of the Jews, signed by Anglican Archbishop Frederick Head of Melbourne, Bishop Donald Baker of Bendigo and various state political leaders, among others.[27] A further petition on 1 December 1938 signed by religious and cultural leaders, Arthur Burdeu (the President of the Australian Aborigines' League) and various heads of left-wing and labour organizations, called on the government to protest the November pogrom.[28]

A much-celebrated expression of anger took place in Melbourne on 6 December – relatively late when contrasted with other, more immediate responses – when a deputation from the Australian Aborigines' League also sought to convey a resolution in person to Drechsler at the German Consulate. The deputation was refused admittance, but a letter requesting that Drechsler forward the resolution to the German government was left at the Consulate. The wording was without precedent: it voiced 'on behalf of the aborigines [sic] of Australia, a strong protest at the cruel persecution of the Jewish people by the Nazi Government and asks that this persecution be brought to an end'.[29]

Led by Yorta Yorta elder William Cooper, the Secretary of the League, it was not the first expression of First Nations protest at the Nazi persecution of the Jews – that had been on 1 December, by Arthur Burdeu – but in this instance it was undertaken solely by the League on behalf of the Aboriginal people as a whole.[30] Still, it was a remarkable initiative on behalf of the Jews by an Indigenous group itself suffering discrimination and, often, persecution at the hands of a broadly unsympathetic Australian society.

Discussions in Parliament

By the end of 1938, the general response to such Jews who had arrived in Australia came to be reflected in the amount of Parliamentary activity taking place because of their presence. An early example occurred in the Senate on 12 October when Senator John Armstrong (Labor, NSW), commenting on immigration and the economy, attacked what he said was the government's position:

> For many years this Government has shown particular anxiety to attract as many migrants to Australia as possible, irrespective of the class of migrant or the repercussions which a wholesale influx would have upon the national economy. Undoubtedly the interests which support this Government are anxious to encourage a large influx of migrants because a surplus of workers would enable them to secure cheap labour. This of course would result in the lowering of living standards generally in this country.[31]

Armstrong alleged that protests had been raised by 'every section of the community' over the number of alien migrants entering the country.[32] He declared there was no doubt that they were undermining living standards, and that 'colonies of aliens' were growing up in various parts of the Commonwealth. This, he asserted, compromised the White Australia principle.[33] The major problem was one of absorption; the government wanted to bring out migrants when there was simply no room for them given existing conditions. Senator Harry Foll, for the government, rejected the suggestion that migrants were being deliberately brought to Australia to create a pool of cheap labour. When Armstrong retorted that the government was at the very least *encouraging* migrants, Foll was moved to reply, 'No; migrants coming to this country are very carefully selected, and they have to survive a difficult test before they are admitted.' It was, he said, 'a tribute to Australia that these people want to come here.'[34]

At this, Armstrong modified his approach. Wishing to clarify his personal position, he stated:

> I do not wish to be misunderstood. I have the utmost sympathy with these people, many of whom have had a terrible time. I am, however, more concerned with the effect of their coming here on the social life of this country unless their entry is carefully supervised. I am not condemning any Jew, whether he comes from

Germany, Austria or elsewhere, who has been forced to leave his country, but I say that we must guard against the establishment of foreign colonies in this country. ... Committees of Jewish people which have been set up in Australia have repeatedly informed the public that the numbers of newcomers will be small and that the persons will be carefully selected. It is clear, however, that is not so, and that the restrictions have been ignored, with the result that hundreds of Jewish refugees are flooding Australia.[35]

He concluded by urging the government 'to take steps to prevent the unrestricted immigration of Jews to this country'.

A few weeks later, the consequences of a Jewish presence were addressed in the Lower House, in a question put to John McEwen on 9 November 1938. John Jennings, the UAP Member for Watson (NSW), questioned whether the Minister was aware 'that there is considerable apprehension in the public mind regarding the influx of migrants'. He inquired whether the government's existing immigration law 'provides sufficient supervision over the entry of aliens and their activities in the Commonwealth'.[36] McEwen's answer was positive on both counts. He responded that he was aware of 'some apprehension in the minds of certain people with regard to the migration of aliens to Australia'. Based on that knowledge, he reported that 'the Government has framed and administered its policy with regard to alien migration'. The system of immigrant selection and admission was rigorous; a landing permit was not issued to an alien 'until he has supplied many particulars ... as to his character, health, financial standing, the amount of money he is able to bring with him, and the employment he proposes to engage in, or the avocation he proposes to follow, after his arrival in Australia'. Only after the Minister was convinced, would a permit to land be issued.[37] McEwen concluded that in his position as Minister for the Interior he was satisfied 'that there is no need for alarm as to the number of aliens coming into Australia at present, and that those granted permits are of a desirable type'. The House was not entirely assured, and doubts would continue to be expressed in succeeding weeks.

As a direct result of *Kristallnacht*, Albert Peters anticipated that a new wave of immigration applications from Germany and Austria would swamp Canberra as soon as the next mails from Europe arrived. He admitted the Department's plight in a frank discussion with civil libertarian Winston H. Burchett in mid-November, commenting that the Department was 'hopelessly understaffed'.[38] At the same time he was also reported as saying that the Department was 'hampered by the lack of a clear policy from the Government'.[39]

The events of 9–10 November 1938 thus compelled the Australian government to evaluate its existing policy and justify its adopted course publicly. A Parliamentary debate on immigration policy was soon organized. The debate opened with a statement from the Deputy Leader of the Opposition, Frank Forde, on 22 November 1938. Summing up the thoughts of many, he asked Prime Minister Lyons whether he could inform the House whether any undertaking had been given by the Federal government concerning Jewish refugees, or whether a request had been received from the British government that a commitment be made by Australia.[40] The question neatly encapsulated the concern that the UK, after several years of pursuing a policy of appeasement towards Nazi Germany, might now offer Australia as a land where Germany could deposit its unwanted Jews. The timing of Forde's question was ironic, for on that same night a cable was received from Stanley Bruce in London suggesting Australia declare its policy internationally as a pre-emptive measure before the UK began applying any sort of pressure.[41]

Several other questions relating to immigration were asked that day: Joseph James (Joe) Clark (Darling, NSW), on the types of checks being carried out to ensure that alien immigrants were not obtaining employment at the expense of Australians; E. J. (Eddie) Ward (East Sydney, NSW), on what the principles were for determining whether applications for admission from refugees were granted or rejected; Adair Blain (Northern Territory), on whether the Minister for the Interior would consider an investigation to ascertain the extent to which 'the Nordic population of Australia is being pushed out of primary production by aliens'; Thomas Sheehan (Cook, NSW), on how the Minister intended to stop aliens congregating in districts not deemed suitable; and H. P. (Bert) Lazzarini (Werriwa, NSW), on whether the Minister possessed any information 'as to the average number of migrants who come to Australia for the one 50 pounds'.[42]

All these questions carried with them more than a tinge of party politics. None demonstrated any measure of concern for those who were under discussion – the refugees themselves. Yet neither the day nor the opportunity was to pass without a sympathetic reference being made to the plight of the Jews in Germany and Austria, and to a call for the alleviation of that plight. When the proposal to adjourn the House was put late on the night of 22 November, nobody was prepared for the impassioned plea that came from the Member for Melbourne Ports, Edward James (Jack) Holloway, regarding Jewish refugee immigration. He had been moved to raise this issue, he began, because it was becoming 'more and more important to the people of Australia'. He spelled out his concern: 'I refer to the ruthless manner in which some of the anti-democratic countries have been hounding native Jews out of their respective countries.' He then said why he was raising the issue now, and what should be done about it:

> Recently I have been worried by individual heartrending appeals of people asking for help to get their relatives in some of those central European countries admitted to Australia. I imagine that to deal with these individual appeals must be becoming a nightmare to the Minister for the Interior (Mr. McEwen). I suggest that the Government, in the interests of all of us, should consider what Australia's attitude shall be towards this international appeal to the humanitarian instincts of the people of democratic countries. Australians have always been regarded as democratic people, but if we do not play our part in some small way to meet the circumstances that have arisen in this connexion, we shall soon lose our reputation.[43]

The present circumstances, he told the House, were 'very unique and extraordinary'. Regardless of the events which led to the refugees being forced to leave their homes, the fact was that now they 'have to live somewhere'. Consequently, 'the Australian Government should consider whether or not it is justified in taking some small quota of Jewish refugees of a type suitable for absorption in this country'.[44] It was clear, he argued, that the system of individual admissions could not continue. Dealing with them was 'becoming a nightmare ... Men and women from the St. Kilda district come to me night and day and plead with me to urge the Minister to endeavour to get Landing Permits for their relatives in order to save them from the concentration camps.' He urged the government to take a stand and make a commitment to taking an appropriate quota of refugees.[45] John Jennings, the UAP Member for Watson (NSW), sought to scoring a political point interjecting with the question, 'Would it be part of Labour's [sic] policy to permit these people to come here?'[46] Holloway could sound good by making speeches of this nature but did not have to worry about putting his words to the same test of public mood as he would if Labor were in government. Holloway ignored Jennings's barb, declaring:

> I make this submission purely on my own account on behalf of many people in my own electorate. I unhesitatingly say that I would support the Government in any reasonable attitude it might adopt in order to relieve the sufferings of these unfortunate people who have no place in which to lay their heads.[47]

Ironically, Holloway's call for a quota was short by about a week, for on the same day Bruce in London sent a telegram to the Prime Minister suggesting precisely the same thing.

The increase in Parliamentary activity over the refugee issue suggested that events were building to a climax. The pressure the government faced from Australia House, from both sides of Parliament, and from the weight of applications being received was rapidly forcing the government to reassess its position. John McEwen, responding to Holloway's speech, was aware of this, and his words, while appearing sincere, nonetheless came across as a rear-guard action in defence of the government's existing policy.

He began by identifying the issue as one which was 'very important, very disturbing and very difficult'. He was able to assure Holloway, however, that:

> As the policy of the Government stands to-day, and as it is administered, regard is definitely paid to the needs of these particular people to whom he has referred this evening. I am glad to be able to assure him that, acting directly within the limits of the Government's immigration policy as it affects white aliens, it is possible for us to admit to this country annually some few thousands of the class of people on behalf of whom he has made his plea.

At this point an interjection was made by the veteran Labor Member for Kalgoorlie (WA), Albert E. (Tom) Green, who called out 'They will grab your farm if you let them in.'[48] McEwen continued:

Permits are being issued at the rate of several thousands per annum to refugees seeking permission to enter Australia from central European countries, where to-day there is political discrimination against those of the Jewish race. We are able to select from these applicants persons who, as individuals, comply with the requirements of our immigration laws, and to admit several thousands of them each year.[49]

The major problem lay in maintaining standards despite the very great personal tragedies this generated. McEwen found it difficult, he said,

to withstand the requests made day after day on behalf of persons of this refugee class who are not able to comply with the standards we set for white aliens. I have the very sad duty almost every day of having to interview people in my office, who, with tears in their eyes, plead for admittance of relatives at present, perhaps, confined in concentration camps where, my interviewers explained to me, they are enduring a living death. One would wish that it were possible, while upholding the standard which we have set for ourselves, to admit many more of these people. I assure the honourable member that the Government is fully aware of their needs, and is doing everything it can.[50]

The next two weeks were to demonstrate that the government was in fact doing only what it wanted. When presented with the opportunity to make a definite contribution to the problem it would renege, and, in so doing, demonstrate its true stance on the matter.

The Department of the Interior had, it should be remembered, already established that only about 10 per cent of applications from non-guaranteed refugees were being accepted. This was not because the applications were in any way deficient, as Victor Thompson had noted in his memorandum to Cabinet of 17 August 1938. It was simply untrue for McEwen to declare, therefore, that refugees were not being admitted to Australia in greater numbers because they were 'unable to comply with the standards we set for white aliens', or that the government was doing 'everything it can'. The Department of the Interior had already agreed that many Jewish refugees met the prescribed standards but were still having their applications deferred or rejected. McEwen, as Minister, knew this, yet he misled Parliament into believing that only those refugees who did not meet the government's standards were being denied permission to enter, when in fact the Department of the Interior was seeing to it that over 90 per cent of applicants who met the government's prescribed standards were being refused permits. This reflected the government's bigoted position and highlighted its active closure of options for Jews to arrive in Australia. His deception was not picked up by the opposition, nor was it questioned by his Cabinet colleagues or noted by a public uninformed of the policy of rejection.

As the refugee immigration issue was not one in which politicians generally sought to become embroiled, the Department was left to administer policy unhampered. Broadly speaking, most Parliamentarians could not have cared less about the refugee issue until it assumed proportions making it relevant to electorates – and thus to the winning or losing of seats. The period between July and November 1938 therefore saw an increase in the level of control exercised by the Departmental experts. They did not make policy, but it was their decisions over its execution that held firm and provided its character. While the politicians were debating the issue, and the Nazis were destabilizing Europe and intensifying their persecution of the Jews, the bureaucrats found themselves subjected to an increasing amount of paperwork and the moral decisions accompanying it. The task was far from pleasant for a small and thoroughly overworked staff. As a result of the increased tensions prior to and including November 1938, therefore, the Department took a significantly stronger grip on the Jewish issue, so that *any* refugee matter – from immigration, to security, to employment, to external relations – was passed through it as a matter of course.

Stanley Bruce proposes a new initiative

On 21 November 1938, Stanley Bruce at the High Commission in London sent a cable to Prime Minister Lyons in which he outlined his appreciation of the state of international feeling 'owing to the wave of indignation consequent upon the treatment of Jews in Germany'. Such feeling, he wrote, was particularly prominent in the UK, the United States, Scandinavia, the Netherlands and France, and he noted that these countries considered that 'an international effort on an unprecedented scale must be made to find means whereby refugees can be absorbed'.[51] Of concern was that 'Many impracticable schemes are being put forward and impossible suggestions made especially with regard to the possibility of the absorption of great numbers in underdeveloped areas of the Dominions.' He noted that among these, 'Australia is more particularly mentioned'. The 'very well connected' High Commissioner[52] noted that there were already ominous rumblings at Westminster concerning the colonial Empire and the Dominions, and Australia could soon find itself in an embarrassing position 'if no public statement is made as to our attitude'.

Bruce hoped that the Commonwealth government would thus make a unilateral declaration of its policy and by doing so end 'the present and growing suggestions as to what Australia might do'. It would also have the effect of increasing the 'goodwill towards and the prestige of Australia as the country that made the most practical and sympathetic contribution towards the solution of a problem that is causing the gravest concern to the Government and arousing increasingly popular feeling'. This would also be beneficial within Australia, for 'an immediate announcement of a definite policy, even if a bold one, would probably be accepted'. If, on the other hand, the opportunity passed, 'even the present number of refugees to whom we are granting permits may prove an embarrassment to the Government in the future'.[53]

Bruce then took the step of suggesting that the government consider establishing a quota for refugees of 30,000 over the next three years. Provided a proper method of selection could be established and instituted, he felt that this figure 'could be filled to the benefit of Australia', especially as the 30,000 need not 'be taken evenly over three years but could be related progressively to Australia's capacity to absorb'.[54] Later that day he forwarded a separate cable to Canberra with a fully developed draft statement for the Prime Minister's consideration.[55]

This was couched in terms tailored for the international audience. It was, of course, only a draft for consideration, but the proposal, in principle, was accepted. Bruce's statement was both clear and logical, outlining why the Commonwealth government should be interesting itself in this matter, and stating what could be done to help alleviate the distress of at least some of the refugees. After announcing the figure of 30,000 over three years, Bruce summarized how such a scheme would look:

> the Government will regulate the proportion of non-Aryan and Aryan which will be admitted to the Commonwealth each year and will prescribe the numbers which will be accepted from the several countries in which refugee populations exist. It will also only receive those classes whose entry to Australia will not disturb existing labour conditions. Farm workers and domestic workers will be given preference. Special consideration will be given to individuals who have capital and experience necessary for establishing and developing industries not already adequately catered for and in particular those industries which would command a market both within and outside Australia for their products.

The draft statement concluded with the assurance that this new initiative held no hidden dangers for the future wellbeing of Australia:

> In arriving at the figure of 30,000 over [a] period of three years the Government has been influenced by the necessity that the existing standards of living should not be disturbed and of reconciling with the interests of refugees the interests of its own present population and of the people of the British race who desire to establish in Australia.[56]

Bruce had thought long and hard about what he was suggesting. An earlier cable, on 8 November, had already signalled to Canberra that Australia House wished to have input into the resolution of the refugee problem; now, considering *Kristallnacht*, he was attempting to force his way into the decision-making process.

The day after he had sent his 21 November cable, Bruce visited the Parliamentary Under-Secretary for the Dominions, the Duke of Devonshire (Edward Cavendish), to discuss Australia's position on the refugee issue. He explained his impatience at Canberra's slow progress in resolving the problem of late, and enlightened the Duke of the proposal he had put to the Australian government the day before.[57] At this stage, of course, he had no idea how his suggestion had been received in Canberra; but, according to Devonshire, he had made the suggestion 'very forcibly'.[58] Bruce held out hope until the end of the month that his suggestion would be accepted by the Australian government. On 29 November he spoke with the Dominions Secretary, Malcolm MacDonald, and informed him that he was 'urging on' the Australian government to 'announce their readiness to take 30,000 refugees from Germany'.[59] Bruce would have mixed feelings about the outcome when news finally did arrive.

In Canberra, Bruce's suggestion was transmitted from the Prime Minister's Department to the Department of the Interior. Joseph Carrodus, immediately aware of its significance, investigated the matter personally, and within two days had prepared a long and detailed memorandum for the Minister outlining what he thought the Department's attitude should be.[60] This memorandum is a key document in the development of Australia's refugee policy. It acknowledged that 'the refugee problem is one quite apart from the general question of immigration', but should be considered as such where Australian policy was is concerned. He stated that refugee admission 'should conform to the same principles as those governing the entry of white aliens generally'.[61] There was nothing startling there; that served merely to reinforce a practice that had prevailed since 1933. Carrodus expressed the view, however, that 'refugees should not be admitted without regard to the question as to whether they are of a type that could be absorbed with the minimum amount of difficulty'. He identified that ideal 'types' in this regard would be 'non-Aryan Christians' and 'Aryans', who were deemed to be 'more easily assimilated than Jews, who preserve their own religious and racial characteristics'.[62]

Further to this, Carrodus asserted that without formal Australian reception organizations 'refugees would drift about Australia until they found employment, and would be an embarrassment, not only to the Commonwealth, but to the general community'. Moreover, a 'great proportion' of the refugees would thus have to start life afresh once they arrived, and large-scale refugee immigration would have an effect on both the 'racial composition of the people of Australia and the economic condition of the Australian community'. Given this, it was therefore considered – yet again – 'that the Commonwealth should [only] authorise the introduction of refugees to the extent that they can be absorbed into the Australian community without detrimental effect to Australian workers'.

Unaware of Bruce's 21 November recommendation to Lyons, some Australian newspapers had already sensed that changes might be needed soon, stimulated, no doubt, by a genuine revulsion over *Kristallnacht*. By the end of November 1938 there was much speculation that an alteration in Australian policy was imminent. Newspapers such as *The Argus* and the *Sydney Morning Herald* began referring to an impending government review of its refugee immigration policy, which must have come as a shock to some in the government who had not even begun to think about it. *The Argus* began on 23 November, noting that the swell in immigration applications had forced the government to 'investigate the whole matter'.[63] It had sounded ministers out on the possibilities of such an investigation, finding divergent views. Some identified that 'grave political repercussions' and 'minor economic repercussions' would accompany 'the unrestricted admittance to Australia of large numbers of Jewish immigrants'; others were of the opinion that Australia, 'in common with other democratic countries, should do a part in providing a refuge for Jews'.[64] *The Argus* maintained its position, however, that Cabinet would decide to provide facilities for an increase in Jewish admission; of this, one could be 'particularly certain'.[65]

The *Sydney Morning Herald* also took it as fact that the government was about to introduce a new policy. In a typically hard-hitting editorial on 24 November, the *Herald* outlined all its hopes and demands for the new direction:

> The conscience of Australians will expect that there shall be something more than the earmarking of a certain number of permits for Jewish refugees in the total of alien migrants that normally comes to these shores. The Cabinet should make up its mind on the number of admissions that it considers a creditable contribution to the problem. Having done so, it should leave the selection of the refugees to the High Commissioner, Mr. Bruce. It would be intolerable if, while the unfortunate Jews try to hide themselves from mob fury in Germany, or gaze pathetically at the frontier posts, their applications for permits to enter this country were permitted to make their leisurely progress from desk-tray to desk-tray at Canberra.[66]

It was heady stuff, but more rhetorical than real. Of greater substance was a report in London's *Daily Telegraph*, in which more precise issues confronting the Australian government were aired – together with the Australian proposal for their remedy:

> The Cabinet of Mr. J. A. Lyons has decided to review sympathetically the whole question of Jewish immigration in view of the sharp rise in the number of applications from Austria and Germany.

> Ministers agree that Australia must do her utmost to help within her absorptive capacity. There is a determination to prevent foreigners of any nationality from forming minority pockets or the concentration of Jews in large cities. Preference will therefore be given to migrants desiring to engage in agriculture.

> The Cabinet is likely to consider a quota system, giving preference to Jews to the extent of half the total alien immigration.[67]

This was nothing but a guess, as there was no hint of any quota or of the nature of any presumed policy modification. On 29 November, *The Argus* speculated that the main features of any revision would see a 'preselection of migrants according to character and ability, preference for those who are likely to introduce new industries and crafts, and precautions against group settlement or displacement of Australian workers'.[68] It was, however, a stab in the dark: *The Argus* had no real idea as to what the government was about to do. It even went so far as to suggest that a quota of 5,000 might be established for refugees – while at the same time intimating that 'the quota that is fixed will [possibly] be less'.[69] The degree of speculation over this issue was to remain widespread until John McEwen made a special announcement in Parliament a few days later.

Carrodus's memorandum to McEwen of 24 November contained the major foundation of what that announcement should be. In essence, he agreed with Bruce that Australia could take more refugees but differed on one vitally important point – how many refugees could be introduced. Bruce's suggestion had been for the admission of

30,000 refugees over a three-year period. Carrodus rejected this figure unequivocally. Under existing conditions, he wrote, 'even with efficient voluntary organisations to assist in their absorption, Australia would not be able to absorb nearly as many refugees as 30,000 in the next three years'. Rather, he estimated that the limit of Australia's absorptive capacity over that period would be no more than 15,000.[70] This was not based on any specific economic or social evidence – an important point given that nine in ten of all those acceptable for entry were being rejected on 'racial' grounds – only justifying himself by reference to the desire of Australia to absorb 'as many British migrants as possible under the assisted migration scheme'; Interior's proposals for the increased 'stimulation of immigration from Holland, Denmark and Scandinavian countries'; and the 'general desire on the part of nationals of certain European countries to migrate to Australia'. This was exclusive of refugees, and clearly discriminated against Jews from Germany and Austria.

The discrimination was reinforced, furthermore, by the categories of Jewish refugees Carrodus believed should be drawn up to help keep numbers down and ensure that only those deemed economically or socially suitable be granted admission. He suggested that entrance to Australia be confined to certain selected classes of immigrants: persons with at least £1,000 capital; persons whose maintenance was guaranteed by the Australian Jewish Welfare Society; persons without guarantors in Australia, 'but whose admission is recommended' by the AJWS, and for whom the AJWS would undertake to find employment after arrival; and 'cases of a special nature', which would be limited in number and be approved by the Department without reference to the AJWS.[71] The first criterion here was important: it increased the minimum amount of landing money for non-guaranteed Jews from £200 to £1,000. Jews without guarantors in Australia, or who were not approved by the AJWS, would henceforth be required to possess this amount – at a time when the maximum amount of currency permitted to be taken out of Germany by emigrants was 10 Reichsmarks (the equivalent of £1 sterling) per person. The existing regulations concerning the amount of landing money for all other non-guaranteed white aliens would remain unchanged throughout 1939.[72] This stipulation enabled the Department of the Interior to exercise its prerogative in deciding who should be allowed entry to the Commonwealth. The criterion of wealth, rather than need, was thereafter to assume joint dominance with 'race' in determining Jewish refugee admission.

CHAPTER 7
LIBERALIZATION?

Refugee admissions 'increase'

Prior to making the anticipated announcement, John McEwen first sought to relieve any public anxieties over a possible increase in refugee admissions. Such concerns had swelled when a report in the *Sydney Morning Herald* on 4 November 1938 announced that the Norddeutscher Lloyd liner *Berlin* was due to sail from Europe for Melbourne and Sydney with several hundred Jewish refugees on board. According to the shipping company, the vessel would only be carrying migrants who fully complied with the Australian government's immigration criteria and possessed landing permits.[1] The prospect of so many refugees on one ship worried officials in the Department of the Interior, who brought immediate pressure to bear against Norddeutscher Lloyd to stop the *Berlin* sailing to Australia. The ostensible reason was that Australian policy allowed only a few Jewish refugees on each ship – and that Norddeutscher Lloyd, knowing this, ignored the regulations by permitting such a large number to book passages. The ship did not sail; the refugees did not arrive. Pressed on the matter, the company said later that many of those who were booked for travel did not actually possess landing capital or landing permits,[2] but this backdown betrayed the reality of the situation. The refugees did not sail because Interior did not want them to arrive.

The Department's argument was simple; the more frequently concessions were given to 'exceptional' cases, the more frequently its carefully constructed policy of restriction would be circumvented. By the end of the month McEwen was ready to throw his hands up in despair. Interviewed by Melbourne's *Argus* on 25 November, he admitted that the position in Europe had become so acute that:

> increasing numbers of refugees are approaching people in authority in an endeavour to persuade them to use their influence to gain their admittance to Australia. People are coming to Canberra to speak to members on behalf of refugees, and large numbers are endeavouring to see me personally or speak to me by telephone.[3]

He knew, of course, that existing procedures allowed for a potential total of 5,100 Jews annually; he also knew that this figure was well known outside Canberra,[4] and that a dispute was underway between Stanley Bruce and Joseph Carrodus the outcome of which would either double that figure or set it in stone. The issues were far from clear-cut. A new policy direction, though desirable in many quarters, was not something to be automatically assumed. It would be difficult to find a solution acceptable to everyone because the government had little real idea of what the majority would tolerate. The bureaucrats knew that a general announcement – any announcement – would be contentious but decided that the best course of action would be to proceed with the original plan suggested by Bruce and halved by Carrodus.

McEwen presented the proposal to Cabinet on 28 November. One short comment was enough to gain Cabinet assent:

> in view of the conditions prevailing in Europe the Commonwealth should authorise the introduction of refugees to the extent that they can be absorbed into the Australian community without affecting living standards and without detrimental effect to Australian workers. It is considered that for the reasons set out …, the limit of Australia's absorptive capacity over the next three years would be *up to 15,000*.[5]

The phrase 'up to' was important, allowing for no more than the stipulated figure and implying less than that. Three days later McEwen announced this new direction in Parliament and Bruce, in London, was informed immediately.[6]

The day before McEwen's announcement, there was one final question to be answered in the House of Representatives. This was put in three parts by Percy Spender, the UAP Member for Warringah (NSW). Spender asked whether it was true that 'no record of any description is kept by the Commonwealth as to the number of Jews' admitted to Australia over the previous year. If such a record did exist, he sought to know of its nature, and how many Jewish immigrants had been admitted. He ended by asking 'What particular steps are being taken by the Commonwealth to ensure that the immigrants are not likely to and do not throw Australians out of employment, lower the living standards of the Australian workers, or disregard industrial conditions?'[7]

McEwen answered the first two questions together. 'It is not the policy of the Commonwealth,' he said, 'to inquire into the religion of any person desirous of emigrating to Australia. Persons admitted to Australia are recorded according to their nationality.' He admitted, however, that 'persons of Jewish race represent the great majority of aliens who are at present seeking permits to come to Australia.'[8] Spender's question then gave McEwen the chance to reassure the House that the government had the immigration issue well under control, and that no undue admission of Jewish refugees was likely to disadvantage Australian workers or living standards. 'Apart from dependent relatives,' he said,

> for the introduction of a white alien, inquiries are made as to the type of employment the nominee would engage in after arrival and whether there is opportunity for employment without detriment to Australian workers. If the result of the inquiries is not satisfactory, the application is refused. Applications made by white aliens overseas are considered on their merits. The persons concerned are required to furnish information as to their present occupation and as to their intended

occupation. If it is considered that they are likely to engage in an occupation for which there are no opportunities for their absorption without detriment to Australian workers, the applications are refused.[9]

If McEwen's intention was to set minds to rest, he was successful. This enabled him to create a climate for the acceptance of the statement he knew he would be making to the House the next day.

When McEwen rose to speak on 1 December 1938,[10] the House realized that this was the anticipated declaration of policy. He began mildly, with an account of the plight of the refugees, and what the government believed could be done in concert with other countries to 'alleviate the conditions of these unfortunate people'. He announced solemnly that the government was about to take a major step which other nations should emulate, informing the House that 'if a solution to this problem is to be found, countries must be prepared to receive a proportion of those to be expatriated, in relation to the capacity of the countries to assimilate them'. He then disclosed what everyone had been waiting for – the future policy direction Australia would adopt:

> In recognising this obligation, and after careful examination of the position, the Commonwealth Government has decided that Australia should assist to the extent of receiving up to 15,000 refugees over a term of three years.
>
> In arriving at the figure of 15,000 over a period of three years, the Government has been influenced by the necessity that the existing standards of living should not be disturbed
>
> The Commonwealth Government hopes that various public bodies throughout Australia will co-operate in establishing a body for the purpose of helping Aryan and non-Aryan Christian refugees after their arrival.
>
> In all cases, permits for the admission of these refugees, within the limits of the number which I have mentioned, will be granted strictly in accordance with the Government's white alien immigration policy.[11]

McEwen then showed just how far the Department of the Interior did not appreciate the gravity of the situation facing the refugees: 'Desperate as is the need of many of these unfortunate people, it is not the intention of the Government to issue permits for entry influenced by the necessity of individual cases.' Rather, Australia could play its part by absorbing a reasonable quota of Jewish refugees 'while at the same time selecting those who will become valuable citizens of Australia'.[12] This meant, in effect, that the Australian government was not concerned about how or why the refugees needed to come to Australia, simply that they were applying to do so. As a result, the government's attitude would be to take only those who appeared to have the best potential for contributing to the Commonwealth. McEwen continued with a further piece of clever propaganda: 'The quota which I have stated means that there will be some increase, but not a very great increase, of the rate at which permits have been issued to people of the refugee classes during the last six months.'

This was not true. As long ago as 17 August 1938 Victor Thompson had related to Cabinet the various ways in which Jewish refugees could enter Australia, and even at that stage it was realized that the potential aggregate of these schemes formed an approximate yearly total of 5,100.[13] Since then, there had been no change in policy to allow for the admission of greater or lesser numbers of refugees into Australia, and on 1 December 1938 this potential was still the current maximum. Given there would be no diminution of that figure, by introducing a quota of 15,000 over three years the government was effectively *reducing* the possible number of all refugee immigrants by 300. Far from there being 'some increase', as McEwen told Parliament, the new policy served effectively to decrease the options available for Jews trying to come to Australia and, by amplifying the competition for permits, ensure that only those whom the Department of the Interior deemed to be desirable could gain entry. The announcement of 1 December 1938 was to stamp the government as humanitarian, welcoming and liberal, whereas it used the opportunity presented in the aftermath of *Kristallnacht* to curtail whatever trend there had previously been towards a growth in refugee admissions.

Reactions to the announcement

The Argus took delight in announcing the policy the next day, for it was now clear that the government was not going to allow the unrestricted entry into Australia of Jews, as the quota 'will cover refugees other than Jewish refugees'.[14] Such an interpretation suited McEwen's purpose, for he could at last point to an expression of opinion from mainstream middle-class Australia endorsing the government's stance. Henceforth, everyone would know where they stood.

McEwen's announcement was accepted without hesitation by the Labor Opposition. Soon after he finished his speech, ALP leader John Curtin rose to commend the Minister for the undertaking to which he had just committed Australia. He informed the House that 'the principles involved will be acceptable to the people of Australia',[15] and his reply to McEwen's speech contained nothing but admiration:

> The Opposition feels, and I believe the country feels, that Australia is a place where lovers of liberty should be welcome, and where those suffering from the inflictions of despotic authority should be given an opportunity to live lives which will enable them to realize their own highest and best future, and at the same time assist in the building of Australia into a great democratic power and a centre of civilization in its best cultural sense. I believe that the Commonwealth is anxious that, in accepting these refugees, there will not be involved any deterioration of standards in Australia. The quota suggested by the Minister seems to me to be a reasonable one. I feel also that the vigilance exercised by the Government over these people will be sufficient to prevent the formation of racial colonies in

Australia. The imposition of conditions under which refugees will be permitted to land in Australia conforming generally to the admittance of white aliens, is a perfectly sound arrangement. I welcome the statement made by the Minister.[16]

With such support, announcement of the government's position must have delighted the officials in the Department of the Interior. It was as much their victory as it was McEwen's, as it meant that regulation of immigration was well and truly back in their hands.

A second major response to McEwen's announcement came from Thomas White, Australia's representative at the Evian Conference back in July. Speaking in Parliament on the afternoon of 2 December, he gave a brief account of his experience as Australian delegate at Evian, and then proceeded to justify McEwen's stance on the refugee matter 'in line with what I said at Evian'.[17] This was, of course, nonsense; White at Evian made no statement concerning numbers, and explicitly rejected any possibility of an increase or liberalization of policy. Alluding to the sub-committee of which he was Chairman at Evian, he noted that:

> not all the representatives were Jewish. There were representatives of the Quakers and other peace-loving organizations, and many non-Aryan Christians, the part-Jewish types, and others. I know from the evidence given there … that there is a great scope for establishing new industries in Australia by the immigration of skilled artisans, of types that we have never had before. They would do a great good to the Commonwealth.[18]

The crux of White's message was that Australia should now accept refugees out of altruistic motives: those who could bring skills to the Commonwealth in which native industry was already lacking should be especially selected, but in such a way and at such a rate that 'we shall maintain the predominance of Britons in our population and have the right kind of man-power to ensure safety and progress'.[19]

It summed up the attitude of many. Australia was still a predominantly British community, and, unlike the United States, did not have a melting-pot tradition. The concern that Australia should keep the alien population at a reasonable level so as not to upset its British character was, for many Australians, perfectly justifiable.

White's references to his participation at the Evian Conference, and the fact the announcement of 1 December followed that meeting, created an impression that the two were somehow linked. As shown earlier, nothing could be further from the truth. At Evian, White went out of his way to demonstrate that Australia was prepared neither to relax the immigration machinery nor to accommodate the needs of the refugees. On 1 December 1938, McEwen announced that Australia was going to accept refugees and 'increase' numbers. The linkage between the Evian Conference and 1 December remained, however, and over time the two became merged in the public mind.

Another mistake, believed in 1938 and never publicly refuted by politicians or officials, was that the quota allowed for 15,000 *Jewish* refugees. The popular assumption usually read the word 'refugees' as implying Jews, but in the announcement of 1 December McEwen never said they would be. In fact, his comments concerning Aryans and 'non-Aryan Christians' should have signalled to observers that he had in mind other refugees as well as Jews. The misreading of the situation has remained, and commentators have since frequently referred to '15,000 Jewish refugees', a mistake that has been often repeated down to recent times. It was in that context that popular reactions were expressed in December 1938 and January 1939.

In London, Bruce's initial response was one of profound disappointment. He confided his feelings to Dominions Secretary Malcolm MacDonald on the evening of 30 November, at about the time McEwen was making his announcement in Canberra.[20] He informed MacDonald that regardless of how he felt personally, however, '15,000 was quite a respectable figure in comparison with the efforts of, for instance, the United States'.[21] Yet Bruce had not forgotten his earlier battle with Joseph Carrodus. Angry at having his proposals halved, he had leaked the figure of 30,000 to the Australian press. Thus, the *Sydney Morning Herald*, in an editorial dated 3 December, related the following:

> Australia House, it is reported, could supply us with at least 30,000 refugee migrants within three months. Considering this demand, the special circumstances of the refugee problem, and the expectation of the world for a generous contribution by us towards its solution, the 15,000 quota for the three year period must appear as the least rather than the most that we could offer. Australia is doing its share, but the share could be more handsome. It can be improved, perhaps, in the future.[22]

The British government saw little immediate significance in McEwen's announcement, identifying it as nothing but a confirmation of the existing situation. A memorandum from W. J. Garnett at the Dominions Office indicated that Australian policy had long been interpreted as permitting refugee admissions at the rate of approximately 5,000 annually. According to Garnett, Bruce's initiative of 30,000 was the new departure, as it suggested that existing arrangements should be doubled.[23] It appeared to Garnett that the Australian government had 'not been able to see their way clear to adopt the higher figure recommended by Mr. Bruce', and that the prevailing situation would be retained.

In Australia, McEwen's announcement of 1 December 1938 was met with suspicion in some quarters. The Labor and populist presses, for instance, were most concerned. *Labor Call* found economic reasons to object. While Melbourne Jews were admired 'for giving aid to their burdened fellows in other lands', the paper saw sinister capitalist motives in McEwen's new policy: 'It was not generosity of heart ... which prompted the Lyons Government to open the gates to foreign refugees, but, rather, to go the limit in undermining the living standards of the workers in Australia' by allowing 'cheap foreign labor to be used to displace Australians in industry'.[24]

The Australian Council for Civil Liberties (ACCL), which had an impeccable record in advocating on behalf of refugees and seeking to improve existing policy, found itself thrown off balance by McEwen's announcement. It acknowledged its vital concern with measures 'to safeguard the rights of refugee immigrants', but also declared its obligation to the rights of Australian workers.[25] The opinion was expressed that the Council was 'not concerned with questions of the absorption of refugees under the Commonwealth Government's quota scheme', but owing to the overlap between refugee reception and labour conditions, it stressed that 'it is urgently necessary that a positive programme should be agreed upon as soon as possible'.[26] The year 1939 was to be filled with examples of the ACCL lobbying in favour of refugees.

The populist press capitalized on McEwen's announcement. On 10 December *Smith's Weekly*, as outrageous as ever, coined a new word which gained currency in some quarters of Sydney: 'Refu-Jews'.[27] *The Bulletin* did not immediately object to the quota provided there was scrupulous compliance,[28] but tempered its endorsement with a loosely veiled threat to the Australian Jewish population:

> Australians have never had any cause for anti-Semitic feelings. It will be an extraordinary achievement, and one that will be especially creditable to Jews already in Australia, if that still holds good after the coming 15,000 are safe here from further persecution. ... It is too much to expect that they will be able to shed their ingrained hatred overnight. It would be a great service to them, as to Australia, if their fellow-Jews already here could bring it home to them, by advice and example, that in this country they are in a free-and-easy and friendly land, in which there is no general deep or inborn hatred of any other country, and where that sort of thing isn't wanted.[29]

The message was clear: if the assimilation of the refugees did not work out, it would be the fault of the Australian Jewish community, which had the enormous responsibility to see that refugee arrivals were as smooth and trouble-free as possible. Implicit in *The Bulletin's* analysis was a comment on the refugees themselves; their 'ingrained hatred' was presumably something so foreign to Australians that it must be stamped out quickly, as it would not do to have the newly arrived Jewish refugees influencing 'friendly' Australians against another country.

Such thinking was the major theme of those who wrote directly to the government. And, though the intended recipients of such letters were usually the Prime Minister or the Minister for the Interior, any official was fair game. The Postmaster-General, Archie Cameron (Barker, SA), was the recipient of one such letter dated 10 December. The author, Lionel S. Norman of Sandalwood (SA), felt the necessity of issuing 'a warning' to Cameron, in the hope that it would be passed on to the appropriate quarters.[30] This did not concern employment or industrial considerations, nor was it based on racial criteria. Rather, it focused on the nature of the Jewish refugees and expressed the fear that 'each of these immigrants could be a Communist agent painting for Jewry the red dawn it painted in Russia in 1917, and spoiling for us the British Empire'. Their intention was to 'batten on society'. Norman asked Cameron:

> Is it really a matter for us how these minority problems of other nations are settled? Of course, I am aware of the usual answers to this objection, such as tolerance, and

home for matyrs [*sic*], and all the rest of sentimentalism. But the point I want to get is, is it worth while to accept another country's minority problem, and so make another for ourselves?[31]

This was now a familiar line. More than ever before, opponents of Jewish immigration began speaking of the negative consequences of a Jewish presence in Australia, for now their worst fears were, they felt, about to be realized. An anonymous letter signed 'Australia First!' informed John McEwen that, 'While deploring the suffering meted out to the innocent, I fail to see why you should add to Australia's burdens and trials an evil that will not be long in maturing.' The writer continued that 'Jews will not remain on the land here and will gravitate into the cities to get a stronger strangle-hold on our economic life'; this would not be difficult for them to do, as already there were 'Powerful Jews' who were 'forwarding their Zionist propaganda and ambitions' and 'using the British Empire for their own ends'.[32]

Albert Carlyle Willis, a citizen from Sydney, also wrote to McEwen. On 13 December 1938 he once more emphasized the inassimilable aspects of Jews. Willis declared that the policy of 15,000 Jewish refugees would be vastly different from 'that of any non-Jewish influx', for even if such an influx were 'constituted of the poorest class of southern Europeans it would be preferable'.[33] This, given the negative feelings held towards southern Europeans throughout the interwar period, was an interesting perspective. The size of the influx was, Willis felt, fortunately not too worrisome for the moment:

To you or to me the Jewish newcomers do not matter, nor to your children or mine. But ultimately when these people multiply they will create a problem for future Australians. They will grow in money and power by living on those who create. And they will always racially be Jews, never becoming Australians.[34]

The problem, then, was not the quota itself but the impact it would have on Australia's racial composition.

It is difficult to gauge how far politicians took note of letters sent to them by concerned citizens. Correspondence circulating through the bureaucracy was almost always minuted or referred to higher sources, indicating that at least someone took notice of them. The extent to which letters swayed the thinking of those in government is uncertain, though all such letters received attention as expressions of how some in Australia were thinking. The issue of how representative they were was reflected only in the volume of mail the government received. All opinions were treated equally, but rarely acted upon directly; their importance lay in the fact that they were being made at all.

Options and possibilities for block settlement

For the officers of the Department of the Interior, public opinion in isolation counted for little. The only facts worthy of consideration were that the refugees were still coming to

Australia and that, with a dam wall of regulations constructed, a way had been found to stem the tide. In this they were not helped by the arrival of the SS *Aorangi* in Australia which listed 144 Jewish migrants on board. This was the largest number of refugees yet to arrive in Australia on a single ship,[35] and did little to relieve the Department's feelings of unease. If it were to oversee the new policy with rigour and efficiency, it would have to see to it that such anomalies did not recur in 1939.

Albert Peters had already foreseen the pitfalls of McEwen's 'liberalization'. On 5 December 1938 he wrote to the Passenger Superintendent of the Orient Shipping Line in Sydney to the effect that 'the Commonwealth Government have decided to reimpose visa requirements for holders of German and unexpired Austrian passports as from 1 January 1939'.[36] This effectively meant that British passport control officers in Europe had been requested by the Australian government 'to refrain from granting visas for Australia in favour of aliens whose admission has not been authorised, but who claim to be tourist or business visitors' – unless their credibility could be guaranteed and that they could legitimately return to their country of origin.[37] In other words, German and Austrian nationals now had to obtain visas for entry to Australia, plus an undertaking from the German government that it would accept their return. They were also still required to obtain landing permits, regardless of whether they were legitimate tourists or business visitors. This was the final nail in the coffin for those who sought to circumvent Interior's regulations as 'tourist-refugees'.

Henceforth, if a Jew sought to emigrate to Australia from Germany or Austria, then it was *only* as a refugee that he or she could apply. If evidence could not be produced guaranteeing a return to Germany or Austria, that person would be prohibited from landing in Australia. Refugees from Nazism were, slowly but surely, being administered out of an Australian option for their deliverance.

Similarly in line with this 'no exceptions' attitude was a strict opposition to queue-jumping. No amount of urgency or extenuating circumstance sufficed to budge the Department, as McEwen outlined in a statement to the Sydney-based *Hebrew Standard* in mid-December. So far as he was concerned,

All applications will be dealt with on their merits, and representations from any interested source will have no influence. Applications will be dealt with no more expeditiously as a result of personal interviews with representatives of the Department. All applications will be dealt with in the order that they are received. They will be dealt with as quickly as possible.[38]

This was to be an across-the-board rule. McEwen had originally raised it in response to the serious allegation of middlemen claiming to purchase 'landing permits or otherwise lobbying Ministers and departments on behalf of refugees'.[39] He pointed out that there was no business to be made in handling applications for landing permits; those attempting to do so were doing a disservice to the refugees, whose cause was being sufficiently looked after owing to the merit system of dealing with applications.

There was thus no need to try to circumvent the system provided people waited their turn calmly and presented a good case.

One area in 1938 in which people showed that waiting in turn for consideration of individual applications might not be necessary concerned proposals for the formation of large-scale group settlements of colonies of refugees in areas remote from the major population centres. Australian governments had always been opposed to this, on the ground that colonies of aliens did not support individual assimilation. The increase in Italian immigration after the Depression, plus the refugee problem, combined to render the Lyons government more tenacious than any of its predecessors in its opposition to group settlement. Numerous schemes were put forward throughout 1938, but none were to see the light of day – though some were to receive serious and favourable consideration by state governments.

In August 1938, a Jewish settlement was proposed for South Australia. Unclear as to the Federal position on such matters, Richard Butler, the Premier, asked the Prime Minister for advice. The response was that as the scheme envisaged the settlement of Jews in specific areas, the Federal government would not grant authority for it to go ahead.[40] This served as a precedent for a later attempt to establish a Dutch settlement in South Australia.[41] The Department of the Interior noted on this occasion that 'Dutch migrants are of a type which would be more readily assimilated into the Australian community than Jewish migrants', but felt itself tied to the position that 'any settlements having as their object the settlement of aliens in a specific area without a leavening of Australians' would be undesirable. The proposal was rejected.[42]

Other suggestions included one which would see Jews established in New Guinea, where they would 'in a very short time make New Guinea a thing of prosperous beauty'. Such a settlement would be good for Australia: 'as the Jews are not a warlike race we need never fear invasion from them', and, added to this, 'the wealth of International Jewry' could be used 'in conjunction with our own ability (but lack of finance) to produce both arms and aeroplanes to defend Australia and New Guinea jointly'.[43] More general suggestions advocated the establishment of colonies in Queensland and Western Australia.[44] A private proposition put to the Premier of New South Wales by a resident in London began: 'As Australia is so sparsely populated and there is so much waste and barren land which is never likely to be inhabited or cultivated by Australians themselves, may I suggest that the Jews may be allowed to settle in those parts.'[45] M. A. Westland, an Australian living in Ceylon, wrote to the Prime Minister along the following lines:

Couldn't it be possible to make another State in the north and call it North Australia and hand this new state over to the Jews than [sic] to compensate all present property holders. This State to have its own local laws as now exist in all present States with the condition that the language spoken to be English than [sic] to have Federal laws as the other States. They could start a cotton industry as cotton grows there so well. Another condition must be that no foreign Jew could own property out of the Northern State. This State could hold a million Jews.[46]

Akin to this scheme was a suggestion from Adair Blain, the Member for the Northern Territory. On 13 December he suggested that 'a section of the Katherine River should be made available to Jewish refugees to settle and develop agriculture'.[47] This suggestion, like all the rest, was noted by the Department of the Interior but not developed further. The government's long-standing antipathy towards group settlement schemes was a major factor here, but all such projects were too vague to be considered further, in any case. Establishing a population in an area with none of the infrastructure necessary for twentieth century European subsistence was a task requiring enormous foresight and planning together with a vast reservoir of capital. The suggestion that the government could work out the finer details of a plan scribbled on a single sheet of paper did little to endear the bureaucrats to such proposals. Having tied up refugee immigration through the 'Fifteen Thousand' policy, there was little likelihood that any settlement proposals would receive favourable consideration.

For all these there was one exception, which could be dated back to April 1938. This was the celebrated 'Kimberleys Scheme' put forward by the Freeland League for Jewish Territorial Colonisation. Established in London in 1935, this organization had the goal of finding an area under British rule in which to plant a large-scale settlement of suitable German-Jewish refugees who would develop into a self-supporting agricultural community. It did not take long for branches to form in Poland, France, the Netherlands and the United States. After considerable study, the League arrived at the conclusion that an area in the Kimberley of far northern Western Australia would be suitable.[48] The proposal was first suggested to the Australian government on 4 April 1938, when Bruce cabled Lyons from London that he had been approached by Freeland League representatives regarding 'the possibility of the settlement of European Jews in Australia',[49] focusing on the placement of 'larger groups of … refugees in the Kimberley section of Western Australia'. After outlining what he had been told, Bruce ventured that 'it seems to me possible that, provided the Jews were themselves satisfied as to the settlement possibilities in the Kimberleys, on strategic and other grounds there would be much to say for the Commonwealth and Western Australian Governments adopting a sympathetic attitude towards the idea'.[50] He was not alone. There soon emerged a strong groundswell of support for the scheme from many sectors, so much so that in mid-1938 Australia's Deputy Prime Minister, Sir Earle Page – at that time visiting London – contacted Lyons with a request that he make an early decision on the matter 'because of his concern that it would be raised as a possibility at the Evian Conference'.[51]

The Freeland League made its initial contact with the Western Australian government on 7 April 1938,[52] but the response it received was not immediately favourable. It did not take long, however, for the Premier, John C. Willcock, to change his mind 'once the advantages for Western Australia became more obvious'.[53] In the meantime, the Freeland League pressed on. One scholar has noted that towards the end of 1938 the Freeland League's proposal took a more concrete form. It contemplated a Jewish refugee settlement of some 50,000 refugees on the seven million acres which [the landowning firm of] Connor, Doherty and Durack were offering for sale in the eastern Kimberley at a price of 180,000 pounds. It was proposed that some five to six hundred pioneers would construct roads, housing, irrigation works and a power station and that the balance of the colonists would arrive to establish both primary and secondary industries.[54]

Predictably, the Department of the Interior was opposed, basing itself on the well-worn precedent that colonies were undesirable. In London, the Freeland League knew that its proposal would have little progress if there was no-one present in Australia to fight on its behalf, so at the beginning of 1939 it decided to send its Secretary, Isaac N. Steinberg, to Australia. The purpose of this was to 'investigate the Kimberleys and to mobilise Australian support for the resettlement scheme'.[55]

A great amount of support was indeed mobilized, but ultimately the scheme was rejected – not by the Lyons government, but by a later Labor government which made its decision at the end of the Second World War, when circumstances were vastly different to those prevailing in 1938 and 1939.[56] This was no fault of Steinberg or the viability of his suggestions, but rather on account of the traditions which Labor had inherited from earlier governments. In this, the announcement by John McEwen on 1 December 1938 played a key role. The relationship between the Kimberley settlement scheme and Australian refugee policy was shared, though not interdependent. McEwen rarely if ever had anything to say on the matter, but because the Kimberley proposal existed the Department of the Interior found it was forced to justify its existing attitude not only in 1939 but throughout the war. And, because it was forced to justify current practices, the Department found newer and better reasons to retain a tight grip on policy execution. McEwen's policy direction of 1 December 1938 thus remained crucially important to the future regulation of refugee immigration.

The end of the Freeland League settlement initiative in the Kimberley had a tragic consequence at the other end of Australia in mid-1942, when Melbourne-born Critchley Parker, Jr., who had been inspired by Isaac Steinberg's hopes for a Jewish homeland, took up the cause of finding a suitable location in southwestern Tasmania. The proposed settlement, in the Port Davey area, was to be called Poynduk (from the Indigenous name for the local black swans); it was, however, never built, despite elaborate plans for its success. Steinberg had already discussed the Freeland League's proposals with Tasmanian Premier Albert Ogilvie and his wartime successor Robert Cosgrove, and each had responded favourably. As interest waned over the Kimberley, Parker saw Tasmania as an ideal alternative. Setting out to explore the rugged region, however, he lost his life as the forbidding cold attacked a body stricken with pleurisy (and possibly, tuberculosis). His lifeless form was found four months after his death in the winter of 1942; when he died, he was aged just thirty-one.[57]

The Liberalization myth

Two conclusions can be drawn from a reading of Australian refugee policy during November and December 1938. The first is that there was no relationship between Australia's participation at the Evian Conference and the announcement on 1 December 1938 that the Commonwealth would accept 15,000 refugees over the next three years. The government made up the policy of 15,000 piecemeal, and it was unquestionably not part of Australia's refugee strategy when it attended the Evian Conference. The second point concerns the figure of 15,000 refugees over three years. Notwithstanding the fact that Stanley Bruce in London sought a figure twice the size, and that he hoped an Australian statement would anticipate a British request that could be even higher, the Department of the Interior settled on a number which effectively reduced the potential number of Jews who could achieve entry under existing arrangements, from 5,100 Jews annually to 5,000 for all refugees – who included non-Jews. The idea of liberalization, therefore, is erroneous. There was nothing liberal about the announcement of 1 December 1938. Prior to July 1938, the Australian government had been content to treat refugees in the same way as other white alien immigrants, with little or no distinction paid to their status as refugees. From December 1938 onwards, the government so strictly categorized the refugees that, even though they might comply with existing regulations, their Jewish origin acted detrimentally to their chances of entering the country.

After the Evian Conference, the Australian government began slowly to move towards a policy of increased admission of refugees commensurate with what it believed could reasonably be absorbed. Yet when pressure was placed on the government to increase refugee admissions – from applicants in Europe seeking to come to Australia, from within Parliament and in advance of perceived international pressure – the government reacted by announcing an 'increase' in refugee intake over the next three years. That the figure at which it arrived was half that originally proposed by High Commissioner Bruce was not revealed. That specifying the number of 15,000 effectively reduced the potential total of admissions under the existing system was also not revealed. That the government, despite its avowed commitment to an immigration policy which did not discriminate between the white races, was in fact actively discriminating against Jews, never came to public light. That 90 per cent of non-guaranteed refugees who satisfied the government's immigration criteria were being rejected was never made public. In establishing the future direction of Australia's refugee policy, the bureaucrats of the Department of the Interior were to set the scene for innumerable personal tragedies to follow in 1939.

The Australian government, by dint of its gesture of 1 December 1938, saw the year out with an enhanced reputation as a caring (and careful) administration. That gesture, however, was yet another method of migration restriction which, in the hands of a clever government, was portrayed, and accepted, as a humanitarian freeing of existing regulations. Examination of the motives behind the announcement shows it to have been hypocritical rather than humanitarian. When the year ended the bureaucrats in the Department of the Interior would be able to set about turning the situation more to their advantage than ever before.

CHAPTER 8
TOTAL RESTRICTION

Into the New Year

The period immediately following John McEwen's announcement of 1 December 1938 saw a great deal of activity. Implementing the 'Fifteen Thousand' policy, however, coupled with a delay in the processing of applications and the necessity of dealing with matters other than refugees, limited the Immigration Branch's ability to carry out the government's policy efficiently. This period also demonstrated the deficiencies of an immigration policy based on a system of individual landing permits. Above all, early 1939 showed that the Australian government, despite its public face on the issue, continued to lack sensitivity towards the refugees and their need to find sanctuary.

In the immediate aftermath of McEwen's announcement, officials in the Department of the Interior, though delighted with their victory over Bruce's original proposal, were at first unsure how to proceed. The Department had to establish a workable procedure for executing the new direction in an environment where general immigration policy remained as before. For example, discussions continued to take place over the introduction of 'desirable' non-Jewish Dutch immigrants throughout the final months of 1938 and the early part of 1939.[1] The Dutch case was not unique. In July 1939 it was announced that arrangements had been made between the Australian and Swiss governments for the introduction of an indefinite number of non-Jewish Swiss citizens, 'particularly domestic workers, skilled craftsmen, and metal workers'.[2] In accordance with this scheme, the applications for entry would be submitted by an emigration office in Switzerland to the Swiss Consul-General in Sydney, who would then refer them to the Department of the Interior.[3] The discriminatory nature of the arrangement caused a great deal of disquiet through Jewish circles in Geneva, London and Sydney, but the relationship remained intact until the outbreak of war in September 1939.[4]

Jewish refugee migration was now placed into a separate category altogether. It was the Department's task to identify the limits of that separateness and how it could be administered in accordance with the general rules. Its officers faced immense problems, chief among them being the logistics of how to process the enormous number of applications now arriving. His daughter recalled later, for example, that Albert Peters, who never took a single day of sick leave throughout his long career, would rise at 4.00 am each day to work on refugee cases.[5] By 9 February 1939, Joseph Carrodus acknowledged in a statement to the press that it was 'physically impossible to cope with the flood'.[6] The Immigration Branch was then receiving some 2,000 requests for admission each week, and Carrodus declared that the existing staff, which had recently been increased to twenty-one, was still inadequate.[7] The *Sydney Morning Herald* remarked in its editorial on 16 February 1939 that:

> The 'hand-picking' of emigrants which is the Australian Government's 'fixed policy' is so far providing work chiefly for extra Civil Service clerks; the circumlocution process is too painfully slow to effect admission into Australia of any appreciable number of approved immigrants within reasonable time. To recommend themselves to our reluctant officialdom these unfortunate people are at present required to show such special qualities as 'substantial capital,' special trade skill which will not displace Australian artisans, ability to found new enterprises for which local initiative has so far been lacking, or friends to guarantee their support here for an almost prohibitive period.[8]

Carrodus denied that the policy was that narrow. On the day after the editorial appeared, in a meeting with representatives of the Victorian International Refugee Emergency Committee (VIREC), a body established through the League of Nations Union and local churches,[9] he disavowed the suggestion that only those with capital would be admitted.[10] He also promised to find ways of speeding up the admission procedure – but noted that some delay was inevitable to avoid the country being 'flooded' with immigrants. While poor people could be admitted, there was no suggestion of establishing a ratio between impoverished refugees and those with capital. Carrodus affirmed he could not guarantee first preference to those who were currently imprisoned in concentration camps but offered to give a measure of preference 'all things being equal.'[11]

About the only area where Carrodus did not have satisfactory answers was that of labour displacement, which remained a significant matter for concern. *Labor Call* came close to the heart of this issue on 5 January 1939 when it stated that 'the Trade Union Movement will not submit quietly to foreign refugees allowing themselves to be used by employers to reduce wages and the already low living standards of the workers.'[12] The attitude had changed from one of general opposition to the refugee presence to concern over the potential displacement of Australian workers an influx might bring. The paper again raised the issue a few weeks later when it asked, 'how in all creation are refugee workers to get jobs without Australian [*sic*] being tossed out of their occupations?' A 'vast crowd' of refugees were arriving and Australians were 'going out on their ears!'[13] The Federal leader of the Australian Labor Party, John Curtin, signalled the Party's viewpoint on 8 February 1939 with a warning that the refugee issue must be handled carefully on the grounds that 'Industrial standards in Australia must be maintained.'[14] By March, *Labor Call* offered the comment that 'Jews, as such, are not objected to (in the strictly religious sense) … The objection is mainly economic in origin and not religious.'[15]

Questions of efficiency dogged the Department of the Interior in early 1939, and the increase in applications saw a renewed effort at granting Australia House a measure of autonomy in determining approvals. The *Sydney Morning Herald* had waged a long campaign for this, and now found a more reasonable justification for again pursuing the matter:

The lack of officials with full power in London means that few applications are seen personally by British Consular or even Australian officials. The selection is virtually being done by Jewish organisations and leading British Jews are constantly going to Germany to interview and select refugee migrants, whose papers are then sent to Australian Jews in Sydney for a further sifting.[16]

The situation was to be compared to that of Canada, which had inspectors 'at Paris, Hamburg, Rotterdam, Antwerp and Gdynia (Poland) who interview and report on all intended foreign migrants'.[17] Stung into action, Carrodus conceded that while Australia House currently had no power of selection, 'it may be necessary to give it that power in the near future to expedite matters'.[18] On 17 February Cabinet announced that it would transfer to Australia House 'most of the authority for the selection of refugee-migrants seeking to enter Australia under the government plan for the admittance of 15,000 refugees in three years'.[19] The idea was quite simple:

All applications from refugees for admittance to Australia, except those sponsored in Australia, will go to the [proposed] London branch, where they will be examined. Applicants that are considered satisfactory will then be sent to Canberra for Ministerial approval, but when an applicant is regarded as unsatisfactory he will be informed immediately by the London officials.[20]

The new method was not to become operative for some time. Meanwhile, the Assistant Secretary of the Department of the Interior, Tom Garrett, would be sent to London on a fact-finding mission to investigate the establishment of an immigration presence at Australia House and report back to Canberra.

The 'fifteen thousand' policy in practice

The Department of the Interior needed to implement measures to ensure that the 15,000 refugees would be introduced as smoothly and inconspicuously as possible. A working definition of the term 'refugee' had first to be created so that everyone knew, in accordance with the terms of the quota, precisely whose admission was under consideration. Albert Peters endeavoured to do this in a memorandum dated 12 January 1939. He stated that the Immigration Branch was working from the presumption that the government's refugee policy 'is intended for the present to apply to Jews and non-Jews who are suffering disabilities as a result of action by the German Government', and although reports of specifically antisemitic activity were coming in from other European countries, 'it would not appear that the Jewish residents of those countries could be classed as refugees unless they were former nationals of Germany, or Austria, and cannot claim the protection of the Government of the countries in which they reside, or any other Government'.[21] He identified that a more general definition of the word 'refugee' was based around this: refugees were 'Residents, or former residents, of territory occupied by Germany, who did not enjoy the protection of the German Government, or of any other Government'.[22] He considered that so far as Jews and 'non-Aryan Christians' were concerned the definition would apply to persons 'whose nationality is shown as Austrian, German, or Stateless'.

He then raised a further issue that would be significant when assessing the status of foreign Jews then in the Third Reich, noting that:

> cases arise where applications are received from Jews in Germany, or former Austria, whose nationality is shown as Polish, Czechoslovakia, etc. They are under obligation to leave Germany and, in some cases, there may be uncertainty as to whether or not they can claim protection of any other country, but, if applications by non-refugee Jews are dealt with on the same general lines as those by refugees, there should be no serious objection to classifying the uncertain cases as non-refugees.[23]

The entire memorandum was a convoluted way of clarifying that the only Jews the Department considered to be 'refugees' were those of German or Austrian nationality. It was approved by John McEwen on 13 January 1939.

Crucially, the Department then split up the yearly quota for ease of administration and to keep a reasonable racial 'mix' over admissions. It began by apportioning two sub-quotas: refugees who were Jewish would be allowed into Australia to the total of 4,000 annually, with 1,000 non-Jews granted entry.[24] By cutting the annual quota for Jews to 4,000, the government was effectively *reducing* the Jewish intake even further, remembering that the existing system before 1 December 1938 allowed for a potential annual admission of 5,100 Jewish refugees.

The Department then worked out an interim five-point programme for the yearly immigration of the 4,000 Jewish refugees. This saw the following numerical allotments:[25] migrants with not less than £1,000 capital, 900; migrants with less than £1,000 who, after reference to the Australian Jewish Welfare Society were considered to have satisfactory prospects of absorption, 1,500; migrants guaranteed directly by the AJWS, 750; migrants guaranteed by other than the AJWS, 600; and those without guarantors but presenting special features, 250.

Analysis of this breakdown provides several insights about the Department's priorities. Most obviously, the old financial guarantee of £200 landing money had effectively been eliminated for non-guaranteed Jews. The major criterion was now £1,000 (or less, if guaranteed by the AJWS) which covered 2,400 of the 4,000 Jews. The only chance of entry for those not possessing this amount (but at least £200, as before) was to be included among the trifling figure of 250, on the proviso that their cases were 'of a special nature'. This small allocation of 250 persons, coupled with this special condition, was calculated to suffice for what was the major avenue of all refugee applications. It will be recalled that Victor Thompson's memorandum of 17 August 1938 had already identified the government's receipt of some 10,000 acceptable applications from this source per year. The November Pogrom in 1938 served to increase that number substantially, but according to the Department's breakdown only a relatively minute number, even of those eligible to enter, could do so. The Department justified this by drawing Cabinet's attention to the excess of applications over quota places, stating that it would be 'possible to select from amongst the applicants considerably more than the quota who could be regarded as desirable immigrants', and that it would, in fact, even 'be possible to fill the quota with immigrants (including their dependent relatives) who could introduce 1,000 pounds capital or more'.[26]

A second feature of the Department's five-fold division was the amount of discretion given to the Australian Jewish Welfare Society. It was given 750 cases for guarantee per year – an increase of 250 from March 1938, when Cabinet approved the entry of 500. More important was the authority given to the Society to oversee an additional 1,500 cases and recommend their entry or rejection. This had the effect of removing a good deal of individual contact between the refugees in Europe and the government. Most refugees now had to deal with the AJWS, like it or not. Only 850 places were allocated to Jewish refugees with less than £1,000 who sought admission to Australia and were unable or unwilling to deal with the AJWS.

By the end of June 1939, the Department of the Interior provided the Society with very definite instructions concerning who should be recommended. They would have to be under forty years of age, skilled artisans capable of absorption into the Australian workforce without disrupting existing conditions, and not engaged in textiles, sales, or as clerks or bookkeepers.[27] In addition, the Society was directed not to pressure the Department into giving immediate decisions on applications.[28] The government had for some time been troubled by the Society's requests to hurry applications along. At the start of the year the AJWS had sent a letter to Tom Garrett requesting that applications in Canberra which had not yet been dealt with should be investigated to advise applicants in various parts of Europe whether they would eventually be granted permission to enter Australia.[29]

The government also cautioned the Welfare Society to refrain from requesting the reopening of cases that had previously been rejected.[30] That the Society thereafter abided by this request is reflected in a letter from Rabbi L. A. Falk of Sydney's Great Synagogue to a Viennese refugee. The original application having been rejected, Falk, as a member of the AJWS executive, was asked to intervene. All he could do was affirm that it was not within his power 'to compel the authorities to act contrary to their considered judgement'.[31] The Society was itself only too aware that it could not push the government too far and informed the broader Jewish community that it was unable to obtain landing permits for friends and relatives of those already in the country. Moreover, no advantage could be gained by applying to firms or private individuals to approach the Department of the Interior at Canberra directly.[32]

The Department was resolute that there would be no queue-jumping on the part of the Welfare Society, which had, after all, been established to work with the government rather than against it, reaffirming its position on the processing of applications on a first come, first served basis. Although this introduced a certain measure of impartiality, it resulted in genuinely desperate cases having little hope of an early consideration. The

Welfare Society was required to implement this process, and as early as 8 February 1939 was sending printed pro forma letters of rejection to unsuccessful applicants in Europe stating that its allocation for the year was full and had been instructed to refrain from sending any further applications to Canberra.[33]

Interior did prove flexible on one count, however: the introduction of elderly parents of refugees. The Department decided they should receive consideration 'on humanitarian grounds' – provided there was 'no doubt that satisfactory provisions can be made for their maintenance in Australia'.[34] A memorandum was prepared for Cabinet noting that the introduction of parents guaranteed by children already in Australia would 'more than absorb' the quota of 600 allocated to those guaranteed by a person or persons in Australia and in possession of £50 landing money. The memorandum noted two other points: 'It would be most undesirable to have this quota filled by aged persons to the exclusion of many younger nominees of a desirable class' and 'The parents may be generally regarded as non-competitors in the labour market.' It also remarked that the presence of such people once in Australia 'would be useful from the economic point of view, because they would be consumers, and money would be kept in Australia which otherwise, in many cases, the children would have to send abroad to keep their parents'.[35] Approval was sought for the proposal that 'applications by refugees already established in Australia for the admission of their parents be treated as not coming within the quota laid down by the government, provided the male parent is 55 years of age or over.' The proposal received Cabinet assent on 14 February, with a note that up to 500 parents of the type referred to could be admitted annually.[36] This had the effect of raising the maximum unrealized number of Jews for entry from 4,000 to 4,500 – still 600 below what the potential figure had been before 1 December 1938.

In January 1939, the government established a special external committee composed of organizations such as the AJWS, the European Emergency Committee (formerly the German Emergency Fellowship Committee) and Christian denominational bodies. This external group was tasked with assisting various refugee bodies 'in the welfare of their fellow religionists' upon their arrival in Australia. The Welfare Society, keen not to have any new Jewish refugee committees on the scene, hastened to reaffirm its ties with the Department of the Interior. In February, however, a new, unknown organization calling itself the Austro-Australian Relief Committee came forward with its own proposals on how Jewish refugee entry could benefit the Australian rural economy.

The general tenor of its representations were threefold: a policy of placing refugees in jobs was undesirable, as 'every man so placed must either replace an Australian or occupy a position that could be filled by an Australian'; the aim of any activity should be the introduction of new industries by refugees in country areas; and acceleration of such industries should take place to provide work for Australians.[37] The Department of the Interior was sympathetic to these proposals, particularly concerning the introduction of rural industries, but suggested the Austro-Australian Relief Committee 'should merge in some way with the Jewish Welfare Society' because the Department preferred to deal with one Jewish refugee organization only. The AJWS, unsurprisingly, endorsed this suggestion,[38] and Carrodus recommended to McEwen that the Austro-Australian Relief Committee be informed that the Department would not be prepared to accept any applications made by it for the admission of refugees unless such applications were agreed to by the Australian Jewish Welfare Society. McEwen agreed to this on 3 March 1939.[39]

Canberra and London: More activity

In setting down refugee policy after 1 December 1938, a reassessment of the role played by Australia House had also to be made, and the Department attempted to do this in a submission to Cabinet early in the New Year. Among other things, it made a revealing statement regarding the annual quota. While it had earlier been established that Jews were to comprise four-fifths of the quota and non-Jewish refugees the rest, the statement was now made that the government had decided the quota 'may be exceeded in the case of Aryans and non-Aryan Christians'.[40] It is not clear when or how this decision was reached, but it was henceforth the case that while the Jewish figure was fixed and immovable, non-Jews now had no such restriction placed over their entry.

The Department of the Interior, in a switch from its earlier position, also sought a larger role for Australia House, declaring that 'the preferable course' would be to utilize the services of the High Commissioner's Office for the purpose of (a) investigating the suitability of applicants, (b) receiving all applications by refugees without guarantors in Australia, and (c) in certain cases, being given the authority to refuse or approve applications.[41] This final concession was a surrender of at least part of Interior's power of selection, as the work needed could now be reduced and dealt with more expeditiously.

The conditions permitting Australia House to operate did not cover all situations. Cases which were 'obviously ones for refusal' could be rejected by Australia House and the applicants notified forthwith: at the other end of the scale, it could authorize the issue of landing permits for Jewish refugees who were able to introduce at least £3,000 capital (the equivalent of around £170,000 today) where there was 'no doubt as to the suitability of the applicant in all respects'. In the case of Aryans and 'non-Aryan Christians', Australia House could authorize landing permits for those with not less than £1,000 capital where there was no doubt as to the applicant's suitability, and also those who could introduce between £250 and £1,000, provided the authorities at Australia House were satisfied that the refugees could be 'absorbed after arrival in Australia without detriment to Australian workers and without the aid of some person or organisation in Australia to give them a helping hand'.[42] In return for these concessions, Australia House would be required to ascertain, in every case submitted to it, whether the applicant was Jewish, Aryan or 'non-Aryan Christian,' or Catholic. This information was to be transmitted to Canberra for the purpose of alerting the refugee organizations and/or obtaining their advice on specific cases.[43] Following through on the changes, in April 1939 Assistant Secretary Tom Garrett was sent to London to take charge of activities and prepare a report for Canberra at first hand on the refugee situation. Australia House was warned in March that 'action to give effect to the decision of the Government [should] be held in abeyance until then'.

February 1939 saw a flurry of activity between London, Sydney and Canberra, prompted by the worsening position in Europe and the urgent need of Jewish organizations to rescue as many Jews as possible. On 1 February the London-based Council for German Jewry cabled the Australian Jewish Welfare Society in Sydney urging that it appeal to Canberra for a more generous quota, imploring it to 'redouble your already great efforts'.[44] The AJWS replied that it intended to approach Canberra and request an increase in the number of permits for guaranteed cases.[45] This was made in a meeting between officers from the Welfare Society and Joseph Carrodus on 27 February. After much discussion he agreed to take 250 refugees from the non-guaranteed category and 'give' them to the AJWS, thus making its quota now an even thousand. Of the remaining 1,250 non-guaranteed refugees, an arrangement was made to reserve 250 places annually for orphans – though this sub-quota was never filled owing to a lack of suitable children who could be found in Germany.

While at first glance it might seem that the Department had softened its policy, in fact it was not really accepting more migrants but rather mixing up the existing quota and shuffling refugee numbers to where they could be filled in a less hit-or-miss fashion. The Council for German Jewry in London did not really understand this, thinking instead that the Australian government had allocated *all* refugee places to the AJWS. Given this, it had already started bringing refugees to Britain from Germany in anticipation of transhipment of Australia.[46] The AJWS was quick to send a letter to London advising that at this juncture the Council should only bring refugees out of Germany 'in cases where they had received definite advice that Permits would be eventually granted', as there was 'no guarantee that the Commonwealth Government would endorse all the applications submitted to them by the AJWS'.[47]

Restriction of refugees: Complete closedown

By early 1939 the difference between immigration procedures for Jewish refugees and other white immigrants had widened considerably. While all the elaborate strategies for the implementation of the 'Fifteen Thousand' policy were being worked out, the criteria for everyone else remained as they were. For Jews, the rules would become even more severe. Early in March 1939, in a memorandum concerning the Inter-Governmental Committee on Refugees (then sitting in London), Albert Peters let slip news of a proposal currently being worked out by the Immigration Branch suggesting a restriction would be placed on the number of landing permits issued to *all* Jews, even those who were not refugees.[48] John McEwen presented a detailed proposal on this to Cabinet on 16 March, arguing that if a Jewish problem was not to arise in Australia and an accompanying antisemitism, 'a limit should be placed on the total number of Jews admitted annually'.[49] He suggested that only 1,000 non-refugee Jews, from all sources, be admitted to Australia each year. This special quota would be made up of 200 'dependent relatives of Jews already settled here', and 800 others whose number would include both guaranteed and non-guaranteed migrants.

This was designed to tighten up the admission of Jews from eastern Europe, particularly Poland. Polish Jews did not fall within the Department's definition of 'refugees', and it will be recalled that the Department had a long-standing aversion to Polish Jewish admission. With this measure, any hope the Jews of eastern Europe may have had to escape to Australia was gone. A total of 4,000 Jews from Germany and Austria (4,500 including dependent parents) were to be admitted annually, but only 1,000 Jews of all other descriptions, provided they were of a sufficient standard, were to be allowed entry (presuming their acceptance in line with the prescribed criteria). McEwen saw the dangerous ground upon which he was walking, but declared:

> It is realised that approval of this recommendation would amount to discrimination against a particular race. It is considered, however, that, in the special circumstances, the proposed action would be justified. It is most desirable, in the interests of the composition of the future population of Australia, that as far as possible the immigration policy of the Commonwealth should be selective.[50]

There it was at last: an admission of selectivity and discrimination against all Jews seeking entry to Australia, and a policy guideline to back it up. Although Polish or other eastern European Jews were not counted among refugees by the government, their Jewishness was sufficient to lock them into a quota which was acknowledged by the government as being racially determined. Prior to this, non-refugee Jewish admission – though made difficult through bureaucratic restrictions – was not subjected to policy. Now every Jewish migrant application was controlled by a quota which, once filled, would deny entry to even the most 'desirable' applicant.

Although McEwen's policy announcement of 1 December 1938 was intended to show the world that Australia was playing a valuable role in the refugee crisis, the months immediately following saw the policy hijacked by the Department of the Interior as the finer details of its execution were worked out. The period in question was only short – just over three months – but it was to be crucial for the Jews of Europe. By manipulating the 1 December 1938 quota both the officials and their Minister demonstrated their negative feelings towards Jews. They showed, moreover, their keenness to discriminate actively to keep them out of Australia. So far as the Department was concerned, the period from January to the end of March 1939 saw the high point of its campaign to restrict a Jewish influx into Australia. There was no reason to suppose that future events could in any way modify the level of control achieved.

A new regime at the Department of the Interior

On 7 April 1939 Joseph Lyons, leader of the United Australia Party (UAP) and Prime Minister since 1932, died in office. In the weeks following, his UAP-Country Party coalition broke up, and on 26 April a new UAP government, under the leadership of Robert Menzies, took office. With the dissolution of the coalition, the portfolio for the Interior was now bestowed upon Senator Harry Foll, who displaced John McEwen, a Country Party member, as Minister.

The change provided the Department of the Interior with an opportunity to relieve some of its immense workload. Albert Peters identified this backlog as a major retardant to the smooth functioning of the Immigration Branch. 'The Department', he wrote on 27 April, 'is receiving applications from Jews, both refugees and non-refugees, far in excess of the quota limits, and great difficulty is being experienced in confining … approvals within the limits' set by the government.[51] What he proposed, therefore, was nothing less than a temporary *increase* in the number of Jews to be admitted to Australia for the current year, taken from the overall triennial quota of 15,000. He recommended that 'the quota for Jews this year be increased from 5,000 (including 4,000 refugees and 1,000 non-refugees) to 6,000'. In his first act as Minister for the Interior, Senator Foll gave his approval to this proposal on 1 May 1939.[52]

This remarkable instance would appear to be unique. A conscious and deliberate decision was made to ease the conditions prevailing for Jews seeking to enter Australia. For the first time, the Department acknowledged the part it could play in alleviating refugee distress and took the opportunity to give immediate help within the confines of its administrative operations. Yet it must be emphasized that the overriding reason for this turnaround was intended to ease the workload of the Department, *not* to help Jews enter Australia. The general rules about landing money, permits, guarantees and adherence to the quota remained. Most applications received were still rejected.

Approval of this measure was Senator Foll's first action as Minister for the Interior. His arrival did not, however, characterize the rest of his tenure, which was to prove a disappointment for Europe's Jews. The pressure under which the Department was working called for a flexible approach, the ability to take tough decisions and a good deal of sympathy. On this issue, Harry Foll, who was broadminded in many other respects, was not so endowed. As early as 9 May 1939 he signalled the likely tenor of his approach in a statement highlighting the determination of the government that no 'minority problems' would arise in Australia. The procedure, in his view, was simple: 'in general our policy is to select carefully from individual applicants for admittance, thus ensuring that the migrants admitted are of a type that can be readily assimilated in the Australian community.'[53] The issues were clear-cut, and although Foll was to adhere to this simplistic approach, the matters with which he was dealing were to become more and more complex throughout the second half of 1939.

Ministerial statements and new rules in June and July demonstrated further that Senator Foll was determined to adopt a strict letter-of-the-law approach. The first of these, on 5 June, set the tone for those to follow. The topic concerned landing permits for families separated temporarily within Europe. Foll instructed the Department to refuse permission for wives and children to proceed to Australia ahead of the husband or father where permission had been granted for the entry of a whole family.[54] An exception could be made for a husband to travel to Australia in advance of his wife and family, and in such cases 'an official letter in lieu of a separate Permit may be issued to enable the wife and children to embark for Australia within three months of the husband's departure'.[55] There was, however, a catch; if permission was sought to extend the period beyond three months a new (and separate) landing permit would have to be obtained for the wife and children.

The implications were severe for many Jews, as the concentration camps contained men for whom family permits had been granted but who remained imprisoned and could not leave. Their wives and children might have been able to emigrate, but the Australian government would not accept them unless they were accompanied by the husband or father. Where the situation was reversed, and the man could come to Australia leaving his wife and children behind, new landing permits would have to be requested after three months – at a time when they were being handed out grudgingly and in order of application. It could take years for a family to be reunited in Australia, if at all.

On 29 June 1939, Foll made a further statement to the effect that no direct approach to officials in Canberra could influence the Department in considering an application. Whereas it 'may have been the habit of officials a few years ago to grant interviews to intercessors or agents who sought verbally to press the claims of individual Germans who wished to obtain permission to land in Australia', this practice was now to stop.[56] Officials in the Department of the Interior were simply too busy to listen to personal appeals. Foll then sought to cut Jews out of an Australian option by refusing the entry of refugee doctors on 24 July. Announcing the decision, he stated that all applications for landing permits from foreign medical professionals were being refused 'because of the difficulty of their engaging in practice' in Australia.[57] He added, 'In the last two months about 29 applications by refugee doctors, all of high qualifications and including eight of outstanding ability, had been refused.'[58]

On the same day, speaking of refugee immigration generally, Foll informed the nation that some 20 per cent of all applications were now being granted.[59] This was certainly an improvement on Victor Thompson's figure of 10 per cent from August 1938, and must be acknowledged as evidence that the processing of applications according to a specific quota was helping the Immigration Branch catch up on its paperwork. It is perhaps no surprise, therefore, that new Prime Minister Robert Menzies should say in Adelaide on 8 July 1939 that the government's attitude towards the refugees had been generous, and that it was 'unlikely' any extension would be made to existing arrangements.[60]

Observing the government's efforts

Australian public attitudes were, as always, mixed, though sympathy for the Jewish refugees was becoming more apparent. Much of this came from Sydney, where many refugees were settling. The reasons often stemmed from an impatience at what were seen to be the government's frail attempts at facilitating refugee immigration. The *Sydney Morning Herald*, in an editorial dated 20 June, summed up this attitude when it stated:

The plain truth is that the Federal Government has not yet tackled the whole problem of the refugees with that vigour and enthusiasm which it demands. Facilities for the selection and assistance of migrants, especially at the London end, still seem to be niggardly and in urgent need of improvement.[61]

Another frustration stemmed from the fact that the Department of the Interior refused to provide explanations when refusals were given. One correspondent to the *Sydney Morning Herald* asked of the Department, 'Do they know themselves just what they are doing?'[62] Often, it seemed, they did not. The daunting task of immigrant selection saw frequent instances of premature rejection before the full facts were known. An example of this can be seen in the case of a Warsaw Jew, Mordka Nejman. His brother-in-law, Norman Seidel, had emigrated to Australia years earlier, and had settled in Hobart where he soon became established in soft goods manufacture. In 1938, owing to the situation prevailing for Jews in Poland, Nejman decided to sell his flourishing electrical business and move to Australia. Seidel arranged employment that would not displace an Australian, and with assured landing capital of £500 together with Seidel's maintenance guarantee, Nejman made his application to come to Australia. This was refused without Interior providing any reasons.[63] The Tasmanian Premier, Albert Ogilvie, took up the case personally, and in a letter to the Prime Minister on 14 March 1939 he sought favourable consideration of Nejman's application.[64] On 26 May Ogilvie received news that, upon further reflection, the application of Nejman, his wife and children, had now been approved.[65] In view of the ease with which reconsideration was given to the case, there is every likelihood that with a little more care in Canberra the application would have been approved in the first place.[66]

Despite the pressure under which the Department was working, it still sought to conceal its activities whenever possible to avoid interference from outside. When it decided to divide the quota of 15,000 into Jews and non-Jews, for example, Joseph Carrodus minuted that such an action was regarded as 'a departmental instruction which might be varied later', and that consequently 'it would not be advisable to make it public'.[67] When the proposal to limit non-refugee Jews to an annual quota of 1,000 was mooted, Carrodus similarly suggested that it would not be advisable to refer to it publicly, as Australia's Jewish population 'may regard it as unreasonable discrimination'.[68] Even the measure concerning the parents of refugees was subjected to careful treatment. On 24 May, Gerald Mahoney, the Labor Member for Denison (Tasmania) asked in Parliament 'whether any age limit' was being applied to migrants or refugees wishing to enter Australia. Should there not be one, he sought 'immediate steps' to prevent the entry of aged persons.[69] Interior had an advance reply prepared. The response of John Perkins (himself a former Interior Minister), for the government, was that 'No age limit operates, but the facts in individual cases are considered by the Minister before admission is granted'. In some cases, where parents were already naturalized, their children were admitted, while in others, 'young people secure permits for their parents'. Perkins observed that, overall, 'we do what we can to meet the wishes of those desirous of becoming citizens of this country'.[70] The meaning of all this, in practical terms, was that no news of the refugee parent scheme was discussed in Parliament, and the Department of the Interior was again left to run its affairs without scrutiny from outsiders.

To some observers, the Department's bias against Jews became obvious as 1939 progressed, and gestures such as the 1 December 1938 announcement began to appear empty. Many people, Jews and non-Jews alike, began to question the foundations of the government's refugee policy, and although there was never agitation for a wholesale revision of selection procedure, public statements voiced criticism of the landing permit system. One of the most caustic of these came from Dr. J. Leon Jona, presiding at the Zionist Federation of Australia's Annual Conference in Melbourne on 5 March 1939. While keeping his comments general, there was little doubt as to the direction in which they were being steered:

> When the history of the Jewish people of the early decades of the 20th century comes to be written, it will be found that the greatest curse of the Jewish people was not the tyrants and their murderous henchmen, but the permit system, which prevented these refugees, driven from one land, from entering another – One of the most cruel and vicious inventions of this generation.[71]

Jona was to be in for more disappointment. The following month, it was announced that the Department of the Interior had amended the wording of the forms required to be completed by all applicants. Henceforth, every application for admission to Australia, regardless of the applicant's country of origin, would be required to attest whether the applicant was 'of Jewish race'. This would force the Department to retreat from its set position – the only occasion on which outside pressure had this effect throughout the entire Nazi period.

CHAPTER 9
THE LAST DAYS OF PEACE

The 'Jewish race' clause

Regardless of an applicant's origin or circumstances, applications for foreign immigration to Australia were filled out on one of two official forms. Form 40 was headed 'Application for Admission of Relative or Friend to Australia', and was submitted to the Department of the Interior in Canberra by an Australian resident guaranteeing an immigrant's maintenance after arrival. The migrant would be permitted to come to Australia after showing that he or she (but usually he) was of acceptable health and character standards and was in possession of at least £50 landing capital.

Form 47, a more general 'Application for Permit to Enter Australia', was to be filled in by all non-guaranteed intending migrants. The amount of landing capital required by these people was at least £200, but as 1939 progressed the migration authorities began to take the term 'at least' to mean almost any figure over £200, and up to £3,000 was required in certain instances later in the year.

In March or early April 1939, both Form 40 and Form 47 were revised. This was well after the 'Fifteen Thousand' decision and coincided roughly with John McEwen's recommendation on 16 March 1939 that a quota be placed on the entry of all Jews regardless of their refugee status. The amended forms required intending immigrants, from anywhere other than the British Empire, to state whether they were 'of Jewish race'.

Some government officials responded negatively to the new form. Inspector Roland S. Browne of the Commonwealth Investigation Branch, for one, considered the Department of the Interior's position thoroughly unjustifiable. He declared that it could even be unconstitutional, suggesting that if the Department wanted to elicit certain information from the applicants it should simply ask what race the person in question was. Browne was concerned that the amendment would 'raise a controversy as to what is the Jewish race', as even 'Eminent scientists hold that the Jewish race is a myth'.[1] Would Australia, he asked, be about to accept Hitler's definition of a Jew? This would be nonsensical if only since there are 'thousands of mixed marriages among the refugees, and the Jews are as mixed a crowd as the English'. Browne recorded that the amendment was:

an amazing and disquieting departure, for a Government form, and the question is impossible to answer in a great number of cases, that is answered with any degree of authority. ... If such discrimination is to be shown, will the Department go a step further and logically define what is the Jewish race? I should think even the most ardent Nazi will praise the author of this form, who, modest in the fame which his work brings, may desire to add a new line such as 'Roman Catholic or not,' or 'Salvation Army or not.'[2]

As an officer of the law, he advised that 'the wording of the form is bound to invite strong criticism on the purest democratic and ethical grounds', and while he thought the Department of the Interior had its reasons for wanting to know the race to which an intending migrant belonged, 'one can only ponder over the mentality which inspired the wording as it is'. Browne's letter to Albert Peters concluded with the hope that 'for the sake of Australia's good name' the form would be immediately withdrawn, as 'it is monstrous, offensive, quite absurd and provocative'.[3]

The Director of the Commonwealth Investigation Branch, Harold E. Jones, took up the issue with the Department of the Interior at once, and had a reply from Albert Peters within a week showing that the Department had already reconsidered its position. Jones was informed that:

Exception has been taken by some members of the Jewish community to the use of the words 'Jewish race' and it is, therefore, desired that the words 'of' and 'race' should be crossed out on the forms already distributed, so that the phrase reads simply 'is/is not Jewish.'

If inquiry is made as to how a nominee should be described who is of Christian faith, but Jewish extraction, the reply could be to the effect that such person could be shown as 'not Jewish.'[4]

Peters commented that it was desired to bring the new forms into operation forthwith and invited Jones to 'kindly issue the necessary instructions to your Inspectors and request them to withdraw from use stocks of the form hitherto used'.[5]

The exception taken by 'some members of the Jewish community' had been transmitted to Peters from no less a source than the Australian Jewish Welfare Society. In a letter dated 21 April, the Secretary of the Society accepted that the wording used on the form 'greatly facilitates the working of the Department in determining those applicants who would come under the category of Jewish refugees and be included in the special quota'.[6] He noted, however, that the Society had:

received numerous protests from members of the Australian Jewish Community in Victoria and New South Wales, who have taken great exception to the words 'JEWISH RACE.' They are most emphatic in their protests and wish to point out that they are *BRITISH SUBJECTS* of *JEWISH FAITH*, and the word 'RACE' especially, is most obnoxious to them.[7]

The Department backed down immediately, and in a subsequent letter of 27 April Joseph Carrodus informed the AJWS that 'in view of the objection taken to the use of the phrase "JEWISH RACE" it will be arranged for the word "RACE" to be deleted and the form amended to read simply "is/is not Jewish".[8] This was sufficient for the AJWS, which neither broached the subject again nor demonstrated any objection to the continued employment of the discriminatory categorization. Moreover, the only objection made by the Welfare Society was that Jews were being classified as a 'race'; there was no opposition to the general idea of a Jewish identifier appearing on immigration forms, as the AJWS saw benefits to the selection process if Jewish applications could be known in advance.

Opposition, however, came from the Victorian Refugee Immigration Appeals Committee (VRIAC). This body had been established by the Australian Council of Civil Liberties and the trade union movement as a watchdog organization overseeing the rights of refugees and had brought individual cases (including those rejected without apparent reason) to the attention of the Minister. When news of the new Form 40 reached VRIAC, a vigorous exchange of correspondence began between the Honorary Secretary, Marjorie Coppel, and the Department of the Interior. In her first letter, dated 4 May, Coppel noted that VRIAC had been made aware that the new Form 40 was to be replaced and that insertion of the 'race' clause was due to a mistake. On behalf of the Committee, she hoped that no discrimination based on race or religion would be introduced into immigration application forms. The issue of who was to be classed as 'of Jewish race' was important here:

> As the distinction between Jewish and non-Jewish members of the Australian community is solely a religious distinction, we cannot understand any Government Department imposing a different significance to the term 'Jew', when it deals with persons coming into the community. On the other hand, discrimination on a religious basis would be repugnant to the spirit of religious tolerance on which our constitution is based.[9]

The Department tried to downplay this by reassuring Coppel that her fears were misplaced. On 14 May, Carrodus wrote back that the AJWS had only disapproved of the use of the word 'race', and that it had no objection to the Jewish clause remaining on the form. He went on to state that 'no discrimination is shown against an intending immigrant merely because of his religion', though in the case of refugees, certain information was necessary which intending migrants had not hitherto been required to give. Such information was mainly for 'statistical purposes'.[10]

Coppel was far from convinced. A further letter to Carrodus dated 25 May stated that VRIAC did not feel 'that its protest against the racial or religious discrimination, involved in this new departure, has been satisfactorily met'.[11] VRIAC, she wrote, was not making its protest 'particularly on behalf of the Jews', but rather 'for the interests of the community, which we do not think are served by a discrimination of this sort'. She requested that her letters be placed before the Minister, commenting that 'If the Government persists in this discrimination, our Committee feels that such a vital matter concerning refugee immigration should be brought before the public.'[12] By way of closing, she sought the definition of the term 'Jewish' according to which the Department operated. This, among other things, was included in the response which followed.

Albert Peters contended that the term 'Jewish' was intended to apply to 'persons who would ordinarily describe themselves as being Jews, and not to persons who may be of partly Jewish blood and who could be classed, for example, as non-Aryan Christians'.[13] Beyond this, he was very guarded. 'The broad distinction', he wrote, 'as to whether an intending migrant would class himself as Jewish or non-Jewish will serve the immediate purpose of the Department'.[14] If further information was required, the subject could be interrogated later. In an aside to Carrodus, Peters then remarked cryptically that 'we don't want to confine the term merely to persons of Jewish blood and faith'.[15]

Marjorie Coppel persisted. In another letter to Carrodus on 23 June, she stated that VRIAC was not concerned with the number of Jews admitted under the quota. It was only concerned 'that there should be no discrimination on the grounds of race or religion against the refugee and that the sole criterion of admissibility should be absorptive capacity'.[16] This was the opportunity Interior needed to bury the can of worms Form 40 had become. In a letter drafted by Peters on 7 July 1939, all the circumstances under which an immigrant may be permitted entry to Australia were recounted. These ultimately fed back to the issue of maintenance guarantees, the financial standing of the guarantors, landing capital and the nature of the industry or occupation in which the immigrant proposed to seek employment.[17] This did not remove the offending clause in Form 40, but it did serve to eliminate Coppel's concerns over whether the government was operating a discriminatory policy. A letter of acknowledgement and thanks that the issue had been explained and clarified in such detail followed for Carrodus on 11 July,[18] and all opposition to the revised Form 40 ended.

The question as to how far the 'Jewish race' clause was discriminatory is open to debate. Perhaps it was introduced to facilitate the entry of Jews to Australia; alternatively, it could have been used negatively. It was, moreover, retained until November 1952 at the behest of the Australian Jewish Welfare Society, at a time of booming post-war immigration. Indeed, it will be recalled that the Welfare Society's objection to the clause in 1939 focused only on the use of the term 'race' as applied to Jews; it did not object to the underlying concept of the clause itself which possibly might have been introduced in 1939 to assist Jewish refugees.

The motives of the Department of the Interior must, however, be viewed critically. It was the Department which drew up the forms and put them into operation. Given Interior's earlier history of opposition to Jewish entry, that raises some questions over the reason for the existence of the form. That the move to amend Form 40 and Form 47 and insert the 'Jewish race' clause arose and at a time when the main aim of the Department was seeking ways of reducing or at least slowing refugee admission, is also a matter for questioning the adoption of the amendment. Finally, until the introduction of the amended forms there was no fixed way of ascertaining whether an applicant was Jewish: the forms as altered now required any white person desiring to migrate to Australia – from Europe, the United States, European territories abroad or anywhere else – to state whether he or she was (or was not) Jewish. That would provide to the Department accurate figures of how many Jews, from all sources, were applying to come in, and intensify or relax its restrictive practices accordingly.

It could be concluded that the Department of the Interior was acting unreasonably and tried to camouflage its obviously discriminatory ploy by subterfuge. The Australian Jewish community, through the AJWS, was deceived by the line that the clause was introduced to assist refugee Jews to come to Australia; so also, were the Board of Deputies of British Jews and the London-based Jewish Refugees' Committee.[19] After the war the clause was retained, ostensibly to assist the selection of Jewish immigrants. However, any discussion of the post-war administration of the Jewish race clause should not overlook its overtly racist foundations from 1939.

A diversion: Refugees from the Spanish Civil War

The Department of the Interior at this time was also faced with another refugee issue. Since July 1936, the forces of fascism and republican democracy were locked in a life-and-death civil war in Spain that would ultimately claim up to 500,000 dead.[20] Refugees from the conflict poured into France and sought to resettle permanently either in that country or in lands in the Americas and elsewhere. In Australia, an organization known as the Spanish Relief Committee[21] sought to alleviate the distress of Spanish refugees and make representations to the government for some form of limited admittance. Its communications fell directly within the jurisdiction of the Department of the Interior, which was – with all the problems associated with Jewish refugees – unprepared for another refugee crisis involving white aliens.

The Department of the Interior had not considered the problem of Spanish refugees before the Spanish Civil War ended in early April 1939. On 6 April Carrodus asked Peters whether the Department had yet received any advice regarding the plight of Spanish refugees, or any official request from the Minister 'to do something for them'.[22] This was a less-than-subtle hint to Peters that he should investigate the matter and draw up a few suggestions as to how the issue should be handled.

The memorandum he produced as a result was comprehensive.[23] Noting that some organizations had suggested Spanish refugees be included within the 'Fifteen Thousand' policy, Peters commented that 'There is no need for such a course.' His justification was that it would make the problem of authorizing their admission more difficult, as 'ten times more applications' were already being received from Jewish refugees than could be approved. He suggested that special consideration might be given to the admission of Spanish children whose maintenance was guaranteed, but beyond this 'each application should be dealt with on its merits in accordance with the general rules,' and that 'many of the Spanish refugees are Communists and precautions are desirable against admitting any who are likely to be political extremists'.[24]

Upon reading the memorandum, Senator Foll ordered that it be redrafted for Cabinet with definite policy recommendations. Carrodus instructed Peters to rework the document but only list the options available; Cabinet itself would then decide which option would become policy.[25] At the same time, Peters was also directed to prepare an additional statement for Senator Foll 'giving reasons *against* [any] proposal' to admit Spanish refugees.[26] Accordingly, Foll was informed as follows:

It is doubtful whether more than a very few Spanish refugees would be able to comply with the landing money requirements, or to find suitable guarantors in Australia, but it is not considered advisable that special facilities should be granted for their admission.

It is not unlikely that many of the Spanish refugees would be Communists.

It is not considered desirable to include Spanish in the quota for refugees. The latter are not actually securing special concessions for admission as regards landing money requirements, etcetera. They are mostly Jews and the number of applications is far in excess of the number which the Government is prepared to grant.[27]

Foll, in turn, considered that the Spanish refugee issue did not merit special attention. Five weeks later Cabinet assented to the proposal that 'no special action be taken to encourage Spanish refugees'.[28] The government's response to the question of refugees from Spain was thereby settled.[29] The term 'refugee' could now only mean refugee Jews from Nazism, with those falling outside that category – such as those from Spain, Poland, Hungary or elsewhere – not considered deserving of special treatment.

Assistance beyond the government

Most Jews fleeing Nazism and seeking refuge in Australia had very few chances to enter. Often all they had by way of support were the efforts of well-intentioned Australians who tried to convince the government to modify its policy, but such favourable circumstances were exceptional. Frequently, personal representations, even to highly placed individuals, did not achieve positive results. Yet practical help did take place, and at a faster rate as the danger became more discernible. Some Australians did their best to circumvent or confront government policy.

Some known instances have already been mentioned, such as the intervention of VRIAC over the revision of Form 40, the formation of the German Emergency Fellowship Committee by Camilla Wedgwood and agitation for a systematization of refugee policy by the AJWS throughout 1938. These are key illustrations of the practical work that was undertaken by those pushing against the government's restrictive policy. Other examples keeping the Department of the Interior apprised as to how members of the public were thinking occurred almost daily. On 11 March 1939, Brian Fitzpatrick, in his role as Deputy Chairman of VRIAC, wrote to the Department with a question as to whether Jews and 'non-Aryan Christians' were required to prove that they were in possession of a greater amount of landing capital than non-Jewish immigrants.[30] Additional concern was expressed around the urgent necessity of processing applications in a timely manner.

Many representations were made to the Department in 1939 with this in mind, but none were so pointed as that from Harry Lesnie, the Honorary Secretary of the AJWS, on 22 May. Having earlier raised the issue with Senator Foll personally, Lesnie indicated that the Society:

would deeply appreciate your favourable consideration of the suggestion that a decision after an application for a permit had been made could be given with the least possible delay. As already explained, we find it necessary to ask for this on account of the tremendous number of individuals who have died either in the Concentration Camp or otherwise while waiting for the issue of a permit, or any advice that a permit will not be granted.[31]

Foll's reply sought only to justify the delays. He affirmed that 'a tremendous number of ... applications are being received and the officers of my Department are working at high pressure in order to cope with them, and of necessity some delay must occur ... [while] every precaution is taken to ensure that no unnecessary delay takes place in reaching a decision'.[32] He did not refer to Lesnie's reason for bringing the matter up, namely, that people were dying in concentration camps while the government procrastinated.

Foll found it difficult to dismiss representations from other Parliamentarians. The example of Tasmania's Albert Ogilvie has already been mentioned; another state politician, David Drummond, the Minister for Education in New South Wales, also sought to assist the cause of refugees in a personal entreaty to John McEwen prior to his departure as Interior Minister. Writing to him 'as one Country Party colleague to another and not in an official capacity', Drummond was concerned specifically with the case of a German Jewish refugee named Hans Wolfgan [sic] Cohen, 'a man ... with exceptionally fine qualifications who has sought entrance to Australia, but whose entrance has been denied by your Department on the score that he was not guaranteed employment'.[33] This case had been brought to Drummond's notice by Sydney's Rabbi L. A. Falk. Drummond informed McEwen he had an assurance from Rabbi Falk that in this specific case he was prepared to guarantee that Cohen would not become 'a burden on the State'.[34] Drummond then suggested that McEwen arrange to meet with Rabbi Falk when next in Sydney to discuss the matter, but regardless of whether he did this, if he could 'spare thought' and bestow 'a favourable decision' to the introduction of such refugees, 'I am sure you would be doing something that would help us to get citizens of the right type into our country'.[35]

On 18 April 1939 McEwen wrote directly to Rabbi Falk, advising him that he had received Drummond's letter. He invited Falk to correspond freely with him.[36] There is no record of any successful outcome of the application. It will be recalled that the Department of the Interior was poorly disposed to personal intercessions on behalf of refugees.

Rabbi Falk, on his part, made numerous attempts to secure the entry of Jews from Europe. One example concerned a Hungarian Jew seeking to enter Australia, Dr. Laszlo Roth. Rigorous efforts were being made from Hungary to secure his entry; Chief Rabbi

Simon Hevesi of Budapest and other rabbinical figures had written to Falk in the hope that he could obtain a permit for Roth's entry, but on every occasion, Falk had been forced to reply in the negative. In explaining the situation to Hevesi, Falk outlined that Roth could not enter because 'our community cannot yet find suitable employment for him' and that, 'as he is not a skilled tradesman, I cannot find anyone who would guarantee him employment, as required by the Commonwealth of Australia'. Finally – and perhaps most importantly – Jews from Hungary did not come under the category of refugees.[37] Despite this, Rabbi Falk hastened to assure the Chief Rabbi that other ways were being investigated to acquire the necessary landing permit, asking Chief Rabbi Hevesi whether 'you could assure me that [Roth] is capable of acting as a teacher of Hebrew and religion. *It would not mean that it is necessary for him to be able to speak Hebrew*.'[38] This was one of many avenues established to facilitate the entry of individual Jews, but there is no record of Roth entering Australia.

On occasion, bodies other than welfare or religious organizations tried to serve their own interests by recommending specific cases to the government. The Advance Ballarat Association (ABA) was such an organization. On 27 April 1939 the ABA's Honorary Secretary, G. S. Hendy, wrote to the Minister of the Interior with 'a plan for Ballarat' involving 'certain selected refugee migrants with capital and experience' who could be introduced to the city 'for the purpose of opening new industries'.[39] The ABA had prepared its proposal carefully. A complete examination had been made of several applicants who had stated their willingness to settle in Ballarat, and of these it selected eighteen whom it considered to be highly desirable. The Australian Jewish Welfare Society had been contacted, and it agreed to obtain 'suitable written undertakings from each of the specified applicants to make genuine endeavours to settle in this district'. The ABA assumed responsibility to render assistance to the refugees 'in the choice of industrial sites, and advice regarding labour, transport, raw materials, water, electricity and the like', and declared it would 'welcome those admitted and assist them to become absorbed in the Australian community'.[40]

The ABA named the specific immigrants it sought to settle in Ballarat and noted that all of these had already been proposed to the government by the AJWS. Upon consideration of the 'capital, industrial experience, and character of the ... applicants, and employment likely to be provided for Australians by their admission', the ABA respectfully recommended their applications to the Minister for favourable decision. The Association had decided that the refugee situation could be employed to benefit the city and emphasized that in taking this action it had 'not allowed itself to be swayed by humanitarian motives'. In making its final choice of eighteen refugees, Hendy stated that the Association 'was guided solely by the need to stimulate the economic development of this locality'.

The ABA's application was one of many similar proposals sent to the Department of the Interior by concerned citizen groups, but due to the government's antipathy towards any proposal that even hinted at the possibility of 'group settlement', none of these offers were taken up. The ABA's proposal was rejected. It transpired that most of the refugees it selected had made earlier applications which the Department of the Interior had refused.

The applicants had also been refused support by the AJWS, further weakening their cases.[41] The ABA was informed that the Department of the Interior would authorize the entry of only two of its eighteen nominees; the applications of all the other refugees were rejected for a variety of unstated reasons.[42]

Australia House and the Garrett Report

By the middle of 1939, the processing of refugee applications had been eased by the introduction of specific sub-quotas and the continued cooperation of the AJWS. One of the most important avenues of relief had come from the decision to grant some discretionary powers to Australia House. Tom Garrett had been sent to London in April 1939, charged with the task of working with the staff there and preparing a detailed report at first hand on the refugee situation. The report, when completed, would then form the basis for the future implementation of Australia's refugee policy.

Working closely with Major Reuben H. Wheeler, the Chief Migration Officer at Australia House, Garrett soon found that the work being undertaken there was 'quite different from what it is in Australia.'[43] While refugees already in Britain presented little problem owing to their being able to visit Australia House in person, German-based refugee organizations were considered to be of dubious merit as they had to 'work closely under the eye of the Gestapo . . ., which is apt to exert pressure on them from the point of view of getting rid of Jews'.[44] By being closer to the scene, a new London-based migration office might be able to administer refugee applications with greater insight.

Garrett's relationship with the local Jewish relief organizations in London was, in his words, 'stormy'.[45] During the very first meeting, in fact, a deadlock was reached over numbers of Jews to be allowed into Australia, which was only resolved after a week's adjournment during which both sides cooled down. The chief problem, as Garrett saw it, lay in the relationship between the Jewish Refugees' Committee (JRC) and the Australian Jewish Welfare Society, for the British body 'holds the purse and wants to call the tune'.[46] That tune involved the JRC trying to 'fill the quota at all costs, irrespective of whether the people could be placed in Australia in a gainful occupation which would not be detrimental to our own people'. Garrett found he had no course but to inform the JRC that 'the adoption of these tactics was the surest way to close the refugee movement to Australia'.[47]

One of the most pressing matters Garrett wished to clear up concerned eastern European Jews, particularly those from Poland, Hungary and Romania. After spending time in London – and prior to undertaking a field trip to the Continent – Garrett concluded that in many cases their desire to emigrate to Australia had little to do with economic conditions, but, rather, they were 'apprehensive that political changes in the various countries in which they are resident may render their continued living intolerable'. Those from Poland, Hungary and Romania were 'not in fact refugees', but 'they may be regarded for practical purposes as coming within that category'.[48] Did this suggest that Jewish applicants from eastern Europe were about to be classified as refugees within the terms of the quota? This question, Garrett felt, would have to depend upon what he saw during his fact-finding visit to the Continent.

This trip, which began on 10 July 1939, caused a major headache for the British Foreign Office given that its objective was to consult with British consular and passport control officers, and to learn at first hand the reality of the Jewish position. The Foreign Office was concerned over the question of whether Garrett and Wheeler could be accorded diplomatic status while abroad; this was especially important as Australia did not have any diplomatic representation other than the High Commissioner's Office in London. British diplomats in all the major European centres to be visited were informed that they should provide Garrett and Wheeler with every assistance,[49] but the Foreign Office was more concerned about the lack of assistance the Australians might encounter at an official level, especially should war break out while they were in Italy or Germany[50] and the British government could not confer diplomatic status on the two Australians.

The Australians thus proceeded to the Continent under somewhat precarious circumstances. They were aware of the risks but adopted a business-as-usual approach which kept them too busy to concern themselves unduly about the international situation. Their trip took them to the Netherlands, Germany, Poland, Bohemia and Moravia (which Garrett referred to in his Final Report as 'Czecho'), Austria, Slovakia, Hungary, Romania, Switzerland, France and Belgium. The journey allowed Garrett to see at first hand the condition of Europe's Jews and liaise with British officials who would be in the front line of migration enquiries. Those observations are of greater interest than Garrett's major recommendations, which can be summarized briefly.

Garrett's first proposal was that 'the whole of the immigration work at Australia House, embracing assisted migration and alien migration, be centralised under the control of the Chief Migration Officer'.[51] This would establish the framework for all future activity: the existing Migration Branch at Australia House should be strengthened; each application received at Australia House could be examined by this improved Migration Branch; applications that were 'obviously ones for refusal be refused by Australia House, and the applicants notified forthwith'; applications not submitted through approved refugee organizations 'be referred to such organizations, where considered necessary, for advice'; applications considered worthy of examination be (a) vetted by Migration Branch officials at Australia House where the applicant resides in Britain, Germany, Bohemia and Moravia, Austria or Hungary, or (b) vetted by British passport control officers where the applicants reside elsewhere in Europe; applicants considered unsuitable by either of these authorities be refused by the officers at Australia House; applications considered suitable be approved by Australia House subject to landing money provisions (for Jews, at least £3,000, and for Aryans and 'non-Aryan Christians,' at least £200); all other applications not covered in the above be submitted to Canberra in classifications of (i) Jews, (ii) Aryan and 'non-Aryan Christians' who are Catholics and (iii) Aryan and 'non-Aryan Christians' who are not Catholics.[52]

Garrett acknowledged the tenuousness of his proposed process when he commented that if war should break out, 'the whole of my proposals for the time being at any rate would be skittled', but he did not consider his proposals unworkable. Far from it. In his opinion, the whole issue of refugee immigration could be resolved if his suggestions were adopted, as they 'would enable us to cover virtually the whole Jewish field which, after all, is refugee migration'.[53]

Garrett's perceptions of the Jewish population under discussion were thrown into sharp relief during his trip to the Continent, with his portrayal of Polish Jews faring worst of all. The tone of his comments was set in an informal letter to Carrodus covering the final report. Polish Jews, in his estimation, were 'the poorest specimens outside blackfellows that I have seen'.[54] His views grew in intensity as he was escorted through the Jewish districts of Warsaw by a British passport control officer:

> We visited several Ghettos. The types of individual seen and the conditions under which they live are almost indescribable and unbelievable to a westerner. They are undoubtedly as low a class of white people as we have seen.[55]

Garrett concluded that it would be 'especially desirable' that 'no landing permits should be issued to any of these people unless they have been vetted',[56] and that 'the greatest care should be exercised in the selection of Polish Jews'.[57]

After this came a distinct ranking order of Jewish 'types.' Thus, 'the further east one proceeded in Europe the poorer was the type of Jew'.[58] Other observations verified this: 'The Polish Jew is the worst, then come the Hungarian and Roumanian in that order';[59] 'Jews in Hungary are not to be relied upon. They are smart but crooked';[60] 'the Polish Jew is the worst type of Jew in Europe';[61] 'the type of Jew seen [at Bratislava] was very poor, although slightly better than those seen at Warsaw'.[62] Judgements such as these highlighted to the Department of the Interior that it should maintain the strictest scrutiny over applications from eastern European Jews, and that no application, irrespective of how attractive it appeared, should be taken at face value.

Garrett also had misgivings about the Jews remaining in Germany or German-occupied areas. While 'the German Jew is easily the best type',[63] nonetheless 'as time goes on, the refugees, especially in Germany, Austria and Czecho, will deteriorate from the point of view of quality; speaking generally, the best have already left those countries'.[64] By now, many Jewish refugees seeking landing permits in Berlin were creating an unfavourable impression when they called for visas at British passport control offices.[65] This was also true of Garrett's own experience, for in London he had had dealings with a number of refugees who were, he said, 'very slippery gentlemen'.[66] The overall conclusion to be drawn about German Jewish 'quality' by mid-1939 was that 'some' were 'excellent types' but, on the other hand, 'many would not be regarded as suitable for Australia'.[67]

Officials in the Department of the Interior received all this news with abundant interest. The Garrett Report and the notes accompanying it were read very carefully, handwritten notations indicating that it was referred to constantly in the years following 1939. Yet there was no time to implement its recommendations owing to the rapid deterioration in the state of international affairs in August 1939. Joseph Carrodus agreed with the report's main suggestions and retained Garrett in London awaiting further instructions about the establishment of the new Migration Office. He would remain there until war broke out on 3 September 1939, and only returned to Australia in October 1939.

The outbreak of war

On 3 September 1939 came the declaration of war which had for so long been threatened. Prime Minister Robert Menzies issued a statement regarding refugees before the end of the war's first week:

> As we have a fair number of aliens living in our midst, I consider it my duty to appeal to the Australian people at this time to avoid treating as enemies those persons who are ready to live peacefully among us and exhibit loyalty toward the Australian constitution and our political traditions.
>
> Many of the aliens in Australia must now be classed as enemy aliens, but that does not mean that they are sympathetic toward or owe any allegiance to the Nazi Government. Indeed, some of these people have been forced to leave Germany and Austria and as refugees they have sought asylum in Australia. If they are willing to be friendly to us, I see no reason why we should deny them the right of asylum despite the fact that a state of war exists between the country of their birth and the British Empire.[68]

The refugees thus passed from being exiles into enemy aliens, but the initial attitude at war's outbreak was of goodwill and an outstretched hand. There would, of course, be some who disagreed with this position, and others who would seek to overturn it altogether.

That said, while Jewish immigration had increased after 1 December 1938, it remained questionable whether the increase was matched in tolerance, understanding or humanitarian feelings. There was no reason it should have shifted. The refugees were still foreign, still Jewish and still applying to come in what were, for some, alarming numbers. No government could hope to legislate tolerance or approval: that could only come through wholehearted commitment and education, but there was nobody within the Australian establishment with that level of commitment. For most Australians, there was a world of difference between admittance and acceptance; one was a technical matter, the other an attitudinal one. No authority in the interwar years could tell the Australian people what attitude they should adopt over any issue – least of all one concerning foreigners, the outside world or the future ethnic composition of the country.

The majority of the refugees who were permitted to enter Australia came in 1939, and at the outbreak of war were thus more alien and less assimilated that the significantly fewer numbers who had arrived in the preceding five years. Still, the figure was by no means a flood, and did not consider non-Jewish refugees – though it may be stated that there were less of these. The refugee problem had always been seen as Jewish; now, with the outbreak of war, it became an 'enemy alien' problem. This would see new grounds for opposition to entry or acceptance. As the war progressed, most remained at large as free persons. Prejudice and intolerance remained – towards them as Jews, as foreigners, as economic competitors and now, as enemy Germans or Austrians. There would be no guarantee that the Australian people would willingly depart from their cherished standard of a 97 per cent British Australia. Yet the presence of the refugees, small though it was, would play an important part in the future approach of Australians towards the wider world. It was that presence which signalled to Australians that other groups of people existed who were just as eager to help build the country as they were. Despite the bigotry, xenophobia, insularity and apathy of many Australians, the refugee presence had a large say in helping to determine the future intellectual disposition of Australians and was thus a major contributing factor to the development of a multicultural Australia in the second half of the twentieth century.

CHAPTER 10
RESPONSES TO JEWISH REFUGEES

Acceptance? Rejection? Absorption?

On 14 July 1939, the *Sydney Morning Herald* published a story praising the success of the migration programme up to this point. Total arrivals of central Europeans for all of 1938, the report stated, were 3,585; for the first four months of 1939, the figure was 2,983. The overall position, argued the *Herald*, 'is now well in hand'.[1] The paper reported that most of the new arrivals were 'enthusiastic in their praise of Sydney and its people', though 'some of them have found it difficult to obtain accommodation because of the prejudice against them in certain areas'.[2] Concern was expressed over the degree to which refugees could be successfully absorbed into a British, monolingual, homogeneous and parochial Australia; as a letter to the editor of the *Herald* claimed a few days later: 'Australia is answerable to mankind and to the future generations not for what has been done in Europe, but for what is not being done in Australia.'[3] The process of integration would not be easy, and disapproval would often be loud, even cruel. Yet absorption did take place, and with time a measure of acceptance became apparent.

In early 1940 a memorandum forwarded from the Commonwealth Investigation Branch to Senator Foll outlined the state of refugee absorption as it stood in 1939.[4] It showed that the refugee influx was a cause of concern for many Australians:

> Newspapers recorded, almost every week, that several hundred refugees had arrived; publicity was given to many of the newcomers who usually were described as prominent men in their trades, professions or business and thus easily evoked fear of competition. The appearance of a growing number of foreign-looking and differently-dressed (long overcoats and attaché cases) men in the principal city streets quickly tended to reverse the initial feeling of pity and interest into one of concern.

Despite these misgivings – and the threat that Australia's 'ratio of Jewish population would ... have increased to an extent unparalleled in history and might conceivably have entailed serious racial dangers' – a measure of assimilation took place relatively quickly after the refugees' arrival. It was noted that this was particularly evident for refugee children:

Children of Central European refugees are willing to become assimilated with pathetic enthusiasm. The manner in which they were driven out of their former fatherland is an incentive for them to settle down as quickly as possible in this friendly country. It is common to hear of good results being achieved by refugee children in schools here – particularly in English. Continental – and especially Jewish – children usually develop more rapidly than English children, but the desire of refugee children to become 'fully' English is certainly also a vital reason for their scholastic successes. It is to be hoped that such successes will not engender ill-feeling among the parents of other children – especially Australian.[5]

It was observed that at this time most refugee families tended to mix only among themselves. Perhaps this was due to the age of the refugees, perhaps to the language gap. The report concluded that at present the newcomers 'lack the necessary versatility and adaptability', but this was expected to change with time. The memorandum concluded that the refugees had an overwhelming desire to fit into Australian society.

Many Australians agreed that incorporation into the Australian community should take place as quickly as possible. One correspondent to the *Sydney Morning Herald* noted that the 'desire of the Government and of the refugees themselves is that they should mingle in the community and be absorbed',[6] while another stated that refugees were 'extremely anxious to speak nothing but English, and to understand and conform with all our local customs'.[7] This correspondent painted a highly positive picture of the refugees: 'They are fine types of people, with an education and culture, in many instances, superior to our own, and I say, with confidence, that the time will come when Australia will be even grateful to Nazism for having provided her with such excellent citizens.'[8]

However, not all Australians felt the same way. Indeed, it was observed by one reader of the *Herald* that 'Many of the new foreign immigrants have had a wretched time since arrival in Sydney – rebuffed and insulted when they seek employment, treated with suspicion and resentment, and often not a single friendly door has been held open to them.'[9] Rejecting foreigners was an acute problem, and Jewish Australians were not immune. True to the general interwar approach to all foreigners, the Australian Jewish community adopted a position every bit at one with the majority population; one historian has concluded that the refugees 'were considered inferior by the [Jewish] establishment, even though they came from the centres of European culture and were generally well educated'.[10] Many Australian Jews assumed a patronizing attitude towards the refugees, even going so far as to instruct them on polite behaviour and manners:

If the officials of the [Australian Jewish Welfare] Society make an appointment for you regarding a position [in employment] it should be your positive duty to report the result to the office. If you are registered at the office as a person desirous to obtain a position, please inform the office if you get one in the meantime. If you forget to do so, you are hindering some other person being assisted. ... All immigrants who are anxious to become Australian citizens as soon as possible, should sincerely endeavour to follow the customs of this country and be sure they leave no cause for complaint regarding lack of appreciation of the endeavour made to be helpful to them.[11]

The AJWS issued advice to newly arrived refugees, warning them about their behaviour:

Above all, do not speak German in the streets and in the trams. Modulate your voices. Do not make yourself conspicuous anywhere by walking with a group of persons all of whom are loudly speaking in a foreign language. ... Remember that the welfare of the old-established Jewish community in Australia as well as of every migrant depends on your personal behaviour. Jews collectively are judged as individuals. You personally have a grave responsibility.[12]

Refugees were admonished to behave like other Australian Jews and act as exemplary citizens in the middle-class Australian way. For their own good, they were also urged by Inspector D. R. B. Mitchell of the Commonwealth Investigation Branch to look inconspicuous. At a mass meeting for refugee migrants held at the Maccabean Hall in Sydney in July 1939, he schooled the refugees as to their dress: 'Those flat leather portfolios you carry, those overcoats reaching the ground, may be fashionable in Europe, but in Australia it simply advertises the fact that you are a refugee.'[13]

The question of assimilation aroused much discussion within the Australian Jewish community, and always for the same reason: a fear of the emergence of antisemitism if rapid cultural absorption did not take place. In early 1939, cut paper swastikas were scattered around the Sydney Conservatorium during a recital at which Jews were expected to be present;[14] in April there had been a spate of stone-throwing and window-smashing incidents at the Kadimah Jewish Cultural Centre and Yiddish Library in the inner Melbourne suburb of Carlton.[15] Such incidents caused great concern to local Jews, and prompted the Secretary of the Victorian Branch of the AJWS, Frances Barkman, to write to the President of the Board of Deputies of British Jews for advice on what steps could be taken to deal with antisemitic outbreaks.[16] In response, the Board sent a quantity of printed material to Australia which, it was hoped, would serve as a model for the local Jewish community in the fight against antisemitic propaganda.[17]

The refugees were themselves aware of the strictures Australians placed over their acceptability, and wherever possible they sought ways to demonstrate their loyalty and desire to do well in the new country. This was expressed unmistakably at a mass meeting on 16 April 1939 of Jewish migrants called by their representative organization in Sydney, the Migrants' Consultative Council. In his opening address the Chairman, Walter Hirst, stated that 'we feel at home in Australia'. It was this feeling of being at home

that determines our attitude towards our new country. We do not only feel mere gratitude for having found a 'haven.' We take sincere interest in all vital problems of Australia, we wish to take part in its life, to share citizenship and responsibilities.[18]

Those granted entry to Australia had escaped persecution and found a society in which such evils were absent. Yet the international situation was catching up with them:

> the world has taken a course which did not leave much occasion for 'happiness.' I do not need to stress the present gathering of storm clouds, but I wish to stress that our feeling towards Australia was born under adverse conditions, and is, therefore, genuine and thoroughly sincere. We do not know what the future may hold for the world and for Australia in particular. But we do know, that whatever will come, we shall stand to Australia and shall do all in our power to strengthen her cause, as loyal and active members of her community.[19]

The refugees attending the meeting, of course, did not really need to be told this: their commitment to Australia was as one. In conveying their feelings, the attendees unanimously passed the following Resolution:

> We arrived with the sincere hope that our activities could be devoted to the peaceful development only of our new home country. Should fate, however, interrupt peace, we desire to express our serious wish actively to share the burden of turbulent and unpleasant times.[20]

The Resolution was signed by Walter Hirst, the leaders of all the refugee organizations in Sydney, and no fewer than 700 refugees at the meeting, all of whom appended their names and addresses. On 28 August 1939, with the international situation growing bleaker by the day and war less than a week away, the Migrants' Consultative Council drew Senator Foll's attention to the Resolution, reaffirming the declaration of loyalty and expressing the desire 'to be given the opportunity by the Commonwealth Authorities to show their allegiance to the British Empire in a practical manner by being permitted to participate in any emergency duties and share responsibilities in the same manner as their fellow Australian citizens.'[21]

Neither the government nor the Anglo-Jewish establishment was completely convinced, welcome though such expressions of loyalty might be. On 22 April 1939, the Department of the Interior appointed one of its officers, Arthur L. Nutt, to review immigrant settlement. His specific brief was to investigate 'the congregation of aliens in communities and the prospects of aliens admitted to the Commonwealth',[22] primarily concerned with the location of refugee settlement and the activities in which they were engaging. While not playing a key role in refugee immigration at this stage, his operation as a settlement and assimilation officer would stamp him as a key figure in later years.

As reported in the popular press, the issue of refugees 'congregating in districts' caused major worries for many Australians residing in the inner suburbs of Sydney and Melbourne. Nutt was to investigate such matters and, where possible, do something to stop the refugees from 'congregating'.

The AJWS, too, sought to keep the refugees both under control and at arm's length. This began on 16 May 1939 with an announcement in *The Argus* of a forthcoming refugee census. It was not made clear who would run this, but the report stated that its objective was to offset the possibility that Nazi agents posing as Jewish refugees might be slipping into Australia.[23]

Responses among the Australian public

Australians differed greatly in their attitudes towards the refugees. Negative comments predominated – though some were positive, and expressions of support often came from unlikely sources. For example, the Victorian Education Department published the following guidance to schoolchildren in the August edition of the *School Paper*, a monthly journal of manners, morals and stories: 'Those of you who are fortunate enough to have them [that is, refugee children] as schoolmates can help them to become good Australians by assisting them with their work and by welcoming them to the happy world of the school.'[24] This positive affirmation of goodwill concluded with the instruction that such behaviour 'will give every refugee child a valuable opportunity and added encouragement to live up to their designation – NEW AUSTRALIANS'.[25]

Within the professions, not all seemed as dark as the reception that had earlier been accorded refugee doctors. In February, the President of the New South Wales Chapter of the Royal Institute of Architects issued an appeal to all Australian architects to welcome refugees who were members of the profession, as he saw their appearance as 'nothing but an acquisition to the cultural side of Australian life'.[26] In his view,

Many of our students and brother architects have travelled abroad to broaden their architectural knowledge and outlook by the study of European work, returning with new ideas for our benefit. Now we have the opportunity of returning this 'architectural hospitality' by making welcome architects who are no longer able to practice in their own countries ... We must remember that although we give them much, they will eventually give much more in return.[27]

In May 1939, a further breakthrough took place when the New South Wales Trades and Labour Council recommended the admission of European refugees to membership of its constituent unions.[28] It is unclear whether this was because unemployment had by now declined or because the Trades and Labour Council feared an influx of non-unionized cheap labour. Motive notwithstanding, it was a significant gesture. Subsequently, the *Sydney Morning Herald* published a letter stating that it would now seem 'opportune and incumbent upon those controlling entrance into professional spheres, to see that their decisions concerning professional refugees do not suffer any comparison with this high ethical decision of the workers' council'.[29] The lesson was not lost on the New South Wales Institute of Accountants. In August it suggested that refugees holding German accounting qualifications be exempted from most of the local examinations and thus be eligible to practice.[30]

For its part, the government seemed little interested in the refugees' educational qualifications, considering only those who possessed trade or technical skills of direct use to the Commonwealth. This prompted one comment to the editor of the *Sydney Morning Herald* that the present immigration laws 'make a very large discount on the cultural value of [the] refugees'.[31] Too few Australians were willing to see this: culturally, foreigners were not viewed as being necessarily desirable additions to the fabric of Australian life.

Others saw the issue less subtly. In January 1939, the Australian Natives' Association passed a resolution at its annual meeting in which it called for immediate steps to be taken to ensure that 'only the best type of migrant' be encouraged into Australia.[32] Perhaps not surprisingly, an issue which became increasingly topical throughout 1939 dealt with unassimilability. In its 6 April edition, *Labor Call* foresaw that 'Continuation of the present suspicion, dangers and fears must result in the development of an anti-foreign, and particularly anti-refugee, psychology among the people'.[33] By 27 April *Labor Call's* scenario had crystallized into something far worse, with reference being made to the possibility of 'riots taking place when least expected'.[34] An unnamed writer for *Smith's Weekly* tackled the problem and came up with the following:

> Only one final solution of the Jewish problem is therefore conceivable; that they should break down their old tribal isolation and inter-marry, on a vast scale, with their Gentile oppressors.
>
> If that happened, Jewish brains would give a distinct lift to the mental quality of humanity in general. And there would be no more pure Jews, handy and unpopular scapegoats, for every brutish and deluded political mob.[35]

Resolution of the whole matter could thus easily take place with the Jews' disappearance as a distinct and identifiable people.

A further response was sent from a resident of Sydney to the Department of the Interior in January 1939, articulating clearly the anti-foreign and economic dimensions of anti-Jewish sentiment:

> I desire to emphatically protest at the continued landing in Aust. of Alien Jews. I have observed their conduct & demeanour & I consider that these people are undesirable. Only people that do manual labour, i.e. produce something, should be allowed in. All my acquaintances are of the same opinion. I suggest an immediate embargo be placed on Jews before the people realise fully what is happening.[36]

One thing was certain: based on letters to politicians, government Departments and the press, there was increasing disquiet running through Australian society that the presence of the refugees in large numbers would lead to racial friction and communal strife for which the Commonwealth was unprepared.

The front-line areas in which all the dramas of assimilation were played out were the inner-Sydney suburbs of King's Cross and Darlinghurst, the eastern suburbs centring around Waverley, and the Melbourne suburbs of Carlton and St. Kilda. So great was the fear of foreign colonies forming that this issue was included among the tasks for investigation in the brief given to Departmental officer Arthur Nutt. His report on the economic condition of the refugees was completed in December 1939, but prior to this these matters had already been dealt with extensively through public expressions reported in the newspapers. Two well-known examples came from the *Sydney Morning Herald* and *Smith's Weekly*. In the first, published on 13 June 1939, an anonymous official of the AJWS stated that 'unless the migrants could be induced to abandon the formation of a "colony," a situation might develop that would be detrimental to the newcomers'.[37] Certainly, the newspaper reported, the congregation of refugee migrants at King's Cross was causing anxiety to local residents, and this was not helped by the fact that 'Many migrant families ... are not trying to learn English', and that 'some parents have refused to send their children to the Public [that is, state] schools'.[38] If it was not bad enough that an official of the AJWS was being quoted in this regard, on 24 June *Smith's Weekly* quoted a Federal government official who said that 'if the drift towards Sydney were not stopped soon, it would become another Shanghai with its 48 different nationalities'.[39]

The AJWS was quick to respond to the allegation made in the *Sydney Morning Herald*,[40] but by then the damage had been done. The Welfare Society had given every encouragement to attempts by the new arrivals to settle in country towns and districts, and the idea of 'congregating' was just as anathema to the existing Jewish population as it was to wider society. It was unfortunate, therefore, that the newspapers carried reports that refugees were opening businesses in certain localities and squeezing out Australian smaller firms, as well as finding success in speculation and investment. One example centred on Leo Grimm, a refugee from Czechoslovakia, who had arrived in Sydney with £7,000 of which £6,500 had been invested in a block of flats in Waverley. The rest was used to establish a pawnbroking enterprise.[41] According to the *Sydney Morning Herald*, the local shopkeepers did not object to newcomers engaging in business, 'but they allege that Australian conditions and local awards are not being observed'.[42]

Arthur Nutt was tasked to examine this issue also. By December 1939 he had scrutinized many aspects of refugee settlement, and in making his report he observed the following:

When walking around the main street of King's Cross it is easy to pick out plenty of refugees, yet a reasonable person could not claim that the area is almost completely given over to them, there are many Australians there too.

While there are objections, perhaps more imaginary than real, to refugees congregating in a section of a large city, after all these people must live somewhere and it is natural for them to choose a district where they may have relatives or friends and where they can enjoy social intercourse with their fellows, rather than to isolate themselves by living in suburbs where they do not know anybody.[43]

This was not the way many Australians saw it, with lower growth economic conditions often establishing hostile local attitudes towards immigration. The Australian Jewish community saw the problem no less clearly than the majority population, as an editorial in the *Westralian Judean* of 1 May 1939 showed:

> The bone of contention is that refugees are displacing Australian workers, and if that were proved to be correct this paper would be the first to issue a strong protest. … We emphatically agree that not one of our employed Australian workers should be permitted to stand aside while preference is given to a refugee migrant. The cry from suffering humanity overseas must not deafen us to the cry from distressed workers in this country, and it is the solemn duty of the Jewish communities everywhere in Australia to co-ordinate their work on behalf of the refugees with an attempt to solve local unemployment problems.[44]

For some Australians, economic displacement had been at the core of opposition to refugee migration since 1933; for others, this apprehension took a little longer. A Melbourne resident who, out of humanitarian motives, had applied for the entrance of a refugee family under his guarantee in May, withdrew his support in July. Having made enquiries, he had concluded 'that there are hundreds of men with the qualifications claimed by these people who are at the present time walking the streets of the capital cities of Australia seeking employment', and it was 'definitely unfair to bring to Australia foreigners who are taking positions our own Australians could well fill'.[45]

A major concern was that the refugees were allowing themselves to be economically exploited and threaten living standards and industrial conditions for all Australians. The Shop Assistants' Union in Melbourne expressed the fear that 'foreign refugees who have come to Australia were being employed in Melbourne at rates far below those stipulated by the award',[46] and that 'foreign workers coming here have earned a reputation for accepting low wages and working long hours, which is economically unsound, and a serious threat to our living standards'.[47] A company manufacturing artificial flowers in Sydney protested against the exploitation of refugee labour in factories, providing unfair competition in a very restricted marketplace, and expressing the hope that strict supervision would be imposed on the refugees in future in order 'to prevent our Standard of living from being endangered'.[48]

Enter Sir Frank Clarke

The most vicious anti-refugee attack to date came from the President of the Victorian Legislative Council, Sir Frank Clarke, on 8 May 1939. Speaking to a branch meeting of the conservative Australian Women's National League in the respectable Melbourne middle-class suburb of Malvern, Clarke shocked the ladies by his reference to the:

Slinking, rat-faced men under 5 ft. in height, and with a chest development of about 20 inches, who worked in backyard factories in Carlton and other localities in the north of Melbourne for 2/- or 3/- a week pocket money and their keep.[49]

His speech, reported widely in the press, contemplated with horror that 'such people would want to marry Australian girls, or even to bring here their own undernourished and underdeveloped women, and breed a race within a race'; he also expressed with consternation that on the wharves at Port Melbourne 'the tongues of Babel could be heard, and in the third-class accommodation of ships there were hundreds of weedy East Europeans'. Medical certificates produced upon landing in Australia 'were apparently dictated more by friendship than the truth', otherwise many of these refugees would not have obtained entry. Clarke suggested that an equal abomination was the nature of the activities in which the refugees engaged once they arrived:

In the back-yard factories in Carlton and elsewhere where they were employed, the Factories Act regulations could not be applied, as a factory was only defined as such when four people or more were employed, and the proprietors of them were careful only to import three aliens. Factory inspectors could not exercise any supervision as to the cleanliness of the conditions under which these aliens, who were breaking down the standard of living in Australia, worked, and union rates of wages did not apply to such establishments. Recently a group of these back-yard factories had been able to quote a big Sydney department store for the supply of 100,000 artificial silk women's undergarments at 7 1/2d each. No firm could do that and pay award wages. This sort of competition was resulting in employees being dismissed from legitimate factories which paid award wages and provided decent working conditions for their operatives.[50]

To combat this, Sir Frank proposed that the legislation should be amended to redefine a factory as 'any establishment where one alien of less than twelve months' residence [is] employed'. Moreover, medical certificates issued in Europe 'should not only state that the refugee was free from disease, but also give details as to the physique and degree of intelligence'. That job, he advised, could only be entrusted to Australian medical officers stationed overseas.

Upon concluding his speech, a vote of thanks was expressed by the United Australia Party leader of the Opposition (and former state Premier) in Victoria, Sir Stanley Argyle. His comments, while not levelling the same sort of charges as those of Clarke, were no less anti-refugee. Argyle referred to the type of aliens described by Clarke as 'the refuse of European countries, where bad living and bad government had developed them into what they were'. He declared that Australia should not be allowed to become 'a receptacle for them', and noted with concern that the Australian people 'should firmly resist an evil such as … [that] described by Sir F. Clarke being built up in our midst'. Both speakers were cheered enthusiastically by the ladies of the Malvern branch of the Australian Women's National League.[51]

Response to Clarke's outburst was swift. *The Age* immediately invited comments from newly installed Prime Minister Robert Menzies, who regarded the allegations as 'very serious'. Announcing that he would personally have them investigated, he declared that 'the policy of the Government is to protect Australian standards, and if we find that they are in effect being broken down we will certainly take every step in our power to prevent such a course'.[52]

The refugee organizations, troubled by the allegations, hastened to refute Sir Frank Clarke's claims the following day. In a joint statement prepared by Isaac H. Boas (Australian Jewish Welfare Society) and Professor Harold Woodruff (Victorian International Refugee Emergency Committee), attention was drawn to the fact that,

Had Sir Frank Clarke inquired from informed sources, he would have found that a large majority of Jewish migrants reaching Australia are not eastern Europeans, but German and Austrian. Those people are of excellent physique, many of the males having served in the armies of their respective countries. They are, moreover, among the best educated types of migrants ever to reach Australia, an outstanding proportion being graduates of universities and technical high schools.[53]

The Honorary Secretary of the Victorian Branch of the AJWS, Frances Barkman, offered similar comments, stressing that those coming into the country under Welfare Society auspices 'were skilled men with occupations, had undoubted testimonials and were carefully hand-picked'.[54] Newman Rosenthal, another Victorian AJWS officer, responded by reminding readers of *The Age* that 'Literature has been prepared [for the refugees] giving details as to Australian arbitration awards, factory legislation and the like'.[55] *The Argus*, on the other hand, took such protestations of innocence with a grain of salt, and basically accepted Clarke's allegations. In an editorial the day after the story broke, the paper stated that 'Most Australians will agree with the strictures uttered by Sir Frank Clarke on Monday concerning the undesirable industrial practices indulged in by an equally undesirable type of foreign migrant', but recognized that 'the Jewish refugees must be taken as they come, mixed lot though they may be'.[56] It added, however, that 'Even objects of pity have certain obligations to their benefactors, and the performance of such obligations should be insisted upon'. It continued:

If it is true, as Sir Frank Clarke has been informed, that the poorer types of Jewish newcomers are meanly taking advantage of loopholes in the law to conduct sweating shops under conditions which are destructive of human rights and repugnant to Australian sentiment, the sooner the law is tightened up the better. No self-respecting nation can allow its hospitality to be abused in this fashion.[57]

The Commonwealth Investigation Branch launched inquiries immediately. By 16 May the Director, Colonel Harold Jones, sent a memorandum on the matter to Joseph Carrodus.[58] It took the form of an account which had been 'received from a person who is very capable of giving an unbiased report'. The memorandum examined the current position of Jews in the clothing industry in Melbourne, their trade practices and the reasons underlying their pursuit of those practices. In all respects it seemed to be well-balanced and visibly free of the antisemitism which characterized many similar documents emanating from other Departments. Addressing Clarke's comments concerning Jewish physique, Jones recorded the following:

> Visiting certain parts of Carlton one sees a population of undersized Jewish people whose looks are anything but confidence-inspiring; they often have the misfortune to look "suspicious." Certainly this is due to the conditions under which they are [*sic*; ?and?] their forefathers have been living in ghettos in miserable townships of Eastern Europe, despised [and] persecuted. ... The poor physique of many of these people, I think, cannot be doubted and finds its explanation in their slave-like work.[59]

This was the situation applying to Jews from eastern Europe – those who came, 'almost exclusively, from Poland, Russia, Lithuania and Roumania'. Jewish refugees from Germany and Austria, on the other hand, were classed to be of a quite different type, most of them having been 'assimilated in Germany for several generations'. Their looks were often 'typically German', they were of 'average height' and they adhered to 'Western European business morality and standard of living'. They did not congregate in Carlton but sought to live in 'better suburbs'. Most of them, the report concluded, 'have only one idea – to assimilate here as quickly as possible'.[60]

While the report was being circulated, the accusations levelled by Sir Frank Clarke were also being aired in Canberra. On 17 May, Senator Don Cameron (Labor, Victoria) asked Senator Foll whether inquiries were being made as to the veracity of Clarke's statements. Foll responded that an investigation had been ordered as soon as Clarke's speech was reported, and that information had already been received to the effect that his evidence was only hearsay. On further questioning, Foll said that Sir Frank Clarke could not verify any of his allegations.[61] He went on to reassure the Senate that 'every effort is being made by the Government to ensure that the state of affairs suggested in the statement attributed to Sir Frank Clarke shall not be allowed to occur'.[62] He was, at this time, still awaiting a full report from the Commonwealth Investigation Branch on the whole matter.

When that report arrived, it refuted every one of Clarke's arguments. Prepared by Inspector Roland S. Browne, the first page established clearly that Clarke's allegations were not based on sound evidence. His sources of information were, as Browne identified them, threefold:

(i)   Persons (unspecified) who had travelled on or had knowledge of immigrant ships (unspecified).

(ii) Some two or three Flinders Lane manufacturers who complained of unfair competition from 'back-yard' factories, but who were naturally enough, unwilling to place themselves in the position of public complaints.

(iii)   Information received about the quoted order for women's undergarments. This information, Sir Frank Clarke intimated, was authentic, but applied to Melbourne and not to Sydney, as stated in the Press Report in 'The Age.' Sir Frank Clarke stated that his source of information was a large financial institution in which he was interested.[63]

Clarke admitted to Browne that except for point (iii), his statements could not be substantiated by reference to any evidence. When Browne asked Sir Frank whether he had taken any steps to verify for himself his statements concerning the physical stature of the refugees, Clarke replied that 'on one occasion he did drive through Little Collins Street during the luncheon hour, when he had seen some appalling types'. Browne inquired whether he had any confirmation that these people were refugees; Clarke answered that he did not.[64]

Examining some of Clarke's other accusations, Browne referred to the point made about medical certificates being issued to immigrants in Europe through friends. He rebutted this by reiterating that, in addition to any such certificates, refugees still had to pass 'the usual medical examination conducted by the Australian authorities at the port of arrival'. As to Clarke's reference to the refugee women who were coming into Australia 'who are apparently so repulsive to him', Browne did not feel it necessary to even go into the matter, 'for his statements are simply not in accord with general fact'. He felt, rather, after much discussion and observation,

that the type of alien refugee women who have sought sanctuary in Australia within the past twelve months from the almost unbelievable persecution and tragedy in Europe will be recognised (when the present era can be looked back upon in its proper perspective), as a body of women whose courage, fortitude, and determination to make a new life with their husbands and children in the country which has given them a new opportunity, stamps them as fine as any who have come to our shores since our own pioneers.

In his defence, Clarke told Browne that his remarks had been given quite unexpected and unmerited publicity, and that he regretted that in certain quarters they had been given a meaning far beyond his 'purpose' – which was, he said, to warn the authorities 'that if the utmost care were not taken in the selection of aliens, a situation would arise in the future which would lead to an unfortunate problem'.[65] Underscoring his assessment of Clarke's assertions, Browne offered a few thoughts of his own concerning the 'types' being admitted to Australia as refugees:

In the city of Melbourne, with a population of a round million of people, it is considered that it would be difficult to readily find even 100 alien people to whom the description of Sir Frank Clarke could apply, but that it would be easy to find 50 to 100 aliens of satisfactory physique for every one of such inferior type as delineated by Sir Frank Clarke.

The landing permit system, Browne believed, was in large part responsible for this tightening of standards, but the nature of the refugee problem had contributed to the improvement in the quality of immigration. The refugees, coming from 'a section of the community who have been successful in their own highly developed countries', were forced to leave through political necessity. They were of 'a far higher grade of mentality than ever before experienced in alien immigrants'.[66]

Browne finally dismissed the controversy stirred up by Sir Frank Clarke with the observation that the refugees 'deeply appreciated' the action of the Australian government in granting them admission. Their loyalty and desire to be good citizens in Australia 'cannot be doubted, and will prevail against the ill-considered outbursts which may be made from time to time'.[67] The report, once circulated through the bureaucracy, served to clarify the position. In Parliament, many of the points raised by Browne were incorporated into a speech on foreign migrants by John Perkins, the Minister for External Affairs.[68]

Hostility in Parliament

The attitude of Sir Frank Clarke and Inspector Browne can each be seen as epitomizing the polarized attitudes that had developed in Australia by the middle of 1939. A further extreme statement of opinion, and uttered in a forum far more significant than the Malvern branch of the Australian Women's National League, came from a Labor Member of Parliament in the House of Representatives on 15 June 1939. Albert Ernest (Tom) Green, the Member for Kalgoorlie (WA), rose to speak during the debate on the Supply Bill, but clearly what he had to say bore no relevance to the matter at hand. Referring initially to the government's execution of the 'Fifteen Thousand' policy, he announced that his opposition to it was 'far stronger than if the immigrants were of the Nordic race, and came from Northern European countries, from the north of Italy or from Jugo-Slavia'. Were immigrants to come from these countries, the development of Australia would be enhanced. Jews, on the other hand, would not develop Australia, as they 'are essentially a trading people...', and the Jews who are coming here will be of no help to a producing country like Australia'.[69] Where Jews were not merchants, they were professionals; this, too, was not suitable for Australia's needs, because 'for every Jew who is given a professional job ... an Australian will be shut out'. Green commented that Jews were not wanted in Australia and asked why it should be necessary for them to leave Europe in any case. In asking that question, he said he was 'not trying to excuse Hitler his persecution of the Jews', but he felt it 'only fair to point out that there may have been some reason for his wishing them to go elsewhere'.[70] He then suggested that the reason centred around Jewish internationalism, economic domination and exploitation, and that with the Jewish presence increasing they were 'trying to dominate Australia'. Green enumerated some of the ways in which they were doing this:

Most of the cut-price tobacco shops in the suburbs of Melbourne and elsewhere are run by Jews, most of them recent arrivals. ... The fur shops are completely in the control of Jews. Even little shops for the mending of stockings, some of them a mere hole in the wall where a little Australian girl can be seen working, have behind them a Jew who controls the business. The mantle shops, where mantles priced at ten and twenty guineas, allegedly exclusive models from Paris, are for sale, are also Jewish-owned, though the Jew's name does not appear, of course. ... There is a well-known mammoth emporium in Melbourne which is controlled by Jews. When trade is slack, the workers are told to take a couple of weeks off, and they are not paid for that period. In Western Australia, there is another great emporium under the control of Jews. In that business Australian workers are being dismissed, and their place taken by Jews. The very press of this country, including the Melbourne evening papers, is controlled by these people who are now stretching out their tentacles to South Australia.[71]

Green concluded his speech by stating that Jews 'are not wanted here; we have enough exploiters among our own people, but these other people are the kings of exploiters'. He then declared his intention to continue his remarks at some future date and resumed his seat.

Green's comments came at a time of concern over the alien presence. Earlier, in March 1939, serious investigations were being undertaken into the charge made by a British citizen 'that the Hun Gestapo Police have appointed Jews as their Agents amongst the Jewish Refugees for sinister purposes'.[72] In London, Australia House conferred with MI5 over the charge, which verified that Jews were being employed as unwilling informants on some occasions.[73] On 3 May 1939 the Member for the Northern Territory (Adair Blain) asked the Prime Minister whether, in view of the fact that the Department of the Interior 'does not keep trace of aliens after they enter this country, but merely admits them', the immigration function could be transferred forthwith 'to the direct control of the Department of Defence, where it rightly belongs?'[74]

At this time a Bill for the compulsory registration of all aliens in Australia was receiving its Second Reading in the Lower House, and numerous Members were expressing their thoughts on what should be happening in relation to aliens control. The Bill had general agreement from both sides, but Labor's Bert Lazzarini found it necessary to raise one highly pertinent issue concerning the policy which allowed aliens into the country in the first place, declaring that the proposal to register all aliens in the country 'suggests that the Government is of opinion that too many aliens are coming into this country, and from this we can assume that a weakness exists in the administration of the Migration branch, or alternatively, that the Government believes it is necessary to tighten up the act'.[75] The government was thus condemned whichever direction it took. If it did not institute a registration measure for aliens, it would be seen to be acting irresponsibly; but by introducing it, the government was opening itself to the criticism that its migration policy was deficient. Such were the dilemmas of office, and the advantages of opposition.

During the debate on the second reading of the Aliens Registration Bill, speaker after speaker rose stressing the need for some form of control.[76] Some did not want aliens in Australia at all. From antisemites such as Green, who did not want refugees because they were Jews, the focus shifted to those who advocated restriction on the grounds of economic necessity. Much of this agitation came from the Labor Party, which sought to protect the interests of workers from any potential ingress into the very tight labour market. On 16 May, Senator Joe Collings – who ironically, was to become the next Minister for the Interior in a Labor government – made the clearest possible statement of Labor's attitude on this issue:

Although I have the greatest sympathy with men and women who have been persecuted through detestable forms of government in other countries, my parliamentary salary is paid by Australians to enable me to do a job in this chamber for Australia. Therefore, I must not allow my sympathy with foreign refugees to make me overlook the fact that my first duty is to Australians. I hope that I shall not be accused of cruelty, but, if I had my way, not one foreign refugee, man or woman, would be admitted until every good Australian had been taken off the dole or relief work, and given a job under award conditions.[77]

At the heart of the registration proposal lay the question of national security. What could be termed the attitude of mainstream Australia was conveyed in the House by Gerald Mahoney, the Labor Member for Denison (Tas.). Referring to aliens generally, he stated emphatically that 'If the migrants are carefully selected, they should become good citizens.'[78] The Australian Jewish Welfare Society had been arguing this since its inception, but even after this there were still many who found little comfort in the prospect of foreign Jews arriving and seeking to take up citizenship.

CHAPTER 11
REFUGEES AND ENEMY ALIENS

War with Germany: What now?

Australian government Departments had made few plans for any imminent conflict prior to war breaking out. In fact, it was only in late August that statutory rules regarding wartime security were enacted under the *Defence Act*. These were then replaced by a new *National Security Act*, which commenced on 9 September 1939 with certain provisions backdated to 25 August. They impacted severely on Jewish refugees already in Australia, given their German and former Austrian nationality.

On 29 August, the High Commissioner's Office in London raised concerns about the effect of war on the refugee exodus. In a cable to Prime Minister Menzies, Stanley Bruce sought policy advice regarding three points in the event of war: first, whether aliens holding landing permits who had not yet sailed for Australia would be permitted to proceed, and whether those en route would be allowed to land; second, what treatment should be given to applications already in Australia and at Australia House; and third, whether new applications could be received at Australia House.[1] Canberra's reply took six days to be sent to London, by which time Germany had invaded Poland and Australia found itself at war. Owing to the changed circumstances, Canberra subsequently adopted a new migration policy covering refugees from enemy or enemy-occupied countries. All applications for landing permits by enemy aliens were to be refused, and refugees already in possession of landing permits would be admitted provided the military authorities had no objection.[2]

This measure was intended to freeze all new landing permits and allow in only those refugees who were on their way to Australia prior to the outbreak of hostilities. This did not stop the occasional refugee almost slipping through the system. Chaskel Kurz, a refugee from Austria, is one such case. Having made his application from France much earlier in 1939, he had to wait in the queue, and when brought before the Department of the Interior his admission was approved. The landing permit authorization was passed on 8 September, a full five days after the declaration of war. The Department, having then realized its mistake, ruled that 'Owing to the existing international situation, … such approval has now been cancelled and the matter deferred indefinitely.' The fate of Chaskel Kurz has not been recorded.[3]

Some issues remaining unresolved after the outbreak of war had also to be tidied up. By 8 December 1939 Tom Garrett, having returned to Australia, produced a memorandum asserting that the coming of war had 'absolved the Commonwealth from its commitment to receive up to 15,000 refugees over the three-year period, in view of the fact that the great majority of refugees had become enemy aliens'.[4] Moreover, he noted, 'Jews in Europe who are at present eligible, under the Commonwealth's immigration policy, to enter Australia, are not as good a type as those who are ineligible on account of their being enemy aliens'. His proposed solution was that landing permits for all European Jews be immediately restricted only to the following classes: (a) dependent relatives of persons already established in Australia, and (b) cases in which it was clearly established that the Jewish refugee's entry would be beneficial to Australia's internal economy or culture, 'or in which exceptional circumstances exist'.[5] Interior Minister Harry Foll approved the proposal on 12 December 1939, with the comment 'I agree with these recommendations. This is the policy we are adopting now'.[6] With that, Australia's Jewish immigration policy was seemingly set for the duration of the war.

The practice of issuing landing permits to refugees of enemy nationality was henceforth stopped. No-one in September 1939 could foresee the horrific fate of Europe's Jews, of course, but even their current plight was of little interest. Since 1933, the Department had based its immigration policy on the principle that 'special precautions should be taken to ensure that the Commonwealth does not receive an undue proportion' of German Jews, and that care should be exercised 'to prevent a serious influx'.[7] In the years prior to the outbreak of war the Department never lost sight of its original brief and stuck to it rigidly whenever possible.

Between January 1933 and September 1939, the Department deliberately manipulated its own rules, compromised its own selection criteria and deceived the public it was employed to serve – and all for the expedient of denying entry to Australia of foreign Jews. The war ensured that this objective was retained. The fact that several thousand Jews had been admitted since 1933 was achieved despite the Department's best efforts, not because of them. The government rejected Jews: because they were Jewish, because they were foreign and because they were viewed as economic competitors. Arguments concerning such issues as the Australian contribution relative to other countries, or the degree to which the refugee presence altered the demographic structure of Australian Jewry, do not exonerate the government. Judged by its own standards, it was found wanting.

The question of precisely how many Jews from Germany, Austria and Czechoslovakia entered Australia before 3 September 1939 cannot be accurately computed. The Department of the Interior did not begin to keep accurate records of Jewish arrivals until mid-1938, and Jews who entered earlier were listed according to their nationality as German, Austrian, Czech, Polish and so on. The Department estimated that perhaps 90 per cent of such arrivals were Jewish, but this is only an approximate figure. It is certain that 5,080 Jews entered in 1939. Just at the time the Department of the Interior was under its greatest pressure and sought (with its best chance of success) to reduce refugee numbers, the vast number of applications that had been made in 1938 but not yet processed came to the surface. This saw previously unfilled totals now filled for the first time.[8]

Refugee Jews become enemy aliens

The greatest anxiety for both the Department of the Interior and security agencies related to refugees who had reached Australia prior to September 1939. How were such people to be regarded under the law? Indeed, to what extent did their situation change because of the war?

The new *National Security Act*, which came into operation on 9 September 1939, gave the Commonwealth extremely broad powers 'for securing the public safety'. It could regulate an enemy alien's property rights and civil rights and the conduct of their trade or business; it could prohibit an enemy alien from 'doing any act or thing', permit the authorities to search any premises in which an enemy alien was present and compel an enemy alien to disclose information 'as to any prescribed matter'.[9] In preparing Regulations implementing these provisions, however, the drafters would base themselves on a misconception as to who comprised the enemy.

The crux of the issue lay in the definition given to the term 'enemy alien'. It was only with the National Security (Aliens Control) Regulations, which came into operation on 13 September, that a working definition was constructed. This defined an alien as anyone over the age of sixteen years, other than a person who was a British subject or having the privileges 'to which a natural-born British subject is entitled'.[10] Following this, the Regulation's definition of 'enemy alien' was wide-ranging: it was a person who, not being either a British subject or 'enjoying His Majesty's protection', possesses the nationality 'of a State at war with His Majesty'.[11] Adoption of this definition effectively classified all those who had entered Australia as refugees from Nazism as posing the same potential threat as all other Germans present in the country. This led to many innocent people being exposed to administrative misunderstandings and severe personal hardships.

On 7 September 1939, the Department of the Interior forwarded a memorandum to the Department of Defence outlining how the immigration freeze would take place, and what the exceptions would be. Included was yet another reference to the special nature of refugees from Nazism: 'The term "refugee" is at present regarded as applying to persons of German nationality, or former German, Austrian or Czechoslovak nationality, against whom there is political discrimination'.[12] Prior to the establishment of the National Security (Aliens Control) Regulations, the Department of Defence seemed sympathetic in its stance, as shown in a memorandum to the Prime Minister's Department on 7 September 1939:

Whilst the national interest must be paramount, sympathetic treatment will be accorded to enemy aliens who, having left their own country on political, racial or religious grounds, or having been in this country for many years, are known to have lost sympathy with the country of their origin.[13]

The National Security (Aliens Control) Regulations of 13 September 1939, however, intervened.

The restrictions varied from place to place and in accordance with geographic and demographic circumstances, yet there were some essentials to which all enemy aliens were subject. These included that an enemy alien 'shall not leave Australia or any Territory of the Commonwealth except with the permission of an approved authority', and could not change his or her place of abode or travel outside the police district in which they were resident 'except with the written permission of an aliens registration officer'. In addition, enemy aliens were required to reside in any place or area specified by the Minister of Defence, were required to report to the authorities at specified times and places, and were forbidden to be outside their place of residence during certain prescribed hours. Beyond this, the Minister could prohibit the holding of any meetings, processions or demonstrations by enemy aliens; prohibit the publication in an enemy alien language of any newspaper or other publication; and require enemy aliens to submit all communications to addresses overseas.[14]

These restrictions were drafted originally to safeguard the community from aliens who were, or had the potential to be, enemies; but German and Austrian refugees from Nazism were included among those to be restricted. There was, furthermore, an internment provision in the Regulations.[15]

The implications of all these restrictions were profound. A refugee might be denied permission to leave Australia and thus enter a neutral country or other place of refuge; he or she could be denied permission to re-establish themselves in a new locale, or reunite with family; moreover, owing to the restriction on travel, those with itinerant occupations might be forced to change their means of earning a living. Refugees could be placed under curfew, and difficulties could thus arise when they sought to help each other in easing the burdens they faced from by the restrictions. They were also potentially barred from writing confidentially to immigration authorities overseas with a view to further migration – which, even if they had been able, may have been denied them due to the prohibition on overseas travel. Finally, the internment provisions could place Jews, socialists and hardcore Nazis together in the same compound – a situation which would have been to nobody's benefit.

All these scenarios took place in varying degrees during the war years. Despite the earlier declarations of tolerance, once the regulations had been passed the military authorities began to implement them robustly, basing their actions on the paramount ideal of national security. After the fall of the Netherlands in May 1940, a fear of spies developed throughout the Commonwealth. A secret Australian Army document from 20 June 1940 drew attention to the possibility of enemy agents 'travelling as refugees on neutral ships', who may acquire 'naval and military intelligence at various ports visited, for transmission to Germany upon arrival at their destination'.[16] Of greater perceived danger were those refugee aliens already in Australia, as highlighted in a personal memorandum prepared by the Chief of the General Staff for the Minister for the Army in October 1940:

It may be stressed that enemy or subversive organisations do not choose stupid men as their tools. Their agents usually keep in the background and perform their duties quietly and efficiently. To handle and prove a case against a clever suspect who may be a refugee, requires those necessary intelligence attributes, patience and perseverance. The absence of sabotage up to date reinforces the view that such activities will take place only as part of a pre-arranged plan. The peril at present may be subterranean, and all precautionary steps affecting many, perhaps legitimate, refugees are taken in the national interest.[17]

The memorandum demonstrated the Army's attitude: while it acknowledged that 'the great majority of the refugees is only too willing to help ours and the Allied cause, which, with the genuine refugee, is also his own', it also observed that 'it is a matter of great difficulty to make the necessary discriminations with justice in every case'. Consequently, 'Where there seems any ground for doubt, authority can take no risks, and we must ask those who are placed under restrictions, which in their case appear to them quite unnecessary and undeserved, to bear with the inconvenience for the common good.' None of this was intended to reflect on their 'avowed loyalty and disposition' towards Australia, 'but military considerations take precedence over all others'. The general policy applied, therefore, was 'that the nation should always be given the benefit of the doubt' in any matter of internal security.[18]

Refugees were thus under suspicion because Nazis may have smuggled themselves into their ranks, but they also posed a potential threat because of their status as refugees. The memorandum pointed out the necessity of realizing that 'virtually all the refugees in Australia from Germany left Germany by definite permission of the Gestapo'. Moreover, while 'it may be presumed that these people left Germany on the avowed condition that they did not return', the issue to be decided was whether there was 'another condition that they should go to certain countries and not be surprised to find certain services required of them'. Refugees therefore posed a security threat owing to their vulnerability:

Some have had their spirits broken by harsh confinement and are therefore ready to work abroad as required. Others have been, one can take it, approached since, and many, perhaps uncertain about the war, treat it as a matter of re-insurance and prudence to do something to establish a claim for Nazi consideration, should the need arise.

What is known of the German procedure is briefly as follows: Nearly every German abroad has relatives in Germany. These are card indexed and the victim can be confronted with by [sic] the exact address and details of his relatives when it is desired to exert pressure. Many Germans abroad are tied financially to Germany; particularly the large number of German trade representatives abroad. This financial dependence on Germany will be made use of in the application of pressure.[19]

Given this, there was little the refugees could do to convince the authorities that the contrary was in fact closer to reality, and no evidence has been found that any such pressure was employed.

As if to underscore the position, the Secretary of the Army prepared his own memorandum for the Minister in January 1941, in which he stated:

> While it is probably true that the majority of those classed as refugees are genuine victims of Nazi oppression who have sought asylum in this country, it is considered extremely unlikely that an efficient Intelligence Service, such as that of Germany, would fail to take advantage of such an opportunity of introducing a certain number of agents into this country in the guise of refugees … It is, therefore, considered necessary that all Jewish Refugees of German or Austrian origin should be subject to the restrictions placed on enemy aliens, which, unless imposed as the result of specific evidence against the individual concerned, are not of a very repressive nature, particularly compared with the degree of control existing in many parts of Europe for some years, including those countries from which the refugees came to Australia.[20]

The refugees' response to their continued classification as enemy aliens was to petition for the Regulations to be revised. Activity was stepped up when it became known that refugees in the UK had been reclassified as 'friendly aliens', giving them the right to participate in the war effort. The Migrants' Consultative Council, a sub-committee of the Australian Jewish Welfare Society, wrote to Prime Minister Menzies in 1941 with a request that refugees in Australia be similarly reclassified, as they were 'equally eager to serve the common cause'. The request was circulated through the Prime Minister's Department, Attorney-General, Interior and the Army. No action was taken.[21] A similar letter from the Migrants' Consultative Council, dated 9 June 1941, met a similar fate.[22] The position of Jewish 'enemy aliens' within Australia was only resolved in favour of the refugees in 1944, when a new definition was constructed acknowledging that Jews who had come into the Commonwealth as escapees from the Nazi regime were in fact friendly to the Allied cause.[23]

Jewish internees sent from overseas: An uncertain fate

Invoking the British precedent did not come as a surprise to the Australian authorities, as they had by 1941 already been involved in a long and close relationship with the British government on the issue of internment and enemy aliens. This did not concern what should be done with Jews already in Australia; rather, in what became one of the most celebrated incidents in twentieth-century Australian Jewish history, was the question of what should be the fate of German and Austrian Jews then residing in Britain. The result would become known as the *Dunera* affair;[24] for at least one author, it would become the '*Dunera* scandal'.[25]

There is little doubt that in the summer of 1940 Britain was fighting for its life.[26] The so-called Phoney War ended on May 10 with the German invasion of the Low Countries and France, and the commencement of Hitler's campaign in the West.

Britain's resources were then stretched even further as Italy entered the war on 10 June 1940, threatening the British Mediterranean lifeline – a matter of potential threat for Australia. New considerations of security began to confront, and then dominate, British decision makers. Immediately after the outbreak of hostilities, the British Home Secretary, Sir John Anderson, declared that the government would draw a clear distinction between enemy aliens and refugees from Germany and Austria. Tribunals had been set up throughout the country to classify Germans and Austrians as either (A) persons to be interned immediately as not being absolutely reliable; (B) persons left at liberty, but subject to certain of the restrictions applicable to enemy aliens under the Aliens Order of 1920; and (C) persons who should be free from all restrictions under the Aliens Order, except those which applied to friendly aliens. Those in both the (B) and (C) categories were classified as refugees from Nazi oppression, and generally considered sympathetically.[27]

On 12 May, in response to the attack on the West, Sir John Anderson ordered that all male Germans and Austrians over sixteen and under sixty (excluding invalids or the infirm) throughout the coastal regions of England and Scotland be interned temporarily. All other male aliens in the same age group, regardless of their nationality, were subjected to restrictions: daily report to the nearest police station; prohibition from using any motor vehicle (other than public transport) or bicycle; and a curfew between 8.00 pm and 6.00 am.[28]

At the end of May, a second order required that all (B) category persons of enemy nationality, male and female, anywhere in the country, should be interned at once. Then, in the last week of June, an order was issued for the general internment of all adult males of enemy nationality between the ages of sixteen and sixty. The vast majority of these were men who had been placed in the (C) category and included many engaged in work of national importance as scientists and educators, as well as students from schools, colleges and universities.

Accompanying the panic measures to intern all enemy aliens were calls to deport as many as possible from Britain to places where they could do the least damage to the war effort through diverting manpower and draining resources. On 3 June Prime Minister Winston Churchill wanted to know why arrangements could not be made to deport 20,000 internees to Newfoundland or St. Helena, and on 7 June the Dominions Secretary, Viscount Caldecote (formerly Sir Thomas Inskip), asked the Canadian High Commissioner in London, Vincent Massey, whether Canada could take some of the internees off Britain's hands. Canada agreed that it could. Subsequently, ships taking internees across the Atlantic departed Britain on 24 June (*Duchess of York*), 30 June (*Arandora Star*), 3 July (*Ettrick*) and 7 July (*Sobieski*).[29] One of the transports, the *Arandora Star*, never reached its destination; it was torpedoed by a U-boat a few hours out of Liverpool, with considerable loss of life. Some 444 survivors were plucked from the water by British and Canadian warships and later re-embarked on board another ship, the 12,615-ton *Dunera*, which left Liverpool on 10 July 1940, bound for Melbourne and Sydney. Altogether the *Dunera* carried 2,732 internees of all ages, most of whom were German and Austrian Jews; mixed in with them were 251 German prisoners of war, several dozen Nazi sympathizers and 200 Italians. There were 141 in the guard detachment and ship's crew.

The Australian government agreed initially to take a total of 6,000 internees,[30] provided its role would simply be one of guarding them and there would be no possibility of them remaining after their British release. It was intended that the *Dunera* would be the first of several transports: in the end, it was the only ship to come from Britain to Australia carrying internees. Mention should be made here, however, of the *Queen Mary*, which came to Australia from Singapore in September 1940 carrying over 200 internees, men, women and children. These people fell into the same general category of 'Overseas Internees' as the men and boys on the *Dunera*.[31]

In all accounts of the *Dunera's* journey, as related by the internees themselves, instances are recorded of the most appalling injustices and mistreatment perpetrated by the ship's British guard detachment. Identifying their prisoners as enemy aliens and thus as Germans – without recognizing that most of them were refugee Jews – some in the guard were responsible for beating, looting, torture, starvation and overall tactics of intimidation.[32]

Having left Liverpool on 10 July, the *Dunera* docked in Fremantle, Western Australia on 27 August. On 3 September the ship arrived in Melbourne (where several the internees disembarked and were sent to camps at Tatura in northern Victoria), and on 7 September it docked in Sydney and offloaded the bulk of the internees. The next day, after a nineteen-hour train trip, they arrived at Hay internment camp in western New South Wales.

There was little reason to suspect that the Australians should have welcomed the arrival of over 2,000 Jews from Britain in September 1940 – and every reason for the government to want them gone again once their internment was over. Yet for the internees, a constant theme running through their entire experience, before they left Britain and after they arrived in Australia, was their desire to be released to be able to contribute to the war effort against the common enemy.

At practically the same time as the *Dunera* arrived in Australia, questions began to be asked in Britain's House of Commons about the arbitrary nature of the arrests that had transformed the refugees into internees in the first place. The upshot of these questions saw a set of exemptions from internment published in a White Paper in October 1940, which affected most of those who had been sent to Australia on the *Dunera*.[33] The British change of heart facilitated the release of thousands within Britain who had been interned and threw open the status of those who had been sent overseas. Considering the new classifications, the British government requested Australia in November 1940 to consider the release of eligible internees for transmigration to the United States, Palestine and other countries.[34] To help facilitate this, the Home Office sent to Australia a liaison officer, Major Julian Layton, who acted as a go-between for the British government, the internees and the Australian authorities.[35]

The British went on to suggest how the releases should take place, with Layton's task being to help facilitate the repatriation of the internees to Britain. Until he arrived, however, the internees had no option but to remain in internment. That had been the arrangement agreed to originally, and there was no logical reason, in the view of the Australians, to depart from it.

It will be recalled that in 1936 Julian Layton visited Australia and was instrumental in liaising with leading members of the Sydney Jewish community in the establishment of the Australian Jewish Welfare Society. Since then, he had gained a great deal of additional experience regarding refugee and internee matters. He visited Germany on numerous occasions and dealt directly with the Nazis in trying to arrange exit visas for Jews. For a time, he also oversaw the Kitchener Transmigration Camp at Richborough, where he had got to know many of those who were later interned. He was known and respected by many in Australia, on both sides of the wire. After arriving in Sydney in March 1941, he learned quickly that the task of internee repatriation was not going to be as simple as he had at first anticipated. The usual bureaucratic inertia which takes place after a mistake has been made had taken hold, and things were going to take time. Undeterred, Layton set about achieving what was possible, and allowing the impossible to work itself out.[36]

Having been sent halfway around the world to redress the situation and arrange for the repatriation and release of the internees, he began a process whereby compensation would be paid by the British government to the internees for the losses they incurred on the *Dunera*. It went out of its way to pay restitution to the internees, a figure of £35,000 (just over £2,000,000 today) eventually being paid out as compensation for physical losses incurred during the voyage. That this took place at a time when Britain was engaged in a war for survival and needed literally every penny for the war effort is strong evidence that the British government was sensitive to the injustices committed against the internees. Back in London, three of the guards who behaved so brutally on the *Dunera* were tried by court-martial on a variety of charges upon their return to the UK; one was found guilty, reduced to the ranks, sentenced to twelve months' imprisonment and dismissed from the Army.

As a result of Layton's efforts, several hundred internees were repatriated from Australia to Britain. Others were able, again with Layton's help, to move to third countries while the war was still in progress. Those who did not want to return to freedom in Britain, or who were concerned that to do so would entail more risks than if they remained in Australia, elected to remain in internment until conditions improved or changed. There was, at this stage, no 'release-into-Australia' option – the Australians stuck by the original arrangement and insisted that the British government rectify its own mistake.

In mid-December 1941 word began circulating among the internees that the Australian Army was contemplating the establishment of a labour unit. Layton had spent much of the year since his arrival trying to recruit internees into the British Pioneer Corps, their best chance of repatriation to the UK. Returning to Britain was hazardous, however; at least four transport ships were torpedoed and sunk on their way back from Australia, with forty-seven of the internees losing their lives. It was clear that a new Australian labour corps could be both a way out of the camp and provide the internees with an opportunity to contribute to the war effort.

The unit comprising men from the *Dunera* and *Queen Mary* was duly formed on 7 April 1942, listed as the 8th Employment Company[37] under the command of Captain Edward R. Broughton, a career officer who had seen service in three armies dating from the time of the Boer War.[38] Upon formation it comprised four officers and 453 other ranks.

The first internees to volunteer were set to work picking fruit in local commercial farms and orchards, while subsequent intakes went straight into the Army. The option to join up remained open throughout the war, with the last internees enlisting in September 1944. Their status was unchanged from the time of their arrival in Australia in 1940; they remained 'enemy aliens' until February 1944, when the government granted them 'refugee alien' status.[39]

Almost all who had not yet returned to Britain took advantage of the opportunity. Most of those who had been on the *Dunera* and *Queen Mary* had been released from internment by the end of 1942, and by 1945 the war service of the men of the 8th Employment Company forced a government rethink on their migration status. By November 1945, some 785 former *Dunera* men were still in Australia, the rest having returned to Britain or transmigrated elsewhere. Of those left in Australia, 417 were in civilian employment and 368 were still in the Army.[40]

After the war, serious consideration was given to allowing the former *Dunera* and *Queen Mary* internees the opportunity to remain in Australia. On 20 November 1945, Frank Forde, in his capacity as Minister for the Army (he had been Prime Minister for seven days earlier in 1945 owing to the death of John Curtin), proposed that the ex-internees should all be repatriated to Britain now that the war with Japan was over.[41] However, the Minister for Labour and National Service, Edward (Jack) Holloway, balked at that idea, writing that 'where any of these people, who have worked loyally and well since being released in Australia, desire to do so, they should be permitted to become permanent residents and citizens of Australia'.[42] Within a week, the new Minister for Immigration, Arthur Calwell, showed less inclination to be welcoming, preferring that 'arrangements be made for the repatriation of these people as soon as shipping becomes available'.[43] By this stage, however, those who had served the country during the war and who sought to remain were accepted and in due course became Australian citizens.

The Jewish internees from the *Dunera* and *Queen Mary* were never intended to add to Australia's domestic internment problems. They were to have had no relationship with the wider Australian population; it was as if they were to remain hermetically sealed, with no contact outside the camps to which they had been sent. They would be *in* Australia but not *of* it, a situation which suited the Australian authorities perfectly. Although this position would change, throughout all of 1941 the situation concerning so-called overseas internees stayed constant until the exigencies of war and the threat of invasion forced a rethink that could simultaneously make use of their manpower and give the internees the opportunity to contribute to the war effort.

Internment and Australian fears of foreigners

Internment of enemy aliens in Australia was always seen as a measure of last resort.[44] The position of the government was to limit internment 'strictly to the minimum numbers necessary for security reasons, and to adopt such a measure only where it is considered that internment is essential because other forms of control are inadequate'.[45] The relative generosity of this policy helps to account for the fact that by the end of November 1940 there were only 574 Germans and 1,544 Italians in internment, together with 76 naturalized British subjects of German origin and 182 naturalized British subjects of Italian origin. This did not, of course, include the *Dunera* or *Queen Mary* internees, who fell into a different category.

At various times during 1940 there was a popular clamour in Australia for the round-up and internment of enemy aliens, but the government was, by and large, able to resist this. The circumstances following the entry of Japan into the war on 7–8 December 1941 were, however, quite different. Within days, people bearing enemy alien nationality were caught in a police internment net which aimed to clear certain areas, particularly in northern Western Australia, Queensland and New South Wales, that might present security problems in the face of a Japanese military advance. As the Pacific War intensified and Allied disasters multiplied in the early months of 1942, a flood of telegrams, letters and petitions demanded total internment from government officials, Cabinet Ministers and Members of Parliament. Many letters did not discriminate between enemy aliens and refugees from Nazism bearing German nationality. In fact, the Australian authorities did not recognize a change in status for refugees from Germany until 1944, when a new definition of refugee alien was constructed acknowledging that Jews who had come to Australia as escapees from Nazism were in fact friendly to the Allied cause.[46] Typical of this attitude was a letter to Prime Minister John Curtin in March 1942:

> Just a few words from the man in the street, re. the present position. Are we fair to the man in the street, when Aliens, and not only Aliens, but enemy subjects, are allowed to carry on business whilst our men are overseas, or in camp? Just how long would you or I be afloat in either Germany or Italy. Just let that sink in. You are not going to get co-operation until such time as every alien Jew or enemy is behind the barbs. Then and not till then will you have the rest of Australia behind you.[47]

During the early months of 1942, organizations demanding general internment included Protestant organizations, such as the Loyal Orange Lodge (especially directed against Catholic Italians remaining at large); rural Shire Councils; and ex-service associations. One letter, from the Enoggera (Queensland) Sub-Branch of the Returned Soldiers', Sailors' and Airmen's Imperial League of Australia, is illustrative:

> In view of the imminent danger of invasion of our country and the knowledge of aliens still at large, we feel that nothing less than total internment is sufficient. In view of the fate of other countries with regards to fifth columnists, we consider

that North Queensland presents a deadly peril in this regard and do not wish to see our gallant men shot from behind as they were in Malaya, Greece and Crete. … The only place for aliens is internment camps. In view of the fact that some may be friendly and as this is total war the innocent are made to suffer as well as the guilty, INTERN THEM ALL without regard to sex before it is too late.[48]

Between February and March 1942, many naturalized Italians were taken into internment together with enemy alien Germans, Hungarians, Finns and others. As the war situation deteriorated, so the number of arrests increased in what was clearly a direct relationship between perceptions of security and the state of the war.

When war was declared, security became paramount. Prior to the war, Australians had been able to define themselves by pointing to those in society who were not Anglo-Australian; now, with war's onset, this was reinforced. Anyone from an enemy or enemy-occupied country was now suspect; anyone from a neutral country could be dubious. At the same time, the necessarily 'British' nature of Australia's allies was continually highlighted, even after the entry of the Americans and Britain's demise in Singapore.

The status accorded enemy aliens during the war was in many respects consistent with the attitudes held towards foreigners prior to 1939. The greatest irony in all this is that when war broke out, the conservative United Australia Party government – which had done so much to restrict refugee arrivals before the war – adopted a relatively mild policy commensurate with national security, while it was a Labor administration in late 1941 and early 1942 that was forced to assume a harsh and all-embracing attitude towards enemy aliens. That these included German-Jewish refugees opposed to the Nazis confused the Australian authorities, who subjected them to administrative restrictions, criminal surveillance and, occasionally, internment. Their Germanness, Jewishness and foreignness all combined to render their position difficult (when not unsustainable) in a time of total war.

All manner of conclusions can be drawn from an investigation of Australian policies during the Second World War: that the authorities were obsessed with legality and 'proper channels' in 1940, but less concerned with these in 1942; that the war acted as a turning point on the road to a post-war multicultural Australia, owing to the increased perceptions Australians had of foreigners;[49] that Australians genuinely panicked in 1942 owing to a fear of invasion from Japan and Australia's isolation in the face of Britain's defeat at Singapore, and hit out indiscriminately at all those who were perceived to be a threat to the nation; and that the internment measures were often accompanied by a narrowness of vision on the part of the Australian authorities. Many of those subjected to measures intended for enemy aliens in early 1942 could have worked for Australia's war effort instead of holding up men and resources at a time when both were desperately needed.

Yet for all this, it cannot be overlooked that Australia's policies were grounded in attitudes towards race and identity that were prevalent in the pre-war period. Examinations focusing on these issues only in their time-and-place context have a great many important things to say but are by and large incomplete if they do not also consider how the Australian people framed their views and ordered their priorities in advance of government action.

CHAPTER 12
WARTIME EUROPE AND AUSTRALIA

Immigration from Europe in wartime

The *Dunera* affair, for all its drama, far from typified Australian wartime immigration. Indeed, the internees from overseas were not considered in immigration reckonings at all, and it was not long after war's outbreak that the government began demonstrating that it was prepared to say one thing and do quite another where migration was concerned. Policy decisions concerning group settlements for non-Jewish Europeans, for example, started being made throughout 1940, despite a long-standing opposition to all forms of group migration dating back to the turn of the century.

At least two of these group settlement schemes emerged out of initiatives made prior to the outbreak of war. The first concerned the Netherlands. According to an agreement made between the Australian and Dutch governments in March 1938, the amount of landing capital required for entry to the Commonwealth would be reduced for migrants guaranteed by the Netherlands Migration Office, though it was stipulated that the more liberal conditions of entry 'would not apply to persons of Jewish race'.[1] In December 1939 Tom Garrett noted that the outbreak of war had prevented the development of this scheme, resulting in a 'suspension of the immigration into Australia of persons who racially are the most desirable'.[2] It was anticipated that once the war ended the scheme would still prove viable and would likely be reinstated.

Of equal interest was a scheme to admit an unspecified number of skilled Swiss toolmakers and machine manufacturing experts. This idea had first been raised in July 1939, when Senator Foll granted approval 'for the admittance to Australia of non-Jewish Swiss migrants'.[3] Nothing came of the proposal immediately, but in July 1940 the matter was brought before Cabinet by Prime Minister Menzies 'in view of [Australia's] shortage of skilled tradesmen'.[4] No landing money would be insisted upon,[5] a significant departure from all immigration procedure since the early 1920s. In another departure from existing practice, the Commonwealth government would be prepared to maintain these people at its expense pending their absorption into industry.[6] The decision was cabled to Stanley Bruce in London on 23 July 1940, with a precise list of the classes of tradesmen to be recruited. There is no record of any of these mechanics arriving in Australia, but they were actively pursued by the government despite its own regulations. The demands of wartime were such that Swiss technicians and toolmakers were highly desirable in the fight against Nazism – provided they were not Jewish.

A second important initiative involving the recruitment of foreign technicians concerned Czech engineers. On 9 July 1940, Bruce cabled Canberra that a list of forty-five Bren gun experts had been forwarded to him, and that the Commonwealth might consider the possibility of admitting them as immigrants.[7] A further list of seventy engineers was soon added. All these men, and their families, were currently marking time in Palestine while awaiting their future; the Department of the Interior observed that it was likely that 'many, if not all of them', were Jews,[8] though on this occasion their Jewishness did not stop the Department from spotting a bargain. Departmental officers felt that definite advantages for Australia's war effort might accrue from the admission of these Czech Jewish engineers. Foll put the matter before War Cabinet on 7 November 1940, and later that day minuted its agreement on the proviso that London could certify 'as to their capacity & loyalty if allowed to come here'.[9] After taking a long time to set up the administrative machinery needed to receive them, however, the opportunity was lost; in January 1941 Bruce cabled that the Czechs had been absorbed elsewhere.[10] When pressed on the matter, it was learned that 'All Czech engineers referred to in earlier cables are now either in India or on route there'.[11] It was unlikely that any more would be available for Australia, though the Department of the Interior sought to have the offer kept open indefinitely in case the opportunity again presented itself.[12] Australian procrastination had led to the loss of a number of highly skilled technical people whose abilities could have greatly assisted the war effort. For the Bren gun project, their Jewish identity would have played no part in their acceptance or rejection and would seem to have been irrelevant in the Department of the Interior's considerations. The government's problem here was one of inertia. If there had been sufficient drive from the Departments of the Army or Supply, a way could have been found to get the Czech experts and their families from Palestine. But the opportunity was not taken up in a timely manner.

Two additional cases reinforce the point that the Australian government was prepared to accept European migrants during the war. On 21 November 1940 Menzies notified Robert Cosgrove, the Premier of Tasmania, of the imminent arrival in Brisbane of 174 evacuees from the Baltic States.[13] No record of these people has been found in Federal government migration records, but they were not refugees in the usual sense understood by the Australian authorities. The British government had agreed to their financial maintenance, and the Commonwealth sought the assistance of the state governments in placing them upon arrival. This suggests that they were not Jewish, as the welfare of Jewish refugees was by now almost exclusively in the hands of the Australian Jewish Welfare Society. How these people came to be on a ship bound for Brisbane is a mystery, but their appearance serves to illustrate the genuine sympathy felt by Australians for the people of the Baltic States after their forcible incorporation into the Soviet Union in late 1939. They were also 'racially desirable', as became evident in many ways after the war.

Another group of non-Jewish Europeans the government was prepared to accept as immigrants was Greek. On 16 December 1941 Cabinet decided to modify its existing policy regarding alien migration so as to permit the entry of Greeks 'whose admission has been sponsored by the Greek War Relief Fund Committee'.[14] This decision related to up to 1,000 immigrants, and was made 'as a gesture in recognition of the gallant service rendered by the Greek nation to the Allied cause'.[15] The month of March 1941 had seen Australians fighting in Greece and Crete, where a close relationship had sprung up between the Australian forces and the Greek population. Perhaps the decision to allow Greeks into Australia was in part to soothe the Australians' feelings at having left Greece to its fate, or, possibly, to reinforce Allied unity, as this measure appeared a week after the entry of Japan into the war. Not that the Greek government-in-exile could have assisted Australia in a dispute with the Japanese; but friends are important for morale purposes, and the Australian government, by showing how it felt about Greeks as immigrants, was in effect acknowledging that everyone on the Allied side was a 'mate'. Greeks were thus now considered among those desirable for entry to Australia – an irony when it is considered that Greeks were among those who were made less than welcome in the pre-war years, being among the small number of nationalities who had a quota imposed on their entry.

So far as Jews were concerned, Australia continued to be as relatively inflexible during the war as it had been beforehand, though the outbreak of war created some anomalous circumstances. Despite the position announced in September 1939, Jewish refugees still on the water in transit to Australia were permitted to continue their journey and land upon arrival. On 7 September, for example, fifty-seven German Jews possessing valid landing permits arrived in Bombay (Mumbai) on the S.S. *Maloja*.[16] The Indian government, unsure of whether to allow the ship to continue Australia, detained the refugees and then cabled Canberra for instructions. On 7 October 1939, the Department of Defence notified the Prime Minister's Department that no objection would be raised to the landing in Australia of the fifty-seven refugees 'provided Department of Interior satisfied validity of visas and landing permits'.[17]

Shipping space was limited, and preference was at this time being given to Australians stranded abroad who were trying to return home.[18] The flow of foreign migrants, now a trickle, was determined by the extent to which aliens could convince the military authorities of their fitness to enter the country. The general expectation was that the supply of foreign migrants – including German refugees, who were being denied entry – would soon dry up.[19] On the surface the government's position was clear, as articulated by Senator Foll in June 1940:

In view of the international situation the issue of landing permits in favour of aliens residing in European countries has been suspended, and, in regard to aliens residing outside of European countries, permits are being issued only in exceptional cases. No further permits are being issued to aliens of enemy nationality.[20]

The situation was further clarified when, in July 1940, a request came from the High Commissioner's Office in London that consideration be given to allowing the transit through Australia of German and Polish Jews en route to Shanghai. The government noted Stanley Bruce's warning that 'some would endeavour to remain' and that many were of an 'undesirable type'.[21] Permission was therefore refused.[22] In January 1941, Bruce sought to know whether the government would admit, for the duration of the war, 180 Polish boys aged between fourteen and eighteen, then in Romania. The Prime Minister's Department cabled London to the effect that the Commonwealth would be willing to admit these boys subject to the Polish government-in-exile paying all expenses.[23] After referring the matter to the Department of the Interior, however, the decision was overturned on numerous grounds – primarily that 'if the Commonwealth opened its doors to a large number of foreign evacuees from Europe, there would no doubt be a considerable revival of applications by residents here for permission to introduce their relatives'.[24] A week later, on 18 January 1941, the High Commissioner was advised that the decision to admit these 180 boys had been rescinded.[25] Most of these boys were not Jewish, but the tardiness of the Australians in checking this saw events in Romania overtake them. On 21 January 1941, the ultra-fascist Iron Guard attempted to overthrow Romania's military dictator Ion Antonescu, and simultaneously conducted a murderous pogrom against the Jews of Bucharest.[26] The Iron Guard's coup was a failure, but Britain, appalled by Antonescu's violent suppression of the rebellion, severed relations with Romania on 14 February. Probably, the boys never got out of Romania. If they did, there is no evidence to suggest that they ever came to Australia.[27]

Finally, as late as October 1944, a request came that such Jews as were then left in Hungary be permitted to apply for entry to Australia. The Minister for the Interior, Senator Joseph (Joe) Collings, adjudged it undesirable that the Commonwealth commit itself to the granting of visas.[28] The continuity between these instances, the negative attitudes of pre-war times and the restrictive policies announced at the war's outbreak would seem apparent. Canberra's attitude could perhaps have best been summed up in the words of a report from the Army's Security Service, dated 3 May 1943:

> When the persecution of the Jews first began most people felt sorry for them and were prepared to welcome them, but their actions since they reached here show that they are no good as citizens and are merely parasites on the rest of the community. It is considered that if a plebiscite were taken, this would represent the opinion of nine out of ten of the community.[29]

Now, as in the past, objections were found for the exclusion of Jews from Australia – this time based on the premise that those who had arrived as refugees before the war were not making good citizens three years later.

From time to time, however, the government showed that it was prepared to assist in the process of Jewish rescue. Take, for example, a case from June 1940, when the government gave permission for the Australian Jewish Welfare Society to introduce 100 'Dutch or Belgian Jewish children between ages seven and fourteen'.[30] This was, it appears, in response to a request from the AJWS to take 500 children from Belgium and the Netherlands. Historian Glen Palmer, who has investigated this episode, has concluded that because of the relationship between the government and the AJWS 'some concessions were made', even though 'the Australian government did not want Jewish children'.[31] Overall, she argues, 'there was consistently little enthusiasm or generosity in the offers – and generally other restrictions or barriers were imposed to ensure few, if any, children would arrive'.[32]

Also worthy of consideration is a Cabinet decision from March 1943, when approval was given for the admission of 150 Jewish children evacuated from Vichy France.[33] On this occasion, Senator Collings acceded to a request from the Australian Jewish Welfare Society that these children, aged between seven and fourteen, be permitted to enter Australia. At present, it was reported, they were under the care of the Roman Catholic Church, though it was not specified whether they had yet been brought out of Vichy France.[34] Of importance was that migration standards would be maintained: steps would be taken to see that only children 'of good physical and mental health' would be selected, and it would be the responsibility of the AJWS (not the government) to arrange and undertake the transport of these children to Australia. The AJWS would, it was automatically assumed, take full care of the children once they arrived.[35] Given the war situation, transportation difficulties and the distances involved, it is almost certain that these children did not reach Australia.

The AJWS requested further assistance from the government nearly a year later. It received such help in the form of block approval for another batch of 150 Jewish refugee children from France who were (it was believed) currently awaiting their fate in Switzerland.[36] The Prime Minister, John Curtin, announced the same acceptance criteria as for the earlier group, adding that the children must also be 'submitted to examination by Australian authorities in Britain' – though precisely how this would take place is unclear. By this stage, the security implications of allowing aliens in from an enemy-occupied (as distinct from enemy-combatant) country had altered. To some extent, the Australians were committing themselves to the rescue of Jewish children who had already been saved, but their transport to Australia, though next to impossible, would not be undertaken by the government. Again, it is highly unlikely that any of these children ever arrived in Australia.

Considering the government's attitude, another anomaly saw the ongoing admission of small groups of Polish Jews from time to time between 1941 and 1944. Discussions began in February 1941. The Australian Ambassador to Tokyo, Sir John Latham, sought the government's approval to allow 'a limited number of Polish citizens' (including Jews), who were then marking time in Japan, to enter Australia.[37] The Department of the Interior took this up and recommended favourably on the matter to War Cabinet in April 1941; after consideration, permission was granted for the entry of sixty-six Polish citizens from Tokyo who were allowed to remain for the duration of the war.[38] (In an aside, the view was expressed that the government was agreeable to the admission of these refugees 'as a gesture to Poland', but that it was 'not desirous of giving effect to the decision if it can be avoided'.[39]) By 5 August 1941 the number had increased, and seventy-two Polish refugees from Japan had arrived in Australia.[40]

Reporting on their arrival in Australia per the *Kasima Maru* a few days later, Melbourne's *Argus* noted that these refugees included a medical doctor, a solicitor, engineers and technical experts. Nowhere did the report state that the refugees were Jewish, though late in the story it mentioned that a reception took place for them at the Kadimah Hall, Carlton, and that it had been arranged by the Australian Jewish Welfare Society.[41] Probably mindful not to panic the population, *The Age* went even further. The refugees' Jewishness was not even alluded to – though their Polish identity was stressed on at least six occasions.[42] Both articles also picked up a portent for the future. The Honorary Consul-General for Poland, Ladislas de Noskowski, had said that another 1,500 'Polish refugees' were still in Japan[43] and had been given until 15 September to leave that country.[44] *The Argus* reported – accurately, as it turned out – that owing to this deadline Polish consular authorities in Australia had asked the Australian government to admit another 200 refugees from Japan for the duration of the war.[45]

At the same time, and for the same reasons, the Polish Ambassador in Tokyo requested that the Australian government take a further group of refugees,[46] which received Departmental approval provided the number did not exceed fifty persons.[47] At the same time, Noskowski's request that 200 Polish nationals from Japan be permitted entry was rejected.[48] Then, paradoxically, on 4 November 1941 a second group of fifty was approved provided their maintenance in Australia was guaranteed by the Australian Jewish Welfare Society.[49] In announcing this measure, *The Argus* noted that this was to be 'the first immigration to Australia permitted for a considerable time'. Reporting the government's position, the paper stated that the measure to allow these refugees entry was 'subject to stringent conditions', and had been accepted 'only as a humanitarian measure to relieve the plight of a friendly ally's nationals'. One of the key conditions was that 'none of the men shall be eligible for service in the Polish army'; another was that they would not be permitted to bring with them more than three accompanying family members.[50]

Reasons accounting for this half-turn in policy are difficult to determine, but two developments between August and November 1941 should be borne in mind. The first concerned a change of government and an accompanying change in Minister at the Department of Interior. On 28 August 1941, the government of Robert Menzies fell when the two Independents giving him the balance of power in the House of Representatives withdrew their support. The leader of the Country Party, Arthur Fadden, became Prime Minister from 29 August until he too lost the support of the Independents on 7 October and John Curtin and the Australian Labor Party took office. Harry Foll was replaced as Minister for the Interior by his opposite number in the Senate, Joe Collings. Although this did not result in a sudden shift in immigration policy, the departure of the hard-line Foll made possible a little more flexibility in policy than had previously existed, and the ascent to office of a Labor government with an avowed social conscience was itself a development offering some hope to those seeking refugee admission.

The second point concerns conditions in Japan, where political instability had been occurring throughout 1941 as a war party sought to take advantage of Allied reverses in Europe by aligning Japan more closely with Berlin and Rome and removing European influence from Asia. The September deadline for the departure of the Polish-Jewish refugees was affected by these developments, as was an ongoing evacuation of British and American civilians from Japan as war clouds began to gather during October and early November. It was, indeed, on the recommendation of Sir John Latham in Tokyo that some of the refugees should be admitted to Australia, as their presence was complicating the task of evacuating the British and American civilians.[51] The fifty refugees made it to Australia just prior to the Japanese attacks on Pearl Harbor, Malaya and Hong Kong on 7–8 December 1941, and the commencement of the Pacific War. Refugees still left in Japan at this time were eventually evacuated by the Japanese to the International Settlement at Shanghai, there to wait out the war with others who had arrived before 1939.

The issue of Polish refugees again surfaced, though in a slightly different way, in September 1941. The Consul-General for Poland in Sydney, Sylwester Gruszka, requested permission to introduce to the Commonwealth all Polish citizens, then in Russia, who had relatives in Australia.[52] This took much longer to resolve, as it was only a year later, on 15 December 1942, that the Department of External Affairs raised the matter with Interior. By that stage the number of likely immigrants had been fixed at thirty, and on 1 January 1943 Albert Peters was able to confirm that their admission had been approved subject to various conditions of health, character and security.[53] The success of this petition emboldened Gruszka to repeat it in November 1943; the upshot saw approval granted for another 100 Polish refugees in Russia to enter Australia.[54] By March 1944 none had yet arrived, though some had made it as far as Tehran, Persia.[55] Thus, as a result of discussions in Cabinet, and taking cognisance of the fact that none of these Polish refugees had yet made it to Australia, the government could feel generous; on 27 March 1944 it approved in principle for the admission of another 100 Poles from Russia.[56] No evidence has been found to suggest that any of these ever arrived.

A final instance of ambiguity in Australian policy came as the result of representations made by Sir Hughe Knatchbull-Hugessen, the British Ambassador in Ankara, on 13 December 1941. A cablegram of that date to Prime Minister Curtin referred to 'about 28 emigres from Germany employed at Turkish educational institutions', and enquired 'as to the possibility of their finding refuge and work in British territory in the event of a German invasion of Turkey'.[57] The Department of the Interior rejected the request without further ado, stating that the Commonwealth 'is not prepared to authorise the admission of the German nationals'.[58] The Army, though concerned to keep them out on security grounds, was nonetheless not quite so dismissive: noting that the request had also been sent to other British Empire countries, the Army Secretary informed the Prime Minister's Department that if the émigrés proved unable to obtain entry to countries such as Canada or South Africa the Army would be prepared, 'at a later stage, when the military situation may have improved, to reconsider the question of the admission of such of them as are not "Aryan" Germans'.[59] Translated, this meant the Army would consider the admission of any Jews who might be in the party.

As it turned out, nothing came of the episode: Turkey was not invaded, shipping became even scarcer after the entry of Japan into the war, and as the war lengthened the British government freed up Palestine visas for refugees in transit through Turkey. The conflicting positions of the Army and Interior would have made for an interesting confrontation, however, had things worked out differently. It also posed the question of which Department was in fact running migration, and how far the opinions of one were to be listened to by the other.

Understanding European events: The view from Canberra

The responses of the Australian government to pleas for Jewish refugee admission during the war years need to be placed alongside its grasp of news coming out of Europe at this time. News in Australian government archives concerning the mass murder of Europe's Jews is sketchy, but points to the fact that enough was known at an official level for the government to have a position on the matter. When, for example, an important declaration of abhorrence at the massacres of Jews was issued simultaneously in London, Washington and Moscow on 17 December 1942, the Australian government was quick to associate itself with its sentiments. The Minister for External Affairs, Dr Herbert Vere Evatt, noted in Canberra that the declaration 'condemned the present coldblooded German campaign to exterminate the Jews', while reaffirming the determination of the United Nations 'to ensure that those responsible met with retribution'.[60] A few days earlier, Evatt's Department received a cable from Clement Atlee, then serving as Secretary of State for Dominion Affairs in London, stating that 'we have little doubt that a policy of gradual extermination of Jews except highly skilled workers is being carried out by the German authorities'.[61] Then, a few days after the Allied declaration, the Department of External Affairs received a cable from a Sydney-based import/export firm enclosing a plea from its parent company in Haifa (Palestine):

> Please use all your influence on authorities to save Jewry in enemy occupied countries whose extermination will otherwise be complete before Allied victory. Allied intervention through neutrals, warnings and reprisals are last hope of victims.[62]

Just what the Department of External Affairs could have done, other than to align Australia with Allied declarations such as that made on 17 December 1942, is uncertain. It was considered that the best hope for the Jews lay in an Allied victory, and the Australians were of course thoroughly committed to that. Beyond this, Australia's role could only be defined through such areas as refugee migration and relief. The military or rescue options would have to be undertaken by those closer to the scene – and Australia did not have troops serving in the European theatre.

That said, the Australians were particularly wary when they learned that the Prime Minister of New Zealand, Peter Fraser, had authorized the admission to that country of 700 Polish child refugees in 1944. Given that their arrival had been announced, the Australian Prime Minister's Department contacted Thomas (Tom) D'Alton, the High Commissioner in Wellington, with a request for information as to what arrangements had been made for the transport of these children to New Zealand. This was desired 'in view strong representations made by Jewish Welfare Society for Commonwealth to arrange transport of Jewish children from Western Europe whose admission has been authorized'.[63] The Department of the Interior received a following reply from Wellington a few days later: 'In no circumstances should the fact of [Mr Fraser's] special representations or arrangements made be transmitted to Jewish

Welfare Society. ... Mr. Fraser is most anxious that this information be regarded as strictly confidential.'[64] The Department of the Interior must have found this response reassuring. If news was released that New Zealand had found a way of rescuing several hundred refugees at a time when the Commonwealth was only occasionally handing out individual permits, the embarrassment might well have been sufficient to place the Department under increased pressure within Australia.

Despite occasional incidents such as this, the two main political parties maintained that Australia was doing all it could – even though each held strikingly dissimilar attitudes towards the victims of the mass murders then taking place. At the annual conference of the Australian Labor Party in December 1943, a clear illustration of its position was given when John Curtin dismissed an item from the agenda: a motion submitted by the Victorian executive of the Party seeking national recognition for the Jews at a future peace conference. The offending part of the motion read:

This conference ... declares (a) that the problem of the Jewish people must not be forgotten at the peace conference; (b) that the Jewish people, through their representatives, be accorded an opportunity at the peace conference to state the Jewish aspirations and problems, with a view, if possible, to the difficulties confronting this people being resolved; (c) that to ensure existence and free development of the Jewish people international assistance should be given for the continued growth of the Jewish national home in Palestine by immigration and settlement.[65]

The Argus reported the next day that most of the non-Victorian delegates considered that adoption of this resolution 'would suggest interference by the Australian Labor Party in a matter which was not the concern of the movement or of Australia'. The Premier of Queensland, Frank Cooper, argued that the question was one 'for the Jewish people to decide for themselves.... [F]or centuries they had had the opportunity to build a nation for themselves' but had instead 'preferred to live with other people'. He concluded that 'rich Jews' had no desire to live in Palestine but sought only to settle 'their surplus population there'.[66] The motion was duly withdrawn from the Federal conference agenda, and the ALP, the party in government, did not express its condemnation of the Nazi atrocities then coming to light.[67]

The same could not be said for the conservative United Australia Party opposition, at least if the words of one of its leading members, Percy Spender, are any guide. On 16 May 1943 he made a guest address to the conference of the Zionist Federation of Australia and New Zealand. That he agreed to do this was itself an admission of identification with the Jewish people's hope for a national homeland, but his comments addressed directly the terrible events in Europe which were by now becoming common knowledge:

In all the sadistic barbaric cruelty displayed by our enemies, nothing could be worse than the fate which has overtaken the Jewish people. I wonder whether any of us here, with sunshine and relative security our fortunate lot, can really have any understanding of their plight. … Perhaps it may be that the extent of the disaster which for the time being has overtaken the conquered peoples of the world, for whose liberation we fight, has prevented us from seeing in its true perspective the unbridled fury which the Germans have in particular unleashed against the Jewish people.[68]

In marked contrast to the Labor perspective, and possibly as a belated apology for its earlier position when in office, the UAP did seem at this stage to be genuinely sensitive to the plight of the Jews of Europe. Spender, a member of the Advisory War Council, spoke with authority as a senior Parliamentary frontbencher, and would not have made comments such as these without considering the wider audience. His final words summed up his own position and, it could be suggested, that of much of middle Australia:

We as a Christian people are vitally concerned in the fate of the Jews. The things which we are fighting for, which our young men are laying down their lives for, are the sacred things which give dignity, freedom and purpose to human life. We have witnessed the terrible spectacle of a people who call themselves civilised, who are in fact the scourge of Europe, whose fanatical cruelty is driving them to mass murder in cold blood, men, but not only men, but women and little children of the Jewish faith. Not to be deeply concerned with the fate of the Jewish people would be to deny the cause for which we are fighting.[69]

The Labor and UAP attitude towards the horrors coming to light in 1943 was thus strikingly different. Whether the UAP would have adopted a policy at variance to that of Labor if in office is questionable: its previous record, from 1933 to 1941, does not inspire confidence that it would have done so, but as the alternative government it was certainly making all the right noises, while carefully avoiding any references to migration.

Considerations at the end of the war

In January 1944 President Franklin D. Roosevelt of the United States established in Washington a new body called the War Refugee Board.[70] Its express purpose was to take immediate action for the 'rescue from the Axis Powers of as many as possible of the persecuted minorities of Europe'.[71] In a diplomatic note dated 23 March 1944 from Nelson T. Johnson, the American Ambassador to Australia, the cooperation of the Commonwealth to effectuate this policy was sought. After consultations between External Affairs and Interior, the Australian government conveyed its opinions to the American Ambassador along the following lines: (a) the Australian government sympathizes with the victims of Nazi oppression and is interested in all measures to facilitate their escape; (b) the government is giving active consideration to what its immediate post-war migration policy will be, and reaffirms its preference for taking Europeans; (c) a resumption of the pre-war scheme to accept 15,000 refugees from Nazism is receiving consideration; (d) the Australian government has permitted some 750 refugees ('mostly Jewish'), sent to Australia from Britain for internment, to remain; and (e) the Australian government has an excellent recent record of accepting Jewish refugee children, which it is willing to maintain provided welfare organizations in Australia guarantee the maintenance of any increased numbers.[72] With this, Australia promoted the message that it was already doing as much as it could to alleviate Jewish distress in Europe.

This message was pushed throughout the rest of the year. To cite one example, on 7 August 1944 the Minister for War Organization of Industry, John Dedman, deputized for the Prime Minister in a letter to former Minister for Home Security Joseph P. (Joe) Abbott. Recalling that Australia was a member of the Intergovernmental Committee on Refugees set up after the Evian Conference, Dedman argued that Australia had granted refuge to European immigrants 'on a basis commensurate with national welfare'.[73] There is little doubt that some sectors of the government were sincere in their view that everything was being done in the circumstances and that any suggestions that more should or could be done would be met by reference to the Curtin Labor government's record since assuming office in 1941.

Despite this, it became clear that Australia would need to look at the future of immigration and foreign settlement once the war ended. The trauma of total war, coupled with a well-held opinion that the small Australian population would not have been sufficient to stave off a Japanese invasion had one eventuated in 1942, led to a 'populate or perish' mentality which appeared continuously in letters columns throughout 1944 and early 1945. There was related interest about the economic stimulus an expanded population would give to the development of Australian industry, as well as to a decreased dependence upon Britain and the United States for future defence needs.

These considerations accompanied Prime Minister Curtin when he commenced a trip to the United States, Canada and the UK in April 1944. His primary aim was to attend a conference of Dominion Prime Ministers in London in May, much of which was taken up with discussions relating to Imperial foreign policy, trusteeship of colonial territories and the progress of the war. Yet these were not the only topics on the agenda, and migration was also discussed. Curtin was able to draw on the recommendations of an earlier Australian Inter-Departmental Committee on Post-War Migration, which Cabinet had authorized in October 1943 mainly for the purpose of investigating the feasibility of recommencing large-scale British immigration to Australia. There was little discussion in Curtin's briefing notes about Jewish migration, however, other than a recommendation that the often-discussed settlement scheme in the Kimberley be not pursued in the post-war period.[74] Of deeper significance, perhaps, was a related series of notes drafted by Albert Peters at the request of Senator Collings one year later. It is worth looking at these notes in detail, as they contain much on which future Australian migration policies would be based.

The Inter-Departmental Committee's final report had been read by the then Minister for Information, Arthur Calwell, whose interest in migration would soon see him appointed Australia's first Minister for Immigration. Seeking clarification of several points included in the report, Calwell contacted Collings on 4 May 1945 with a request for information. Peters drafted the reply, 'Notes on Points Raised by Honourable A.A. Calwell – White Alien Immigration.' This was a good indication of how the Department of the Interior viewed matters at the end of the war, at a time when news about the newly liberated concentration camps was dominating public discussion. Regarding refugees (who were not referred to as Jews), Peters wrote:

> Compared with the situation when the decision was arrived at to admit 15,000 refugees spread over a period of three years, the position after the war will be so different that it will be reasonable, and preferable for administrative purposes, to put the former 'refugee' class on the same footing as other Europeans, i.e. to deal with each application for admission strictly on its merits.[75]

In a more general sense, Peters emphasized the necessity of moving 'cautiously' over the admission of aliens from Europe during the early post-war period. In view of the 'changed circumstances', he wrote, 'the admission of the former refugee class should be governed by the same principles as apply to aliens generally', meaning that approvals should be confined 'to those who can be satisfactorily absorbed'.[76] Australia should also proceed with its pre-war plans to establish a migration presence closer to the scene, for one fundamental reason:

> Prior to the war, when many thousands of applications were being received from Europeans of the refugee class for landing permits, it was found very difficult to decide the merits of numerous cases by the applications alone. Some of the most undesirable type of Jewish applicant could make the best show on paper.[77]

Australia should therefore take the opportunity of attaching migration officers to the new legations in Europe which were being proposed as a part of the post-war expansion of the Department of External Affairs.

By 1945, the question of Europe's Jews had taken on a new dimension, as the fate of concentration camp survivors began to be discussed throughout the Commonwealth and elsewhere. This opened a new chapter in the history of the Jews and Australia, but its roots lay within the confusions apparent in the policies of the Australian government during the war years. Was Australia possessed of an antisemitic policy which aimed to keep out all Jews? If so, how could the agreement to admit tiny groups of Jewish children or Polish Jewish adults from Japan be explained? Was the retention of the 'Jewish race' clause in immigration forms intended to assist Jewish entry or deny it? Was the desire to renew and expand British migration in the post-war era planned in such a way as to shut out Jews who were then wasting away in Displaced Persons' camps? The definitive question was whether Australia had done all it could to assist Jews during the war years, and whether the policy of restriction would continue once the war was over.

By and large, the Jewish plight in Europe was kept on the backburner in Australia throughout the war. Sometimes its temperature was raised, but even then, it was through default as the changing circumstances of the war stirred consciences into action. The

Department of the Interior was under considerable strain throughout the war and addressing the overall problems of European Jews was a luxury the Department could not afford. The most realistic appraisal that can be made about Australian Jewish policy during the war years is that the Commonwealth would only act when it affected Australia's interests directly – and even then, there were occasions when it acted too slowly to be effective. As in pre-war times, policy regarding the Jewish situation in Europe was haphazard, uncertain and inconsistent.

CHAPTER 13
NEWS ABOUT THE HOLOCAUST

The Australian newspaper press during the War

Within days of the German attack on Poland in September 1939, the first measures were taken by the invaders against Jews in German-occupied territory. Over the next six years, millions of Jews were killed as a deliberate result of Nazi antisemitic policy, the intention being nothing less than the annihilation of every Jew in Europe. How was this news transmitted to the Australian public? Did the principal vehicle for news dissemination, the newspaper press, publish much in the way of news about the atrocities as they occurred? Indeed, did they themselves know enough about what was going on to be able to inform Australians with accuracy?

An examination of the role of the newspaper press can establish the extent to which the Australian people – including the politicians and bureaucrats – were apprised of the situation in Europe. From that information, it can be discerned how the government responded and, perhaps, what the reaction of the Australian people was.

Consideration will be given here to these issues through a detailed examination of four leading Australian newspapers between September 1939 and May 1945. The newspapers selected for close study, in alphabetical order, are the Adelaide *Advertiser*, the Melbourne *Age*, the Melbourne *Argus* and the *Sydney Morning Herald*. These papers, all morning broadsheets, have been chosen for several reasons. Ownership was an important initial determinant. *The Age* was operated by the family of Ebenezer and David Syme, who owned and ran the paper from 1856 until it became a public company in 1948. It was to a large extent the newspaper read by Victoria's business leaders and educated elite, and thus commanded some degree of influence among those holding sway in the decision-making process. In 1941 it had an average daily circulation of 99,400. *The Argus*, like *The Age*, was the successor of one of the first newspapers in the Port Phillip District and was regarded as the voice of middle-class conservatism throughout Victoria. It had a reputation as a 'cause' newspaper, vigorously crusading on behalf of old-time values, the monarchy, the British way of life and social stability. It was owned by the heirs of early proprietors Edward Wilson and Lauchlan Mackinnon, and, surprisingly for a paper that was such a power in Australian politics and business, was not directly affiliated with any other press organizations until 1949, when it was purchased by the *Daily Mirror* group from the UK. In 1936, Wilson and Mackinnon became a public company; in 1941 the paper had a daily circulation outstripping its rival *The Age*, claiming 108,370 of the morning newspaper market. The two broadsheets were in direct competition; they did not compete with Melbourne's other major newspapers, the morning *Sun News-Pictorial* or *The Herald*, the evening paper.

In New South Wales, the *Sydney Morning Herald*, known there colloquially as the *Herald*, was not faced with a quality broadsheet opposition, and in 1941 had a daily circulation of approximately 225,000. It did, however, find competition from three mass-circulation tabloids (*Daily Telegraph*, *The Sun* and the *Daily Mirror*). The *Sydney Morning Herald* was the oldest ongoing Australian metropolitan daily newspaper, having commenced in 1831. From 1853 it was in the sole control of John Fairfax, and the Fairfax family retained this control for the next six generations. An entrepreneurial family, the Fairfaxes owned a large share of the newspaper market through the acquisition of smaller papers in New South Wales and elsewhere. To a large degree the *Herald* fulfilled the same function in Sydney as did *The Age* and *The Argus* in Melbourne: solid, dependable, middle-class and conservative, it was the paper of choice for the leaders of society in New South Wales.

In the smaller state of South Australia, there were only two daily newspapers, *The Advertiser* (morning broadsheet) and *The News* (evening tabloid). Founded in 1858, *The Advertiser* played a similar role in Adelaide as the broadsheets in Melbourne and Sydney, though this was often enhanced by the fact of there being no mass-circulation morning rival. *The Advertiser* often projected an image that was less formal and more sociable than the other papers, which might also be explained through the relative population size of the city, then slightly less than half that of Sydney and Melbourne. In 1891 Sir Langdon Bonython acquired *The Advertiser*; in 1929 he sold it to a syndicate led by Sir Keith Murdoch, and the Herald and Weekly Times Limited (HWT) – of which Murdoch was managing director – controlled some 40 per cent of the stock. HWT was soon to become Australia's most extensive publishing and communications organization, and *The Advertiser* was able to tap into the resources of other HWT newspapers such as Melbourne's *Herald* and Brisbane's *Courier-Mail*. In 1941 the *Advertiser's* daily circulation was 110,931.[1]

All four newspapers – *The Age*, *The Argus*, *The Advertiser* and the *Sydney Morning Herald* – were members of the Australian Associated Press (AAP) foreign cable service, as well as agencies such as Reuters. Papers in the other capital cities included the *Courier-Mail* (Brisbane), the *West Australian* (Perth), the *Mercury* (Hobart) and the much smaller *Canberra Times*, serving the capital city. All of these had either a relationship with the major papers in Sydney, Melbourne and Adelaide, or shared news from the same overseas wire services (as did papers in the regional centres).

News coming out of Europe often appeared in all papers, word for word, on the same day, though what was taken from the overseas wires was at the discretion of individual editors. Australian newspapers thus had access to the same sources of information, except in those rare cases where individual correspondents had been sent (usually to Britain) or hired overseas. Although they were not necessarily superior to each other in their newsgathering or reporting abilities, their readership was much more influential politically than those reading tabloids. The files of the Departments of the Interior and External Affairs in Canberra show that news clippings were taken most frequently from the four key newspapers in Sydney, Melbourne and Adelaide.

The newspapers did not hold to any unanimous collective viewpoint and operated independently of each other. Editorial policy was firmly in the hands of local editors, and where uniformity of storyline occurred it was most often through coincidence. Thus, sometimes news items pertaining to the Holocaust were published in all four papers, and at other times only in one or two. Occasionally, for months on end, no news about Nazi atrocities was forthcoming at all. From time to time, news about the Holocaust was generated locally, as in cases where rescued Jews who arrived in Australia spoke about their experiences to one or other of the newspapers; but mostly, news came straight from the international cable services. How and where it was presented, how it was headlined and whether it was accompanied by any commentary were all local decisions, and it was these which really determined the image Australians received about the events then taking place in Europe.

Reporting Jewish persecution in Europe

Among the deluge of overseas items swamping Australian newspaper offices in September 1939 came the first indication that the Nazis were going to continue the anti-Jewish policy that had already been so widely reported in the cases of Germany and Austria. On 9 September 1939, towards the end of the first week of war, *The Advertiser* printed in its 'Late Cable' column a United Press story concerning alleged Polish atrocities perpetrated against Germans living in Poland. The correspondent wrote that he had seen twenty-five mutilated bodies of German civilians allegedly killed by the Poles but noted that retribution 'would not be long in coming'; many young Poles were already being rounded up by the Gestapo. This journalist had been struck by one case of mistreatment he had witnessed, when a Polish Jew 'came to headquarters and was kicked and struck with truncheons at the hands of SS men'.[2] Whether this would be an isolated incident, or the portent of things to come, was at this stage not known.

A few days later, however, *The Age* published a feature article on Europe's Jews and their need to find urgent sanctuary. 'Almost every day', the report stated, 'some new horror' was being brought to public notice. As an example, 'a few days ago an obscure paragraph announced that the Gestapo in Prague had ordered the expulsion of the entire Jewish population of the "protectorate" of Bohemia-Moravia at the rate of 200 a day'. *The Age* considered that the hardships ahead of 'these unfortunate Czechoslovak Jews will hardly bear thinking about'.[3]

By early October 1939, further reports of Nazi brutality started arriving. At first, the news was general and not particularly shocking: on 9 October, for example, *The Age* reported that Berlin sources had outlined plans for a new Poland that would comprise about 15,000,000 people and would number thirteen Poles for every one Jew. This suggested that some radical restructuring of Poland's frontiers might take place involving mass deportation and resettlement of the people currently living there.[4] The next day *The Age* reported that 'tens of thousands of Jewish refugees from Germany, Austria and Czechoslovakia ... are being subjected to terrible persecution'. In the Polish countryside,

'German fledgling officers and NCOs are now masters of life and death, and are creating a reign of terror'.[5]

Another report on the proposed restructuring of Poland came on 21 October, when *The Advertiser* published a report from Copenhagen stating that Hitler was about to create a new independent Jewish state 'approximately the size of Bulgaria'. Three million Jews 'from all parts of Poland' would be settled in 'a special State in the east, the capital of which would be Lublin'. The Danish correspondent who first picked up this story commented that the Nazis 'would thus be creating the first Jewish State for thousands of years'[6] – a remarkable piece of journalistic naïveté given what was already known about Nazi attitudes towards Jews.

As news came to light about the horror and tragedy of Warsaw's destruction later in October, Jews were mentioned as being among its victims. On 26 October, *The Age* published an account by two American Quakers who had seen the devastation of Warsaw, in which the 'worst havoc was wrought in the crowded tenements of the old city and the Jewish quarters':

Thousands of bodies were still buried in the debris. The survivors had neither homes, money nor work. The Nazi relief organisation was distributing 250,000 hot meals daily. The Jews, however, got nothing. … Gangs of prisoners and Jews had been impressed to clean up the Warsaw streets. Typhoid was spreading, and water was unfit for use.[7]

This same report was picked up and published by Adelaide's *Advertiser*, though in greater detail. It noted that Hitler's attack on Poland had 'degenerated into the forcible expulsion of Poles from Poznan and Pomerania, to accommodate Germans from Estonia and Latvia', as well as 'the constitution of a Jewish reserve' – not now a Jewish 'state' – at Lublin. Moreover, Jews were no longer permitted to trade in textiles and leather, 'thus imposing terrible hardships, particularly at Lodz, where thousands depended on such work'.[8]

It is interesting, given later reportage of the Jewish situation under the Nazis, that news cables could at this stage still be interested in the way Polish Jews earned their living. This not only brought a human dimension to the Jewish population under discussion, but also showed them to be friends, even allies, in the struggle against the Nazis. The image was reinforced by an AAP report in *The Age* at the end of October, where occupied Poles and Jews were shown to be on the receiving end of particularly nasty German methods of colonization:

Owing to their 'impudent and arrogant' attitude, Poles under new regulations are obliged to leave the pavement when German soldiers and Nazi party members pass. Jews are not allowed on the pavements at all, and are forbidden to possess more than 2000 zlotys. All debts to Jews of more than 500 zlotys have been cancelled. They are not permitted to receive Red Cross assistance or to own wireless sets. Shops are required to serve Germans first, then Poles and Jews last.[9]

There seemed to be genuine shock as the Australian public began to learn not only about the nature of Hitler's victims, but also about Nazi brutality.

The end of the year saw reports of new measures taken against Jews under Nazi control. In early November *The Argus* reported that the Jews of Vienna were being forced out of their homes and sent in daily contingents to 'a reservation in Western Poland'; they were departing in separate batches for men and women, while 'younger children are being left behind temporarily in the charge of the remaining members of the Jewish community'.[10] As part of the restructuring for the creation of 'Lublinland', thousands of Poles were reported as being 'forced to leave their homes', while 'pathetic and sometimes terrible scenes' were being witnessed as the Jews were driven out of Polish areas. *The Argus*, in a report on 8 November 1939, described some of the Jews as being 'manhandled and robbed by German guards', then left to fend for themselves. Their pitiable condition was noticed by nearby occupying Soviet troops, who allowed them to cross the border and seek salvation.[11]

Then, on 21 November, the first report came that the Jews of Warsaw were to be segregated from the rest of the city 'by means of barricades'. This report introduced the people of Melbourne to the word 'ghetto', to describe the isolated section that would be 'strictly controlled' by German forces. This control was made with good reason, for 'the ghetto was one of the most dangerous districts for pests and illnesses'.[12] There was no questioning as to why such pests and illnesses predominated in this district, nor any comment made over the injustice of such segregation. This was to become a major characteristic of how such events were presented to the Australian public, with little in the way of further comment or interpretation. Similarly, a short item in *The Age* on 22 November stated without further explanation that 'the Gestapo at Lodz detained 30 Jews, of whom they executed 15. The others were taken to an unknown destination'.[13] Neither the 'unknown destination', nor the reason for the murder of the fifteen, nor even for the original detainment of the thirty, was discussed; indeed, it probably was not known to the Australians.

The most horrible report to date of Nazi atrocities against Jews came in early December, when *The Age* reproduced a story conveyed through the Jewish Telegraphic Agency at Vilna. The report, in full, read:

The Jewish Telegraphic Agency of Vilna (Lithuania) reports that hundreds of Jews have been executed in the German portion of Western Galicia and that almost all the synagogues have been burnt down. Nazis are reported to have massacred 200 Jews at Dynow and 40 at Usciesolne, near Cracow, whilst they shot 19 at Limanowa. The Jewish communities have been almost exterminated at Cracow, Rszezow, Sanok and neighboring districts. Nine hundred families have been expelled from Sanok, and two synagogues and a religious school have been destroyed. A report from Kaunas (Lithuania) states that 53 Jewish inhabitants of a house in Warsaw have been executed allegedly for resisting German soldiers.[14]

While this account was the worst of its type so far, it was hardly the last. As December 1939 moved into January 1940, new revelations appeared in both *The Age* and *The Argus* concerning mass evacuations and resettlements of both Jews and Poles. An *Argus* headline of 12 January 1940 announced: 'Nazis "Move On" 650,000 Jews/Sufferings Kill Many.' The report explained how 'terrible privations' were being suffered by 650,000 Jews from Poznan and Danzig, who were in the process of being sent to Warsaw and Lublin; hundreds had so far died from cold, hunger and epidemics, while others were being forcibly evicted from their homes and transported to other districts.[15] The report ran an item on the Jews of Berlin, scores of whom had been arrested the previous night for curfew violation. *The Age*, which also published the report on the 650,000 Poznan and Danzig Jews, added something which *The Argus* report had missed: 'It is believed that a similar fate is awaiting Jews all over Germany.'[16] As a news story, the presumed process of resettlement seemed to be building towards something big.

This culminated on 24 January 1940 in an *Age* report following a headline proclaiming, 'Typhus Rages in Poland/Horror Follows Nazi Rule'. Readers were confronted by the following:

> Typhus is raging in Warsaw, Lodz and other towns in Poland. More than 250,000 Jews have died in Poland through military operations, disease or starvation since September, and 2500 have committed suicide. ... Eighty per cent of the 1,250,000 Jews remaining in the German occupied section have been reduced to beggary. The institution of a Ghetto in Warsaw in which 350,000 are crammed in a few blocks, and where half the buildings have been destroyed by bombing and fire, has been delayed because of fear of the epidemic spreading. Corpses are still being recovered among the debris.[17]

Although not accompanied by any editorial comment, this was clearly a shocking account demonstrating that Jews continued to receive harsh treatment and were dying as a result. As if to underscore the point, *The Age* published another account in February 1940 in which it pointed out that Czech, Polish and Jewish workers in German territory were being reduced 'to the status of coolies' by new Nazi decrees on forced labour.[18]

For the remainder of 1940 there was scant news published in Australian newspapers on anti-Jewish measures in Europe. Any such news was forced to compete with events which were far more newsworthy for Australian audiences: the fall of Norway, the invasion of the Low Countries, Italy's declaration of war, the Fall of France and the Battle of Britain. Italy attacked Egypt and Australian troops saw action in North Africa for the first time. Everywhere, the war seemed to be expanding – and not to the advantage of British or Dominion forces. Where European Jews were mentioned at all in Australian papers, it was usually regarding their status in Australia as 'enemy aliens' and, as such, as potential fifth columnists or spies. As the bulk of pre-war refugees had settled in Sydney, it was that city's major newspaper which reported differences in public opinion over the 'enemy alien' issue, particularly in June and July 1940. The *Sydney Morning Herald*, holding true to its pre-war record, maintained its support for the refugees, but there was little space left to also discuss or report on atrocities committed against Jews in Europe.

It should also be recalled that the Australian newspapers were dependent upon the wire services overseas. If no news on the Jewish situation in Europe was forthcoming, the newspapers had nothing to print. And although by now it was apparent that Jews were the victims of atrocities, it was accepted that Europe was in a state of war, that in war people are killed, and that because of Nazi racial ideology it had long been clear that the rights of Jews caught by the Nazis would not be respected. By the end of 1940, a full year of war had already desensitized many people to persecution and horror, and the treatment faced by Jews was regarded as a natural part of the war being fought against a brutal enemy who had also committed atrocities against many others as well. There was, at this stage, nothing seen to be unique about the sufferings of the Jews.

A tiny article in the *Sydney Morning Herald* on 7 January 1941 provides a good example. Quoting London's *Daily Express* Stockholm correspondent – Stockholm then being one of the few neutral windows on the Third Reich – the report stated: 'About 100,000 idiots, incurable lunatics, and hopeless criminals in Germany will be executed in 1941 as part of a programme to exterminate useless citizens,'[19] a reference to the so-called Euthanasia or T-4 campaign, by which the Nazis sought to annihilate those who were physically and mentally handicapped. There was no mention of Jews here, but then, there was no reason for there to be; if the story could be employed as a further example of Nazi barbarity, it did not matter who the victims were. To readers of the *Herald*, the point would be sufficiently made if it was realized that mass killings of obviously innocent people were taking place.

The months of October and November 1941 saw the first extensive coverage of the Jewish situation in Nazi Europe since late 1939. In the meantime, the cataclysmic event known as Operation Barbarossa – the German invasion of the USSR – had taken place, and the scope of Nazi industrial killings had been expanded to far greater dimensions than before. Accompanying the invading German troops were SS detachments known as *Einsatzgruppen*, specifically charged with rounding up and eliminating local Jewish communities in occupied areas; in the months that followed, hundreds of thousands of Ukrainian, Belarussian and Russian Jews were annihilated. News of these massacres took time to reach the West, but the amount of press activity by October 1941 was a clear indication that the Nazis' anti-Jewish persecution was intensifying. The only direct reference to Nazi measures in the USSR came on 22 October, when the *Sydney Morning Herald* and *The Advertiser* both observed that all Jews who had been found in Kiev after its capture by the Nazis had been deported 'to an unknown destination'.[20] It was not known at this time that the 'unknown destination' was a ravine just outside Kiev known as Babi Yar, where, according to the official SS report, 33,771 Jews had been machine-gunned over the two days of 29–30 September 1941.[21] Detailed information of this action only reached Australian newspapers in November 1943, when the *Sydney Morning Herald* reported the Soviet discovery of tens of thousands of corpses in the ravine.[22]

Australian newspapers received information of smaller-scale persecutions which seemed to intensify throughout October 1941. *The Advertiser* reported that in Prague seven Czechs – 'including three Jews' – had been executed.[23] A few days later, *The Argus* outlined that 10,000 Jews living in Bratislava were ordered to assemble for deportation 'to concentration camps in the Slovak mountains'.[24] On 22 October the *Sydney Morning Herald* announced that all adult Jews had been ordered to leave Bohemia and Moravia.[25] It seemed as though the earlier deportation of Polish Jews in 1940 was now being repeated in Czechoslovakia.

This became even more apparent when cables were received from the Polish News Agency stating that 25,000 Jews from Berlin, the Rhineland and Vienna had been deported to Poland. The first arrivals had already been settled in the ghetto at Lodz, and other groups were on their way.[26] Reporting in greater detail a few days later, *The Age* commented that Germany planned to deport 70,000 Jews from Germany by the end of the month, and that before 1941 had finished '196,000 of the 240,000 Jews in Germany and the Czech Protectorate' would have been relocated in Poland and Ukraine.[27]

The month of October 1941 ended with more brief accounts of Jewish deaths. On 24 October, the *Sydney Morning Herald* published an item declaring that 200 Jews had been executed in Belgrade in reprisal for an attack on two German soldiers.[28] On 31 October *The Age* announced (via AAP, British Beam Wireless and Reuters) that over 1,000 Jews had been massacred near the Polish city of Lomza: 'The Jews were ordered to descend into trenches, where they were forced to kneel in rows, three abreast, whereupon they were machine-gunned.' A similar massacre 'of several hundred Jews' had been reported from Rzeszow, in southern Poland.[29]

With massacres such as this, Nazi policy towards Jews had undergone a change from the earlier measures in ghettos. Not only were Jews from Poland being deported to Warsaw, Lublin, Lodz and other major centres, but so also were those from Germany, Austria and Czechoslovakia. A report from mid-October 1941 showed that the Nuremberg Laws on Race were now being applied in the Netherlands, where Jews were being stripped of their civil rights and facing an undetermined future.[30] By the end of 1941 Australians would have reached the conclusion that Hitler was adopting measures against Jews which went beyond brutal occupation policies such as in Poland, Russia, Yugoslavia and elsewhere. From the newspaper accounts it was evident that Jews were being singled out for treatment different to other subject peoples. The next year, 1942, would see the horrible realization of just how different that treatment was.

Witnessing and reporting mass murder

On 27 May 1942, the Reich Protector of Bohemia and Moravia, SS General Reinhard Heydrich, was ambushed in Prague by two Czech agents who had been parachuted into Czechoslovakia by Britain's Royal Air Force. Critically wounded in the attack, he died on 3 June. Even before his death, Nazi retribution had begun, and on 4 June 1942 *The Age* reported that already some 132 Czech citizens had been executed. Those among them included Jews, seven having been killed the day before.[31] At this stage news of Heydrich's death had not yet come through, but in the days and weeks following there were numerous reports in all newspapers of reprisals against Czech citizens – including many Jews – for Heydrich's assassination. And not just Czechs; a report in *The Argus* on 16 June stated that rabbis and other Jewish leaders in Berlin had been informed that 'if any further attempt were made to harm a single German 5,000 Jews in Berlin, Vienna and Prague would be executed'.[32] Even prior to the attack on Heydrich, 258 Jews in Germany had been executed for their alleged complicity in planting five bombs at an anti-Bolshevik exhibition in Berlin;[33] the Nazis were now obviously concerned at any examples of resistance. Although Heydrich's assassins were not Jewish, the blind fury following his death struck at any groups or individuals targeted by the SS.

Much worse was to come. On 17 June, *The Age* relayed a message from Stockholm to the effect that between 7 and 20 May 1942 'the German-controlled Lithuanian police had executed 60,000 Jews at Wilno' (Vilnius). The report stated, matter-of-factly:

the police began persecuting Jews and Poles after an announcement towards the end of April of the so-called autonomous status of the Baltic nations. The Jews were rounded up in a ghetto, and were taken to the suburbs of Wilno, where they were machine-gunned. The victims included women and children.[34]

This report was a forerunner of a more detailed statement a few days later. On 26 June 1942, *The Age* republished a London *Daily Telegraph* story to the effect that 'over 700,000 Polish Jews have been slaughtered by the Germans in the greatest massacre in the world's history'. In the most comprehensive account of Nazi atrocities so far, the report continued:

The Germans are also reported to be carrying out a system of starvation, from which the total deaths are expected to be nearly as high as those from the extermination.

The massacres began in eastern Galicia last year, and the procedure has everywhere been similar. Boys and men, whose ages ranged from 14 to 60 years, are assembled, usually in a public square or a cemetery, where they are knifed, machine-gunned or grenaded after digging their own graves.

The death totals include 300,000 at Wilno and the Lithuanian Kovno district, and 15,000 at Rowne in three nights.

In Chelmno from November to March, 5000 civilians from four towns and 35,000 from the Lodz Ghetto were killed in vans fitted up as gas chambers, into which 90 people were crowded at a time.

Other death totals included Lvov, 30,000; Stanislawow, 15,000; Slonim, 9000; Tarnopol, 5000; and Brzezany, 4000.

In March 25,000 Jews were taken from Lublin in sealed waggons, after which all trace of them was lost.[35]

While most Australians had never heard of these places, the horror of vast numbers of innocent people being killed would have appalled many. For the first time, too, news came of Jews being gassed to death at Chelmno. The story was repeated, in a slightly abbreviated form, by *The Argus* on the same day. It also referred to the massacre as the greatest in history.[36] Becoming aware of further information, *The Argus* reported a week later that in addition to the 700,000 Polish Jewish deaths, fully one million Jews had been wiped out since the war began in September 1939.[37] That figure was again stated in *The Argus* and *The Age* on 7 August 1942.[38] From this time on, there could be no doubt that the worst excesses of Nazi violence were in train, and that Jews were being systematically murdered.

That same day, 7 August 1942, news was published in *The Advertiser* and the *Sydney Morning Herald* of drastic measures being taken against the Jews of France.[39] Basing its information on AAP and a London-based representative, *The Advertiser* began: 'A pogrom as terrible as any in Germany has been launched against Paris Jews.' Thousands of male Jews had been arrested: 'they are believed to have been sent to slave labour battalions in Germany.' This had come about because of Nazi pressure placed on the French collaborationist Premier, Pierre Laval, who had agreed to surrender to the Germans 'all Jews of so-called foreign origin in the occupied zone, and in addition 10,000 Jews from the unoccupied zone.' The report detailed horrible things that were being done to French Jewish children: 'Young children are being torn from their parents and sent to workhouses, where all trace of their identity is being systematically suppressed. ... Jewish children arrested in the big German round-up ... are reported to be undergoing sterilisation.'[40]

The *Sydney Morning Herald* reported the same story, adding that those arrested 'have been flung into concentration camps and left without food'.[41] The *Herald* then responded in a rare editorial on the Jewish situation. There was no point in excoriating the Nazis for these horrors: their actions no longer needed explanation. But the *Herald* was furious at the apparent willingness of the French to collaborate in the murder of Jewish children:

> The horror felt by civilised people at the latest Nazi outrage against Jews will be the greater because a French Government is a party to it. ... The pretext offered that the Jews might support an Allied landing is obviously hollow. To remove all potential aid for a second front in France, it would be necessary to deport most of the French people. The real reason is the Nazis' determination to exterminate all Jews in Europe, and the shame is that any Frenchmen should be aiding this outrage on human liberty.[42]

The ultimate destination of the French Jews had not been announced, but the *Herald* posited that it might be Poland or Russia. And for the first time came the suggestion that this could also be the fate of Jews from other countries such as the Netherlands and Belgium beyond just France, Germany and Austria.[43] Within days this was to be shown to be correct, when *The Argus* published news to the effect that Dutch Jews 'who do not obey immediately the summons to work in Germany will be arrested and sent to a concentration camp at Mauthausen, in Austria'. The report was accompanied by the chilling news that of 1,200 Dutch Jews who had recently been sent to Mauthausen, 740 had already been reported as having died.[44]

While these measures were being carried out, the threat to French Jews was intensifying. A report in *The Advertiser* on 29 August 1942 noted that Jews of foreign nationality who had entered France since 1936 had been rounded up in the unoccupied zone and deported to eastern Europe, while Jews of French nationality were having their names erased from municipal registers, depriving them of the rights accorded French citizens. Prime Minister Pierre Laval, in the meantime, had rejected representations from the Vatican to stop the deportations, sealing their fate.[45]

Returning to Poland, a report on 17 August in the *Sydney Morning Herald* noted the suicide on 23 July of Adam Czerniakow, leader of the Warsaw *Judenrat* (Jewish Council). Having been ordered by the Nazis to prepare a list of 100,000 Jews 'for deportation to an unknown destination in eastern Poland', he had chosen death rather than submit to the Nazi demands.[46] Though not directly connected, the same report also announced the existence in eastern Poland of 'a common grave nearly a mile long containing the bodies of many thousands of Jews who had been massacred by the Germans'.[47]

And so it went on. Although hampered by a lack of information concerning the daily activities of the Nazi extermination machine, enough was revealed throughout the middle of 1942 to indicate to Australians that the wholesale extermination of Europe's Jews was underway. The words 'systematically exterminated' were indeed used in an *Age* report on 26 November, the observation being made that only in Italy, Sweden, Hungary and Switzerland were Jews being spared; the rest were in the process of being annihilated.[48]

By now, an occasional murmur of public disquiet in Australia began to be heard as news of the Nazi atrocities was received. One of the strongest public statements came from the Lord Mayor of Melbourne, Sir Thomas Nettlefold, on 12 December 1942. In a letter timed to coincide with an Empire-wide Jewish Day of Mourning the following day, Sir Thomas addressed the citizens of Melbourne in terms that were both unequivocal and poignant:

> Although the war has blunted our sensitivity to suffering, the magnitude of these horrors cannot fail to stir us to the depths of our being. While the victims of aerial attacks may seek shelter, while the soldier in the front line may fire until he is overwhelmed by sheer weight of arms, Europe's Jews are helpless and defenceless. The most primitive rights and privileges are denied them, and their present terrible fate in the huge concentration camps of Poland and other European countries has no parallel in history.[49]

Sir Thomas Nettlefold was not alone; by 17 December 1942 it was apparent that he had the entire weight of Allied opinion on his side, for on that day a simultaneous announcement was made in London, Moscow and Washington condemning, 'in the strongest possible terms', what it described as the Nazis' 'bestial policy of cold-blooded extermination'.[50]

This was a major statement of Allied awareness of the Holocaust, and had not been made without a painfully long attempt at verification of the news that had been coming from occupied Europe. It was endorsed not only by Britain, the Soviet Union and the United States, but also by the governments-in-exile of Belgium, Czechoslovakia, Greece, Luxembourg, Holland, Norway, Poland, Yugoslavia and the French National Committee (despite Roosevelt's reluctance to recognize it as a government-in-exile). Canada, South Africa and Australia quickly made common cause with the other Allies, though only one of the newspapers under examination here – *The Argus* – reported news of the United Nations declaration.[51] Still, from now on there could be no doubting the Allies' attitude or the kind of language to be employed to describe what was taking place to the Jews under Nazi domination: 'transportation' or 'deportation' to Poland meant extermination. The German authorities were 'now carrying into effect Hitler's oft-repeated intention to exterminate the Jewish people in Europe'.[52] Before the year was out a further report appeared that Axis countries had responded to the Allied declaration by an intensification of their anti-Jewish program, with both Vichy France and Italy announcing further measures against Jews.[53]

The year 1943 began with an *Argus* story about a new form of 'sport' in Hungary, where Jews were being made to run around over minefields to explode undetected mines. A diary, reportedly found on a dead German, confided that such practice was 'great fun'.[54] Other *Argus* reports from January 1943 included one referring to a slaughter of Jews in Tripoli just prior to the German departure from the Libyan capital;[55] news picked up from Zurich that several large convoys of Jews had been transported to the fortress of Terezin (Theresienstadt) prior to their deportation to eastern Poland;[56] and a related report in February declaring that 30,000 Jews from Germany had been killed since 15 October the previous year.[57] On 9 March came one of the first newspaper references to the 'notorious German concentration camp at Oswiecim' (Auschwitz), which had become 'a mass graveyard for Poles', and where 'Mass executions are continually being carried out'.[58]

The month of April 1943 was crucial for the persecuted Jews of Europe. Two major events – the Warsaw Ghetto Uprising and the meeting of Allied leaders at the Bermuda Conference on refugees – both began on the same day, 19 April. Although it had been reported for some time previously that the Nazis had been systematically deporting the Jews of Warsaw, a report in *The Argus* on 20 March attested to the fact that 'Liquidation of the Warsaw Ghetto is being speeded up by the Germans, who intend to empty it altogether and to close it before the spring'.[59] On 19 April the Jewish underground in Warsaw began to fight back, and momentarily turned the Germans onto the defensive. The first anyone in Australia read of a rebellion in the Warsaw Ghetto, however, only came on 24 May, long after it had been crushed and SS General Jürgen Stroop had announced to a relieved Berlin government that the Warsaw Ghetto had ceased to exist.[60]

The same could not be said of the Bermuda Conference on refugees. *The Advertiser* gave a good deal of coverage to the meeting, which was attended by delegates from the United States and Britain. Prior to its commencement, *The Advertiser* reported that there was little information available regarding the scope of the discussions, though it was believed that 'the temporary transfer of large numbers of refugees' could not be achieved owing to a severe shortage of shipping.[61] No direct reference was made to Jews, though it was acknowledged that Britain and the United States might be compelled to seek new havens for 'persons who, because of race, creed or political beliefs, are at present threatened with persecution or extermination by the Nazis'.[62] As it turned out, a pre-conference meeting had agreed that Jews would not be discussed as an issue separate from the general problem of refugees: the conference achieved precious little in the weeks and months following. *The Advertiser* quoted comments from the Bermuda representative of the Associated Press of America that the conference signified 'the impossibility of a large-scale evacuation of Jews and other oppressed people from occupied Europe, because of the transportation problem and difficulty of negotiating with the enemy'.[63]

Australian newspapers showed one area in which practical help could be given to Jews facing death, however, when in early October 1943 reports came that the Nazis had targeted the Jewish population of Denmark as the Holocaust's newest victims. The first report came in the *Sydney Morning Herald* on 4 October, with a comment that Sweden had protested persecution of Danish Jews and offered to provide sanctuary for any who managed to escape.[64] This news was by now old, for the last two days of September and the first two days of October had already seen the quiet smuggling of over 7,000 Danish Jews across the Kattegat to Sweden.[65] The *Sydney Morning Herald*, *The Argus* and *The Advertiser* all carried the story on 5 October, though the Australian Associated Press cable had only quoted 1,000 Jews as having made the escape.[66]

By the end of 1943, most of the Jews caught in the Holocaust had already perished. The year had seen the martyrdom of the Warsaw Ghetto, the abortive Bermuda Conference, the rescue of Denmark's Jews and a vast number of lesser stories which built on what had been revealed during 1942. The news conveyed to Australians was patchy and often out of date, but enough pieces of the jigsaw puzzle had arrived to give a fairly accurate overall picture of what the Nazis had been doing to Europe's Jews throughout four years of war.

By now it had become apparent that Germany was beginning to lose the military supremacy it had enjoyed only a year before. Although the Holocaust – and the war – still had a long way to go, German forces were now in a long retreat that would only end in the ruins of Berlin in May 1945. The piecemeal communique aspect of reportage on the Holocaust was about to end. As the armies of the Soviet Union began to reclaim ground in 1944, discovery of the evidence of mass murder would come to dominate what Australians learned about the Jews. There was to be, however, one major exception: the fate of the last major Jewish community in Europe still untouched by the Holocaust, the 800,000 Jews of Hungary. Their story would be related to the Australian people months after the worst excesses of Nazi violence had already taken place.

The Holocaust revealed

The last eighteen months of the war saw more revelations, beginning at the end of January 1944 with a report stating that more than 3,000,000 Jews had been killed since the Nazi rampage began, with 'not more than a few hundred thousand starving people ... left out of 3,300,000 Jews in Poland'.[67] The portents were not good and seemed to be worsening when news came in March that the Jews of Hungary were now at risk. Germany had occupied Hungary on 19 March 1944, installing a puppet regime under Dome Sztojay as a means of keeping the Hungarians in the war. On 25 March, *The Argus* reported that the Germans were already looking at the future of the Hungarian Jews: the German News Agency had 'boasted' that 'more than 1,000,000 Jews in Budapest will now be "politically and economically eliminated, along with unreliable Hungarian elements".'[68] By now the Australian public could be under no illusions as to what this implied, though there were no further reports about the fate of the Jews of Hungary for another three months. When news did arrive, it came in the form of a verbatim report of an Associated Press of America account published in *The Advertiser*. Although Australian readers had not received any news about events in Hungary, they were treated to the following statement from the American House of Representatives Foreign Affairs Committee:

> Events show that the tide of military battle has turned in favor of the United Nations. Let Hungary at this historic moment stem the tide of inhumanity towards helpless people within her borders.
>
> We are not merely content to speak with horror at the barbarism of the Governments involved. ... We are determined that the criminals guilty of such treatment shall be brought to justice.[69]

To provide a context, *The Advertiser* informed readers that Hungary was mistreating its Jews, and that 'the lives of almost a million hang in the balance'.[70] In fact, mass deportations to Auschwitz had been well underway for over two months prior to this report, and by the middle of July some 400,000 Hungarian Jews had already been murdered.[71] The only news received in Australian newspapers was another report in *The Advertiser* like the earlier one: a statement from US Secretary of State Cordell Hull denouncing Nazi atrocities and noting that 'the entire Jewish community of 1,000,000 persons in Hungary was threatened with execution'.[72] The Australian public would learn no more from its newspapers about the extermination of Hungarian Jewry until after the war.

In January 1944 President Roosevelt of the United States established the War Refugee Board, a government instrumentality intended to find ways of rescuing the remnants of European Jewry.[73] Much later, on 27 November 1944, its reports acted as the foundation for stories appearing in *The Age*, the *Sydney Morning Herald* and *The Advertiser*. *The Age* account, headed 'Death by Torture/An Organised Campaign', told of the atrocities that had been uncovered at Auschwitz-Birkenau, where 'up to 1,765,000 were murdered in ... torture chambers' between April 1942 and April 1944.[74] Referring to the War Refugee Board, the report continued that 'it was an undeniable fact that the Germans deliberately and systematically murdered millions of innocent civilians, Jews and Christians alike, throughout Europe'. The number of deaths transcended that discovered earlier at Lublin,

The Age continued, where the world had been shocked to learn of the murder of 1,500,000 people.[75] The *Sydney Morning Herald* report was identical to that in *The Age*.[76]

The Advertiser's coverage was longer and more detailed. Included with the War Refugee Board story was a report smuggled by the Polish underground to the American Jewish Labor Committee. *The Advertiser* showed that this contained accounts of 'Demoniacal terrorisation and extermination of Jewish men, women and children, including the use of Jewish women as human guinea pigs in scientific obstetrical experiments'.[77] The most pathetic accounts of the fate of Jewish children were then recounted by a woman who had smuggled her observations out to the wider world:

> There were six crematoriums at Birkenau, … and they were always working. One saw every day thick smoke coming from their chimneys. I saw 4,000 Jewish children from Czechoslovakia passed through our concentration camps to be gassed and a quarter of an hour after they had been suffocated they were burning in the crematorium.

> All of them were not actually killed by the gas; they were merely rendered unconscious. Guards ordered the gas to be used sparingly, because it was very expensive. The weaker children were killed, but the stronger ones regained consciousness on the cart taking them to the crematorium, and they were burned alive.[78]

It had been a long time since any of the major Australian newspapers had recounted atrocities committed against Jews so graphically, but the new year would show that this account was but a foretaste of things to come.

By the time of the persecutions against the Hungarian Jews, the extermination camps at Belzec, Treblinka and Sobibor had long been closed. Only Majdenek and Auschwitz remained to carry out the massacres of April–July 1944, but even Majdenek had begun to wind down its operations by the time of the Hungarian operation. Auschwitz now became the sole killing centre, and as the Red Army advanced westward in the latter half of 1944 the position of that camp itself began to look less certain. On 26 November, the evacuation of Auschwitz was ordered for 17 January 1945. When the first Soviet troops arrived on 22 January, there were fewer than 3,000 sick and dying inmates left in the camp.

The prisoners who had been evacuated from Auschwitz were marched westwards, deeper and deeper into Germany and away from the Russians. They joined other inmates then being evacuated from other camps, and while on their journey thousands perished. Dumped down in camps such as Belsen, Dachau, Buchenwald and Mauthausen, there was little they could do but wait for Allied liberation or death. Many had no choice and did not live to see the arrival of American or British troops in April and May.

As the Allied armies swept through Germany in the last days of the war, military correspondents relayed to the world graphic images of what was being uncovered. Sam White, *Argus* special correspondent (engaged by Sydney's *Daily Telegraph*) embedded with the American Third Army, had an account of his observations at the recently liberated Ohrdruf camp published on 11 April 1945. He began:

> This is written for all those people in England who asked me when I was there recently: "Are those atrocity stories really true?" No doubt such people exist in Australia, too. They should have been in Ohrdruf, a village in central Germany, today. They should have been there with 28 Germans of the town whom officers of the 4th Armoured Division took on a tour of a near by concentration camp. This is what the Germans saw as they stepped out of the pine forest into the bright sunshine. They saw lying on the ground the emaciated bodies of 75 former inmates of the camp, some almost nude, some wearing filthy pyjamas, some with bits of blanket around them, and each lying in a pool of congealed blood. The villagers were ... then shown a burial pit near the camp, in which the burned bodies of inmates were dumped after cremation, carried out on grills improvised from railroad rails. About 10 charred bodies were still distinguishable on the grill. According to prisoners who escaped from the camp, nearly 4,000 were burned or buried in the pits. Human ashes were scattered about the edges of the pit, and from one blood-tinged pool of rain water a foot protruded.[79]

White's story was a long one. Readers of *The Argus* were most likely appalled by what they were seeing; people could envisage 75 dead bodies, and the impact would be more telling than the figure of 4,000 that was also mentioned. That the seventy-five were depicted in their appalling condition would also have aroused people's pity – the more so given that, on the same page as this story appeared, was another headline declaring that 'German People are Unrepentant/No Sense of War Guilt'. Within days, newspapers all over Australia were displaying their disgust, whether through editorial opinions, juxtaposition of stories or the writing of emotive headlines.

Soon after the liberation of Buchenwald, for example, *The Advertiser* published an editorial damning the Nazi state which could have created such a place:

> No cure could be too drastic, no purge too violent, for a country in which the infamy of the Buchenwald concentration camp was possible. And Buchenwald, as there is altogether too much reason to believe, merely typifies the Nazi terror. There were dozens of other concentration camps and kindred institutions in which German barbarism found expression in prolonged and systematic atrocities that stagger the mind and sicken the soul.[80]

In a revealing statement, the editor then highlighted the fact that although Nazi atrocities were already known in Australia, no-one had expected the reality to be as reports now coming in revealed:

> [A]s those Allied correspondents know who have seen the Buchenwald camp, in particular, there is no evidence to be compared with that of one's own senses.

Buchenwald is a testimony to Nazi devilry that excludes every possibility of doubt, and admits of no word of palliation.[81]

The next day, 20 April 1945, *The Age* published a London *Daily Telegraph* opinion which said much the same thing: 'Nazi concentration camps have always been a synonym for horrors, but the worst ever reported or imagined about them, is far outmatched by the realities being disclosed daily to the eyes of the Allied troops.'[82] *The Age's* own comment was that 'if all the world's greatest picture-fakers got together they could not produce anything remotely resembling this'.[83] An editorial in the *Sydney Morning Herald* the next day echoed the theme of the German people's moral debasement, claiming that the concentration camps represented 'convincing evidence of national degeneracy'.[84]

On 19 April 1945 it was Bergen-Belsen's turn to receive Australian media attention, with a *Sydney Morning Herald* story of how some of the prisoners, crazed with hunger, had turned cannibal to get something to eat.[85] Then on 21 April, *The Argus* published a feature article on 'How Able-bodied SS Brutes Wreaked the Fuhrer's Will'. Readers were taken on a long tour around Belsen and introduced to some of the inmates who described what life was like in the camp. The article ended with some telling words from the journalist who wrote it, Ronald Monson: 'You might not like to believe this, but I do. Come to Belsen and you will believe anything.'[86] To illustrate the same point, the *Sydney Morning Herald* published a whole page of photographs from Belsen on 23 April, under the heading 'German Camp Horror which has Shocked the World'.[87]

In the last days of April, and then into early May, newspaper reporting evolved into discussions of what should be done with Germany now that the war was coming to an end and the ghastly legacy of the concentration camps had to be addressed. The editor of *The Advertiser* sought justice rather than vengeance, basing himself on St. Paul's admonition to the Romans that this could only be delivered by God (Romans 12:19). There was one concern, though: 'If dispassionate justice only must be done, how, in the circumstances, is justice to be made dispassionate?'[88] Quiet and reasonable consideration of the issues in this matter masked an indignation which seemed both sincere and genuine.

The Argus was nowhere near as controlled, raging against both the Nazis and the German people in evocative terms such as 'Satan', 'the beast', 'monsters', 'devils', 'sadists' and 'demon-ridden'.[89] This anger continued in another editorial a month later. By this time, the first newsreel footage of Belsen, Dachau and Buchenwald had begun showing in Australian cinemas, and *The Argus* – along with other newspapers – urged that all Australians should make a point of seeing them. Such films, *The Argus* warned, were 'not entertainment'; every adult Australian should see them, however, 'as a matter of duty', for if any doubts remained as to the veracity of the stories coming out of Europe these films would convince once and for all. *The Argus* argued that the leaders of the United Nations 'have a solemn duty to spurn maudlin sentimentality and administer stern justice to the Nazi criminals, from the highest to the lowest'. The films coming out of the camps would serve the purpose of alerting public opinion to the truth and help them believe what the written word had told them throughout the war – 'That is why the people should view for themselves the evidence upon which the guilty "master race" is to be convicted.'[90]

Although far from being the last word on the Holocaust reported in Australian newspapers, later references sprang from either of the two strands of revelation or retribution. The war over, it remained for the Allies to determine what would happen next, and in this process Australia's role was to be comparatively puny. There was a good deal of advice proffered, however, *The Argus* in the forefront. So far as the European conflict was concerned, the end had come, and henceforth reconstruction would be the major goal for the Australians. Immigration would play a major part in this, and the newspapers were able to look back on their wartime indignation as a source of inspiration when framing attitudes towards those who would next be allowed into the country. The early post-war period would demonstrate a marked and continuing sympathy for the Jewish victims of Nazism. This was, however, tempered increasingly by a growing distaste at Jewish methods against the British presence in Palestine leading to an obvious confusion in the minds of many over Jewish 'victims' and Jewish 'terrorists'.[91]

What overall conclusions can be drawn about Australian press reporting of the Holocaust while it was in progress? Three major themes stand out. In the first place, given that Australian newspapers were dependent for their news on overseas sources, reports were usually piecemeal, frequently late and often incomplete. The picture that formed for the Australian public was therefore patchy, built over nearly six years of war. It was only when Western reporters could see the evidence for themselves that detailed accounts began to be published in April and May 1945. Stemming from this inconsistent supply of information is the second theme, an acceptance of the stories coming out of Europe despite the relative paucity of information. Often, months would pass without reference to the Jewish situation, but when a spate of reports arrived on, say, the Danish Jews or the deportations to Poland, the newspapers were prepared to publish them and anticipate that they could be contextualized by the Australian public. Perhaps this was due to the final theme characterizing Australian newspaper attitudes: the tacit appreciation of the fact that from 1942 onwards oppression of the Jews formed a distinct element of Nazi policy and was different from other persecutions. Taken together, these three features coalesced into what may be described as an educated – even sophisticated – understanding of what was happening to Jews in Europe between 1939 and 1945.

Where it broke down was in the fact that none of these newspapers on its own provided this understanding. It was only by reading all of them that a broad composite picture could be constructed, and most Australian citizens did not possess the means to do so. There were some in government service, however, who did; the Department of External Affairs kept newspaper clippings on file, as did the Department of the Interior. It was not uncommon for such items to be minuted and discussed, either within Departments or between them. Put simply, it can be concluded that the government Departments, possessing both the means and the need to establish an integrated picture of events in Europe, were apprised from the newspapers – as well as from their own sources – of what was happening to the Jews of Europe under the Nazis.

CHAPTER 14
AUSTRALIANS VIEW THE NUREMBERG TRIAL

The Nazis face justice

By 1945, the situation facing Europe's Jews had taken on a new dimension as the fate of concentration camp survivors began to be discussed. This opened a new chapter in the history of the Jews and Australia, but its roots lay deep within the confusions apparent in the policies of the Australian government before and during the war years. The definitive question focused on whether Australia had done all it could to assist Jews during the Nazi years, and whether it would increase its commitment once the war was over.

The range of policies Australia adopted regarding Jews between 1933 and 1945, which upheld the ideal of a monolingual White Australia, varied between apathy, opportunism, indifference and, on occasion, outright antisemitism. This was exacerbated by the pressures of wartime and fears of invasion, and it was in this context that Australians considered the immediate post-war fate of Nazism and its captured leaders.

Long before the German Army capitulated it had been decided by the Allies that the leading members of Germany's National Socialist government and military forces would be tried for war crimes. Accordingly, on 20 November 1945 the trial of major Nazi war criminals began at Nuremberg in what was termed the International Military Tribunal (IMT). The Allies had broadcast into occupied Europe for years that punishment would be meted out to those found guilty of violating the generally acknowledged laws of war, with warnings having been delivered from as far back as 1941 and on many occasions since.

The defendants were arraigned on some or all the following counts: (1) 'The Common Plan', that is, taking part in conspiracy to commit crimes against the peace, war crimes and crimes against humanity; (2) Crimes against Peace, that is, participating in the planning and waging of wars of aggression in violation of international treaties and agreements; (3) War Crimes, that is, murder and ill-treatment of civilians in occupied territory or on the high seas, deportations for slave labour, murder or ill-treatment of war prisoners, killing of hostages, plunder, exacting collective penalties, wanton destruction and devastation, conscription of civilian labour, forcing civilians to swear allegiance to a hostile Power and Germanization of occupied territories; and (4) Crimes against Humanity, that is, murder, extermination, enslavement, deportation, other inhumane acts committed against civilian populations before and during the war, and persecution on political, religious and racial grounds in the common plan mentioned in count 1. The tribunal sat in the Palace of Justice at Nuremberg during 1945 and 1946.

Despite the avowed purpose of the trials, an impression has developed ever since that their central focus had something to do with the Holocaust and other atrocities committed by the Nazis against innocent populations in occupied Europe. Indeed, these events did form a major part of the indictments and were covered in count 4. Yet right from the outset it is important to record that the IMT was not established to punish the leaders of the Third Reich for the Holocaust.

On the contrary, its main intention was to try those who were held to have been responsible for bringing about the Second World War, and to hold them accountable for all the damage and loss of life that had been caused because of it. Because of the shocking nature of the revelations made during the trials about atrocities committed against Jews, however, Nuremberg came to be seen from an early date as a tribunal judging the anti-human evils perpetrated by the Third Reich. The Crimes against Humanity indictment became the count which most clearly represented the abhorrence held by people around the world at what they understood Nazism to mean.[1]

In view of the Australian public's awareness of the finer details of the Holocaust, how was this event viewed?[2] In what was generally considered to be a momentous trial eclipsing any other ever held, was there much interest shown by the Australian government to the proceedings taking place at Nuremberg? An immediate answer is no, as a thorough investigation of the available government archives reveals that the major focus of attention was directed towards Japanese war criminals rather than Nazis,[3] and that, on those rare occasions where Nazis *were* involved, the Australian government was only interested in relatively junior prisoner-of-war camp officers of German camps where Australian servicemen had been held.[4] So far as the Australian government was concerned, the International Military Tribunal was none of its affair. In fact, even members of the Federal Parliament showed little interest in the proceedings, only one reference being made to the trials – and this, some three weeks after those condemned to hang had gone to the gallows.[5]

That said, there was one tiny aspect in which Australia was represented. As *The Age* reported on 21 November 1945, Australia was 'the first and at present the only British Dominion to appoint a special representative at the tribunal'. Major Joseph Lenehan, an Australian Army solicitor originally from Sydney, had been attached to the Australian military staff in London for the previous eighteen months. At Nuremberg, *The Age* wrote, he 'will be given all the privileges of the highest ranking personages at the trial, and will stay at Nuremberg's Grand Hotel, which is reserved for distinguished visitors'.[6] Lenehan's role would be to assist the British delegation by drawing on his experience gained in the prosecution of Japanese war criminals. *The Argus* reported that 'Although of comparatively low rank', Lenehan was treated as a celebrity 'and has been allocated a seat in the second row of the distinguished visitors' gallery'.[7] While both the Melbourne papers, as well as the *Sydney Morning Herald*, were keen to demonstrate to the public that Australia was an actor at Nuremberg, the reality was that it was only a bit player in a much, much larger drama.

This is not to say that Australians had no interest in the general notion of putting a defeated enemy on trial for war crimes. On the contrary, Australia was at least equal with much larger Powers in prosecuting war criminals after 1945. No less than 275 separate trials were conducted by Australian military authorities in pursuance of the *War Crimes Act 1945*, resulting in 644 convictions and 148 executions. But these were Japanese; if not for the presence of Major Lenehan at Nuremberg, Australia would play no part in the trial of European war criminals.

The fundamental reason for the difference is not too difficult to discern. Although Australia had originally gone to war against Germany, Australian ground troops had not fought in Europe other than Greece and Crete in 1941. They had confronted Germans and Italians in major campaigns in North Africa, and Vichy French in Syria, but the 'real' enemy was always seen as the menace to the north, Japan. It was the Japanese who might have invaded Australia; certainly, they had bombed its towns from the air and brought the war into Sydney Harbour. Most importantly in the public consciousness, the Japanese were responsible for horrific acts against Australians within the theatre of war, such as machine-gunning nurses in the waters off Java, executions by means of beheading, and the perpetration of innumerable and sustained horrors against captured Australian soldiers at Changi, on the Burma Railway and elsewhere. Against this, the crimes of the Nazis, though of course shocking, seemed a long way away. What happened in Europe was terrible, but it happened to other people. The atrocities of the Japanese happened to *us*, and therefore commanded the greatest part of *our* attention, *our* legislation and *our* spirit of vengeance.

For all this, the country's press response regarding the German war crimes issue after 1945 was not the same as the official face. Newspapers saw a story at Nuremberg – a big one. Those responsible for the war in Europe were now being put on trial (apart from Hitler, presumed dead, and Goebbels and Himmler, undeniably so), and all the press outlets realized quickly that this would be far more momentous than the otherwise predictable expedient of punishing Japanese war criminals. There, real questions concerning justice, responsibility and complicity would be explored, and all the world would see the degree to which Nazism should be held accountable for the corruption of Western civilization and the evils perpetrated in its name.

On the opening day of the Nuremberg tribunal, Tuesday 20 November 1945, Adelaide's *Advertiser* published a story from the renowned American correspondent William Shirer. Focusing on the educative aspect of the trials, Shirer observed that:

We Allies can learn much by following the Nuremberg trials.

We can learn why we had to fight this last time. We can learn the real nature of the Germans, who came so close to beating the Allies and conquering the world ... .

How many people sitting in their peaceful, comfortable homes realise even today the enormity and bestiality of the Nazi crimes?[8]

Evidence introduced during the trial would tell them. Earlier, the *Sydney Morning Herald* had introduced a word of caution by noting that 'some way must be found through the absurd technicalities which "fair trial" is allowing defending counsel to put forward',[9] even though, as noted by Perth's *West Australian*, the official Australian position approved the procedure to be adopted by the United Nations.[10]

Revelations at the trial

The first day of the trial was certainly newsworthy. The lead headlines in the major Australian newspapers said it all: 'History's Greatest Trial Opens' (*The Advertiser*); 'Great Nazi Trial to Open To-Day' (*Courier-Mail*, Brisbane); 'Men who Loosed War on Trial' (*The Mercury*, Hobart); 'German Criminals on Trial To-Day' (*The Age*); 'Nazi Gangsters Face Judges' (*The Argus*); and 'Trial of Top Nazis Opened' (*Sydney Morning Herald*). The general assumption was that this would be a mammoth effort in which blame would be fixed on those who had plunged the world into war, and everything else would spring from that.

Editorials in some of the newspapers expressed the hope that the accused would be convicted and suffer the maximum possible penalty. Hobart's *Mercury*, for example, argued that:

the Allies will present a case which rests primarily on the premise that aggressive war is an international crime. … Every individual who can be proved a party to that violation is guilty of the most terrible of all crimes – the crime against peace.[11]

The Argus, in Melbourne, looked at the issue as one of simple morality:

It is fitting that the chief criminals should be tried *en masse*. Whatever their individual guilt – and that is a heavy enough load – their collective responsibility for murder and destruction is symbolic of the beastly organisation that they directed: a system in which the individual is dwarfed by the mass and human ethics are lost in the ramifications of an infernal doctrine.[12]

The Advertiser's editorial referred to the trial as 'the most sensational and significant *cause célèbre* in history', marking 'the slow but inexorable progress of the machinery of post-war justice'. It also acknowledged that the trial was taking the world down an as-yet untrodden path, with no precedent upon which to base itself:

The trial promises to be an extraordinary affair, in a courtroom described as 'a sort of mixture between a cinema and a telephone exchange.' The law that will be administered is a compromise acceptable to Britain, America, France and Russia. The tribunal will be presided over by representatives of these four Powers; even the bench, therefore, will have no common language. To add to the difficulties of the interpreters, evidence will doubtless be adduced in all the tongues of Europe. Proceedings that were slow to begin, will almost certainly be slow to develop.[13]

This drew readers' attention to the dilemmas of a judicial process of this kind, but while guilty verdicts would of course be sought, there was no suggestion that justice would not be seen to be done. A lengthy trial, in which all the legal arguments were canvassed, might well be the best solution. The *Sydney Morning Herald* topped things off with a nicely crafted assessment:

> This is the first time that the primary authors of aggression – the real warlords – have had to answer at the bar of world justice for the misery they caused; there is no modern precedent for the trial of an aggressor nation's leaders. … The trials due to begin today will demonstrate finally that the rulers of an aggressor nation are answerable for the crimes committed in their name, and that even the head of a State can be arraigned as a common criminal and forfeit his life. Hitler has cheated justice, but his henchmen have been brought to its bar.[14]

Sentiments such as these mirrored the superb – and now, legendary – opening words of the United States lead prosecutor at the tribunal, Justice Robert Jackson. These set the tone for the direction the tribunal would take, and are worth repeating:

> The privilege of opening the first trial in history for crimes against the peace of the world imposes a grave responsibility. The wrongs which we seek to condemn and punish have been so calculated, so malignant, and so devastating, that civilization cannot tolerate their being ignored, because it cannot survive their being repeated. That four great nations, flushed with victory and stung with injury stay the hand of vengeance and voluntarily submit their captive enemies to the judgment of the law is one of the most significant tributes that Power has ever paid to Reason.[15]

Although Jackson's primary concern lay with the guilt of the Nazi regime for its waging of aggressive war, his comments regarding the Jews showed both his awareness and his rage. Noting that 'The most savage and numerous crimes planned and committed by the Nazis were those against the Jews', he drew attention to the fact that there was 'a plan and design, to which all Nazis were fanatically committed, to annihilate all Jewish people'.[16] The crimes in question 'were organized and promoted by the Party leadership, executed and protected by the Nazi officials', leading to persecution that 'was a continuous and deliberate policy'.[17]

Shocking revelations concerning Nazi Jewish policy began coming to light in court on 27 November 1945. Press headlines in Australia ranged in their coverage of the topic. While the *Sydney Morning Herald* led with 'Nazi Leaders on Jew-Baiting', *The Age* headed its story 'Diabolical Nazi Plan to Eliminate Jews'.[18] The story was identical in both cases and concerned a verbatim record of a meeting of high Nazi officials presided over by Hermann Göring held in Berlin on 12 November 1938 (two days after *Kristallnacht*). The reference was to the elimination of Jews from German economic life at that time, rather than its ultimate expression during the war, which was by now well known to Australians.

Much worse concerned the screening of so-called horror films at the trial, as reported on 29 November 1945. Both the *West Australian* and the *Canberra Times* referred to the court seeing films showing 'thousands of corpses rotting in Nazi concentration camps and S.S. men beating helpless women and children'.[19] With this report, the perception that the accused were on trial for the war alone diminished; henceforth, it would be assumed that the tribunal was also sitting in judgement on a system allowing for brutality and degradation against innocent people who had been singled out by the Nazis for such hideous treatment.

The theme of concentration camp horror films persisted in the Australian papers for several days. The *Sydney Morning Herald* sought to convey to its readers a spirit of what was being shown to the court and referred not only to the individual camps highlighted in the films, but also to some of the crimes that took place in them. On 1 December 1945 it also recounted some of the responses of the accused as they sat and watched these films.[20] Newspapers in other states examined the same responses, quoting the observations of two Allied psychiatrists present in Nuremberg. The consensus was that the Nazis were shamed by what they were viewing. While not stating it outright, there was an implication that this was the effect the prosecution sought. *The Age* and *The Mercury* both noted that:

All the defendants were obviously affected. The majority felt profound shame at what they realised was Germany's disgrace before the world.

The accused mostly reacted with amazement and depression, and showed the effects of severe emotional strain.[21]

A few days later, as part of a more general report on Nuremberg, the *Canberra Times* noted that the Allies had located the wife of Rudolf Franz Hoess, former commandant of Auschwitz, 'with a house full of clothes and jewellery taken from Jews sent to their death in the Auschwitz gas chambers'.[22] The alignment of the Holocaust with the International Military Tribunal was becoming more apparent as each day dawned.

As the tribunal moved during December 1945 to the involvement of the SS, its role was highlighted in the Australian press. Hence, on 5 December, the *West Australian* published details of a concentration camp in Poland 'where Germans were said to have made soap from human bodies and purses and ersatz leather goods from human skin'.[23] In the middle of the month, a number of similar reports came in concerning evidence presented of a shrunken human head and a piece of human skin that had been taken from the Buchenwald concentration camp.[24] These items, however, were but a prelude to news of the prosecution's case regarding the systematic mass murder of Jews, reported from 15 December onwards. Quoting a series of German documents released at Nuremberg, several Australian newspapers outlined the details of 'a calculated plan to starve millions of Jews to death by shutting them off from supplies and stopping them working land from which they might get food'.[25] Under the heading 'Done to Death/6,000,000 Jews', the *West Australian* printed a story in which an affidavit from SS General Wilhelm Hoettl stated that he had helped to compile a report for Heinrich Himmler 'estimating that the Germans had killed 6,000,000 Jews in Eastern Europe'. Further references were made in the story to the 1940 Madagascar Plan for the Nazi resettlement of the Jews, and to Himmler's wish to kidnap 'Aryan-looking' children 'from inferior faces' [sic].[26]

Further stories were accompanied over the next few days by a retrospective on Nazi antisemitic policy during the 1930s. In what was clearly a mistake, all newspapers carried the account of US prosecutor Colonel Robert Storey, who referred to the *Kristallnacht* pogrom against Jews taking place in Germany on 9 October 1938 (rather than the correct date of 9 November). These accounts were harrowing.[27] To a reader perusing the morning paper, there could be little doubt as to what *Kristallnacht* represented: all one needed to do was consider headlines such as 'Murder of Jews was Condoned'[28] or 'Organised Murder/Hounding of Jews',[29] and it was apparent that a deliberate policy rather than a spontaneous outburst was under discussion. The point was reinforced when newspapers followed these stories with references to the destruction by the SA of thirty-five German and Austrian synagogues in a forty-eight-hour period.[30]

Adelaide's *Advertiser* then weighed in with a report on further concentration camp atrocities, and immediately prior to the court going into a Christmas recess told of Gestapo methods against Jews in Ruthenia in October 1941, where a senior German officer had complained about the burial of seriously wounded Jews who were not yet dead. It was, the officer exclaimed in a written report at the time, 'such a base and filthy act that the incident should be reported to the Führer'.[31] *The Mercury* and other papers were able to add numbers to this grisly anecdote, quoting 'liquidations' in which 37,180 Jews had been killed; another 3,145 Jews had been shot in Zhitomir in Ukraine because 'they were regarded as carriers of Bolshevik propaganda and saboteurs'.[32]

The revelations continued when the court resumed in early January 1946. In the first report, *The Advertiser's* headline captured the essence of what was to come: 'S.S. Reign of Terror/Mass Slaughter of Jews'.[33] With gripping detail, the report outlined the testimony of SS General Otto Ohlendorf, Himmler's chief of security. Under cross-examination, Ohlendorf revealed the nature of Jewish murders by means of gas vans in Poland and Russia and admitted that it was his idea to institute a policy of deception so there would be no panic among the victims. A few days later further murderous images were reported, as testimony was taken of conditions at the Mauthausen and Natzweiler concentration camps, as well as in German-occupied Oslo.[34]

While reports on Nuremberg in Australian newspapers focused on the complicity of the Nazis in promoting war, nonetheless for many Australians the Crimes against Humanity indictment was now synonymous with Nazism. As early as 1 March 1946 an *Advertiser* editorial, commenting on the fact that the prosecution's case had closed, offered the following insight:

> It is quite unnecessary to say that no other story was ever related. No comparable horrors were so much as dreamed of, indeed, in the pre-Hitler era, even in a criminal lunatic asylum. ... Even today, after three months of proof officially produced at Nuremberg, it is difficult to believe that the worst of the Nazi atrocities

are more than an abominable nightmare. The normal human mind does its best to reject the conclusion that men could ever have been so infinitely vile. It is the virtue of Nuremberg that it sternly forbids incredulity and denial. The evidence has been as overwhelming as it has been revolting.[35]

This summarized the Australian public's position generally. The Nazis in the dock were guilty of deliberately planning and starting the war, and for all the death and destruction brought about because of it. As Justice Robert Jackson stated in his closing argument in words that were as unequivocal as they were brilliant:

It is against such a background that these defendants now ask this Tribunal to say that they are not guilty of planning, executing, or conspiring to commit this long list of crimes and wrongs. They stand before the record of this trial as blood-stained Gloucester stood by the body of his slain King. He begged of the widow, as they beg of you: 'Say I slew them not.' And the Queen replied, 'Then say they were not slain. But dead they are … ' If you were to say of these men that they are not guilty, it would be as true to say there has been *no war,* there are *no slain,* there has been *no crime.*[36]

That included the annihilation of Europe's Jews – a conclusion that did not need to be stated as it was obvious to anyone who considered the issue.

For at least one man, however, the issue was not so straightforward. The words of the American Associate Counsel at the International Military Tribunal for the Far East, Owen Cunningham – who served as Defence Counsel to the former Japanese Ambassador to Berlin, General Hiroshi Oshima – were reported at length in Brisbane's *Courier-Mail* on 28 September 1946. This was only days before the IMT at Nuremberg was due to hand down its verdict. Cunningham's comments, reported around the world, must have come as a shock to many in Australia who had followed the trials and who believed they were witnessing the pursuit of true justice:

The Nuremberg court was not much interested in the discussion of legal propositions. The full theory of rule by law, rather than rule by force, has taken a holiday as in few other periods in our history.

If there were no Jewish question and no persecution of minorities, there would not be a very strong case against the German accused. Otherwise this war was not much different from hundreds of others.[37]

These were startling comments, to say the least, and certainly the first words of dissent over Nuremberg that had been displayed in the Australian press since earlier debates over what the fate of arrested Nazi leaders should be. The *Courier-Mail* was the only major Australian paper featuring Cunningham's outburst in any detail. Hobart's *Mercury* quoted London's *Daily Mail* correspondent on the story but did not provide the content of Cunningham's statements other than to say that some in official circles regarded them as 'highly indiscreet'.[38]

Australians assess the verdicts

When the judges of the International Military Tribunal handed down their decision at the beginning of October 1946, there were few surprises. Six of the accused were found guilty on all four counts and sentenced to hang; another six were similarly sentenced after having been found guilty of some of the counts. Those sentenced to be executed were to die by hanging. They were Hermann Göring, Joachim von Ribbentrop, Wilhelm Keitel, Ernst Kaltenbrunner, Alfred Rosenberg, Hans Frank, Wilhelm Frick, Julius Streicher, Fritz Sauckel, Alfred Jodl, Artur Seyss-Inquart and Martin Bormann (*in absentia*). Others received long prison terms ranging from life to ten years: Rudolf Hess (life), Erich Raeder (life), Walter Funk (life), Albert Speer (twenty years), Baldur von Schirach (twenty years), Konstantin von Neurath (fifteen years) and Karl Doenitz (ten years). Three of the accused, Hjalmar Schacht, Franz von Papen and Hans Fritzsche, were acquitted and after some delay, released.

In Adelaide, *The Advertiser* was meticulous in summarizing each individual sentence, as well as in describing the scene at Nuremberg as the verdicts were read out. Of greatest interest was its editorial comment, in which it argued that the trial had given the Nazis the fullest opportunity to defend themselves during a process in which a genuine attempt had been made by the Allies to render the day of reckoning a day of justice as well.[39] The paper summed up its position as follows:

> The guilt of these blood-stained men, who, with the justice-cheating Hitler, became living symbols of hatred, terrorism and violence, and who plunged the world into six years of unexampled human misery, has been established beyond the shadow of doubt. There will be little pity for them, now that retribution has finally overtaken them at the bar of world justice. Any vestige of sympathy for them can hardly survive the memory of concentration camp bestialities, of annihilation on an unparalleled scale, of the horrifying treatment of slave laborers, of the loss of millions of lives and the ruination of millions of homes, and of the impoverishment of whole States.

The editorial then concluded with an attempt at a last word on the matter:

> The fate of these men as individuals is now of little consequence to the world. There is no doubt, however, that the trial has been of immense value, not only in placing on record the criminal nature of the Nazi regime, so that its terrible lessons may be learned by mankind, but in creating international machinery which must help to promote the cause of peace. The trial represents a significant contribution to the law of the future world community.[40]

There was no doubt that Nuremberg resulted in landmark judgements. Never had a tribunal of victor nations sat to deliver verdicts over a vanquished foe, and never had there been such a vast set of compromises made across often competing legal systems to reach a convergence of opinion.[41] In rendering its decisions, the tribunal reached three important legal milestones. First, it rejected the contention that only a state could be found guilty of war crimes, arguing that crimes of international law are committed by people rather than states, and that only by punishing the individuals who commit them can international law be enforced. Second, it rejected the argument that it was an illegitimate court because it was sitting *ex post facto*. The acts being tried had been regarded as criminal before the outbreak of war and had continually been drawn to the attention of Germany and its allies throughout the conflict. In this context, the accused were answering for crimes against existing international law. Finally, the International Military Tribunal rejected the defence that obeying superior orders was legitimate, provided a moral choice was available. The tribunal held that there are certain standards in Western society to which everyone must adhere, and that one of the cardinal rules in this regard is that obeying criminal orders renders the perpetrator just as guilty as the person giving the order. This finding, the so-called Nuremberg defence, has since become one of the major legacies of the trials handed to posterity.

The tribunal's major objective was to bring to justice those who had upset the international order by waging aggressive war – not those who had expressly committed crimes against humanity and war crimes. That these took place during the Nazis' war only served to highlight further the criminal nature of the regime, but nothing was seen in the first instance as being more criminal than the foisting of aggressive war upon a world which had been clearly committed to avoiding it.

A few days before the scheduled execution of the condemned Nazis, one of the very few public pronouncements on Nuremberg by a major Australian public figure was made when the Catholic Archbishop of Melbourne, Dr. Daniel Mannix, expressed the view that carrying out the death sentences might have the effect of making the Nazis into martyrs for the German people. His preference was that they avoid the noose, and instead be sent 'to a place where they would be harmless for the rest of their lives'. This Napoleonic solution should be taken in view of the fact that 'the Germans were not alone in their guilt of murder and rape', and that – in a direct slap at the Soviet judges on the tribunal – 'some of the people who sat in judgement might have been trying their own nationals'. Archbishop Mannix finished his statement by venturing the opinion that 'extreme penalties did not always bring about the desired end'. His speech, reported in *The Age*, was made at the opening of a new church hall in the small rural town of Drysdale, in Victoria.[42]

Others may have agreed with Archbishop Mannix, but such expressions rarely made it into the opinion pages of the newspapers. Only Melbourne's *Argus* allowed free rein in the letter columns, and this took the form of claims that the execution of convicted criminals either was or was not in keeping with Christian doctrine. One letter-writer, a clergyman, ventured the comment that the execution of the Nazis 'would not deter others from doing what these men have done'[43] – a clear refutation of the point regarding deterrence that had been made on many occasions by others during the trials.

The revelations about the Holocaust were a centrepiece of the evidence presented during the trial. They were crucial to the prosecution's case concerning the indescribably brutal nature of the Nazi regime and were of course locked directly into counts 3 and 4. The alignment of Jewish horrors with the IMT became closer as each new day dawned. News of Nazi atrocities was broadcast all over the world and rapidly became the central theme justifying Nuremberg.

The editorials appearing in Australian papers after the verdicts had been handed down all shared the view that Nuremberg represented a landmark in world justice, and that here was a real mechanism for the pursuit of international peace in the future. Almost alone among the major Australian newspapers commenting specifically on the Nazi genocide of the Jews, however, was the *Sydney Morning Herald*, which referred to it in an editorial on the day of the executions. Among other things, the *Herald* remarked:

> At the patient and impartial trial which, to their own surprise, they were accorded, their real accusers were not the Allied prosecutors but the six million Jews whose extermination they sanctioned, … the men and women of Belsen, Buchenwald and Dachau. The evidence against these evil men, with its record of murder and torture coldly employed as instruments of German policy, is so terrible that the human mind finds it hard to compass its enormity. There can be no pity to-day for those who knew no pity.[44]

Few newspapers approached the stance of the *Herald* in its articulation of this point. Brisbane's *Courier-Mail* noted simply that the doomed men 'had to die because they were once so powerful in Nazi Germany',[45] while the *Canberra Times*, furious at the suicide of Hermann Göring just hours before he was due to hang, used the opportunity presented by the Nazi executions to ask for like treatment to be also handed out to the Japanese.[46] The trials and the executions, once over, were then allowed to fade away – their message not lost, but put to one side until some future occasion.

Assessing the overall position of the Australian press regarding the International Military Tribunal leads to the conclusion that the whole process provided both good copy for the newspapers and an opportunity to pronounce upon the evils of Nazism, while simultaneously reinforcing the absolute integrity of the Allied cause throughout six years of war. Further, as the Australian newspapers had been dependent upon external sources for their foreign news, from the end of the war onwards the major papers began employing their own correspondents at key overseas postings. The days of a full-scale foreign bureau were a long way off, but the war years broke forever the previously total Australian reliance on overseas sources to inform readers of what was happening in other parts of the world. Nuremberg provided a good testing-ground for this; several papers had correspondents covering the trials, while others employed local stringers to do on-the-spot reporting on their behalf.

It should be emphasized that the Australian newspapers were able to express their views based on sound information (for the most part) and the understanding that they were communicating with an enlightened readership. The six years of war had prepared Australians well for appreciating Nuremberg, particularly, though not exclusively, in matters concerning anti-Jewish atrocities. Australians were by now quite clear about what the Holocaust was, and what it represented *vis-à-vis* Nazism and the evils that had originally propelled them into the fight way back in September 1939. With the execution of the leading Nazis on 16 October 1946, however, the curtain came down on this phase of reportage. Henceforth, attention was directed elsewhere – to atomic arms development, to the Chinese Civil War, to the struggles of the Dutch in Indonesia – such that news having nothing to do with Nazism or Europe now began to come into its own.

If the newspaper press comes out of the whole process looking good, the same could not be said for the Australian government. For long an opponent of Jewish refugee migration, the aftermath of the Holocaust may be classed as a period during which the official Australian position was one of sympathy for Europe's Jews coupled with a preference not to become too committed to any single stance relating to their deliverance. The admission of any Jews after 1945 would be such a departure from all previous policy as to appear an aberration over what had been the case before the war.

The newspapers' indignation at the Nazi horrors, and their subsequent coverage of the Nuremberg trials, thus served the government's needs to the letter. Attention could be directed away from the Commonwealth's poor pre-war record by focusing on wartime Germany. Moreover, the very ideals which formed so much a part of how Australians saw themselves, such as fair play, equality for all, a helping hand and comradeship, could all be worked on in government citizenship campaigns through pointing to Nazism as the antithesis of everything Australia stood for. Such a technique worked brilliantly. The aftermath of the Second World War saw an urgent desire on the part of Australians to settle down, raise families, realize the Great Australian Dream of home ownership, reinforce a patriarchal nuclear family structure, and create a stable domestic environment in which everyone knew their place and was happy to stay there.

Awareness of Nazi atrocities, when coupled with Australian understandings of what was at stake at Nuremberg, combined to show the population why democracy – even at its worst – was better than dictatorship at its best. By shifting attention from Australia's previous record, moreover, this appreciation was also eminently suitable for further transformation into a rationale for confronting dictatorship (now converted into expansionist Soviet communism) wherever it appeared. Even as the Nuremberg tribunal was sitting, the Cold War was beginning to take shape in the polarized attitudes of the major Australian political parties and the phenomenon known as 'modern Australia' was commencing. The understandings coming from the Second World War, no less than the trauma of fighting it, were to leave Australia totally and permanently changed in the decades to come.

CHAPTER 15
AFTERMATH: THE HUNT FOR NAZI WAR CRIMINALS

Post-war immigration and displaced persons

When the Australian mainland was attacked from the air and sea by the Japanese during the war, fears of the white Australian population being swamped by an Asian enemy, prevalent throughout the previous 150 years, seemed about to be realized. With victory, hopes to meet any such future challenge were summarized by Arthur Calwell, the Minister of the newly created Department of Immigration, in a speech in 1947: 'We must populate or we will perish. ... We must fill this country or we will lose it. We need to protect ourselves against the yellow peril from the north.'[1] Earlier, in 1945, Calwell had written that the nation's first task 'is to ennoble motherhood',[2] but Australian birth-rates were low and not about to rise suddenly. This led to a second preference – a vast post-war immigration programme ideally composed of British and Irish settlers, who would be given preference to arrive and settle through the provision of assisted passages to Australia.

Despite the incentives, it was soon apparent for various reasons that British and Irish immigrants were not arriving in anywhere like the desired numbers, and a third option was set in motion: the encouragement of racially and politically desirable continental Europeans. Given the concerns that were so frequently expressed about European aliens before the war – and the uncertainties regarding all foreigners during it – selling the idea to the Australian public was not going to be an easy proposition. In the immediate short term in late 1945 discussion on this could be avoided by reference to the need for shipping to repatriate Australian military personnel from overseas, but this could not last long. The pill could be sugared through reference to Europeans who had served as allies during the war; but most of those were Poles, and the Australian public had a memory of Poles as immigrants from before the war that was far from positive. There were others who had been victims of German occupation, but while these included Dutch citizens, they also included Greeks and Yugoslavs – hardly the blond and blue-eyed ideal so often extolled earlier. A further alternative existed, however, as Calwell informed Parliament on 25 September 1945: 'There are at least 1,000,000 people who have left the Baltic states of Latvia, Estonia, and Lithuania. In Sweden and Norway also, there are great numbers of people who would make admirable Australian citizens.'[3]

At the same time, a genuine concern surfaced regarding the fate of those who had survived the Holocaust. In February 1945, even before war's end, the Executive Council of Australian Jewry, a roof body established in August 1944 to represent the interests of Australian Jews nationally, submitted a memorandum to Prime Minister John Curtin seeking government approval for the admission to Australia of Jewish survivors on a humanitarian basis.[4] On 22 August 1945, Arthur Calwell issued a directive that 2,000 landing permits would be made available for close relatives of Jews already living in Australia.[5] These would be limited to parents, siblings and children then in Europe, and would be admitted 'provided they had spent the war years in Europe in concentration or forced labour camps or had been deported from their usual place of residence or had carried on a clandestine existence in occupied Europe'.[6] Added conditions were that guarantors in Australia had to underwrite those admitted for a period of five years after arrival; that the government would not provide any shipping assistance; and that priority transportation would be given to returning ex-service personnel.

While this was a positive step, it was not met with acclamation from some sectors of the Australian population. Despite the challenges of wartime, the old arguments relating to assimilability resurfaced, posing a problem for the government as it approached a Federal election called for 28 September 1946. Given mounting public opposition to the arrival of Jewish refugees, continuation of the humanitarian programme became an election issue. Although the government won the election by a landslide, the programme did not survive, and was abandoned on 23 January 1947. Henceforth, Jewish immigrants were subject to the same rules for entry as everyone else, with one condition: from February 1947 onwards, ships leaving Europe for Australia were to contain a manifest numbering no more than 25 per cent Jews on board.[7]

With the end of the war, more than eight million people throughout Europe found themselves displaced from their homes, including more than 250,000 Jewish Holocaust survivors. Many had either no homes to which to return, no countries who wished their return or did not themselves seek to do so. How to house, clothe, feed and provide medical services (both physical and psychological) became an Allied nightmare. As a way around this, so-called Displaced Persons (DP) camps were established throughout Germany, Austria, Italy and other countries formerly occupied by the Nazis. At their maximum level of operation, those housed in the camps included Armenians, Croats, Czechoslovaks, Estonians, Greeks, Latvians, Lithuanians, Poles, Russians, Serbs, Slovenes, Ukrainians and Yugoslavs. The plight of the Jewish refugees, however, often saw them in the same camps, where antisemitism grew, up to and including violence. Ultimately, in many situations, this necessitated their segregation into separate accommodation.

On 1 October 1945 the United Nations Relief and Rehabilitation Administration (UNRRA) took charge of camp activities. Relatively quickly, once camp life assumed a reasonable measure of stability and routine, the residents themselves were hard at work, establishing temporary synagogues and churches, newspapers, and cultural and educational endeavours. Yet these remained stop-gap measures (though all too often, lasting for lengthy periods). The preference for many was emigration away from Europe, and to secure homes elsewhere.[8]

For Calwell this provided an excellent opportunity to pick and choose the 'best' immigrants, and in July 1947 the Australian government entered into an agreement with the International Refugee Organisation (IRO) according to which Australia agreed to accept 4,000 DPs for the remainder of the year, and another 12,000 during 1948.[9] The Australian government sent officers to Europe to scour the camps and select those who were suitable for migration. These did not include Jews, who the government 'secretly sought to exclude … out of fear that they would not fulfil their two-year work contract'[10] (one of the criteria for acceptance). When Australian Jewish leaders protested to Calwell about Jewish DPs being deliberately excluded from the IRO scheme, he assured them that this was an unfortunate oversight but would be corrected. As shown by historian Suzanne D. Rutland, 'this assurance did not eventuate'. Jewish DPs, she affirms, were excluded 'completely'.[11]

Over the next few years Australia would accept a disproportionate share of IRO refugees, adding to the many thousands who arrived from various European countries as immigrants rather than refugees. Populating the country was much more than an ideal: it was fast becoming a reality in which the 'New Australian' took his or her place alongside older Anglo-Australians. As historian Ben Shephard has concluded:

> After the improvised beginning, Australia adopted a far more aggressive and successful strategy for luring DPs (the right kind, of course) to immigrate. Books, pamphlets, films, and posters were distributed around the camps extolling the wonders of Australia as a land of good wages, housing, food, fine weather, and so on. All that was required was that the prospective immigrants meet age and health criteria and remain for two years in the type of employment selected for them.[12]

From the end of the war in 1945 until December 1951, the overall Australian population grew from 7.4 million to 8.5 million, most of the increase due to migration.[13]

For all this growth, however, there was a catch: in their keenness to attract migrants, the Department of Immigration under Calwell and his conservative successor from the Liberal Party, Harold Holt, was not always scrupulous when it came to screening the pasts of those it was so keen to allow in. Government policy was that 'in theory both war criminals and Nazi collaborators were barred from the benefits of immigration to Australia', but there were various ways in which 'it proved easy to circumvent the restrictions'. Australian politicians and officials, it has been argued, 'did not implement effective procedures to exclude was criminals, 'often deliberately turning a blind eye and even denying the facts known to the authorities'.[14] The immigrants themselves often lied about their wartime activities during the entry screening process as well as on official documents and in interviews. When queried as to their activities during the war, they most frequently claimed to have been subjected to forced labour and deportation to Germany. Since a great many of those seeking entry came from countries that were now behind the Iron Curtain, they were viewed as likely to be anti-communist, and thus acceptable politically given the Cold War context of the time. It has been concluded that 'ill-informed and blinkered Australian politicians and officials did little to question or probe their credentials and histories'.[15]

Despite restrictions, bureaucratic delays and the shortage of migrant ships, estimates suggest that between 1946 and 1954 some 16,300 Jews arrived in Australia.[16] Most succeeded in rebuilding their shattered lives, sometimes in dramatic and extraordinarily successful ways. Yet even within this environment, ongoing rumours regarding the arrival and acceptance into Australia of Nazi perpetrators of the Holocaust persisted. Six months after the DP scheme commenced in 1947, the Commonwealth Investigation Service (CIS) – the successor to the Commonwealth Investigation Branch and the forerunner of the Australian Security Intelligence Organisation – alerted Calwell that enquiries 'suggested that some DPs were former SS men'.[17] At this, Calwell flew into a rage, describing the allegation as 'a farrago of nonsense'.[18] The head of the Department of Immigration, Tasman Heyes, wrote to the CIS that investigation of all prospective migrants was a matter for his Department, not of Security. Further, any hasty conclusions 'do much harm not only to worthy people but also to our immigration plans'.[19]

The idea of upsetting the grand migration scheme was uppermost in the mind of both Arthur Calwell and Harold Holt. Each turned a blind eye to the possibility of war criminals having entered Australia as part of the post-war migration programme. For Calwell, 'the issues at stake were far too important to let a few "bad apples" disrupt a program which could secure the very existence of a prosperous and basically "white" Australia'.[20] Where Holt was concerned, by 1950 the economic benefits of widespread immigration had begun to make themselves felt, to say nothing of ensuring that anti-communists predominated among the migrants. Upsetting the programme was clearly anathema, and so, whether because of deliberation or inefficiency, former Nazis and war criminals arrived in Australia during the late 1940s and early 1950s.

The Menzies Inquiry

On 25 January 1990, a resident of Adelaide, Ivan Polyukhovich, was arrested by Australian Federal Police on a charge of killing 25 men, women and children and being involved in the murders of some 850 Jews during the Second World War.[21] In many respects it was the culmination of a process that had begun four years earlier, prompted by the research of an Australian investigative reporter.

Mark Aarons, a presenter of radio documentaries for the government-owned Australian Broadcasting Corporation (ABC), had, 'in one form or another',[22] been investigating the subject of Nazis in Australia for ten years prior to the first broadcast of his findings on 13 April 1986. His interest developed from the realization that, with so many immigrants from all sources coming into Australia after 1947, it would have been 'almost a miracle' if some Nazis had not slipped in among them.[23] Working with documentary material from several countries in Europe, as well as Australia, the United States and Britain, Aarons painstakingly pieced together a tightly argued and thoroughly sourced case showing how and to what extent Nazi war criminals had come to Australia during the post-war migration programmes of the Chifley and Menzies governments.

The result was a succession of radio documentaries produced for the ABC Radio *Background Briefing* series entitled *Nazis in Australia*, broadcast for five weeks from Sunday 13 April 1986. Even before the first of the programmes went to air, Aarons had announced his preferred outcome:

> I think that, for a start, some form of official investigation is required, because there is always the danger that innocent people will be accused. It has to be done in a scientific, methodical way ... It is for the good of Australia that the facts be presented to the Australian people; if presenting the facts results in a judicial process whereby some of these people [that is, convicted war criminals] are sent back, so be it. But I think that's a secondary consideration. There is no statute of limitations for the crime of murder. I would hate to think that the Nazis are going to die leading a comfortable existence. They should at least know that there are people who are trying to bring them to justice as Australia can.[24]

The allegation that there were Nazis in Australia was greeted with a mixture of shock, revulsion and, in certain sectors, denial, but the response from the Federal government was swift. The last of the radio programmes having gone to air on 11 May 1986, on 25 June the Special Minister of State, Mick Young, authorized a review to be undertaken of material relating to the entry of suspected war criminals into Australia. The brief was placed in the hands of Andrew C. Menzies QC (no relation to the late Prime Minister Sir Robert Menzies), a former senior official with the Commonwealth Attorney-General's Department.

In his study, Aarons referred to demands by the Australian Jewish community that the government follow the lead of the United States and Canada 'in belated action to investigate the charges',[25] and there were certainly calls from other sectors that the government do something either to refute or verify the assertions he had made. Some began calling for definite action, such as a Royal Commission or a judicial inquiry, but the government of R. J. L. (Bob) Hawke decided first to make a quiet investigation of the available documents to see whether there was any validity to Aarons's claims. The result was the Menzies Inquiry.

The radio programmes were not the only push leading to the Inquiry, with other events occurring almost simultaneously. A little over a week after the first episode of *Nazis in Australia*, ABC-TV screened a *Four Corners* newsmagazine programme entitled *Don't Mention the War*, which argued many of the same points as Aarons had – perhaps not surprisingly, given that much of the material came from Aarons's own research and had been passed on to the production team at *Four Corners*.[26] Also in the same week as the first of the *Nazis in Australia* programmes, the New South Wales Legislative Assembly resolved the following:

> The House expresses its deep concern at facts revealed by recent U.S. State Department, British Foreign Office and ASIO files which establish:

(1) Large numbers of Nazi War Criminals were knowingly admitted to Australia by the Menzies Liberal Government in the 1950s.

(2) Although records of these Nazis were drawn to the attention of the Menzies Government they were not only allowed to stay but protected even to the extent of that Government misleading the Commonwealth Parliament.[27]

The revelations leading to this resolution were originally made by New South Wales MLA and former State Attorney-General Frank Walker, who had for some time liaised with Aarons and was working from many of Aarons's documents. Such accusations were too serious for any Federal administration to ignore. Overall, the combination of all these inputs, publicized at roughly the same time, resulted in the government's decision to act.

Once it was decided that a review should take place, terms of reference had to be established to give Andrew Menzies guidance so that he would know what to look for and how far his inquiry should go. His brief required that he:

conduct a review of all material, encompassing material held by relevant Commonwealth departments and agencies, relevant records held by the United Nations, or relevant material otherwise supplied to the Review, relating to the entry into Australia of persons alleged to be or suspected of being war criminals …, and to submit a report … embodying as appropriate findings and recommendations, on:

(a) whether war criminals are now or ever have been resident in Australia and, if so, when and how they obtained entry to Australia;

(b) whether the material reveals any breach of law, breach of duty or impropriety by any person or persons in relation to the entry into Australia by any person mentioned in paragraph (a);

(c) whether there was any policy by any Government of Australia to allow or assist the entry of known or suspected war criminals into Australia;

(d) whether further investigations are required.[28]

Put simply, Menzies was to carry out a review of government documents the purpose of which was to ascertain whether further investigations should be made. The terms of reference were narrow; the main emphasis lay in ascertaining whether war criminals were resident in Australia, and whether there had been any improprieties in their entry. This was to restrict Menzies in that it did not provide an opportunity for him to consider any cover-up that might have taken place *after* the entry of the alleged war criminals – which, as Mark Aarons was to assert, lay at the heart of the Australian security authorities' Cold War efforts in the 1940s and 1950s.

In view of the narrowness of his brief, Menzies worked on his review much as a university professor undertaking a research project, investigating records from several archival collections to piece together an authoritative documentary account. He was thus able to conduct his inquiry setting his own agenda (within the terms of reference) and without being answerable to public opinion until the report's release. The period of the inquiry was short; he began on 25 June 1986 and was given until 30 November that year to complete his investigation, only five months in total – and this after Minister Young asked for an extension of time. The review was, in the words of two American scholars, 'more low-key' than others elsewhere; it was 'simpler, much less formalized, [and] not nearly as visible or as susceptible to political pressures', during which Menzies 'did not take it upon himself to act as judge and jury'.[29]

This latter prospect was never an option, in any case. Given the terms of reference, Menzies was only charged with finding out whether anybody had a case to answer and compile a list of possible suspects for whom further investigation might be warranted. He was not asked, moreover, to identify what crimes (if any) the possible perpetrators had allegedly committed, only to ascertain whether there were breaches in the Australian immigration process what would have allowed Nazi war criminals to enter the country during the 1950s.

In assessing the resources Menzies had available to assist him, the word 'modest' is apt. A total of seven individuals assisted him in his research; given that this was not a judicial investigation, he was able to get by with a small group who, acting as a team, gathered and sifted the information necessary to produce a comprehensive review of suspected war criminals in Australia. The secretary to the investigation, Dr H. J. W. Stokes, explained later how the inquiry worked:

> We had to remember at all times that we were conducting an historical inquiry and not a court of law and that our commission was to decide whether there was a case to answer, not to undertake public witch hunts … Essentially we were attempting to answer two questions: were Australian migrant selection procedures sufficiently imperfect to allow war criminals to enter the country and if so who were the criminals?[30]

To recreate the machinery of immigration of the late 1940s and early 1950s, the inquiry had three main resources on which to rely: 'Immigration Department and ASIO administrative records, selection documents relating to individual migrants and interviews with former migrant selection and security screening officers.'[31] There were no specialist reports, no public witnesses and no outside counsel. The investigation team was confronted with an experience 'something akin to a reader being invited to walk into the plot of a murder mystery'.[32] Essentially, they were required to work alone and without the benefit of external input.

Yet although the inquiry toiled way without much publicity, its operations were not completely unmonitored. Critical comments from outside the investigation focused on the perils of group or communal defamation or the moral injustice of prosecuting men who had lived exemplary lives for four decades and now had only the aim of peacefully living out their old age quietly. There was, however, no lengthy period of waiting for findings to be released. Andrew Menzies submitted his report to Minister Mick Young on 28 November 1986; it was tabled in the House of Representatives on 5 December and ordered to be printed as a Parliamentary Paper on 2 April 1987. Announcing the findings of the inquiry in the Senate, Foreign Minister Gareth Evans announced that 'urgent arrangements have been made to study the report and that Attorney General Lionel Bowen would be making a submission to Cabinet in early 1987'.[33] Apart from some further general comments that day in Parliament, that was where the issue stood as the House rose for the summer recess.

That Menzies could produce any sort of authoritative report in just five months was testament to an excellent investigator with sound administrative skills. As befits a government report, he summarized his key findings in an executive summary. The key finding – which all had been awaiting, and which vindicated the initial statements of the 1986 ABC radio programmes – stated, 'It is more likely than not that a significant number of persons who committed serious war crimes in World War II have entered Australia and some of these are now resident in Australia.' He finished by saying that 'the likelihood of this is such that some action needs to be now taken'.[34]

By the terms of reference, he had not been permitted to investigate individual cases of alleged war criminals, though large lists were compiled of names that had been given to the review team from a wide variety of sources. From this, Menzies produced a distilled list of seventy individuals 'known or believed to be still living in Australia'[35] against whom there were allegations of them having committed 'serious war crimes'.[36] This list was kept confidential and has not been published.

The question of what to do in view of this finding, however, provided Menzies with the opportunity to propose to the government three possible courses of action. If Australia possessed an extradition treaty with a country in which an alleged offence took place, that country could be approached by Australia to suggest an extradition request; if no such treaty existed with a particular country, the government could possibly negotiate one. If, on the other hand, that was not deemed to be appropriate, the government could consider the possibility of revoking citizenship followed by deportation; or, in lieu of any of these alternatives, 'the Government should consider amending the War Crimes Act so as to permit a civil court to deal with a war crime'.[37] The agency to do this would be 'a very small unit in the Director of Public Prosecutions' Office' along the lines of the United States Office of Special Investigations.[38] This unit would, Menzies wrote, deal with requests for extradition, continue investigations of alleged war criminals in cases not dealt with by the Inquiry, gather evidence from overseas sources, and provide an opportunity for the suspect to answer the allegations made against him.[39]

As to the question of whether Australian authorities conspired to allow war criminals to enter the Commonwealth after the Second World War, Menzies concluded that there had been no deliberate collusion among ASIO officers or with British or American intelligence operatives, but that 'limitations and gaps' in Australian immigration procedures in Europe 'would have made possible the entry of persons responsible for war crimes'. The essential problem at the time was one of logistics and resources:

There were serious limitations, particularly in early years, in numbers and geographical spread of staff to do the necessary checking and equally serious gaps in the data against which Australian security officers would have made their checks, particularly in relation to non-Germans.[40]

Menzies never intended his report to be the last word on the issue of war criminals. He had made important recommendations that suggested government action in response – and the government could, or could not, decide to act accordingly. In March 1987 journalist Nicholas Rothwell suggested that, more than ever, 'Australia needs a firm framework such as that provided by the recommendations of the Menzies review to guide its steps in any future investigation into the crimes of suspected Nazis'.[41] The generally held view was that the government would simply adopt the Menzies recommendations without debate.[42]

The Special Investigations Unit and war crimes legislation

The adoption of the Menzies Report saw the government swing into action with the establishment in early 1987 of a new Special Investigations Unit (SIU), headed by Robert Greenwood QC, a former Deputy Director of Public Prosecutions and National Crime Authority commissioner. The SIU, based within the Attorney-General's Department, began operating before the passage of any legislation which could give its findings legal sanction, though in October 1987 Attorney-General Lionel Bowen took up Menzies's suggestion of amending the existing *War Crimes Act 1945* to enable prosecutions of war criminals to take place in Australia.

Accordingly, the *War Crimes (Amendment) Bill* was directed at persons alleged to have committed what were deemed 'serious' war crimes between 1939 and 1945, including genocide, murder, manslaughter, rape and internment in death or slave labour camps. (The Bill specified genocide, but this did not make it into the list of crimes finally included in Section 6 of the subsequent Act.) When the Bill was debated in late November it seemed as though it would receive an easy passage, Shadow Attorney-General Peter Reith suggesting that a bipartisan approach could be adopted. The one sticking point with the conservative (Liberal-National) opposition concerned the acceptance of evidence from the Soviet Union and Eastern Bloc countries. When the Bill came before the Senate in December 1987 the Leader of the Opposition in the Senate, Fred Chaney, sought to delay the legislation by asking the Senate Standing Committee on Legal and Constitutional Affairs to consider the procedures for conducting war crimes trials and presenting evidence, particularly from the Soviet Union and Eastern Bloc. Public submissions were called for and hearings took place in early February 1988. The war crimes issue henceforth became 'of the most acrimonious and heated party political debates in recent years'.[43]

The most heated arguments were not held in the Senate or the House, but, rather, outside the confines of Parliament. Ethnic community organizations, individual politicians from all parties, the Returned Services League, civil liberties groups, legal commentators and representatives of the Australian Jewish community all joined battle for almost a year: in the press, through demonstrations, and in public speeches. Debates covered issues such as retrospectivity, the use of Soviet evidence, the amount of time that had elapsed since the alleged events, geographical distance from Europe, the advanced age of those who would be charged, the cost to the public purse of staging war crimes trials, the potential unreliability of eyewitness testimony, and fears of a witch hunt hysteria that could stigmatize entire ethnic communities. The public debate at times took on the guise of a knock-down, drag-out brawl, which newspapers, radio talkback programmes and television news channels lapped up and to some extent encouraged throughout 1988.

The legislation was finally introduced for debate in the Senate on 15 December 1988. After accepting some Opposition amendments, the government was pleased to see the Bill pass through both Houses on 21 December – the last Act to be passed before the summer recess. It completely rewrote the *War Crimes Act 1945*, leaving practically nothing of the original. The debate in the Senate had lasted four days: the final vote was thirty-eight to thirty-three, Australian Democrats and Independents giving the government the crucial votes it needed. The result of the new Act was the arrest of Ivan Polyukhovich in Adelaide on 25 January 1990, with the promise of more arrests to come.

Proceedings in Adelaide

Ivan Timofeyevich Polyukhovich was born in Serniki (Sernyky), Ukraine, close to the Pripjet Marshes. Soon after Nazi Germany's invasion of the Soviet Union in June 1941, Serniki, a village of about 5,000 mainly Ukrainian farming families, was occupied and a ghetto was created to imprison the town's Jewish population. Polyukhovich, like many other Ukrainians, elected to collaborate with the Germans, working as a gamekeeper and forest warden. On 29 September 1942, the Serniki ghetto was liquidated, and approximately 850 Jews were murdered by Nazi *Einsatzgruppen*. While up to 150 others fled to the forest, it was believed that only ten of them survived the war. When the Germans retreated from Ukraine during 1943–1944, Ivan Polyukhovich and his second wife Maria left with the departing German troops and was given work in Germany. On 28 December 1949, Polyukhovich, Maria and his two stepdaughters arrived in Melbourne. In 1958 they obtained Australian citizenship.

The charges against him in 1990 involved his alleged murder of twenty-four people, and complicity in the murders of the 850 who had been gunned down in a pit killing of Jews during the liquidation of Serniki's Jews. What followed his arrest was not a trial, but, rather, a hearing to determine whether he had a case to answer. The Adelaide press had a field day. Sensational images were portrayed daily and employed to the full. They included Nazis, Jews, a befuddled old man who seemed not to know what was going on around him, protesters and, always, the spectre of racial tension. There were photographs of swastikas and barbed wire, as well as sensationalist headlines to tempt readers. Story lines and editorial comments were often questionable in terms of taste, but few people seemed to care; the war crimes circus was exciting, and that sometimes seemed to count for more than media objectivity.

Often, the question was portrayed as an issue between 'Jews' and 'Nazis', with 'the Australians' on the sidelines. From time to time the issue was portrayed as a case of Federal politics intruding on states' rights; almost always, the picture was of an aged and often bewildered Adelaide pensioner, innocent or not, who was being forced to relive the horrors of half a century earlier. No section of the media seemed able to resist adding the word 'pensioner' whenever the accused's name was mentioned. Only rarely did the media report the case as being one of due legal process in accordance with Australian law – a law that had passed through both Houses of Parliament and been upheld by a decision of the High Court of Australia.

To prove the case against Polyukhovich, prosecutors had first to identify the location near Serniki where the massacre had occurred, and investigators from Australia travelled to Ukraine to excavate a mass grave.[44] Soviet authorities cooperated in helping to clear a section of the forest and it soon became clear to investigators that they were indeed at the site, and that the killings had occurred during the Second World War.[45] Back in Adelaide, lawyers for the prosecution sought to present their respective cases professionally and with a genuine concern for the justice they were pursuing, forming a special – even pastoral – relationship with the witnesses they assembled from various parts of the world. Equally, the defence team developed its own close connection with the accused, doing all they could to have him acquitted. Both sides were determined not to allow the case to get carried away in a flood of emotive rhetoric and fought the case strictly on points of evidence and the nature of justice rather than on the red herring of whether war crimes tribunals should or should not have been held.

Over the course of the nine-week hearing, the case against Ivan Polyukhovich became increasingly whittled away by those who presided over the various stages of the trial process. Despite evidence from the mass gravesite and corroborating eyewitness testimony about Polyukhovich's involvement, his defence team was able to pick enough holes in the prosecution's case to secure his acquittal. The evidence was something of a patchwork: some of the witnesses died before they could give evidence; some were not well enough to travel to Australia; and the quality of some of the evidence was undermined owing to translation problems. In the end, the prosecution's case was simply not strong enough. From what had originally seemed like a series of open-and-shut cases of first-degree murder and second-degree participation in mass murder, the court ruled in numerous instances that various aspects of the prosecution's case were inadmissible. This happened with such frequency that in the end there was hardly any case left for Polyukhovich to answer. By 5 June 1992, he was indicted for only six murders, and the rest of the charges were dismissed. On 18 May 1993, he was acquitted by a jury of all charges due to purported difficulties in presenting evidence and questions over witness testimony which struggled to identify the accused with certainty. Under Australian law, it was not beyond reasonable doubt that the perpetrator of the crimes in Serniki was Ivan Polyukhovich, and, as a result, it was found that there was no case for him to answer.[46]

In addition to Polykhovich, two other residents of Adelaide, also originally from Ukraine, were prosecuted under the amended war crimes legislation. Mikhail Berezowsky was arrested and charged on 5 September 1991 under the Act, in that he was knowingly involved in the killing of approximately 102 Jews in the Ukrainian town of Gnivan. It was alleged that Berezowsky's offences occurred between 1 March 1942 and 31 July 1942. Committal proceedings commenced in the Adelaide Magistrates Court on 22 June 1992 and concluded a month later. A total of twenty-five witnesses were called by the prosecution to give evidence (twenty-two of whom came from overseas), but the charges were dropped on the ground that there was insufficient evidence to bring Berezowsky to trial.

The third prosecution involved Heinrich Wagner, who was arrested and charged in September 1991. His offences were alleged to have been committed between May and July 1942 and to have involved the wilful killing of approximately 104 Jewish adults and nineteen Jewish children, all from the village of Izraylovka in Ukraine. Wagner was further charged with a war crime involving the murder of a Ukrainian construction worker near the village of Ustinovka in 1943. Committal proceedings commenced in the Adelaide Magistrates court in June 1992; thirty-seven witnesses were called, of whom twenty-seven came from overseas. Wagner pleaded not guilty.

On 11 December 1993, Michael Rozenes QC, the Commonwealth Director of Public Prosecutions, withdrew the charges against Wagner on grounds of the accused's poor health. The previous month Wagner had suffered a heart attack and doctors advised that a continuation of the case against him could result in his death.[47]

By the end of 1992, Australia's prosecution of Nazi war criminals effectively came to an end. Earlier that year, it was announced by the government of Paul Keating that Federal funding for the SIU would cease as from 30 June 1992, and that further legal proceedings under the war crimes legislation were not expected. The small number of outstanding cases, including the prosecution of a fourth suspect, Karlis Ozols, would not be completed. On 13 September 1993, the SIU published its final report. Over the period of its five-year existence, the Unit conducted 841 investigations, from which it identified twenty-seven cases of suspected war criminals. Because of insufficient evidence, however, none were pursued other than the four cases referred to the Commonwealth Director of Public Prosecutions (Polyukhovich, Wagner, Berezowsky and Ozols).

Indeed, as American-born Nazi hunter and inaugural director of the Simon Wiesenthal Center in Los Angeles, Ephraim Zuroff, has concluded, closing the SIU certainly spared a prosecution of Ozuls, and, in his view, what would have been 'an almost certain conviction'.[48] There was, he has argued, more to the closure of the SIU than just financial considerations: 'It was no doubt also influenced by staunch political opposition by the local émigré communities (whose members were the suspects in question) as well as various politicians and public figures.'[49]

The war crimes prosecutions attracted heavy and ongoing criticism in the media owing to the failure to secure convictions and the $30 million cost of the investigations and prosecutions. Zuroff has concluded that the decision to close the Unit 'was a total disaster', coming as it did just 'at the very same time that the pertinent archives in the former Soviet Union and post-Communist Eastern Europe' were finally being opened, 'with full access granted to Western prosecutors'.[50] It was clear, in his view, that 'the politicians had lost their will to bring Nazi war criminals in Australia to justice and were pulling the plug way too soon'.[51] Eventually, the whole thing simply fizzled out and was largely forgotten.[52]

The SIU's final report recommended the establishment of a permanent war crimes unit covering 'persons who are or who become Australian citizens or residents', noting that it was 'difficult to see any justification for continuing to confine the operation of the Act to war crimes committed in Europe during the Second World War' given that alleged war criminals from other conflicts were likely to enter Australia down to the present day.[53]

This was to see its consummation on 20 November 2020, when a report into possible war crimes committed by Australian military forces in Afghanistan was released. The report, entitled *Inspector-General of the Australian Defence Force Afghanistan Inquiry Report*, was undertaken by Paul Brereton, a New South Wales Supreme Court Justice and Major-General in the Army Reserve. Evidence was found of thirty-nine murders of civilians and prisoners by (or on the orders of) members of the Australian military.[54] The upshot saw the establishment by the government of Prime Minister Scott Morrison of a new Office of the Special Investigator to probe any further criminal conduct and recommend prosecution for those named. In December 2020, Home Affairs Minister Peter Dutton appointed former Victorian Supreme Court Justice and judge of the Federal Court, Mark Weinberg, as the Special Investigator. The inquiry, report and the appointment of a Special Investigator to investigate Australian troops for war crimes while on active service were a clear indication of how far the nation had come in the nearly thirty years since the closure of the SIU in 1992.

Because of the magnitude of the Holocaust, unprecedented in its techniques and the scale of its horror, the wheels of justice should have been spinning with increasing speed to keep pace with the enormity of the crime. This did not happen in Australia until the late 1980s and early 1990s, but even then, what transpired was as much a trial of the Australian legal system as it was of those who had been arrested. In this sense, the hunt for Nazi war criminals was very much an Australian issue, as, indeed, was the Nazi period since 1933 and the Holocaust during the years of the Second World War. It was certainly not – to paraphrase British Prime Minister Neville Chamberlain in 1938 – a quarrel in a faraway country between people of whom the Australian people knew nothing.

CHAPTER 16
MEMORY: THE HOLOCAUST AND ITS PLACE IN AUSTRALIAN HISTORY

The Holocaust was perpetrated by people from many backgrounds. One did not have to be a German to be a Nazi, as witness Jewish experiences at the hands of the Hlinka Guard in Slovakia, the Arrow Cross Party in Hungary, the Iron Guard in Romania, antisemitic Poles who denounced Jews to their German occupiers (and sometimes murdered those they denounced as well), Vichy French police and officials, Ukrainian collaborators and so on. For many people who never saw a German Nazi, the Holocaust was visited upon them by a wide variety of messengers.

It was, however, from first to last a German enterprise. Without Nazism, it would not have happened, or at least, not been played out in the manner it was. In the 1930s, the Nazi goal was for Jews to leave Germany, and many of the government's acts – removing Jews from social and economic life, withdrawing their citizenship and physically intimidating them – were dedicated to that aim. A significant number of German Jews did manage to flee, though relatively late in the decade; it was only after *Kristallnacht* in November 1938 that the writing was on the wall and those remaining saw there was no possibility of an accommodation with Nazism and no future to be had in Germany.

Australia's moves in relation to people seeking refuge in Australia from Nazism – indeed, to European events generally – were tied politically to Britain's appeasement policies; further, despite the information newspapers provided about European events, the attitude of the Australian government remained hardened on racial grounds to the plight of Europe's Jewish refugees, even as their awful fate was made clearer daily.

Where could Germany's Jews go? Why should countries outside Germany feel under any obligation to take them in? It is worth remembering that in the 1930s the death camps and the Final Solution were still some way off, and that the Nazis had not themselves yet thought of extermination as a policy. Still, bureaucratic inertia, political game-playing and an ill-informed public combined around the world to leave Germany's Jews (indeed, ultimately all Jews in Europe) in a dangerously exposed position. By the time war came in September 1939, Jewish options to leave Germany – and places for them to go – were slashed.

Interviewed in 1982, Israeli activist Yitshaq Ben-Ami, who helped smuggle Jews from Europe to Palestine in the 1930s, considered the following formula:

> The recipient countries have made it so difficult for the Jews to get in that they can't go anywhere. Therefore they are left there [in Germany]. If they are left within the

control of the Reich, then the Reich has to find a way to eliminate them. Because they have no value either politically, propaganda-wise, or whatever it is. Actually, it got to the point in the camps eventually, and the gas chambers and the crematoria, that the only value Jews had for Germany was in their residual value. The residual value was gold fillings and hair. And this they collected. And that's all. Now, who brought the Jews into this status, into this level, of having no value? The Western world, not Hitler. The Western world lowered the boom by saying 'they don't exist for us.'"[1]

Australia was one of these Western world countries. As this book has argued, the Australian response to the Jewish situation, both before and during the war, cannot be understood without some appreciation of the various frames of reference within which Australians located their position. And despite the amount of paper generated in the files of the government Departments, it must be concluded that in general terms the Australians set a relatively low priority on the Jewish plight in Europe when balanced against their preferences for the future 'racial' composition of the country.

The Holocaust took place in Europe, but it is part of Australian history – even though it is not seen that way by a population largely unaware of the Australian connection to that horrible event. Admittedly, there is an enormous amount of interest in the Holocaust: each year Australians are exposed to an increasing number of Holocaust-related television documentaries, feature films, background reports and news items. Australia had its own war crimes trials in Adelaide – committal hearings brought by the Federal Attorney-General's Department against three men charged with war crimes against Jews in eastern Europe. However, Holocaust denial continues to attract adherents, particularly from among a younger generation who seem to be confused as to the veracity of the accounts upon which their parents and grandparents were raised. Swastikas and Stars of David are used to attract attention on book covers and in magazine articles, and projections of barbed wire are employed as backdrops to reports on Israel, racial crimes and the Second World War. The Holocaust and its symbols have become an inescapable part of popular culture and historical awareness in Australia.

For those coming after the Holocaust, its memory has produced powerful responses. Its legacies are manifested through memorials, museums and popular culture. Perhaps most visibly within the Australian Jewish community, education about the Holocaust is in the forefront of collective awareness. The expansive Jewish day school movement has to a large extent been crafted as a living monument to the inheritance of the Holocaust. Beyond this, some state high school curricula have seen Holocaust education mandated, while elsewhere individual teachers seek to increase offerings on the Holocaust as electives. Many Australian universities offer undergraduate courses on the Holocaust, often as part of a broader human rights agenda.

The moral challenges posed by the Holocaust were at once immense, profound and deeply challenging, and in a Jewish community that boasts the largest survivor and survivor-descent population per capita outside of Israel, this is frequently expressed through religious belief and observance. Memorial Days such as *Yom Hashoah* (April) and International Holocaust Remembrance Day (January) are marked as solemn occasions observed with reverence across the entirety of each state's Jewish community.

As the Holocaust generation ages, the children of survivors – known collectively as the Second Generation – play an increasingly crucial role in keeping alive the memory and legacy of the Holocaust experience. In recent times, consideration has also been made of the grandchildren of Holocaust survivors, the last generation of Jews who will have had any sort of direct biological link to the Holocaust.

Holocaust memorialization can be a complicated affair. How the Holocaust is publicly commemorated depends very largely on practical considerations, and in planning a memorial several logistical concerns abound. For example, who is commissioning the memorial? Is the intended location available, and, if so, is it appropriate? What is the budget within which those who are planning the memorial can operate? How is the memorial to be designed, and how are decisions to be made concerning its realization? Most importantly, in whose name does the planning committee speak – and to whom is the memorial directed? Memorials are silent testaments to victimization and persecution and embrace a wide variety of types ranging through monuments, plaques, sculptures and other public spaces designed to memorialize the Holocaust or people associated with it (such as e.g. the monument to Raoul Wallenberg in Melbourne). An understanding of the Holocaust is also incorporated in film, art, music, theatre and other artistic creations.

The two most important Holocaust museums in Australia are Melbourne's Jewish Holocaust Centre (established by survivors in 1984) and the Sydney Jewish Museum (1992). While acting as key places for educational initiatives and the display of artefacts, both institutions have been instrumental in collecting and recording memoirs and testimonies from survivors before they are lost. In 1990 the Holocaust Institute of Western Australia was inaugurated in Perth, with a huge financial boost announced in August 2020 from the Western Australian government that will lead to a significant expansion. On 9 November 2020 – the anniversary of *Kristallnacht* – the Adelaide Holocaust Museum and Andrew Steiner Education Centre was opened, while Federal government funding to assist in the creation of other Holocaust museums was announced for Brisbane (October 2020), Canberra (January 2021) and Hobart (March 2021). As the decade of the 2020s proceeds all Australian state capital cities, and the national capital, will have places dedicated to Holocaust memorialization and education.

Despite all the interest in (and sometimes, fascination with) the Holocaust, however, at no time – other than within the Jewish community itself – has the Holocaust itself ever been seen as an issue pertinent to Australia. Indeed, apart from the efforts of a narrow range of university academics and some journalists and media commentators, the role of Australia during the Holocaust has never entered the mainstream of Australian historical consciousness. One of the main foci for arguments during the committal hearings of the men charged with war crimes in the 1990s was that any crimes they may have committed took place decades ago, outside Australian territory and beyond Australian jurisdiction. Such reasoning tended to absolve Australia from having any direct interest of its own in the Holocaust, along the way also removing considered analysis of the Australian role between 1933 and 1945.

The facts, however, speak for themselves. Australia *did* have a part to play, regardless of its own preference for isolation from the world's problems. Jewish refugees from Europe were a considerable inconvenience to the governments of Joseph Lyons, Robert Menzies and John Curtin. Civil service officials did all in their power to mitigate the effects of international and domestic pressure in finding an Australian solution to the refugee problem. Along the way, they provided the Ministers responsible for immigration with the explanations – and often the means – to restrict a refugee ingress in ways that were contrary to, and in breach of, existing migration regulations, and to mislead the public about such actions. As we have seen, the reasons for this restrictiveness can be found in an anti-foreign and antisemitic bias prevalent among some key personnel in the government Departments, which possibly echoed the views of a substantial number of Australians across the period in question.

Tracing the record of the Australian government towards refugees from Nazism is no simple task, with many questions needing to be addressed. How, for example, did it discern between refugees and other immigrants? What were its racial or ethnic priorities? Was there, indeed, a distinct refugee policy? Did a bias exist towards certain types of would-be immigrants? How did Australians react to the foreign presence once refugees began appearing on the streets of Australian cities? The resolution of these questions is often a matter more of contextual interpretation than of accepting Ministerial statements at face value. One thing is certain, however. Contrary to the government's own standards, acceptable Jewish refugees from Europe were excluded in vast numbers from 1933 to 1945 solely on the grounds that they were Jewish. There is good reason to believe that the Australian government, which did not really have a well-established refugee policy until late 1938, generated its refugee options impetuously – often fearful of public backlash – throughout most of the 1930s. When war broke out in September 1939, questions of security were exploited as the means to further exclude Jewish refugees, a policy incongruous alongside government pronouncements condemning Nazi atrocities during the early 1940s.

That this should have been the case is perhaps not too surprising given the prevailing attitudes of the time. For most of the period, the Australian government saw itself pursuing an immigration policy, not a refugee policy. In line with what it understood to be the wishes of the electorate, a policy was framed and administered ensuring that foreign European migrants should not come into the country in numbers greater than what the nation could digest. Australians, even at that stage of their history, had a long tradition of suspicion towards foreigners, and during the period of the Third Reich they would not have tolerated a government policy which opened the gates to a significant number of Jewish refugees. The government policymakers were thus set a challenge: if Australia accepted refugees, the country's racial homogeneity would be diluted. Worse in some quarters was the fear that Australia would fall under 'Jewish domination', and that as a result the Australian standard of living for ordinary workers would drop dramatically.

On the other hand, if the Australian government deliberately excluded refugees, it seemed clear that the Commonwealth would miss the opportunity of acquiring some useful skills and capital brought to the country by potentially 'good' Jews who did not fit the negative stereotype. Australia would then also lose the chance of adding to the country's white population at a time of considerable apprehension about its relative underpopulation and the increased fear of Japanese expansion.

After weighing the pros and cons, Australian governments adopted a compromise position, in which *some* Jewish refugees would be accepted. In this way the government would not be seen as renouncing its humanitarian obligations, while the nation's racial composition would remain intact. This would be done by carrying out a covert policy of discrimination against Jewish admissions, with the bureaucracy playing a major role in shaping and executing policy decisions.

One of the few occasions on which the Australian government did set a definite policy course, after some deliberation and with full knowledge of its ramifications, was the much-vaunted policy announcement of 1 December 1938, when John McEwen declared that Australia would take in up to 15,000 refugees over the next three years. Superficially this measure seemed quite generous. Closer scrutiny, however, showed that the government was more tight-fisted than generous: the figure of up to 15,000 did not refer specifically to Jews (who, under previously existing arrangements, could have come into Australia to the potential aggregate of 15,300 over three years), and the new quota reserved an initial 3,000 places for non-Jews. Later, in 1939, this sub-quota for non-Jews was left open-ended. For Jews, moreover, their newly reduced quota of 12,000 was to include all individuals, not, as the case had been, just heads of households. This further reduced the potential number of Jewish refugees who could come to Australia. In 1939 there were just over 5,000 refugee Jews – German, Austrian and Czechoslovakian – admitted to the country. That figure should not, however, be taken too literally as a demonstration of the new quota in action: a great many had applied to come in 1937 and 1938 and had had their cases rejected. The only reason for their acceptance in 1939 was that for the first time the potential number of admissions was being realized. Still, Jewish immigration did increase after 1 December 1938: the figures show that for the five years prior to this, no more than an estimated 2,500 in total managed to gain admission.

It is highly questionable whether this increase was matched in tolerance, understanding or humanitarian feelings. There was no reason, on the surface, it should have been. The refugees were still foreign and still Jewish. No government could hope to legislate approval: that could only come through wholehearted commitment and an intensive education program. Such approval, however, had to wait for the shock of war and the trauma of possible invasion. For most Australians, there was a world of difference between admittance and acceptance.

The outbreak of war and the threat of imminent invasion by Japan gave the Australians a need to stand back and re-evaluate the need for building their population through immigration. Awareness of the horrors of the Holocaust while it was being reported sensitized Australians to the needs of Jews still alive in Europe to find a place of refuge, and discussion in 1944 and 1945 from time to time raised the possibility of Australia admitting some of the survivors after the war. The bureaucrats, however, were not completely convinced, and referred continually to the 'Fifteen Thousand' policy having been discontinued because of the war. This renunciation, incidentally, had never been discussed – let alone ratified – by Cabinet. The Department of the Interior simply made the statement soon after war was declared, and in the absence of any challenges it then became the assumed position of the government until 1945.

Throughout the war, propositions for the rescue of small groups of Jews were put to the government. Hardly any of these were actualized – not only because the war prevented shipping from Europe (even supposing people could get out), but also because of bureaucratic inertia, reluctance to admit Polish Jews and unaccompanied Jewish children, and simple indifference at a time when important matters such as the security of the country had to be addressed.

Even after the war, when revelations at the Nuremberg trials reinforced for Australians the nature of the regime against which they had been fighting and the character of the values they had been seeking to uphold, the government was less interested in the fate of Europe's Jews than the newspaper press, which, by contrast, showed immense interest. It was only four decades later, when that same press brought to public attention the failures of the past and the likelihood that previous governments had let in Nazi war criminals, that the Holocaust became a clear and present reality. It did not last long, however, with the Special Investigations Unit wound up barely five years after it began, and with no convictions in its wake.

Notwithstanding this, the question of Australia's immigration record across the Third Reich period must be considered, as it was this record to which Australian governments kept pointing. Had, in fact, Australia done enough for the Jews of Europe? Objectivity is crucial here. It is one thing to say that Hitler's aims could have been foreseen and that the Allies should have taken steps to ensure that Europe's Jews were rescued from the Holocaust before the mass murder programme came into being, but such an approach simply does not accord with the realities of history. To suggest that Australia should have – or even could have – admitted more Jews because of the Final Solution has no bearing on any analysis of the Commonwealth's pre-war refugee policy, during which time the Australian Jewish population increased by a third. Proportionately that can be seen as a worthwhile contribution, though in global and numerical terms it was of course quite small. If Australia did all it could – as governments and bureaucrats maintained – then according to whose criteria did it do so? The Australian immigration authorities would say the Commonwealth did well; detractors would argue that more could always have been done.

Indeed, the only way to approach the issue is to consider the Australian record from the perspective of the prevailing immigration regulations and the standards of the day. If the government, according to its own criteria, is then revealed to have operated with a bias against Jewish immigrants solely because of their 'race', a credible case can be made that Australia did not do all in its power to assist those needing a place of refuge. The details set out in this book point to the fact that such was the situation. Whether because of indifference, antisemitism, xenophobia or economic fears, Australia adopted a policy towards Jewish refugees across the entire period of the Third Reich that sought to keep as many Jews as possible, even those clearly eligible in accordance with its own criteria, from entering. It should be remembered that in 1938, 90 per cent of eligible non-guaranteed refugees were refused entry after having met all Australian immigration standards, solely because of the stated 'racial' dimension.

Overall, somewhere in the vicinity of 10,000 Jews did manage to enter Australia between 1933 and 1945 (if we include the internees from overseas who stayed after the war) despite the bureaucracy's best efforts, but the position of Australian governments cannot be assessed in a favourable light when measured against its own avowed benchmarks.

The end of the Second World War saw the creation of a large-scale migration programme to be administered by the newly established the Federal Department of Immigration. The result was that between 1945 and 1965 more than two million new arrivals entered Australia.[2] Many, particularly from Britain, arrived as assisted immigrants, in which the Commonwealth government paid most of their fare in return for which they agreed to remain for at least two years and work in whatever jobs the government found for them.[3] Then, despite the 97 per cent British or British-descent composition of the country's population, Australia also actively encouraged the migration of non-British European immigrants. In 1955 the one-millionth post-war immigrant arrived in Australia, and after the brutal repression of the Hungarian Revolution in 1956, Australia – in a twist from the 1930s – opened its gates and took in a total of 14,000 refugees.[4] In 1973 the government of Prime Minister Gough Whitlam ended the White Australia policy, allowing the entry of immigrants from non-European countries.[5]

The question must therefore be asked: how far have attitudes towards refugees come in the three generations since the end of the Second World War? There is no easy answer, but some prominent signposts can be considered. The war was an important watershed in Australian immigration history, as the threat of Japanese invasion in early 1942 forced the Australians to reappraise their previous immigration targets in the post-war environment. At first, they envisaged almost exclusively British migrants, but soon realized they would have to broaden the sources of migration – such that in the decades that followed they would ultimately welcome all Europeans as well as Turks, Arabs, Asians, Africans and Americans (from both continents). The blending of so many nationalities in such a concentrated time frame forced Australians to adjust many of their previously held views about foreigners, and the Australian version of multiculturalism became a model for other countries around the world to follow or adapt.[6] At the same time, this was accompanied by a growing sense of gratitude that newcomers could help to develop the country further and launch it into the new century. Ongoing public outcries at the disastrous situations such places as Somalia, Ethiopia, East Timor, Sudan, Iraq, Bosnia-Herzegovina, Kosovo, Sri Lanka and Myanmar (among many others) have demonstrated that Australians (though not always their governments) are at last participating in the 'global village' and 'brother's keeper' concepts, ideals prevalent in other parts of the world.

On the refugee issue Australia has begun to live up to the treaty obligations it has adopted as binding on humanitarian and civilized societies – though sometimes it still guards its gates through an inconsistent approach to defining refugee status if the problem appears to be difficult.[7]

What can we conclude about Australian attitudes towards refugees when we compare the policies towards Jewish refugees in the 1930s with the recent past? Clearly, we are looking at two highly distinct periods bearing little resemblance to each other – one in which the earlier focus was on ethnic or racial preference, the other, of late, on genuine need irrespective of race, religion or ethnicity. The period between 1933 and 1945 was concerned with the domestic ramifications of taking in refugees; the years since then, with the humanitarian effects of not doing so. In both periods, however, policies were built on the premise that a refugee problem must be faced up to and acknowledged as an issue for government consideration. Australians in the 1930s might have said that that problem was not one for their country to solve alone, while several decades later most would endorse the view that no man or woman is an island; but both positions would clearly find themselves on the same ground in appreciating that the problem requires both a government position and a public response. The recognition of a common humanity by governments is a vital first step towards reducing distress. Declaring that one group or another has refugee status is an assessment of the political environment of the state from which the people in question seek refuge. It is not always an easy political decision to make – as the appeasement period of the 1930s indicated clearly.

Soon after Adolf Hitler came to power in Germany in 1933, Australia's Department of the Interior was charged with the task of seeing to it that no 'serious influx' of Jews entered the Commonwealth. Twelve years later, a fully fledged Department of Immigration was established, and Albert Peters received his reward for decades of devoted service as a senior public servant and Head of the former Immigration Branch. In advance of a permanent appointment being made, he was elevated to Acting Secretary of the new Department, retiring in that position in 1946. He could look back with satisfaction on his tenure at the Immigration Branch during its period of greatest challenge. He ensured that the brief to which he was entrusted was complied with to the letter, and there had been no invasion of Jews from Nazi Germany.

The team of Albert Peters, Tom Garrett and Joseph Carrodus took on the policy tasks required of them without demur, and there was little indication throughout the years following 1933 that the fundamental premise of their original brief had changed. These men strove to ensure that the policy direction handed to them was translated into practice, and for the most part they were extraordinarily successful. The time and place circumstances determining their approach did not allow for much deviation. Today, several decades and numerous genocides later, governments still struggle to weigh up moral considerations alongside of the interests of the Australian people and the expectations of the international community. It remains a difficult balancing act; but then, it always was.

NOTES

Chapter 1

1   F.K. Crowley, *Modern Australia in Documents*, vol. 1, *1900–1939*, Melbourne: Wren, 1973, p. 557, citing *Labor Daily* (Sydney), 24 July 1931.

2   Ibid.

3   Andrew Markus, *Australian Race Relations, 1788–1993*, St. Leonards (NSW): Allen and Unwin Australia, 1994, p. 153.

4   E.M. Andrews, *Isolationism and Appeasement in Australia: Reactions to the European Crises, 1935–1939*, Canberra: Australian National University Press, 1970, p. 4.

5   Ibid.

6   Ibid., p. 194.

7   Ibid., p. 200.

8   A concise chronological account of the colonial period can be found in Suzanne D. Rutland, *Edge of the Diaspora: Two Centuries of Jewish Settlement in Australia*, Sydney: Collins Australia, 1988, chapters 1–6 *passim*.

9   For a detailed study of the inner workings of communal life in Melbourne – soon to become Australia's first capital city – see Sue Silberberg, *A Networked Community: Jewish Melbourne in the Nineteenth Century*, Melbourne: Melbourne University Publishing, 2020.

10 On the Russian pogroms and Australia, see Hilary L. Rubinstein, 'Australian Jewish Reactions to Russian Jewish Distress, 1891–1913', *Australian Jewish Historical Society Journal and Proceedings*, 9:6, 1984, pp. 444–56.

11 A good account of the relationship between Jews and non-Jews in late colonial Victoria can be found in Frank Fletcher, 'The Victorian Jewish Community, 1891–1901: Its Relationship with the Majority Gentile Society', *Australian Jewish Historical Society Journal and Proceedings*, 8:5, July 1978, pp. 221–71.

12 P.Y. Medding, *From Assimilation to Group Survival: A Political and Sociological Study of an Australian Jewish Community*, Melbourne: Cheshire, 1968, pp. 1–2.

13 Jens Lyng, *Non-Britishers in Australia: Influence on Population and Progress*, Melbourne: Macmillan/Melbourne University Press, 1927, p. 154.

14 Within this context, the record of Australian Jews during the Great War stands out. From an overall Jewish population in 1914 of about 17,000, nearly every Jewish man capable of volunteering for service did so: a figure of 2,304 has been given, representing nearly 13 per cent of the entire Jewish community. See Harold Boas, *Australian Jewry Book of Honour: The Great War, 1914–1918*, Perth: Lamson Paragon, 1923. See also Rodney Gouttman, *In their Merit: Australian Jewry and WWI*, Melbourne: Xlibris Australia, 2015 and Mark Dapin, *Jewish ANZACS: Jews in the Australian Military*, Sydney: NewSouth Publishing, 2017, pp. 56–146.

15 George Blaikie, *Remember Smith's Weekly? A Biography of an Uninhibited National Australian Newspaper*, Adelaide: Rigby, 1966, pp. 2–3.

16 Keith Amos, *The New Guard Movement, 1931–1935*, Melbourne: Melbourne University Press, 1976. The leader of the movement, Colonel Eric Campbell, has left his recollections in *The Rallying Point: My Story of the New Guard*, Melbourne: Melbourne University Press, 1965. See also Rutland, *Edge of the Diaspora*, pp. 197–8.

17 Bruce Muirden, *The Puzzled Patriots: The Story of the Australia First Movement*, Melbourne: Melbourne University Press, 1968.

18 Rutland, *Edge of the Diaspora*, pp. 199–200.

19 See especially G. Kinne, 'Nazi Stratagems and Their Effects on Germans in Australia up to 1945', *Royal Australian Historical Society Journal*, 66, June 1980, pp. 1–19.

20 Andrews, *Isolationism and Appeasement in Australia*, p. 129.

21 NAA A434, file 49/3/3196, 'Admission of Jews to Australia', Home and Territories memorandum (*Polish Jews*) prepared by A.R. Peters, 30 September 1925.

22 Ibid.

23 Ibid., handwritten minute by F.J. Quinlan, 30 September 1925.

24 In 1933, Rabbi Freedman was appointed by the Australian government to be its substitute representative at the 14th Assembly of the League of Nations in Geneva. This was a unique distinction not only for Australia but also for the League, as never before had a rabbi been commissioned as a representative of any of the member countries. See *Jewish Chronicle* (London), 28 July 1933, p. 11.

25 Charles A. Price, *Jewish Settlers in Australia*, Canberra: ANU Press, 1964, Appendix 1.

26 Andrews, *Isolationism and Appeasement in Australia*, p. 26.

27 For an extended treatment of the Australian immigration administration between the wars, see Paul R. Bartrop, 'Foreign Immigration between the Wars: The Role of the Public Service', in J.J. Eddy and J.R. Nethercote (ed.), *Towards National Administration: Studies in Australian Administrative History*, Sydney: Hale and Iremonger, 1994, pp. 157–67.

28 Bill Gammage, *The Broken Years: Australian Soldiers in the Great War*, Ringwood (Victoria): Penguin Books, 1980, p. 279.

29 CPD, H. of. R., vol. 89, 10 September 1919, p. 12179.

30 Michael McKernan, *The Australian People and the Great War*, Melbourne: Nelson, 1980, p. 207.

31 NAA A1, file 34/4359, 'Germans. Removal of Restrictions on', Home and Territories memorandum (*Germans and other Former Enemy Aliens*) prepared by A.R. Peters, 20 November 1925; typewritten minute to Prime Minister, 24 November 1925.

32 NAA A457, file Q400/2, 'Restrictions. Non-British Immigrants. General Papers', Secretary, Department of Home and Territories, to Secretary, Prime Minister's Department, 29 July 1922.

33 See Peter Cochrane, *Best We Forget: The War for White Australia, 1914–18*, Melbourne: Text Publishing, 2018.

34 The best historical works dealing with the White Australia policy are: Myra Willard, *History of the White Australia Policy to 1920*, Melbourne: Melbourne University Press, 1967 (first published in 1923); A.T. Yarwood, *Asian Migration to Australia: The Background to Exclusion, 1896–1923*, Melbourne: Melbourne University Press, 1964; Andrew Markus, *Fear*

and Hatred: Purifying Australia and California, 1850–1901, Sydney: Hale and Iremonger, 1979 and A.C. Palfreeman, The Administration of the White Australia Policy, Melbourne: Melbourne University Press, 1967. A valuable account of the development of restrictive immigration policies in the nineteenth century is to be found in Charles A. Price, The Great White Walls Are Built: Restrictive Immigration to North America and Australasia, 1836–1888, Canberra: ANU Press, 1974. See also Cochrane, Best We Forget.

35 Smith's Weekly, 17 June 1922, p. 19.

36 Ibid.

37 Ibid., 5 July 1924, p. 9.

38 Ibid.

39 Labor Call, 5 February 1925, p. 2.

40 NAA A458, file P156/I, 'Immigration Restrictions. Australian Policy General File', Notes of a Deputation from the Australian Natives' Association Which Waited on the Prime Minister, 8 December 1927.

41 CPD, H. of R., vol. 116, 17 November 1927, p. 1567.

42 The Age, 1 April 1925, p. 11.

43 NAA A367, file C3075 AG, 'Report of Interdepartmental Committee on Migration and Control of Aliens', Interior memorandum (White Alien Immigration) prepared by J.A. Carrodus, 2 August 1937.

44 Lyons Papers, National Library of Australia, MS 4851, Box 1, folder 7, UAP Subcommittee on Policy, 1931.

45 The Argus, 6 July 1927, p. 27.

46 G.L. Kristianson, The Politics of Patriotism: The Pressure Group Activities of the Returned Servicemen's League, Canberra: Australian National University Press, 1966, p. 68.

47 NAA A458, file P156/1, 'Immigration Restrictions. Australian Policy General File', W.M. McHugo (Hon Secretary, Sailors' and Soldiers' Fathers' Association of Tasmania) to Prime Minister Bruce, 3 February 1925).

48 Labor Call, 14 July 1927, p. 10.

49 The literature on Australian policy towards Britain during the interwar years is immense. Some suggestions for further reading include: P.G. Edwards, Prime Ministers and Diplomats: The Making of Australian Foreign Policy 1901–1949, Melbourne: Oxford University Press, 1983; John McCarthy, Australia and Imperial Defence 1918–39: A Study of Air and Sea Power, St Lucia: University of Queensland Press, 1976; E.M. Andrews, The Writing on the Wall: The British Commonwealth and Aggression in the East 1931–1935, Sydney: Allen and Unwin, 1987 and R.F. Holland, Britain and the Commonwealth Alliance 1918–1939, London: Macmillan, 1981. An interesting approach can also be found in Anthony Clayton, The British Empire as a Superpower, 1919–39, London: Macmillan, 1986.

50 In this regard, see Christopher Waters, Australia and Appeasement: Imperial Foreign Policy and the Origins of World War II, London: I.B. Tauris, 2012. For views of the Australian public, see Andrews, Isolationism and Appeasement in Australia.

51 For a perspective on the events surrounding Australia and the 'insurance policy' approach, see David Day, The Great Betrayal: Britain, Australia and the Onset of the Pacific War 1939–42, Sydney: Angus and Robertson, 1988. See also Peter J. Dean (ed.), Australia 1942: In the Shadow of War, Melbourne: Cambridge University Press, 2013.

Notes

Chapter 2

1 South Australian State Archives, Adelaide Hebrew Congregation files, SRG 162/2 vol. 6 (Committee Minutes), minutes of committee meeting, 1 June 1933.

2 *Sydney Morning Herald*, 7 June 1933, p. 15.

3 In this regard, see Christopher Waters, *Australia and Appeasement: Imperial Foreign Policy and the Origins of World War II*, London: I.B. Tauris, 2012 and E.M. Andrews, *Isolationism and Appeasement in Australia: Reactions to the European Crises, 1935–1939*, Canberra: Australian National University Press, 1970.

4 *Sydney Morning Herald*, 28 April 1933, p 4.

5 Ibid., 29 May 1933, p. 8.

6 NAA A367, file C 3075 I, 'Central European Migrants (Stateless German Refugee Jews)', Draft report 'The German Jew', unsigned, to Roland S. Browne (Commonwealth Investigation Branch), 15 September 1933.

7 Ibid.

8 Ibid.

9 Ibid.

10 L.J. Louis and Ian Turner (ed.), *The Depression of the 1930s*, Melbourne: Cassell, 1968, p. 89.

11 NAA A434, file 49/3/7034, 'Admi. of German Jews – Cabinet Decision re', Interior memorandum for Cabinet, 2 June 1933.

12 Ibid., handwritten minute by Sir George Pearce.

13 NAA A1, file 34/2551, 'Sweating by Aliens in Clothing Trade', Interior memorandum of 21 August 1933; handwritten minute by J.A. Carrodus, 22 August 1933.

14 Ibid.

15 NAA A433, file 43/2/3378, 'National Council of Jewish Women of Australia – Information re Jewish Immigration, etc', J.A. Carrodus to Dr. Fanny Reading, 22 May 1936.

16 NAA A434, file 49/3/7034, 'Admi. of German Jews – Cabinet Decision re', Interior memorandum for Cabinet, 2 June 1933.

17 An example concerns the issuance of travel documents for refugees who were accepted into Australia and who then wished to travel abroad. Even though the policy adopted enabled such people to travel overseas on special exit and re-entry permits, it was stated:

> Owing to the geographical position of Australia and the strict control exercised over alien immigration into this country, it is expected that there will be very few cases where it will be found necessary for this Department to issue travel documents to refugees coming from Germany

NAA A1, file 34/4275, 'Travel Documents for Refugees from Germany. Issue of', Secretary, Department of the Interior to Assistant Secretary of External Affairs, 7 August 1934.

18 NAA A461, file M 349/3/5, 'Jews – Policy. Part 1', Interior memorandum for Cabinet, 9 March 1936.

19 Ibid.

20 Ibid.

21 NAA A461, file A 349/1/2 Part II, 'Immigration Policy', extract from Cabinet Minutes, 16 March 1936.

22 NAA A367, file C 3075 AG, 'Report of Interdepartmental Committee of Migration and Control of Aliens', Interior memorandum (*White Alien Immigration*) prepared by J.A. Carrodus, 2 August 1937.

23 CPD, H. of R., vol. 150, 6 May 1936, p. 1246.

24 NAA A433, file 43/2/3378, 'National Council of Jewish Women – Information re. Jewish Immigration, etc', J.A. Carrodus to President, National Council of Jewish Women of Australia (Dr. Fanny Reading), 22 May 1936.

25 NAA A434, file 49/3/7034, 'Admi. of German Jews – Cabinet Decision re', T.H. Garrett to J.A. Carrodus, 6 August 1936.

26 Imperial War Museum (London), Department of Sound Records, Accession no 004382/03, transcript of interview with Julian David Layton OBE, no date (hereafter Layton Interview).

27 Ibid.

28 On the German Jewish Relief Fund, see Anne Andgel, *Fifty Years of Caring: The History of the Australian Jewish Welfare Society, 1936–1986*, Sydney: Australian Jewish Welfare Society/Australian Jewish Historical Society, 1988. An additional source, albeit from a Victorian perspective, is Rodney Benjamin, *A Serious Influx: A History of Jewish Welfare in Victoria*, St. Leonards (NSW): Allen and Unwin, 1998.

29 Layton Interview. Layton's activities in selecting German refugees for settlement in Australia were not relied upon solely by the Jewish leadership in London. The Council for German Jewry also sent a representative, Dennis Cohen, to Germany for the purpose of interviewing potential immigrants for Australia. Cohen's visit took in Berlin, Hamburg, Leipzig, Frankfurt and Cologne, and involved some 150 separate interviews along similar lines to Layton's (TNA HO 213, file 250, 'Report by Mr. Dennis M. Cohen on His Visit to Germany, January 1937').

30 This notwithstanding, the activities of the German Jewish Relief Fund were considerable, the minutes of the organization recording innumerable instances of liaison with London over such issues as permits, landing money, contact with governments and so on. See AJWS Archives, *Minute Book, German-Jewish Refugees Fund NSW Appeal* (March 1936–October 1936).

31 NAA A434, file 49/3/7034, 'Admi. of German Jews – Cabinet Decision re', Interior memorandum (*Question of Admission of Jews into Australia*) prepared by A.R. Peters, dated 14 July 1936.

32 Ibid.

33 AJWS Archives, Minute Book, Executive Committee of German-Jewish Relief Fund (November 1936–February 1939), Minutes for 26 November 1936.

34 Ibid.

35 Ibid.

36 Ibid.

37 TNA DO 35, file 705/M529/1, Dominions Office to Dr. A.C. Don (Chaplain to the Archbishop of Canterbury), 27 April 1937.

38 NAA A373, file 3075, 'Alien Migration Policy', confidential memorandum from Inspector D.R.B. Mitchell to Director, Commonwealth Investigation Branch, 7 June 1937.

39 Ibid.

40 *Smith's Weekly*, 12 June 1937, p. 2.

41 CPD, H. of R., vol. 153, 28 June 1937, p. 49.

42 NAA A367, file C 3075 AG, 'Report of Interdepartmental Committee on Migration and Control of Aliens', Interior memorandum (*White Alien Immigration*) prepared by J.A. Carrodus, 2 August 1937.

43 Ian Jobling, 'Australia at the 1936 Olympics: Issues and Attitudes', *Canadian Journal of History of Sport*, 13:1, May 1982, p. 25.

44 On Australia and the Berlin Olympics, see Larry Writer, *Dangerous Games: Australia at the 1936 Nazi Olympics*, Sydney: Allen and Unwin, 2015.

45 *The Argus*, 2 October 1937, p. 9.

46 NAA A461, file T349/3/5, 'Immigration – Poles', Sdmerek Perle (Poland) to Prime Minister J.A. Lyons, 9 June 1937.

47 NAA A461, file M.A. 349/3/5 Part 1, 'Jews. General. Part 1', Dawid Henenfeld (Poland) to Prime Minister J.A. Lyons, 29 October 1937.

48 On the Polish Jewish Relief Fund, see Benjamin, *A Serious Influx of Jews*, chapter 4, pp. 62–78.

49 NAA A461, file M 349/3/5 Part 1, 'Jews Policy. Part 1', Interior memorandum for Cabinet, 1 November 1937.

50 NAA A434, file 41/3/1039, 'Polish Jewish Relief/Migration of Children', Interior memorandum for Cabinet, 1 November 1937; handwritten minute by J.A. Lyons dated 7 April 1938.

51 Ibid., extract from Cabinet Minutes, 7 April 1938, confirmation of Lyons's handwritten minute.

52 Ibid., Interior memorandum for Cabinet, 1 November 1937; handwritten minute by J.A. Lyons dated 9 June 1938.

53 NAA A445, file 235/5/2 Part 2, 'Admission of Jews Policy Part 2', Interior memorandum (*German Jews*) prepared by A.R. Peters, dated 5 August 1937.

Chapter 3

1 NAA A445, file 235/5/2 Part 2, 'Admission of Jews Policy Part 2', 'Notes of Interview of Mr. Paul A. Cohen, Hon. Secretary, Australian Jewish Welfare Society, with Hon. V.C. Thompson, Minister Assisting the Treasurer', Sydney, 3 February 1938.

2 Ibid., recommendation by Thompson to Minister for the Interior, for submission to Cabinet (*Admission of German-Jews into Australia*), 8 February 1938.

3 Ibid., Interior memorandum (*Immigration of Jews into Australia through the Medium of the Australian Jewish Welfare Society*) prepared by A.R. Peters, 10 February 1938.

4 Ibid.

5 Ibid., Interior draft memorandum for Cabinet, 4 March 1938; handwritten minute by John McEwen dated 7 March 1938.

6 Ibid., Paul A. Cohen to Secretary, Department of the Interior, 19 April 1938.

7 Ibid., handwritten minute by A.R. Peters, 3 May 1938.

8 Ibid., Interior memorandum (*Admission into Australia of Jews under the Auspices of the Australian Jewish Welfare Society*) prepared by T.H. Garrett, 4 May 1938; handwritten

endorsement by J.A. Carrodus, 4 May 1938; Ministerial approval minuted by John McEwen, 9 May 1938.

9   Ibid., J.A. Carrodus to Paul A. Cohen, 13 April 1938.

10   Ibid., Frank Strahan (Secretary, Prime Minister's Department) to Secretary, Department of the Interior, 8 April 1938.

11   *Sydney Morning Herald*, 17 March 1938, p. 11.

12   Ibid.

13   Ibid., 18 March 1938, p. 14.

14   E.M. Andrews, *Isolationism and Appeasement in Australia: Reactions to the European Crises, 1935–1939*, Canberra: Australian National University Press, 1970, p. 128.

15   NAA A461, file A 349/3/1 Part 2, 'Foreign Migration Policy Part 2', cablegram from Prime Minister's Department to High Commissioner's Office, London, 8 July 1938.

16   *Sydney Morning Herald*, 4 February 1938, p. 13.

17   Ibid.

18   NAA A445, file 235/5/2 Part 2, 'Admission of Jews Policy Part 2', Interior memorandum (*Immigration of Jews into Australia*) prepared by A.R. Peters, 14 April 1938.

19   Ibid.

20   Ibid.

21   Ibid., J.A. Carrodus to Minister for the Interior, 19 April 1938 (emphasis added).

22   Ibid., Interior memorandum (*Immigration of Jews into Australia*) prepared by A.R. Peters, 14 April 1938; handwritten minute by John McEwen, undated.

23   NAA A461, file A 349/1/2 Part 3, 'Immigration Policy', Interior memorandum (*White Alien Immigration*), unsigned, 16 March 1938.

24   Ibid.

25   Ibid.

26   NAA A461, file M 349/3/5, 'Jews – Policy Part 1', draft Interior memorandum for Cabinet, no precise date, but prepared in July 1938.

27   NAA MP 729/6, file 22/401/2, 'Control of Aliens', secret memorandum from Secretary, Department of External Affairs, to Secretary, Department of Defence, 10 January 1938.

28   NAA A445, file 235/5/2 Part 2, 'Admission of Jews Policy Part 2', V.C. Farrell, British Passport Control Officer, Budapest, to Secretary, Department of the Interior, 29 March 1938.

29   Ibid.

30   Ibid.

31   TNA DO 35, file 705/M529/20, Lord Stanley to Major Sir Ralph Glyn MP, 21 May 1938.

32   Ibid., minute to the Secretary of State, 27 May 1938.

33   See in this regard Andrews, *Isolationism and Appeasement* and Christopher Waters, *Australia and Appeasement: Imperial Foreign Policy and the Origins of World War II*, London: I.B. Tauris, 2012.

34   TNA, DO 35, file 705/M529/24, British High Commissioner (Sir Geoffrey Whiskard), Canberra, to R.A. Wiseman, Dominions Office, London, 23 June 1938.

35   Ibid., file 716/M576/1, Memorandum to His Majesty's Government in the United Kingdom, from the Embassy of the United States, London, 24 March 1938.

36 Ibid., Reuter's news bulletin, 31 March 1938, issued at 10.00 pm, quoting a Press Statement from J.A. Lyons of that date.

37 *The Argus* (Melbourne), 5 April 1938, p. 11.

38 Ibid., 11 May 1938, p. 6.

39 NAA A434, file 50/3/41837, 'Refugees from Austria: Special Committee Proposed by U.S.A., Evian', Interior memorandum for Cabinet (*Immigration of Jews into Australia*), 25 May 1938.

40 Ibid. (emphasis added).

41 Ibid.

42 Ibid., handwritten minute by Prime Minister J.A. Lyons.

43 Ibid.

44 Ibid. (emphasis added).

45 Ibid., Prime Minister Lyons to the High Commissioner, London, 22 June 1938.

46 NAA A981, file Migration 48, 'Migration Restrictions – Australia. Italians, Policy', Interior memorandum (*Statement Regarding Alien Immigration into Australia*), April 1938.

47 Ibid.

48 Ibid.

49 CPD, H. of R., vol. 155, 4 May 1938, p. 784.

50 NAA A367, file C3075 I, 'Central European Migrants (Stateless German Refugee Jews)', Commonwealth Investigation Branch document, 'Notes on Jewish Migration from Central Europe', unsigned, undated (April 1938?).

51 Ibid.

52 Ibid.

53 Ibid.

54 *Daily Telegraph*, 18 January 1938.

55 *The Bulletin*, 21 April 1938, p. 13.

56 NAA A434, file 49/3/3196, 'Admission of Jews to Australia', Peter Ferrier (Runcorn, Brisbane) to John McEwen, 11 February 1938.

57 While other letters expressing antisemitic attitudes had appeared throughout the 1920s and 1930s, hardly any had opposed Jewish immigration on purely antisemitic grounds. The usual objections revolved around economic rivalry, competition for employment or fear of alien intrusion – all of which were applied at one time or another to alien migrants of every European nationality. Extensive examination of protest letters sent to the Department of the Interior (NAA A433, A434, A659), the Prime Minister's Department (NAA A2, A458, A461, A1608), the Commonwealth Investigation Branch (NAA A367), the External Affairs Department (NAA A981, A989) and the Attorney-General's Department (NAA A1, A432, A472) in the years following 1918 indicate that the letter from Peter Ferrier was one of the first of its kind, certainly since the accession to power of Hitler and the Nazis in January 1933.

58 NAA A1, file 38/11509, 'German Emergency Fellowship Committee Admin. of non-Aryan Christians of Jewish Extraction', Interior memorandum (*German Emergency Fellowship Committee*) prepared by J.A. Carrodus, 2 June 1938.

59 Ibid.

60 Ibid., Interior memorandum (*German Emergency Fellowship Committee: Question of Facilities to Introduce non-Aryan Christians*) prepared by A.R. Peters, 6 June 1938.

61 NAA A461, file R349/3/5, 'Immigration. Catholic Refugees from Germany and Austria', Cardinal Hinsley to J.A. Lyons, 23 May 1938.

62 Ibid., Lyons to Cardinal Hinsley, 4 July 1938.

63 NAA A1, file 38/25491, 'Catholic Refugees from Europe', Interior memorandum (*Roman Catholic Refugees from Austria and Germany – Question of Facilities to Migrate to Australia*) prepared by A.R. Peters, 15 August 1938.

64 Andrews, *Isolationism and Appeasement*, p. 10.

65 Ibid., p. 12.

66 Ibid., p. 14.

67 Ibid. On the Catholic papers in New South Wales, see also Rachael L.E. Kohn, 'The Catholic and Anglican Church Press of New South Wales and the Jews, 1933–1945', in Paul R. Bartrop (ed.), *False Havens: The British Empire and the Holocaust*, Lanham, MD: University Press of America, 1995, pp. 159–85.

Chapter 4

1 For a single-volume treatment of the Evian Conference, see Paul R. Bartrop, *The Evian Conference of 1938 and the Jewish Refugee Crisis*, London: Palgrave Macmillan, 2017. A more general survey, arguing that Evian precipitated the Holocaust, is Tony Matthews, *Tragedy at Evian: How the World Allowed Hitler to Proceed with the Holocaust*, Newport (NSW): Big Sky Publishing, 2020. In German, see the superb resource edited by Winfried Meyer et al., *Geschlossene Grenzen: Die Internationale Flüchtlingskonferenz von Évian 1938*, Berlin: Zentrum für Antisemitismusforschung der Technischen Universität Berlin/Gedenkstätte Deutscher Widerstand, 2018.

2 Michael R. Marrus, *The Unwanted: European Refugees in the Twentieth Century*, New York: Oxford University Press, 1985, p. 170.

3 TNA DO 35, file 716/M576/1, memorandum to His Majesty's Government in the United Kingdom, from the Embassy of the United States, London, 24 March 1938.

4 Ibid.

5 Ibid.

6 TNA FO 371, file 22321, minute by R.M. Makins (Foreign Office), 25 March 1938.

7 Ibid.

8 Ibid.

9 TNA DO 35, file 716/M576/1, Foreign Office to B. Cockram Esq. (Dominions Office) 25 March 1938.

10 Ibid., draft memorandum, undated, unsigned.

11 Ibid., minute on file by W.J. Garnett, 30 March 1938.

12 Ibid., R.A. Wiseman (Dominions Office) to the High Commissioner for Australia, London, 1 April 1938.

13 Ibid., V.C. Duffy (Official Secretary, Australia House) to the Under-Secretary of State, Dominions Office, 5 April 1938.

14 NAA A461, file M349/3/5, Part 1, 'Jews – Policy Part 1', cablegram from S.M. Bruce to Prime Minister J.A. Lyons, 5 April 1938 (received 6 April 1938).

15 Ibid. As it turned out, by early April the nations that had agreed to attend included Belgium, France, Sweden, Argentina, Brazil, Columbia, the Dominican Republic, Guatemala, Haiti, Mexico, Nicaragua, Paraguay, Peru, El Salvador and Uruguay (TNA FO 371, file 21748, C.R. Price (Dominions Office) to the Official Secretary, Australia House, 8 April 1938). By the time the conference took place in July 1938, fifteen other states plus the United States and Britain had joined them.

16 NAA A461, file M349/3/5 Part 1, 'Jews – Policy Part 1', cablegram from S.M. Bruce to Prime Minister J.A. Lyons, 5 April 1938 (received 6 April 1938).

17 Ibid., cablegram from J.A. Lyons to S. M. Bruce, 8 April 1938.

18 NAA A445, file 235/5/2 Part 2, 'Admission of Jews Policy Part 2', memorandum from Frank Strahan, Secretary, Prime Minister's Department, to Secretary, Department of the Interior, 8 April 1938.

19 NAA A461, file M349/3/5 Part 1, 'Jews – Policy Part 1', cablegram from J.A. Lyons to S.M. Bruce, 8 April 1938.

20 Ibid.

21 TNA FO 371, file 21748, Herschel V. Johnson (Counsellor, Embassy of the United States of America, London) to Viscount Halifax (Foreign Secretary, His Majesty's Government in the United Kingdom), 26 May 1938.

22 TNA FO 371, file 21749, Foreign Office minute by Roger Makins, 13 June 1938.

23 Ibid., from the record of the interdepartmental committee meeting held at the Foreign Office on 8 June 1938.

24 Ibid.

25 TNA DO 35, file 705/M529/20, Dominions Office minute for Secretary of State, 27 May 1938.

26 TNA FO 371, file 21749, Foreign Office minute by Roger Makins, 13 June 1938.

27 See Christopher Waters, *Australia and Appeasement: Imperial Foreign Policy and the Origins of World War II*, London: I.B. Tauris, 2012, chapter 4.

28 TNA FO 371, file 21748, Foreign Office minute by Roger Makins, 7 April 1938.

29 Norman Bentwich, 'The Evian Conference and after', *Fortnightly*, 144, September 1938, p. 289.

30 *The Argus*, 8 July 1938, p. 2.

31 *Sydney Morning Herald*, 6 July 1938, p. 16.

32 Ibid.

33 NAA A434, file 50/3/41837, 'Refugees from Austria: Special Committee Proposed by U.S.A., Evian', High Commissioner's Office, London, to Secretary, Department of External Affairs, 13 July 1938.

34 Board of Deputies of British Jews Archives, file E3/282/1, 'Inter-Governmental Conference on Refugees Held at Evian, 6 July 1938', unsigned report (henceforth 'Board of Deputies Evian Report').

35 Ibid.

36 The countries attending the conference were, in alphabetical order: Argentina, Australia, Belgium, Bolivia, Brazil, Canada, Chile, Colombia, Costa Rica, Cuba, Denmark, Dominican Republic, Ecuador, Eire, France, Guatemala, Haiti, Honduras, Mexico, New Zealand,

Netherlands, Nicaragua, Norway, Panama, Paraguay, Peru, Sweden, Switzerland, United Kingdom, United States, Uruguay and Venezuela.

37 NAA A434, file 50/3/41837, 'Refugees from Austria: Special Committee Proposed by U.S.A., Evian', *Inter-Governmental Committee on Refugees held at Evian, 6–15 July 1938: Summary of Proceedings*.

38 Board of Deputies Evian Report.

39 Martin Gilbert, *Exile and Return: The Emergence of Jewish Statehood*, London: Weidenfeld and Nicolson, 1978, p. 202.

40 G. Warburg, 'None to Comfort the Persecuted: The Failure of Refugee Conferences. Evian, July, 1938', *Wiener Library Bulletin*, 15:3, 1961, pp. 43–7.

41 NAA A434, file 50/2/41837, 'Refugees from Austria: Special Committee Proposed by U.S.A., Evian', *Speech by Lieut.-Colonel the Honourable T.W. White, Delegate for Australia at Evian-les-Bains Conference on 7th July 1938* (emphasis added).

42 Ibid.

43 *The Bulletin*, 13 July 1938, p. 13.

44 Ibid. E. M. Andrews has shown how Catholic spokesmen in Australia held similar views on the relationship between Jews and communism throughout the 1930s, to the point where the *Catholic Freeman's Journal*, on 7 July 1938, opposed the entry of refugees 'thinking it wrong to give opportunities to people "who, for one reason or another, are not content to remain in their native land"'. See E. M. Andrews, *Isolationism and Appeasement in Australia: Reactions to the European Crises, 1935–1939*, Canberra: Australian National University Press, 1970, p. 151.

45 *Sydney Morning Herald*, 9 July 1938, p. 16.

46 Ibid.

47 Ibid., 13 July 1938, p. 12.

48 Ibid., 15 July 1938, p. 10.

49 *The Argus*, 9 July 1938, p. 9.

50 This was composed of Brazil, Canada, Chile, the UK, the United States, France, Haiti, the Netherlands and Switzerland. Its brief was to 'hear in confidence the statements of laws and practices of the participating governments, statements of the number and types of immigrants each is prepared to receive and consider the question of documentation'. See S. Adler-Rudel, 'The Evian Conference on the Refugee Question', *Leo Baeck Institute Yearbook*, 13, 1968, p. 251.

51 Board of Deputies Evian Report.

52 Norman Bentwich, *My 77 Years: An Account of My Life and Times, 1883–1960*, London: Routledge and Kegan Paul, 1962, pp. 147–8.

53 Board of Deputies Evian Report.

54 Board of Deputies of British Jews Archives, file E3/282/1, Council for German Jewry Report (*Report on the Governmental Conference at Evian*) prepared by Norman Bentwich, no date.

55 NAA A981, file Refugees 4 Pt 1, 'Refugees – General Inter-Governmental Committee (Including Evian Conference) Pt 1', Alfred Stirling to W.R. Hodgson, 17 July 1938.

56 Adler-Rudel, 'Evian Conference', p. 254.

57 Ibid., p. 255.

58 Bentwich, *My 77 Years*, p. 148.

59 Ibid.

60 Board of Deputies Evian Report.

61 NAA A981, file Refugees 4 Pt 1, 'Refugees – General Inter-Governmental Committee (including Evian Conference) Pt 1', Alfred Stirling to W.R. Hodgson, 17 July 1938.

62 Ibid.

63 Alfred Stirling, *Lord Bruce: The London Years*, Melbourne: Hawthorne, 1974, pp. 73–4.

64 NAA A981, file Refugees 4 Pt 1, 'Refugees – General Inter-Governmental Committee (including Evian Conference) Pt. 1', Alfred Stirling to W.R. Hodgson, 17 July 1938.

65 Stirling, *Lord Bruce*, p. 74.

66 Indeed, Hitler referred explicitly to this in his closing speech at the Nuremberg Party Rally on 12 September 1938, lampooning the hypocrisy of the democratic countries who, while bemoaning 'the boundless cruelty' of countries such as Germany and Italy, now offered 'nothing but laments'. See Norman H. Baynes (ed.), *The Speeches of Adolf Hitler, April 1922–August 1939*, vol. 1, New York: Oxford University Press, 1942, pp. 719–20.

67 See, for example, Australian Population and Immigration Council (APIC), *Population Report 3* (prepared by the Committee of APIC on Refugee Issues), Canberra: Australian Government Publishing Service, 1979. See also, influential editor of the *Australian Jewish News*, Sam Lipski, in his 'Partisan' column from early 1988: 'When I was six months old, the representatives of 31 countries met at Evian-les-Bains on the French shore of Lake Geneva to discuss refugee problems. Most governments did little or nothing. Among the few positive results was the agreement by Australia, which had permitted few immigrants, to receive 15,000 Jewish refugees over the next few years'. (*Australian Jewish News*, 29 January 1988, p. 11. The claim has been repeated continually through to contemporary times.

68 This was even repeated in the official history of Australia at the bicentenary in 1988. See Janis Wilton, 'Refugees', in Bill Gammage and Peter Spearritt (ed.), *Australians 1938*, Sydney: Fairfax, Syme and Weldon Associates, 1987, p. 408: 'as a result of the Evian Conference, the Australian government agreed to accept 15,000 Jewish refugees who were fleeing Austria and Germany as a result of Hitler's anti-Semitic policies'.

69 The bogus document in question can be found in NAA A981, REF part 1, 'Refugees – General – Intergovernmental Committee (including Evian Conference)', Alfred Stirling to Department of External Affairs, 16 April 1940.

70 Much discussion has focused on the 'offer' by the tiny Dominican Republic at Evian to take in 100,000 Jewish refugees; however, this was not the case. The delegate from the Dominican Republic, Virgilio Trujillo Molina (the brother of Dominican dictator Rafael Leónidas Trujillo) declared at Evian that his country could provide land, seed and technical advice to arriving colonists, offering 'specially advantageous concessions to Austrian and German exiles' provided they were 'agriculturalists with an unimpeachable record who satisfy the conditions laid down by Dominican legislation on immigration'. Further, the government 'would also be prepared to grant special conditions to professional men immigrating who, as recognized scientists, would be able through their teaching to render valuable service to their Dominican colleagues'. His address led almost immediately to a myth stemming from a major misunderstanding on the part of many commentators, who have read into the speech a declaration made on 12 August 1938 – over a month later – in which the same Molina communicated an offer of land for the settlement of 100,000 refugees in the Dominican Republic. The two events were related but quite distinct. See Bartrop, *The Evian Conference of 1938 and the Jewish Refugee Crisis*, pp. 67–8 and Marion Kaplan, *Dominican Haven: The Jewish Refugee Settlement in Sosúa, 1940–1945*, New York: Museum of Jewish Heritage, 2008.

Chapter 5

1 NAA A461, file G349/1/2, 'Immigration Encouragement. Landing Money', Prime Minister's Department memorandum (*White Alien Immigration*), 27 July 1938.

2 NAA A1, file 38/30786, 'Jews (British Subjects) Resident in the U.K. Assisted Passages for', Interior memorandum for Cabinet (*Jews (British Subjects) Resident in the United Kingdom – Question as to whether they should be granted assisted passages*) prepared by V.C. Thompson, 29 August 1938.

3 Ibid.

4 Ibid., handwritten minute by Prime Minister J.A. Lyons, 16 November 1938.

5 *The Bulletin*, 27 July 1938, p. 12.

6 NAA A445, file 235/5/6, 'Protests re. Jewish Immigration', H.T. McCrea (Chatswood, NSW) to the Rt Hon W.M. Hughes, 15 August 1938.

7 Ibid., Albert Carlyle Willis (Kirribilli, NSW) to the Secretary, Prime Minister's Department, 31 August 1938.

8 Ibid., A.W. Ross (Melbourne) to 'the Minister in Charge of Migration', 29 July 1938.

9 Ibid., Jack Coyle to the Minister for the Interior, 2 August 1938. The Domain was an area of city parkland inhabited by many unemployed Sydney workers throughout the 1930s.

10 *Sydney Morning Herald*, 28 July 1938, p. 13.

11 Ibid.

12 *The Bulletin*, 27 July 1938, p. 12.

13 NAA A433, file 43/2/46, 'Refugees (Jewish and Others) – General Policy File', Interior memorandum for Cabinet (*Immigration*) prepared by V.C. Thompson, 17 August 1938.

14 Ibid.

15 Ibid. (emphasis added).

16 Ibid.

17 Ibid.

18 NAA A461, file M349/3/5, 'Jews – Policy. Part 1', A.R. Peters to Secretary, Prime Minister's Department, for transmission to High Commissioner's Office, London, 16 September 1938.

19 NAA A445, file 235/5/5, 'Jewish Tourists Seeking Permanent Admission', Interior memorandum (*Jewish passengers on return tickets claiming to the [sic] tourist visitors*) prepared by A.R. Peters, 5 October 1938.

20 *Sydney Morning Herald*, 6 October 1938, p. 13.

21 Ibid.

22 Ibid.

23 Ibid.

24 *The Argus*, 7 October 1938, p. 15.

25 NAA A461, file M349/3/5, 'Jews – Policy. Part 1', cablegram from Department of the Interior to High Commissioner's Office, London, 14 October 1938.

26 NAA A461, file MA349/3/5 Part 1, 'Jews. General. Part 1', cablegram from Department of the Interior to High Commissioner's Office, London, 20 September 1938.

27 CPD, H. of R., vol. 157, 21 September 1938, p. 11.

28 *Sydney Morning Herald*, 17 November 1938, p. 12.

29 Ibid.

30 Indeed, Albert Peters was himself affected, 'agonizing over all the decisions he had to make' and reading 'all those heartbreaking letters'. Estelle Catlow (*née* Peters) to author, 24 September 1995.

31 NAA A461, file MA349/3/5 Part 2, 'Jews. General. Part 2', Oskar Pollak (Prague, Czechoslovakia) to Prime Minister J.A. Lyons, 30 September 1938 (grammar as in original).

32 NAA A461, file MA349/3/5 Part 1, 'Jews. General. Part 1', Hersh Zeil Wozingh (Magdeburg, Germany) to 'the first minister, Canberra', 3 October 1938.

33 Ibid., Fritz Fischer (Vienna, Austria) to Governor-General Lord Gowrie, 11 October 1938.

34 Ibid., Oskar Rosner (Vienna, Austria) to Prime Minister J.A. Lyons, 13 October 1938.

35 Ibid., Maximilian Jacobson (Vienna, Austria) to Prime Minister J.A. Lyons, 10 October 1938.

36 Ibid., Alfred Andermann (Vienna, Austria) to Prime Minister J.A. Lyons, 15 October 1938.

37 NAA A461, file L349/3/5, 'Immigration – Germany Pt. 1', Siegfried Posner (Berlin, Germany) to Prime Minister J.A. Lyons, 10 October 1938.

38 Ibid., Otto Ayrt (Dresden, Germany) to Prime Minister J.A. Lyons, 24 October 1938.

39 NAA A461, file MA349/3/5 Part 2, 'Jews. General. Part 2', Lejzov Kurlander (Kosciuszki, Poland) to 'His Majesty', 14 November 1938.

40 Rabbi L.A. Falk in Sydney received a number of these. Australian Jewish Historical Society Archives, Sydney (hereafter AJHS), Rabbi Falk Correspondence File (file 832), contains several such letters and the Rabbi's responses to them. For an example sent to the government, see also NAA A461, file C349/3/5, 'Migration – Austria-Hungary', Berthe Hekisch (Budapest, Hungary) to 'the Australian Government, Camberra' [*sic*], no date (received at Prime Minister's Department on 26 September 1938).

41 *Sydney Morning Herald*, 6 October 1938, p. 5.

42 NAA A367, file C3075 I, 'Central European Migrants (Stateless German Refugee Jews)', H.E. Jones (Director, Commonwealth Investigation Branch) to the Commonwealth Solicitor-General, 21 October 1938.

43 CPD, H. of R., vol. 155, 28 April 1938, p. 592.

44 Australian Jewish Welfare Society Archives, Sydney (hereafter AJWS), History File, Open Letter to the Jewish community by New South Wales Appeal Committee of the Australian Jewish Welfare Society, signed by John Goulston (Chairman) and H. Vidor (Hon. Secretary), no date (presumably late 1938). For activities in Victoria, see also Rodney Benjamin, *A Serious Influx of Jews: A History of Jewish Welfare in Victoria*, St. Leonards (NSW): Allen and Unwin, 1998, chapter 5, pp. 79–106.

45 AJHS Archives, Rabbi Falk Correspondence File (file 832), L. Schulman (Organising Secretary, Australian Jewish Welfare Society), to Rabbi L.A. Falk, 19 August 1938.

46 AJWS Archives (Sydney), History File, Open Letter to the Jewish community by New South Wales Appeal Committee of the Australian Jewish Welfare Society, signed by John Goulston (Chairman) and H. Vidor (Hon. Secretary), no date (presumably late 1938) (emphasis in text).

47 Ibid., ROTA Committee Meetings – Minute Book (August 1938–November 1938), Minutes for 28 September 1938.

48 NAA A1, file 38/23138, 'Australian Jewish Welfare Society – Proposal re. control of Jewish migration', Sir Samuel Cohen (President, AJWS) to Secretary, Department of the Interior, 6 September 1938 (emphasis in text).

49   Ibid. (emphasis in text).

50   AJWS Archives (Sydney), ROTA Committee Meetings – Minute Book (August 1938–
      November 1938), minutes from 28 September 1938.

51   Ibid.

Chapter 6

1   NAA A433, file 43/2/4588, 'European Refugees. Views of public re. admittance of', Dorothy
     Gibson (Hon. Assistant Secretary, International Peace Campaign) to Prime Minister Lyons,
     21 October 1938.

2   Ibid., L.P. Fox (State Secretary, League for Peace and Democracy) to Prime Minister Lyons,
     2 November 1938.

3   Fitzpatrick Papers, Australian National Library, Series 1, Box 4, Affiliation – Victorian
     Correspondence 1938–9, Resolution Carried at Meeting of Poowong and District Residents
     Held 6 November 1938 (forwarded to B.P. Lazarus, Council for Civil Liberties, by Winston
     H. Burchett on 22 November 1938).

4   NAA A461, file Q349/3/5 Pt 1, 'Immigration of Southern Europeans Pt. 1', H.L. Hanson
     (Secretary, Australian United Empire Party) to Prime Minister Lyons, 6 October 1938.

5   NAA A445, file 235/5/4 Pt 3, 'Admission of Jews Policy Part 3', H.E. Jones (Director,
     Commonwealth Investigation Branch) to Secretary, Department of the Interior, 7 October
     1938.

6   NAA A433, file 43/2/4588, 'European Refugees. Views of public re. admittance of', A.
     Hill (Secretary, Business Brokers' Association of New South Wales) to John McEwen,
     2 November 1938.

7   NAA A445, file 235/5/6, 'Protests re. Jewish Immigration', J.H. Mahony to John McEwen,
     15 October 1938.

8   *The Argus*, 7 October 1938, p. 14.

9   Ibid.

10   *The Age*, 14 October 1938, p. 10.

11   The literature on *Kristallnacht* is large. As a beginning, see Uta Gerhardt and Thomas Karlauf
      (ed.), *The Night of Broken Glass: Eyewitness Accounts of Kristallnacht*, London: Polity, 2012;
      Martin Gilbert, *Kristallnacht: Prelude to Tragedy*, New York: Harper, 2007; Karl A. Schleunes,
      The Twisted Road to Auschwitz: Nazi Policy toward German Jews, 1933–1939, Urbana:
      University of Illinois Press, 1970 and Rita Thalmann and Emmanuel Feinermann, *Crystal
      Night: 9–10 November 1938*, New York: Coward, McCann & Geoghegan, 1974.

12   *Sydney Morning Herald*, 18 November 1938, p. 10.

13   Fitzpatrick Papers, ANL, Series 1, Box 4, Affiliations – ACTU and Trades Hall Council
      Correspondence File, 1936–40, Hon. Secretary, Council for Civil Liberties, to Secretary,
      Melbourne Trades Hall Council, 19 November 1938.

14   NAA A445, file 235/5/6, 'Protests re. Jewish Immigration', Irene L. Couve (Maroubra, NSW)
      to Prime Minister Lyons, no date, but 29/11/[38] minuted in pencil by Department of the
      Interior.

15   *The Argus*, 17 November 1938, p. 12.

16   *The Bulletin*, 23 November 1938, p. 12.

17 E.M. Andrews, *Isolationism and Appeasement in Australia: Reactions to the European Crises, 1935–1939*, Canberra: Australian National University Press, 1970, p. 150.

18 NAA A367, file C3075 I, 'Central European Migrants (Stateless German Refugee Jews)', Commonwealth Investigation Branch memorandum (*Jewish Immigration*), unsigned, 21 November 1938.

19 NAA A433, file 43/2/4588, 'European Refugees. Views of public re. admittance of', Roberta Clapperton (Wooloowin, Queensland) to John McEwen, no date, but apparently November 1938 (emphasis in text).

20 *Sydney Morning Herald*, 18 November 1938, p. 10.

21 Ibid.

22 David S. Bird, *J.A. Lyons – The 'Tame Tasmanian:' Appeasement and Rearmament in Australia, 1932–39*, Melbourne: Australian Scholarly Publishing, 2008, p. 271.

23 Andrews, *Isolationism and Appeasement*, p. 152.

24 Christopher Waters, *Australia and Appeasement: Imperial Foreign Policy and the Origins of World War II*, London: I.B. Tauris, 2012, p. 137.

25 *The Argus*, 18 November 1938, p. 11.

26 Ibid.

27 Ibid., 26 November 1938, p. 9.

28 *Workers Weekly* (NSW), 2 December 1938, p. 3.

29 *The Argus*, 7 December 1938, p. 3.

30 Much has been written and misunderstood about Cooper's action, and the record needs clarification. Contrary to some claims, he was not the first Indigenous Australian to protest Nazi antisemitism, nor was his protest made in his private capacity. Further – in perhaps the gravest ongoing assertion – the League protest was not 'the only known non-government protest worldwide to the events of Kristallnacht'. Such a statement runs contrary to hundreds of protest actions globally. See Barbara Miller, *William Cooper, Gentle Warrior: Standing up for Australian Aborigines and Persecuted Jews*, Bloomington: Xlibris, 2012, p. 229.

31 CPD, Senate, vol. 157, 12 October 1938, p. 593.

32 Ibid., p. 594.

33 Ibid., pp. 594–5.

34 Ibid., p. 595.

35 Ibid., p. 596.

36 Ibid., H. of R., 9 November 1938, p. 1376.

37 Ibid.

38 Fitzpatrick papers, ANL, Series 1, Box 4, Affiliation – Victoria Correspondence 1938–9, Winston H. Burchett to B.P. Lazarus (Council for Civil Liberties), 22 November 1938.

39 Ibid.

40 CPD, H. of R., vol. 158, 22 November 1938, p. 1802.

41 NAA A461, file M349/3/5 Part 2, 'Jews – Policy. Part 2', Secret cablegram from S.M. Bruce to J.A. Lyons, 23 November 1938, received at Canberra, 7.44 pm, 22 November 1938.

42 CPD, H. of R., vol. 158, 22 November 1938, pp. 1803–4.

43 Ibid., p. 1850.

44 Ibid.

45 Ibid., p. 1851.

46 Ibid.

47 Ibid.

48 Ibid.

49 Ibid.

50 Ibid.

51 NAA A461, file M349/3/5 Part 2, 'Jews – Policy. Part 2', secret cable from S.M. Bruce to J.A. Lyons, 21 November 1938 (arrived at Canberra, 7.44 pm, 22 November 1938).

52 Waters, *Australia and Appeasement*, p. 89.

53 NAA A461, file M349/3/5 Part 2, 'Jews – Policy. Part 2', secret cable from S.M. Bruce to J.A. Lyons, 21 November 1938 (arrived at Canberra, 7.44 pm, 22 November 1938).

54 Ibid.

55 Ibid., secret cable from S.M. Bruce to J.A. Lyons, 21 November 1938 (arrived at Canberra, 10.00 pm, 22 November 1938).

56 Ibid.

57 TNA DO 35, file 705/M529/47, Dominions Office minute by the Duke of Devonshire, 22 November 1938.

58 Ibid.

59 Ibid., Dominions Office minute by Malcolm MacDonald, 29 November 1938.

60 NAA A461, file M349/3/5 Part 2, 'Jews – Policy. Part 2', secret Interior memorandum (*Refugees*) addressed to the Minister, prepared by J.A. Carrodus, 24 November 1938.

61 Ibid.

62 Ibid.

63 *The Argus*, 23 November 1938, p. 17.

64 Ibid.

65 Ibid.

66 *Sydney Morning Herald*, 24 November 1938, p. 10.

67 *Daily Telegraph* (London), 24 November 1938.

68 *The Argus*, 29 November 1938, p. 11.

69 Ibid.

70 NAA A461, file M349/3/5 Part 2, 'Jews – Policy Part 2', secret Interior memorandum (*Refugees*) addressed to the Minister, prepared by J.A. Carrodus, 24 November 1938.

71 Ibid.

72 See, for example, NAA A433, file 39/2/174, 'Spanish Refugee Admission', Interior memorandum (*Spanish Refugees*) prepared by A.R. Peters, 24 April 1939: 'It is usual to require that aliens who have no guarantors in Australia should be in possession of at least 200 pounds landing money. If a satisfactory five-year maintenance guarantee is furnished in their favour, the amount may be reduced to 50 pounds.'

Chapter 7

1   *Sydney Morning Herald*, 4 November 1938, p. 10.

2   Ibid., 28 November 1938, p. 11.

3   *The Argus*, 26 November 1938, p. 9.

4   See, for example, TNA DO 35, file 718/M582/2, Dominions Office memorandum (*Settlement of Jewish Refugees in the Dominions*), unsigned, written in September 1938 and circulated on 8 October 1938. The memorandum summarizes the Australian government's policy to that date, by which a maximum possible total of 5,100 Jewish refugees could come to Australia.

5   NAA A461, file M349/3/5 Part 2, 'Jews – Policy. Part 2', Interior memorandum for Cabinet (*Refugees*), 28 November 1938 (emphasis added).

6   TNA DO 35, file 705/M529/47, Dominions Office secret minute (handwritten, initials illegible), 30 November 1938.

7   CPD, H. of R., vol. 158, 30 November 1938, p. 2264.

8   Ibid.

9   Ibid.

10 Ibid., 1 December 1938, pp. 2534–6.

11 Ibid., p. 2535.

12 Ibid., p. 2536.

13 NAA A433, file 43/2/46, 'Refugees (Jewish and Other) – General Policy File', Interior memorandum for Cabinet (*Immigration*) prepared by V.C. Thompson, 17 August 1938.

14 *The Argus*, 2 December 1938, p. 1.

15 CPD, H. of R., vol. 158, 1 December 1938, p. 2536.

16 Ibid.

17 Ibid., 2 December 1938, p. 2626.

18 Ibid.

19 Ibid.

20 TNA DO 35, file 705/M529/47, Dominions Office minute from Malcolm MacDonald, 1 December 1938.

21 Ibid.

22 *Sydney Morning Herald*, 3 December 1938, p. 10.

23 TNA DO 35, file 705/M529/47, Dominions Office memorandum (*Settlement of Jewish Refugees in Australia*) prepared by W.J. Garnett, 6 December 1938.

24 *Labor Call*, 8 December 1938, p. 4.

25 Fitzpatrick Papers, National Library of Australia, Series 1, Box 4, 'Affiliations – ACTU & Trades Hall Council Correspondence file, 1936–40', Brian Fitzpatrick (Honorary Secretary, ACCL) to the Secretary, Trades Hall Council (Melbourne), 12 December 1938.

26 Ibid.

27 *Smith's Weekly*, 10 December 1938, p. 4.

28 *The Bulletin*, 7 December 1938, p. 13.

29 Ibid., 21 December 1938, p. 12.

30 NAA A445, file 235/5/6, 'Protests re. Jewish Immigration', Lionel S. Norman (Sandalwood, South Australia) to Archie Cameron (Postmaster-General, Canberra), 10 December 1938.

31 Ibid.

32 NAA A433, file 43/2/4588, 'European Refugees. Views of public re. admittance of', 'Australia First!' (Toowoomba, Queensland) to John McEwen, 23 December 1938.

33 NAA A445, file 235/5/6, 'Protests re. Jewish Immigration', Albert Carlyle Willis (Kirribilli, New South Wales) to the Minister for the Interior, 13 December 1938.

34 Ibid.

35 *Hebrew Standard*, 22 December 1938, p. 2.

36 NAA A445, file 235/5/5, 'Jewish Tourists Seeking Permanent Admission', A.R. Peters to the Passenger Superintendent in Australia, Orient Line (Sydney), 5 December 1938.

37 Ibid.

38 *Hebrew Standard*, 15 December 1938, p. 3.

39 Ibid.

40 NAA A461, file P349/3/5, 'Immigration Restrictions – Dutch', J.A. Carrodus to Secretary, Prime Minister's Department, 28 October 1938.

41 Ibid.

42 Ibid.

43 NAA A433, file 43/2/4588, 'European Refugees. Views of public re. admittance of', Muriel J. Alexander (Glenelg, South Australia) to Prime Minister Lyons, 12 November 1938.

44 TNA DO 35, file 705/M529/20, Ralph Glyn MP to Malcolm MacDonald, 10 May 1938.

45 NAA A433, file 43/2/4588, 'European Refugees. Views of public re. admittance of', Maude Waller (Knightsbridge, London, England) to Bertram Stevens (Premier, New South Wales), 16 November 1938.

46 Ibid., M.A. Westland (Trincomalee, Ceylon) to Prime Minister Lyons, 12 December 1938.

47 *Sydney Morning Herald*, 14 December 1938, p. 12.

48 J. Steinberg [Isaac N. Steinberg], 'A Jewish Settlement in the Kimberleys', *Australian Quarterly*, 12:1, March 1940, p. 25.

49 NAA A461, file U349/3/5, 'Foreign Migration. Settlement of Jews', S.M. Bruce to J.A. Lyons, 4 April 1938.

50 Ibid.

51 Michael Blakeney, 'The Kimberleys Madness? Wartime Proposals for a Colony of Jewish Refugees in the Kimberleys', *Quadrant*, 27:7, July 1983, p. 17.

52 NAA A1838/T116, file 1531/71/3, 'Immigration. Migration Australia. Settlement of European Jews in Australia', L. Kessler (Chairman) and Dr. I. Steinberg (Hon. Sec.), Freeland League for Jewish Territorial Colonisation, to the Hon. Sir Hal Pateshall Colebatch, Agent-General for Western Australia (London), 7 April 1938.

53 Michael Blakeney, *Australia and the Jewish Refugees 1933–1948*, Sydney: Croom Helm Australia, 1985, p. 255.

54 Ibid.

55 Ibid.

56 See ibid., pp. 270–4, for a description of the events surrounding the final defeat of the Kimberleys proposal. Other accounts of the Kimberleys scheme in 1939 and the war years

can be found in S. Stedman, 'Dr. Steinberg in Australia', *Australian Jewish Historical Society Journal and Proceedings*, 5:4, 1961, pp. 170–86; Wolf Simon Matsdorf, 'A New Jerusalem in Australia – the Kimberley Plan', *Wiener Library Bulletin*, 27:30/31, 1973/74, pp. 24–30; A. A. Calwell, *Be Just and Fear Not*, Adelaide: Rigby, 1978, chapter 13; and I.N. Steinberg's own *Australia – the Unpromised Land*, London: Victor Gollancz, 1948. See also Leon Gettler, *An Unpromised Land*, South Fremantle (WA): Fremantle Arts Centre Press, 1993 and Hilary L. Rubinstein, *The Jews in Australia: A Thematic History*, vol. 1, *1788–1945*, Melbourne: William Heinemann Australia, 1991, pp. 180–96.

57 See Hilary L. Rubinstein, 'Critchley Parker (1911–1942): Australian Martyr for Jewish Refugees', *Journal of the Australian Jewish Historical Society*, 11:1, 1990, pp. 56–68. The full story of Critchley Parker's sacrifice is being recovered in fragments, mainly by amateur historians and journalists in Tasmania. For a digest of these accounts, see https://jewsdownunder.com/2015/02/11/tasmania-new-jerusalem/

Chapter 8

1 NAA A461, file P349/3/5, 'Immigration Restrictions – Dutch.'

2 Board of Deputies of British Jews, Archives, file E1/13/1, Press Statement dated 17 July 1939.

3 *Sydney Morning Herald*, 18 July 1939, p. 10.

4 Board of Deputies of British Jews, Archives, file E1/13/1, correspondence between the Secretary, Board of Deputies, to M. Saly Meyer, Switzerland, 9 August 1939; the Secretary, Board of Deputies, to Miss Frances Barkman (Australian Jewish Welfare Society), Melbourne, 9 August 1939; and Paul A. Cohen (Hon. Secretary, AJWS, Sydney) to Neville J. Laski (Board of Deputies, London), 25 August 1939.

5 Estelle Catlow (*née* Peters) to author, 24 September 1995.

6 *The Argus*, 10 February 1939, p. 11.

7 Ibid.

8 *Sydney Morning Herald*, 16 February 1939, p. 8.

9 Joy Damousi, 'Australian League of Nations and War Refugees: Internationalism and Humanitarianism, 1930–39', *Humanities Australia: The Journal of the Australian Academy of the Humanities*, 8, 2017, p. 76.

10 Fitzpatrick Papers, ANL, Series 1, Box 1, 'Minutes of Meeting of Executive Committee, ACCL', Notes of a Deputation of VIREC to John McEwen and J.A. Carrodus, 17 February 1939.

11 Ibid.

12 *Labor Call*, 5 January 1939, p. 2.

13 Ibid., 2 February 1939, p. 6.

14 *The Argus*, 9 February 1939, p. 1.

15 *Labor Call*, 9 March 1939, p. 2.

16 *Sydney Morning Herald*, 2 February 1939, p. 12.

17 Ibid.

18 *The Argus*, 10 February 1939, p. 11.

19 *Sydney Morning Herald*, 17 February 1939, p. 11.

20 Ibid.

21 NAA A433, file 43/2/46 'Refugees (Jewish and Other) – General Policy File', Interior memorandum (*Question of Definition of Term 'Refugee'*) prepared by A.R. Peters, 12 January 1939.

22 Ibid.

23 Ibid.

24 NAA A461, file M349/3/5 Part 2, 'Jews – Policy. Part 2', Interior memorandum for Cabinet (*Jewish Refugees: Question of Excluding Parents from Quota Restrictions*), 31 January 1939.

25 Ibid.

26 Ibid.

27 AJWS Archives, Sydney, History File, *General Activities and Functions of the Sydney Office of the Australian Jewish Welfare Society*, 29 June 1939.

28 Ibid.

29 Ibid., Executive Committee Minutes (November 1938–April 1939), minutes for 22 January 1939.

30 Ibid., History File, *General Activities and Functions of the Sydney Office of the Australian Jewish Welfare Society*, 29 June 1939.

31 AJHS Archives, Rabbi Falk Correspondence File (file 832), Rabbi L.A. Falk to Sigmund Hechinger (Vienna), 5 December 1938.

32 *Hebrew Standard*, 12 January 1939, p. 3.

33 Judaica Archive, University of Sydney, Max Laserson Collection, file 1, '*Fluchtlingsfragen*', Frank Silverman (General Secretary, AJWS) to Isaac Rosenberg Esq, 8 February 1939.

34 NAA A461, file M349/3/5 Part 2, 'Jews – Policy. Part 2', Interior memorandum for Cabinet (*Jewish Refugees: Question of Excluding Parents from Quota Restrictions*), 31 January 1939.

35 Ibid.

36 Ibid., typewritten minute of Cabinet decision, 14 February 1939.

37 NAA A659, file 39/1/1551, 'Austro-Australian Jewish Relief Committee. Purpose of', Interior memorandum prepared by J.A. Carrodus, 16 February 1939.

38 Ibid., memorandum for the Minister prepared by J.A. Carrodus, 1 March 1939.

39 Ibid., handwritten approval by John McEwen, 3 March 1939.

40 NAA A461, file Y349/3/5, 'Migration – Europe. Refugees', Interior memorandum for Cabinet (*Refugees*), 31 January 1939.

41 Ibid.

42 Ibid.

43 Ibid., typewritten minute of Cabinet's decision, 14 February 1939.

44 AJWS Archives, Sydney, Executive Committee Minutes (November 1938–April 1939), Minutes of Special Meeting, 3 February 1939.

45 Ibid.

46 Ibid., minutes of meeting of 21 February 1939.

47 Ibid.

48 NAA A434, file 50/3/41837, 'Refugees from Austria: Special Committee Proposed by USA, Evian', Interior memorandum (*Inter-Governmental Committee on Refugees Re. Jews Expelled from Germany to Poland in 1938*) prepared by A.R. Peters, 9 March 1939.

49 NAA A445, file 235/5/4 Part 3, 'Admission of Jews Policy Part 3', Interior memorandum for Cabinet (*Immigration of Jews into Australia*), 16 March 1939.

Notes

50   Ibid.

51   NAA A433, file 43/2/46, 'Refugees (Jewish and Others) – General Policy File', Interior memorandum (*Refugees*) prepared by A.R. Peters, 27 April 1939.

52   Ibid., handwritten approval by H.S. Foll, 1 May 1939.

53   *The Argus*, 9 May 1939, p. 8.

54   NAA A433, file 39/2/807, 'A[ustralian] J[ewish] W[elfare] Society. Question of using separate landing permits for (a) husband and (b) wife and children', Interior memorandum (*Landing Permits – Families Temporarily Separated*) for Collectors of Customs at Brisbane, Sydney, Port Adelaide, Fremantle and Hobart, 5 June 1939.

55   Ibid.

56   *Sydney Morning Herald*, 29 June 1939, p. 9.

57   *The Argus*, 25 July 1939, p. 9.

58   Ibid.

59   *Sydney Morning Herald*, 25 July 1939, p. 11.

60   Ibid., 8 July 1939, p. 17.

61   Ibid., 20 June 1939, p. 10.

62   Ibid., 18 July 1939, p. 7.

63   TSA PD 1/607/55/1/39, 'Applications for admission to the Commonwealth of Australia (From Europe)', Basil G. Jones (solicitor) to T.G. de L. D'Alton (Tasmanian Chief Secretary), 10 March 1939.

64   Ibid., Premier A.G. Ogilvie to Prime Minister J.A. Lyons, 14 March 1939.

65   Ibid., J.A. Perkins for Prime Minister to the Premier of Tasmania, 26 May 1939.

66   For an account of the refugee-relief activities of the Ogilvie government, see Paul R. Bartrop, 'The Premier as Advocate: A.G. Ogilvie, Tasmania and the Refugee Crisis, 1938–39', Tasmanian Historical Research Association Papers and Proceedings, 35:2, June 1988, pp. 49–57. Ogilvie had earlier visited Germany and other European countries and was horrified by what he witnessed there. Regarding the visit, see Michael Roe, *Albert Ogilvie and Stymie Gaha: World-Wise Tasmanians*, Hobart: Parliament of Tasmania, 2008 on Ogilvie and Jewish refugees, see especially pp. 232–4.

67   NAA A461, file Y349/3/5, 'Migration – Europe. Refugees', handwritten minute from J.A. Carrodus to 'Mr. Campbell' (?), 3 May 1939.

68   Ibid.

69   CPD, H. of R., vol. 159, 24 May 1939, p. 667.

70   Ibid.

71   Zionist Federation of Australia and New Zealand Papers (Melbourne), Presidential address delivered by Dr J. Leon Jona at the opening of the Eighth Zionist Conference at Melbourne, 5 March 1939.

Chapter 9

1   NAA A367, file C3075, 'Miscellaneous: Admission of Aliens, Forms, Instructions, etc', Inspector Roland S. Browne to Director, Commonwealth Investigation Branch, 19 April 1939.

2   Ibid.

3   Ibid.

4   Ibid., Interior memorandum (*Applications by Persons Resident in Australia for the Admission of Alien Relatives or Friends – Form No. 40*) prepared by A.R. Peters, addressed to Director, Commonwealth Investigation Branch, 26 April 1939.

5   Ibid.

6   NAA A445, file 235/5/9, 'Alleged Discrimination against Admission of Jews [question of Jewish or not on Dep. I Forms]', Frank Silverman (AJWS) to A.R. Peters, 21 April 1939.

7   Ibid. (emphasis in original).

8   Ibid., J.A. Carrodus to Frank Silverman, 27 April 1939.

9   NAA A659, file 39/4641, 'Victorian Refugee Immigration Appeals Committee', Marjorie J. Coppel to J.A. Carrodus, 4 May 1939.

10 Ibid., Carrodus to Coppel, 15 May 1939.

11 Ibid., Coppel to Carrodus, 25 May 1939.

12 Ibid.

13 Ibid., draft reply to Coppel prepared by A.R. Peters, 14 June 1939. Approved for transmission by J.A. Carrodus in handwritten minute, 15 June 1939.

14 Ibid.

15 Ibid., handwritten minute by A.R. Peters to J.A. Carrodus, 14 June 1939.

16 Ibid., Coppel to Carrodus, 23 June 1939.

17 Ibid., draft reply to Coppel prepared by A.R. Peters, 7 July 1939. Presumably approved by J.A. Carrodus for transmission under his name on the same date.

18 Ibid., Coppel to Carrodus, 11 July 1939.

19 See Board of Deputies and Jewish Refugees' Committee correspondence in Board of Deputies of British Jews Archives, file E1/13/1 (September–October 1939), especially the position put forth by the Overseas Settlement Department of the Jewish Refugees' Committee on 12 October 1939. The Australian government did not, in their view, 'have any wish to discriminate against Jewish people'.

20 The huge literature of the Spanish Civil War is best approached by reference to the standard works in English. See, among others, the following: Hugh Thomas, *The Spanish Civil War*, London: Eyre and Spottiswoode, 1961; Paul Preston, *The Spanish Civil War: Reaction, Revolution, and Revenge*, London: HarperCollins, 2006 and Antony Beevor, *The Battle for Spain: The Spanish Civil War, 1936–1939*, London: Orbis, 1982.

21 E.M. Andrews has observed that the Spanish Relief Committee was 'formed as a result of a public meeting in Sydney summoned by the Movement Against War and Fascism and International Labour Defence on 26 August 1936. It was thus, in origin, a typical communist Front, established to influence public opinion, the Labor Party, and government policy, while keeping the Communist Party in the background.' See E.M. Andrews, *Isolationism and Appeasement in Australia: Reactions to the European Crises, 1935–1939*, Canberra: Australian National University Press, 1970, p. 82.

22 NAA A433, file 39/2/174, 'Spanish Refugee Admission', handwritten minute from J.A. Carrodus to A.R. Peters, 6 April 1939.

23 Ibid., Interior memorandum (*Spanish Refugees*) prepared by A.R. Peters, 24 April 1939.

24 Ibid.

25   Ibid., handwritten minute from Carrodus to Peters, 1 May 1939.

26   Ibid. (emphasis in text).

27   Ibid., 'Notes Respecting Spanish Refugees' prepared by A.R. Peters, undated.

28   Ibid., Interior memorandum for Cabinet (*Spanish Refugees*), 11 May 1939.

29   Ibid., handwritten approval by W.M. Hughes, 22 June 1939.

30   NAA A659, file 39/4641, 'Victorian Refugee Immigration Appeals Committee', J.A. Carrodus to Brian Fitzpatrick, 3 April 1939.

31   NAA A1, file 38/23138, 'Australian Jewish Welfare Society – Proposal re. Control of Jewish Migration', Harry Lesnie to Senator H.S. Foll, 22 May 1939.

32   Ibid., H.S. Foll to Harry Lesnie, 25 May 1939.

33   AJHS Archives, Rabbi Falk Correspondence File (file 832), D.H. Drummond to John McEwen, 13 April 1939.

34   Ibid.

35   Ibid.

36   Ibid., John McEwen to Rabbi L.A. Falk, 18 April 1939.

37   Ibid., Rabbi Falk to Chief Rabbi Dr. Simon Hevesi (Budapest), 17 April 1939.

38   Ibid. (emphasis added).

39   NAA A659, file 39/1/1551, 'Austro-Australian Jewish Relief Committee. Purpose of', G.S. Hendy to Minister for the Interior, 27 April 1939.

40   Ibid.

41   Ibid., Interior memorandum (*Advance Ballarat Association*) prepared by A.R. Peters, 24 August 1939.

42   Ibid., H.S. Foll to G.S. Hendy, 31 August 1939.

43   NAA A659, file 47/1/2109, 'Report and Proposals by T.H. Garrett. Refugees from Europe – selection of etc.', *White Alien Immigration into Australia from Europe. Establishment of Organisation at Australia House*, T.H. Garrett to J.A. Carrodus, 28 June 1939.

44   Ibid.

45   Ibid., T.H. Garrett to J.A. Carrodus, 24 August 1939.

46   Ibid.

47   Ibid.

48   Ibid., Interim Report (Department of the Interior) prepared by T.H. Garrett, 23 June 1939.

49   TNA FO 371, file 24101, Foreign Office telegram to H.M. Representatives at Berlin, Warsaw, The Hague, Budapest, Belgrade, Rome and Paris, 10 July 1939.

50   Ibid., Foreign Office minute on cover of file, 12 July 1939.

51   NAA A659, file 47/1/2109. 'Report and Proposals by T.H. Garrett. Refugees from Europe – selection of etc.', *White Alien Immigration into Australia from Europe. Establishment of Organisation at Australia House*, Final Report (Department of the Interior) prepared by T.H. Garrett, 24 August 1939 (hereafter Garrett Report).

52   Ibid.

53   Ibid., T.H. Garrett to J.A. Carrodus, 24 August 1939.

54   Ibid.

55 Ibid., *Brief Notes of Tour of the Continent by the Assistant Secretary, Department of the Interior (Mr. T.H. Garrett), and the Chief Migration Officer (Major R.H. Wheeler) – 10th July 1939 to 1st August 1939* (hereafter, *Brief Notes of Tour*), p. 9.

56 Ibid., Garrett Report.

57 Ibid., *Brief Notes of Tour*, p. 9.

58 Ibid.

59 Ibid., p. 15.

60 Ibid., p. 22.

61 Ibid., p. 13.

62 Ibid., Garrett Report.

63 Ibid., *Brief Notes of Tour*, p. 9.

64 Ibid., *Garrett Report*.

65 Ibid., *Brief Notes of Tour*, p. 4.

66 Ibid., Garrett to Carrodus, 24 August 1939.

67 Ibid., Garrett Report.

68 NAA A1608, file N19/1/1 Pt 1, 'War 1939. Position of Aliens and Refugees – Time of War'. Press Statement issued by Prime Minister Menzies, 7 September 1939.

Chapter 10

1   *Sydney Morning Herald*, 14 July 1939, p. 10.

2   Ibid.

3   Ibid., letter to the editor from 'B.N.M.', 31 July 1939.

4   NAA A433, file 40/2/520, 'Absorption in Australia of Refugees from Central Europe', unsigned memorandum (*The Absorption, in Australia, of Refugees from Central Europe*) written by 'an alien resident qualified to express a reliable opinion', forwarded to Senator Foll by Colonel Harold Jones (Director, Commonwealth Investigation Branch), 2 February 1940.

5   Ibid.

6   *Sydney Morning Herald*, 13 July 1939, p. 4.

7   Ibid., 22 June 1939, p. 6.

8   Ibid.

9   Ibid., 13 July 1939, p. 4.

10 Suzanne D. Rutland, *Edge of the Diaspora: Two Centuries of Jewish Settlement in Australia*, Sydney: Collins Australia, 1988, p. 187.

11 *Hebrew Standard*, 22 December 1938, p. 3.

12 *Sydney Morning Herald*, 13 May 1939, quoted in Suzanne D. Rutland, 'Australian Responses to Jewish Refugee Migration before and after World War II', *Australian Journal of Politics and History*, 31:1, 1985, p. 38.

13 *Sydney Jewish News*, 28 July 1939, quoted in ibid.

14 *Sydney Morning Herald*, 3 July 1939, p. 11.

15 *The Argus*, 6 April 1939, p. 3.

16 Board of Deputies of British Jews, Archives, file E1/13/1, Frances Barkman (AJWS, Victorian Committee) to Neville Laski, President, Board of Deputies of British Jews, 30 June 1939.

17 Ibid., Secretary, Board of Deputies of British Jews, to Frances Barkman, 8 August 1939.

18 NAA A433, file 39/2/402, 'AJWS Sydney. Large numbers of Jewish Migrants desire to enlist in Militia', address of Mr. W. Hirst, 16 April 1939.

19 Ibid.

20 Ibid.

21 Ibid., Migrants' Consultative Council to Senator H.S. Foll, 28 August 1939.

22 *Sydney Morning Herald*, 22 April 1939, p. 18.

23 *The Argus*, 16 May 1939, p. 9.

24 *School Paper* (Victoria), 1 August 1939, reprinted in *Westralian Judean*, 1 September 1939, p. 42.

25 Ibid.

26 *Sydney Morning Herald*, 16 February 1939, p. 9.

27 Ibid.

28 Ibid., 6 May 1939, p. 16.

29 Ibid.

30 Ibid., 1 August 1939, p. 10.

31 Ibid., 4 July 1939, p. 7.

32 NAA A433, file 44/2/1566, 'A.N.A. Annual Conference Sydney. Resolutions Concerning Immigration', H.R. Redding (General Secretary, ANA) to the Secretary, Prime Minister's Department, 16 January 1939).

33 *Labor Call*, 6 April 1939, p. 14.

34 Ibid., 27 April 1939, p. 2.

35 *Smith's Weekly*, 22 July 1939, p. 13.

36 NAA A445, file 235/5/6 'Protests re. Jewish Immigration (1938–1946)', D.G. Simpson, Sydney, to the Secretary, Department of the Interior, 15 January 1939.

37 *Sydney Morning Herald*, 13 June 1939, p. 13.

38 Ibid.

39 *Smith's Weekly*, 24 June 1939, p. 2.

40 *Sydney Morning Herald*, 15 June 1939, p. 13.

41 *Smith's Weekly*, 1 July 1939.

42 *Sydney Morning Herald*, 13 June 1939, p. 13.

43 NAA A433, file 40/2/103, 'Unemployed Refugees – Economic Circumstances', Interior Report for Secretary (*Economic Circumstances of Refugees in Sydney*) prepared by A.L. Nutt, 28 December 1939.

44 *Westralian Judean*, 1 May 1939, p. 2.

45 NAA A659, file 39/1/1551, 'Austro-Australian Jewish Relief Committee. Purpose of', Reginald L. St. John (South Melbourne, Victoria) to Senator Foll, 4 July 1939.

46 *The Argus*, 16 February 1939, p. 1.

47 Ibid.

48 NAA A433, file 43/2/4588, 'European Refugees. Views of public re. admittance of', 'Madame Gennie' (Sydney) to the Secretary, Department of the Interior, 21 February 1939.

49 *The Age*, 9 May 1939, p. 11.

50 Ibid.

51 Ibid.

52 Ibid.

53 *The Argus*, 10 May 1939, p. 2.

54 *The Age*, 11 May 1939, p. 12.

55 Ibid., p. 10.

56 *The Argus*, 10 May 1939, p. 8.

57 Ibid.

58 NAA A433, file 39/2/909, 'Backyard Industries and Sweating amongst Refugees', Commonwealth Investigation Branch memorandum (*Jewish Migration*) to Department of the Interior, prepared by H.E. Jones, 16 May 1939.

59 Ibid.

60 Ibid.

61 CPD, Senate, vol. 159, 17 May 1939, p. 358.

62 Ibid., p. 359.

63 NAA A461, file AA349/3/5, 'Refugees – Representations by Sir Frank Clarke', Commonwealth Investigation Branch memorandum (*Refugee Migrants – Allegations by Sir Frank Clarke*) prepared by Inspector Roland S. Browne, 31 May 1939.

64 Ibid.

65 Ibid.

66 Ibid.

67 Ibid.

68 CPD, H. of R., vol. 160, 16 June 1939, pp. 2130–1. The notes from which this speech was drafted were almost certainly prepared by the Department of the Interior, which would have received a copy of Browne's memorandum.

69 Ibid., 15 June 1939, p. 1965.

70 Ibid., p. 1966.

71 Ibid., pp. 1966–7.

72 NAA A981, file Refugees 10, 'Refugees – General from Germany', J.F. Ramsbotham (Milnthorpe, Westmorland, England) to High Commissioner Bruce, London, 23 March 1939.

73 Ibid., External Affairs memorandum (*Refugees*) prepared by Alfred Stirling (External Affairs Officer, London), 5 April 1939.

74 CPD, H. of R., vol. 159, 3 May 1939, p. 37.

75 Ibid., 5 May 1939, pp. 156–7.

76 See also ibid., 3 May 1939, pp. 55–7, and ibid., vol. 160, 15 and 16 June 1939, pp. 2014–24.

77 CPD, Senate, vol. 159, 16 May 1939, p. 349.

78 CPD, H. of R., vol. 159, 10 May 1939, p. 294.

Notes

Chapter 11

1   NAA A461, file A349/1/2 Pt 4, 'Immigration Policy Pt 4', Cablegram from S.M. Bruce to Prime Minister's Department, 29 August 1939 (arrived at Canberra, 7.32 pm, 30 August 1939).

2   Ibid., Prime Minister's Department to High Commissioner's Office, 6 September 1939.

3   TSA PD 1/607,55/1/39, 'Applications for admission to the Commonwealth of Australia (from Europe)', J.A. Perkins (for Prime Minister) to the Premier of Tasmania, 28 September 1939.

4   NAA A461, file M349/3/5 Pt 2, 'Jews – Policy Part 2', Interior memorandum (*Jewish Immigration*) prepared by T.H. Garrett, 8 December 1939.

5   Ibid.

6   Ibid., minute by Senator Foll for information of Department, 12 December 1938.

7   NAA A434, file 49/3/7034, 'Admi. of German Jews – Cabinet decision re', Interior memorandum for Cabinet, 2 June 1933, and handwritten minute by Sir George Pearce of same date.

8   For immigration statistics, see Suzanne D. Rutland, *Edge of the Diaspora: Two Centuries of Jewish Settlement in Australia*, Sydney: Collins Australia, 1988, p. 399. This data, in its turn, was derived from Konrad Kwiet's research from the Commonwealth Year Books for the years in question; see Konrad Kwiet, 'Die Integration Deutscher-Jüdischer Emigranten in Australien', in B. Bittner and J. Johe (ed.), *Das Unrechtsregime*, Hamburg: Christians, 1986, pp. 237–51.

9   Commonwealth of Australia, *National Security Act*, No. 15 of 1939.

10 Commonwealth of Australia, National Security (Aliens Control) Regulations. Statutory Rules 1939, no 88, section 3 (1).

11 Ibid.

12 NAA MP 729/6, file 65/401/12, 'Alien Immigration, refugees, etc', Department of Defence document circulating statement prepared by the Department of the Interior, 16 September 1939.

13 NAA A1608, file N19/1/1 Pt 1, 'War 1939. Position of Aliens and Refugees – Time of War', Defence memorandum (*Position of Refugees in the Event of War*) for the Secretary, Prime Minister's Department, prepared by F.G. Shedden, Secretary, Department of Defence, 7 September 1939.

14 National Security (Aliens Control) Regulations, 1939.

15 Ibid.

16 NAA A376, file T252, 'Enemy Aliens', Secret memorandum (*Enemy Agents Travelling as Refugees*), Australian Military Forces (Southern Command) to the 4th and 6th Military Districts, 20 June 1940.

17 NAA MP 729/6, file 29/401/273, 'Refugees: Internment, Fifth Columnists', Department of the Army memorandum prepared by the Chief of the General Staff for the Minister, October 1940 (precise date unspecified).

18 Ibid.

19 Ibid.

20 NAA MP 508/1, file 115/703/363, 'Reports from Jewish Migrants', Army memorandum (*German and Jewish Refugees in Australia*) prepared by the Deputy Chief of the General Staff for the Secretary (for transmission to the Minister), 9 January 1941.

21 Ibid., H. Prerauer (Chairman, Migrants' Consultative Council) to Prime Minister Menzies, 14 January 1941.

22 Ibid., H. Prerauer (Chairman) and W.S. Burgheim (Hon. Secretary, Migrants' Consultative Council) to Prime Minister Menzies, 9 June 1941.

23 For a fuller discussion of this, see Paul R. Bartrop, 'Enemy Aliens or Stateless Persons? The Legal Status of Refugees from Germany in Wartime Australia', *Journal of the Australian Jewish Historical Society*, X:4, November 1988, pp. 270–80. On internment generally, see also Margaret Bevege, *Behind Barbed Wire: Internment in Australia during World War II*, St Lucia: University of Queensland Press, 1993.

24 Paul R. Bartrop with Gabrielle Eisen (ed.), *The Dunera Affair: A Documentary Resource Book*, Melbourne: Jewish Museum of Australia/Schwartz and Wilkinson, 1990.

25 Cyril Pearl, *The Dunera Scandal: Deported by Mistake*, Sydney: Angus and Robertson, 1983. See also Benzion Patkin, *The Dunera Internees*, Sydney: Cassell Australia, 1979 and Ken Inglis, Seumas Spark, and Jay Winter (ed.), *Dunera Lives: A Visual History*, Clayton (Victoria): Monash University Publishing, 2018.

26 One excellent account among many is James Holland, *The Battle of Britain: Five Months that Changed History, May–October 1940*, New York: St Martin's Press, 2011.

27 A good general survey of British measures regarding enemy aliens in wartime can be found in a series of essays edited by Richard Dove, See *'Totally un-English?' Britain's Internment of 'Enemy Aliens' in Two World Wars*, Amsterdam: Editions Rodopi BV, 2005. In an otherwise large literature, see also Ronald Stent, *A Bespattered Page? The Internment of 'His Majesty's Most Loyal Enemy Aliens'*, London: William Collins, 1980.

28 A comprehensive account of this process is to be found in Peter and Leni Gillman, *'Collar the Lot!' How Britain Interned and Expelled Its Wartime Refugees*, London: Quartet, 1980.

29 On Canada's agreement to accept the internees and their subsequent reception, see Paula Draper, 'The Accidental Immigrants: Canada and the Interned Refugees', parts 1 and 2, *Canadian Jewish Historical Society Journal*, 2:1–2, 1979, pp. 1–38, 80–112.

30 NAA A816, file 54/301/229, Prime Minister's Department to Dominions Secretary, London, 3 July 1940.

31 The most comprehensive study of the *Queen Mary* internees is Paul R. Bartrop, 'Incompatible with Security: Enemy Alien Internees from Singapore in Australia, 1940–45', *Journal of the Australian Jewish Historical Society*, VI:1, November 1993, pp. 149–69.

32 See, for example, the personal accounts in Bartrop with Eisen, *Dunera Affair*, pp. 151–90; also, Inglis, Spark and Winter, *Dunera Lives*, pp. 65–107.

33 NAA A1608/1, file A20/1/3 Pt 1, Home Office, London: *White Paper on Categories of Persons Eligible for Release from Internment*, October 1940.

34 NAA A1608/1, file A20/1/3 Pt 1, J.S. Duncan, Australia House (London) to the Secretary, Prime Minister's Department (Canberra), 20 November 1940.

35 NAA A1608/1, file A20/1/3 Pt 1, teleprinter message to Secretary, Prime Minister's Department from Secretary, Department of the Army, 10 January 1941.

36 A full account of Layton's role can be found in Imperial War Museum, London, Department of Sound Records, Interview with Julian Layton, Accession No. 004382/03.

37 On the 8th Employment Company generally, see Paul R. Bartrop, '"Enemy Aliens" and the Formation of Australia's 8th Employment Company', in Douglas E. Delaney, Mark Frost and Andrew L. Brown (ed.), *Manpower and the Armies of the British Empire in the Two World Wars*, Ithaca (NY): Cornell University Press, 2021, pp. 134–43.

38 A useful summary of Broughton's life can be found in Inglis, Spark and Winter, *Dunera Lives*, p. 337.

39 Paul R. Bartrop, 'Enemy Aliens or Stateless Persons? The Legal Status of Refugees from Germany in Wartime Australia', *Journal of the Australian Jewish Historical Society*, X:4, November 1988, pp. 270–80.

40 NAA MP742/1, file 255/14/228, F.M. Forde (Minister for the Army) to Ministers for Defence, Immigration and Information, and Labour and National Service, 20 November 1945.

41 Ibid.

42 Ibid., E.J. Holloway (Minister for Labour and National Service) to F.M. Forde (Minister for the Army), 24 November 1945.

43 Ibid., Arthur A. Calwell (Minister for Immigration) to F.M. Forde (Minister for the Army), 30 November 1945.

44 This was also the case where local Australian threats to security saw the internment of native-born extreme-right ultra-nationalists. See the excellent and detailed treatment of this topic in David Bird, *Nazi Dreamtime: Australian Enthusiasts for Hitler's Germany*, Melbourne: Australian Scholarly Publishing, 2012, especially chapter 19, pp. 248–77.

45 NAA MP 729/6, file 65/401/50, 'Control of Enemy Aliens – Request by Canadian Govt.', Department of the Army memorandum (*Control of Aliens: Notes for Reply to Enquiries Made by the Government of Canada*), 16 January 1940.

46 See Bartrop, 'Enemy Aliens or Stateless Persons', for a broader discussion of the changes to status for Jewish refugees during the war years.

47 NAA MP 508/1, file 115/703/520, 'Protest on Enemy Aliens', W.A. Miles to Prime Minister Curtin, 1 March 1942.

48 NAA A373, file 2026, 'R.S.S. and A.I.L.A. Requests for Internment of Enemy Aliens', F.C. Robinson (Hon. Secretary, Enoggera Sub-Branch RSSAILA) to Prime Minister Curtin, 16 March 1942 (emphasis in original).

49 See Paul R. Bartrop and Lois Foster, 'The Roots of Multiculturalism in Australia and Canada', in Kate Burridge, Lois Foster and Gerry Turcotte (ed.), *Canada-Australia: Towards a Second Century of Partnership*, Ottawa: International Council for Canadian Studies/Carleton University Press, 1997, pp. 267–86.

Chapter 12

1 NAA A461, file A349/1/2 Pt 3, 'Immigration Policy (7/1/37-21/9/38)', Interior memorandum (*White Alien Immigration*), unsigned, 16 March 1938.

2 NAA A461, file A349/3/1 Pt 2, 'Foreign Migration Policy Pt 2', Interior memorandum (*Jewish Immigration*), T.H. Garrett to J.A. Carrodus, 8 December 1939.

3 *Sydney Morning Herald*, 18 July 1939, p. 10.

4   NAA MP 729/6, file 67/401/7, 'Swiss Machine Manufacturing Experts and Motor Mechanics – Admission to Australia', F.G. Shedden (Secretary, Department of Defence Co-ordination) to Secretary, Department of the Army, 22 July 1940.

5   Ibid., War Cabinet Agendum (*Swiss Machine Manufacturing Experts and Motor Mechanics – Question of Admission into Australia*), 15 July 1940.

6   Ibid., Interior memorandum for War Cabinet (*Swiss Machine Manufacturing Experts and Motor Mechanics – Question of Admission into Australia*), 12 July 1940.

7   NAA A433, file 40/2/2984, 'Admission of Alien Engineers from Czechoslovakia (1940–1941)', Interior memorandum (*Alien Engineers from Czechoslovakia*), 6 November 1940.

8   Ibid.

9   Ibid., handwritten minute from Senator Foll, 7 November 1940.

10 Ibid., Interior memorandum (*Czechoslovak Bren Gun Experts*), 23 January 1941.

11 Ibid., High Commissioner, London, to Department of the Interior, 22 April 1941.

12 Ibid., T.H. Garrett to Minister of Supply, 13 February 1941; Secretary, Department of Supply, to Secretary, Department of the Interior, 20 February 1941.

13 TSA PD 1/624/55/10/40, telegram from Prime Minister Menzies to Premier of Tasmania, 21 November 1940.

14 NAA A5954, box 253, 'Aliens Internment: Migration; Registration etc.', Press Statement by Prime Minister Menzies (*Greek Migrants*), 16 December 1941.

15 Ibid.

16 NAA MP 729/6, file 65/401/21, 'German Jewish Refugees. Bombay ex S.S. "Maloja"', Secretary to Government of India, Simla, to Prime Minister's Department, Canberra, 28 September 1939.

17 Ibid., Secretary, Department of Defence, to Secretary, Prime Minister's Department, 7 October 1939.

18 *Canberra Times*, 19 October 1939.

19 *The Advertiser*, 19 October 1939, p. 15.

20 NAA A433, file 45/2/3194, 'United Country Party Protest re. Mass Colonisation and Formation of Community Centres by Aliens', Senator H.S. Foll to A. Wilson MP and G.J. Rankin MP, 20 June 1940.

21 NAA A461, file M349/3/5 Pt 2, 'Jews – Policy. Part 2', High Commissioner, London, to Department of the Interior, 15 July 1940.

22 Ibid., Prime Minister's Department to High Commissioner's Office, London, 22 July 1940.

23 NAA A1608, file F19/1/1, 'War – 1939. Assistance to Poland – Migration of Refugees', Prime Minister's Department to High Commissioner's Office, London, 21 January 1941.

24 Ibid., Interior memorandum (*Question of Admitting Polish and Czech Refugees from Nazi Oppression*), 21 January 1941.

25 Ibid., Prime Minister's Department to High Commissioner's Office, London, 28 January 1941.

26 On the Romanian dimension of the Holocaust, see Jean Ancel, *The History of the Holocaust in Romania*, Lincoln: University of Nebraska Press, 2012.

27 On Australian responses to unaccompanied children during the war, see Glen Palmer, *Reluctant Refuge: Unaccompanied Refugee and Evacuee Children in Australia, 1933–45*, East Roseville (NSW): Kangaroo Press, 1997.

28 NAA A461, file MA349/3/5 Pt 2, 'Jews. General. Part II', Interior memorandum for Cabinet (*Jewish Refugees in Hungary*), 23 October 1944.

29 NAA A367, file C3075I, 'Central European Migrants (Stateless German Refugee Jews)', D.A. Alexander (Acting Inspector, Commonwealth Investigation Branch) to Director, Commonwealth Investigation Branch, 3 May 1943, enclosing extract from Security Service Report of 1 May 1943.

30 NAA A981, file Refugees 2, 'Refugees: Offer to Succour Refugees (including permission to leave Australia)', Prime Minister's Department to High Commissioner's Office, London, 14 June 1940.

31 Glen Palmer to author, 24 November 1992.

32 Ibid.

33 NAA A989, file 43/755/6, 'Refugees. Evacuation of Jewish Refugees from Vichy France', aide-memoire of telephone conversation between Department of External Affairs and Department of the Interior, 30 March 1943.

34 *The Argus*, 17 March 1943, p. 12.

35 Ibid.

36 Ibid., 8 February 1944, p. 12.

37 NAA A1608, file F19/1/1, 'War – 1939. Assistance to Poland – Migration of Refugees', J.G. Latham (Australian Ambassador, Tokyo) to Sir Frederick Stewart (Minister for External Affairs, Canberra), 6 February 1941.

38 NAA A1308, file 712/1/53, 'Admission of Polish Refugees from Japan', War Cabinet minute, 9 April 1941.

39 Ibid.

40 NAA A433, file 45/2/660, 'Polish Refugees from Japan, Shanghai and Russia (Part 2)', Department of the Interior notes, *Report of Movement of Polish Refugees through Japan*, 5 August 1941.

41 *The Argus*, 14 August 1941, p. 4.

42 *The Age*, 14 August 1941, p. 6.

43 Ibid.

44 *The Argus*, 14 August 1941, p. 4.

45 Ibid.

46 NAA A1608, file F19/1/1, 'War – 1939. Assistance to Poland – Migration of Refugees', Interior memorandum (*Admission of Polish Refugees from Japan*), 28 August 1941.

47 Ibid.

48 Ibid.

49 Ibid., Secretary to Cabinet to Secretary, Department of the Interior, 5 November 1941.

50 *The Argus*, 6 November 1941, p. 3.

51 Ibid.

52 AA A433, file 45/2/660, 'Polish Refugees from Japan, Shanghai and Russia (Part 2)', Consul-General for Poland (Sydney) to H.V. Evatt, Minister for External Affairs, 11 September 1942.

53 NAA A989, file 43/755/2 Pt 1, 'Refugees. Polish Refugees from Russia. Admission to Australia', A.R. Peters to Secretary, Department of External Affairs, 1 January 1943.

54 Ibid., Secretary, Department of the Interior, to Secretary, Department of External Affairs, 16 December 1943.

55 Ibid., Interior memorandum for Cabinet (*Polish Refugees in the USSR: Question of Admitting a Number into Australia for the Duration of the War*), 15 March 1944.

56 NAA A989, file 44/755/2/1, 'Refugees. Poles – Admission to Australia of FIRST 100 Polish Adults', Secretary to Cabinet to Minister for the Interior, 28 March 1944.

57 NAA A1608, file Q19/1/1, 'Admission to Australia of Aliens during Wartime', Secretary, Department of the Army, to Secretary, Prime Minister's Department, 31 January 1942.

58 Ibid., A.R. Peters (for Secretary, Department of the Interior) to Secretary, Prime Minister's Department, 30 January 1942.

59 Ibid., F.R. Sinclair (Secretary, Department of the Army) to Secretary, Prime Minister's Department, 31 January 1942.

60 *The Argus*, 18 December 1942, p. 12.

61 NAA A981, file Germany 37 Part II, 'Germany – Jews Part 2', Secretary of State for Dominion Affairs, London, to Prime Minister of Australia, 8 December 1942 (received in Canberra, 10 December 1942).

62 NAA A989, file 43/360/4/2, 'Germany – Treatment of Jews', Blok, van Rooyen and Co. Pty Ltd (Sydney) to Dr. H.V. Evatt, Minister for External Affairs, 29 December 1942. This letter covered a cable received from Palestine Frutarom Ltd, Haifa, dated 24 December 1942.

63 NAA A989, file 43/755/3, 'Refugees – General', Prime Minister's Department to Australian High Commissioner, Wellington, 3 November 1944.

64 Ibid., Australian High Commissioner, Wellington, to Department of External Affairs, 11 November 1944 (received at Canberra, 12 November 1944).

65 *The Argus*, 17 December 1943, p. 6.

66 Ibid.

67 See Rodney Gouttman, 'First Principles: H.V. Evatt and the Jewish Homeland', in W.D. Rubinstein (ed.), *Jews in the Sixth Continent*, Sydney: Allen and Unwin, 1987, p. 267.

68 Zionist Federation of Australia and New Zealand archives, Plenary Sessions – ZFANZ Reports to and of Conferences from 2nd–15th Conference 1929-1952, vol. 5, 'Statement by the Hon. P.C. Spender, Opposition Member of the Advisory War Council, Made on the Occasion of the Conference of the Zionist Federation of Australia and New Zealand', 16 May 1943.

69 Ibid.

70 Rebecca Erbelding, *Rescue Board: The Untold Story of America's Efforts to Save the Jews of Europe*, New York: Doubleday, 2018. See also Richard Breitman and Allan J. Lichtman, *FDR and the Jews*, Cambridge (MA): Harvard University Press, 2013, chapter 13, pp. 262–75 and Rafael Medoff, *FDR and the Holocaust: A Breach of Faith*, New York: Wyman Institute, 2013, chapter 3, pp. 79–127, esp. 101–6.

71 NAA A433, file 44/2/1449, 'Refugees – Provision for Reception during Wartime. Enquiry by American Legation', draft War Cabinet Agendum prepared by Department of External Affairs, April 1944.

72 Ibid.

73 AJHS Archives, Miscellaneous Papers, unsorted, J.J. Dedman for Prime Minister, to the Hon. J.P. Abbott, Wingen (NSW), 7 August 1944.

74 NAA A461, file A349/1/2 Pt 4, 'Immigration Policy Pt 4 (1938–1944)', Department of the Interior memorandum for Cabinet (*Post-War Migration*) presented by Senator J.S. Collings, 1 May 1944.

75 NAA A436, file 47/5/16, 'White Alien Migration Policy', Department of the Interior document ('Notes on Points Raised by Honourable A.A. Calwell – White Alien Immigration') prepared by A.R. Peters, no date (7 or 8 May 1945?).

76 Ibid.

77 Ibid.

Chapter 13

1 All circulation figures have been taken from Henry Mayer, *The Press in Australia*, Melbourne: Lansdowne Press, 1964, p. 40. Individual profiles of the newspapers under discussion come from W. Sprague Holden, *Australia Goes to Press*, Detroit: Wayne State University Press, 1961, pp. 235–45.

2 *The Advertiser*, 9 September 1939, p. 10.

3 *The Age*, 12 September 1939, p. 8.

4 Ibid., 9 October 1939, p. 9.

5 Ibid., 10 October 1939, p. 9.

6 *The Advertiser*, 21 October 1939, p. 19.

7 *The Age*, 26 October 1939, p. 9.

8 *The Advertiser*, 26 October 1939, p. 16.

9 *The Age*, 31 October 1939, p. 9.

10 *The Argus*, 2 November 1939, p. 1.

11 Ibid., 8 November 1939, p. 3.

12 Ibid., 21 November 1939, p. 1.

13 *The Age*, 22 November 1939, p. 11.

14 Ibid., 5 December 1939, p. 9.

15 *The Argus*, 12 January 1940, p. 3.

16 *The Age*, 12 January 1940, p. 9.

17 Ibid., 21 January 1940, p. 9.

18 Ibid., 12 February 1940, p. 9.

19 *Sydney Morning Herald*, 7 January 1941, p. 7.

20 Ibid., 22 October 1941, p. 12; *The Advertiser*, 22 October 1941, p. 8.

21 For an account of the Babi Yar massacres, see, for example, Martin Gilbert, *The Holocaust: The Jewish Tragedy*, London: Guild Publishing, 1986, pp. 202–5; Yitzhak Arad, *The Holocaust in the Soviet Union*, Lincoln: University of Nebraska Press, 2009 and Victoria Khiterer, 'Babi Yar, the Tragedy of Kiev's Jews', *Brandeis Graduate Journal*, 2, 2004, pp. 1–16.

22 *Sydney Morning Herald*, 22 November 1943, p. 6. A week later *The Advertiser* described at length the massacre and burning of the bodies as the retreating Germans attempted to cover up their crime, but the location of Babi Yar was not mentioned by name (*The Advertiser*, 30 November 1943, p. 2).

23 *The Advertiser*, 6 October 1941, p. 7.

24 *The Argus*, 17 October 1941, p. 5; *The Advertiser*, 17 October 1941, p. 10.

25 *Sydney Morning Herald*, 22 October 1941, p. 12.

26 *The Age*, 21 October 1941, p. 5. *The Advertiser*, reporting the same story verbatim, reduced the figure to 20,000 (21 October 1941, p. 8). See also *Sydney Morning Herald*, 21 October 1941, p. 8, for the same account.

27 *The Age*, 25 October 1941, p. 11.

28 *Sydney Morning Herald*, 24 October 1941, p. 10.

29 *The Age*, 31 October 1941, p. 7.

30 *Sydney Morning Herald*, 13 October 1941, p. 8.

31 *The Age*, 4 June 1942, p. 1.

32 *The Argus*, 16 June 1942, p. 1.

33 This was a reference to the Jewish resisters known as the Baum Group, who set several fires in and around a Nazi anti-Soviet exhibition at Berlin's Lustgarten on 18 May 1942. See Eric Brothers, *Berlin Ghetto: Herbert Baum and the Anti-Fascist Resistance*, Stroud: Spellmount, 2012 and John Cox, *Circles of Resistance: Jewish, Leftist, and Youth Dissidence in Nazi Germany*, New York: Peter Lang, 2009.

34 *The Age*, 17 June 1942, p. 1.

35 Ibid., 26 June 1942, p. 1.

36 *The Argus*, 26 June 1942, p. 3.

37 Ibid., 1 July 1942, p. 3.

38 Ibid., 7 August 1942, p. 1; *The Age*, 7 August 1942, p. 1.

39 The incident being exposed was the earlier arrest, on 16–17 July 1942, of 13,152 Jews of Paris who were at first concentrated at the Winter Velodrome – hence the name given ever since, the Vel' d'Hiv Roundup. See Claude Lévy and Paul Tillard, *Betrayal at the Vel d'Hiv*, New York: Hill and Wang, 1969 and Maurice Rajsfus, *The Vel d'Hiv Raid: The French Police at the Service of the Gestapo*, Los Angeles: DoppelHouse Press, 2017.

40 *The Advertiser*, 7 August 1942, p. 1.

41 *Sydney Morning Herald*, 7 August 1942, p. 8.

42 Ibid., p. 6.

43 Ibid., p. 8.

44 *The Argus*, 22 August 1942, p. 1. This report also appeared on p. 10 in the *Sydney Morning Herald* on the same date.

45 *The Advertiser*, 29 August 1942, p. 1; *The Age*, 29 August 1942, p. 1.

46 *Sydney Morning Herald*, 17 August 1942, p. 8.

47 Ibid.

48 *The Age*, 26 November 1942, p. 3.

49 *The Argus*, 12 December 1942, p. 2.

50 Martin Gilbert, *Auschwitz and the Allies*, London: Michael Joseph/Rainbird, 1981, p. 103. For a discussion of the genesis and reception of the United Nations declaration, see Gilbert, chapter 11; also, Walter Laqueur, *The Terrible Secret: Suppression of the Truth about Hitler's 'Final Solution'*, Harmondsworth (Middlesex): Penguin Books, pp. 223–8. The text of the

declaration can be found in Paul R. Bartrop (ed.), *Modern Genocide: A Documentary and Reference Guide*, Santa Barbara: ABC-CLIO, 2019, pp. 166–9.

51 *The Argus*, 18 December 1942, p. 12.

52 Ibid.

53 Ibid., 21 December 1942, p. 12.

54 Ibid., 9 January 1943, p. 16.

55 Ibid., 28 January 1943, p. 12.

56 Ibid., 30 January 1943, p. 20.

57 Ibid., 18 February 1943, p. 12.

58 Ibid., 9 March 1943, p. 12.

59 Ibid., 20 March 1943, p. 3.

60 Ibid., 24 May 1943, p. 12.

61 *The Advertiser*, 20 April 1943, p. 2.

62 Ibid.

63 *The Advertiser*, 1 May 1943, p. 1.

64 *Sydney Morning Herald*, 4 October 1943, p. 6.

65 In a large literature, see, for example, Leni Yahil, *The Rescue of Danish Jewry: Test of a Democracy*, Philadelphia: Jewish Publication Society of America, 1969; Emmy E. Werner, *A Conspiracy of Decency: The Rescue of the Danish Jews during World War II*, Boulder: Westview Press, 2002 and Bo Lidegaard, *Countrymen*, New York: Knopf, 2013.

66 Ibid., 5 October 1943, p. 5; *The Argus*, 5 October 1943, p. 12; *The Advertiser*, 5 October 1943, p. 2.

67 *The Argus*, 26 January 1944, p. 16.

68 Ibid., 25 March 1944, p. 1.

69 *The Advertiser*, 23 June 1944, p. 4.

70 Ibid.

71 For possibly the best short history, see Randolph L. Braham, *The Politics of Genocide: The Holocaust in Hungary*, Detroit: Wayne State University Press, 2000.

72 *The Advertiser*, 17 July 1944, p. 4.

73 See Rebecca Erbelding, *Rescue Board: The Untold Story of America's Efforts to Save the Jews of Europe*, New York: Doubleday, 2018.

74 *The Age*, 27 November 1944, p. 1.

75 Ibid.

76 *Sydney Morning Herald*, 27 November 1944, p. 1.

77 *The Advertiser*, 27 November 1944, p. 4.

78 Ibid.

79 *The Argus*, 11 April 1945, p. 16.

80 *The Advertiser*, 19 April 1945, p. 4.

81 Ibid.

82 *The Age*, 10 April 1945, p. 16.

83 Ibid.

84 *Sydney Morning Herald*, 21 April 1945, p. 2.

85 Ibid., 19 April 1945, p. 3.

86 *The Argus*, 21 April 1945, p. 3.

87 *Sydney Morning Herald*, 23 April 1945, p. 5.

88 *The Advertiser*, 24 April 1945, p. 4.

89 *The Argus*, 26 April 1945, p. 2.

90 Ibid., 25 May 1945, p. 2.

91 The best example relates to the aftermath of the attack on the King David Hotel in Jerusalem on 22 July 1946. Australian press responses were unanimous in labelling the ninety deaths caused by the attack as 'mass murder' (see, for instance, *The Age*, 24 July 1946, p. 2 and *The Advertiser*, 24 July 1946, p. 8). One of the most telling statements was a story in Brisbane's *Courier-Mail*, headlined 'Jews Match the Nazis' (24 July 1946, p. 2).

Chapter 14

1 The literature on the Nuremberg Trials is now huge, but solid introductions can be found in Robert E. Conot, *Justice at Nuremberg*, New York: HarperCollins, 1983; Joseph E. Persico, *Nuremberg: Infamy on Trial*, New York: Viking Penguin, 1994 and Telford Taylor, *The Anatomy of the Nuremberg Trials: A Personal Memoir*, New York: Knopf, 1992. Placing the IMT into a broader context, a good discussion is Donald Bloxham, *Genocide on Trial: War Crimes Trials and the Formation of Holocaust History and Memory*, Oxford: Oxford University Press, 2001.

2 A discussion of this can be found in Paul R. Bartrop, 'The Nuremberg Trials and the Holocaust: Crimes against Humanity as Viewed from Australia (1945–46)', *Australian Jewish Historical Society Journal*, XII:3, November 1994, pp. 606–18. For a study of how Nuremberg was received in a single Australian state, see Paul R. Bartrop, 'South Australia and the Nuremberg Trials: Perceptions of Inhumanity and Justice', *Journal of the Historical Society of South Australia*, 22, 1994, pp. 98–112.

3 The Australian dimension of the Japanese war crimes issue has been dealt with in Georgina Fitzpatrick, Tim McCormack and Narrelle Morris (ed.), *Australia's War Crimes Trials 1945– 51*, Leiden: Brill, 2016. The broader picture has also been dealt with elsewhere in Sandra Wilson, Robert Cribb, Beatrice Trefalt and Dean Aszkielowicz, *Japanese War Criminals: The Politics of Justice after the Second World War*, New York: Columbia University Press, 2017.

4 For a detailed perspective on Australians who were prisoners of war of the Germans, see Peter Monteath, *P.O.W. Australian Prisoners of War in Hitler's Reich*, Sydney: Pan Macmillan, 2011.

5 This statement was made by Archie Cameron in the House of Representatives on 7 November 1946. See CPD, H. of R., vol. 189, 7 November 1946, pp. 62–3.

6 *The Age*, 20 November 1945, p. 1.

7 *The Argus*, 27 November 1945, p. 16.

8 *The Advertiser*, 20 November 1945, p. 4.

9 *Sydney Morning Herald*, 16 November 1945, p. 2.

10 *West Australian*, 7 November 1945, p. 7.

11 *The Mercury*, 21 November 1945, p. 3.

12 *The Argus*, 24 November 1945, p. 2.

13 *The Advertiser*, 21 November 1945, p. 6.

14 *Sydney Morning Herald*, 20 November 1945, p. 2.

15 Robert H. Jackson, *The Nuremberg Case*, New York: Cooper Square Publishers, 1971, pp. 30–1 (first published by Alfred A. Knopf, New York, 1947).

16 Ibid., p. 52.

17 Ibid.

18 *Sydney Morning Herald*, 27 November 1945, p. 3; *The Age*, 27 November 1945, p. 2.

19 *West Australian*, 29 November 1945, p. 1; *Canberra Times*, 29 November 1945, p. 1.

20 *Sydney Morning Herald*, 1 December 1945, p. 3.

21 *The Age*, 1 December 1945, p. 1; *The Mercury*, 1 December 1945, p. 2.

22 *Canberra Times*, 6 December 1945, p. 1; see also *West Australian*, 6 December 1945, p. 8.

23 *West Australian*, 5 December 1945, p. 8.

24 *Canberra Times*, 14 December 1945, p. 1; *The Mercury*, 14 December 1945, p. 2; *Sydney Morning Herald*, 14 December 1945, p. 3.

25 *West Australian*, 15 December 1945, p. 9; see also *Sydney Morning Herald*, 15 December 1945, p. 3 and *The Age*, 15 December 1945, p. 1.

26 *West Australian*, 17 December 1945, p. 7.

27 *The Argus*, 19 December 1945, p. 24; *The Age*, 19 December 1945, p. 1; *West Australian*, 19 December 1945, p. 7; *The Advertiser*, 19 December 1945, p. 7.

28 *The Argus*, 19 December 1945, p. 24.

29 *West Australian*, 19 December 1945, p. 7.

30 *Courier-Mail*, 20 December 1945, p. 1; *The Age*, 20 December 1945, p. 1; *West Australian*, 20 December 1945, p. 7.

31 *The Advertiser*, 22 December 1945, p. 1.

32 *The Mercury*, 21 December 1945, p. 2; *Courier-Mail*, 21 December 1945, p. 1; *Sydney Morning Herald*, 21 December 1945, p. 3.

33 *The Advertiser*, 5 January 1946, p. 11.

34 *The Advertiser*, 30 January 1946, p. 7.

35 Ibid., 1 March 1946, p. 8.

36 Jackson, *The Nürnberg Case*, p. 163 (emphasis in text).

37 *Courier-Mail*, 28 September 1946, p. 1.

38 *The Mercury*, 30 September 1946, p. 10.

39 *The Advertiser*, 2 October 1946, p. 10.

40 Ibid.

41 In this regard, the position of the Soviet Union was most at variance with the other legal traditions represented. See Francine Hirsch, *Soviet Judgment at Nuremberg: A New History of the International Military Tribunal after World War II*, New York: Oxford University Press, 2020.

42 *The Age*, 14 October 1946, p. 5; the story was also reported in part in *The Mercury*, 14 October 1946, p. 6.

43 The Reverend Robert H. Green (Richmond, Victoria) in *The Argus*, 5 October 1946, p. 12; see also further correspondence to the editor of *The Argus* dated 10 October 1946 (p. 6), 12 October 1946 (p. 16) and 16 October 1946 (p. 8).

44 *Sydney Morning Herald*, 14 October 1946, p. 2. The language employed here anticipated that of Gideon Hausner, Israel's Attorney-General, in his opening address at the trial of Adolf Eichmann in Jerusalem in 1961: 'When I stand before you here, Judges of Israel, to lead the Prosecution of Adolf Eichmann, I am not standing alone. With me are six million accusers.' See Shabtai Rosenne, *6,000,000 Accusers: Israel's Case against Eichmann. The Opening Speech and Legal Argument of Mr. Gideon Hausner, Attorney-General*, Jerusalem: Jerusalem Post, 1961. Also, Yechiam Weitz, 'In the Name of Six Million Accusers: Gideon Hausner as Attorney-General and His Place in the Eichmann Trial', *Israel Studies*, 14:2, Summer, 2009, pp. 26–49.

45 *Courier-Mail*, 17 October 1946, p. 2.

46 *Canberra Times*, 18 October 1946, p. 4.

Chapter 15

1   Ben Shephard, *The Long Road Home: The Aftermath of the Second World War*, New York: Alfred A. Knopf, 2011, p. 342.

2   A.A. Calwell, *How Many Australians Tomorrow?* Melbourne: Reed & Harris, 1945, p. 66.

3   CPD, H. of R., vol. 185, p. 5859.

4   Michael Blakeney, *Australia and the Jewish Refugees, 1933–1948*, Sydney: Croom Helm Australia, 1985, p. 306.

5   Suzanne D. Rutland, *Edge of the Diaspora: Two Centuries of Jewish Settlement in Australia*, Sydney: William Collins Australia, 1988, p. 229.

6   Blakeney, *Australia and the Jewish Refugees*, p. 306.

7   Ibid., p. 305; also, Rutland, *Edge of the Diaspora*, p. 233.

8   In a large literature, see especially Daniel Nasaw, *The Last Million: Europe's Displaced Persons from World War to Cold War*, New York: Penguin Press, 2020 and Mark Wyman, *DPs: Europe's Displaced Persons, 1945–51*, Ithaca: Cornell University Press, 1998.

9   Rutland, *Edge of the Diaspora*, p. 238.

10 Ibid.

11 Ibid.

12 Shephard, *The Long Road Home*, p. 348.

13 *Historical Population of Australia, 1788 to Future*, available online at http://chartsbin.com/view/eoo (accessed on 12 April 2021).

14 Mark Aarons, *Sanctuary! Nazi Fugitives in Australia*, Melbourne: William Heinemann, 1989, p. xx.

15 Ibid.

16 Ibid., Appendix II.

17 Aarons, *Sanctuary*, p. 92.

18 Ibid.

19 Commonwealth of Australia, *Review of Material Relating to the Entry of Suspected War Criminals into Australia* (hereafter Menzies Review), Parliamentary Paper No. 90/1987, Canberra: Australian Government Publishing Service, 1987, p. 70.

20 Aarons, *Sanctuary*, p. 110.

21 *The Age*, 27 January 1990, p. 1.

22 Mark Aarons, interviewed by Anna Murdoch, 'Are We Harboring Nazi Criminals?' *The Age Green Guide*, 3 April 1986, p. 1.

23 Ibid.

24 Ibid.

25 Aarons, *Sanctuary*, p. xxii.

26 Menzies Review, p. 7.

27 Ibid.

28 Ibid., p. 3.

29 Charles Ashman and Robert J. Wagman, *The Nazi Hunters*, New York: Pharos Books, 1988, p. 252.

30 H.J.W. Stokes, 'The 1987 Eldershaw Memorial Lecture: Diplomats and War Criminals: Some Experiences of an Historian in the Service of the Commonwealth Government', *Tasmanian Historical Research Association Papers and Proceedings*, 35:1, March 1988, pp. 16–18.

31 Ibid., p. 18.

32 Ibid., p. 15.

33 Aarons, *Sanctuary*, p. 290.

34 Menzies Review, p. 177.

35 Stokes, 'Diplomats and War Criminals', pp. 20–1.

36 Menzies Review, p. 177.

37 Ibid., pp. 181–2.

38 Ibid., p. 180.

39 Ibid., pp. 180–1.

40 Ibid., p. 177.

41 Nicholas Rothwell, 'Bringing Nazis to Justice: The Menzies Report', *Quadrant*, 31:3, March 1987, p. 25.

42 This did not stop some from arguing that elderly pensioners should now be left alone. One letter writer to the Melbourne *Age* demanded to know in February 1987: 'Why are Australians expected to forgive the Japanese for atrocities they committed during the 1939–1945 war while *Jews are being aided and abetted to hound and persecute the Nazis for atrocities they committed during the same war?*' See Charlotte Oldfield, letter to the editor, *The Age*, 21 February 1987, p. 12 (emphasis added).

43 Aarons, *Sanctuary*, p. 293.

44 See Peggy O'Donnell, '"Gateway to Hell": A Nazi Mass Grave, Forensic Scientists, and an Australian War Crimes Trial', *Holocaust and Genocide Studies*, 32:3, Winter 2018, pp. 361–83.

45 For a personal reflection on the site investigation by the historian appointed by the SIU – and who travelled to Ukraine for the excavation – see Konrad Kwiet, 'A Historian's View: The War Crimes Debate Down Under', *Dapim: Studies on the Holocaust*, 24:1, 2010, pp. 319–39.

46   A thorough treatment of the Polyukhovich case can be found in David Bevan, *A Case to Answer: The Story of Australia's First European War Crimes Prosecution*, Adelaide: Wakefield Press, 1994.

47   For a detailed study of all three cases, see David Fraser, *Daviborshch's Cart: Narrating the Holocaust in Australian War Crimes Trials*, Lincoln: University of Nebraska Press, 2010.

48   Ephraim Zuroff, *Operation Last Chance: One Man's Quest to Bring Nazi Criminals to Justice*, New York: St. Martin's Press, 2009, p. 64.

49   Ibid., p. 62.

50   Ibid.

51   Ibid.

52   In 2020 Mark Aarons produced a second major work dealing with the issue of war criminals in Australia, in which he charged that governments on both sides of politics not only turned a blind eye to their presence but permitted known killers to be recruited by Australian intelligence services during the Cold War. See *War Criminals Welcome: Australia, a Sanctuary for Fugitive War Criminals Since 1945*, Melbourne: Black Inc., 2020.

53   Commonwealth of Australia, Attorney-General's Department. *Report of the Investigations of War Criminals in Australia*, 13 December 1993, p. 569.

54   The text of the Report can be found at https://afghanistaninquiry.defence.gov.au/.

Chapter 16

1   *Auschwitz and the Allies* (prod. Rex Bloomstein), BBC, 1982.

2   In an otherwise very large literature, see, for example, James Jupp, *From White Australia to Woomera: The Story of Australian Immigration*, Melbourne: Cambridge University Press, 2007 and Janis Wilton and Richard Bosworth, *Old Worlds and New Australia: The Post-War Migrant Experience*, Ringwood (Victoria): Penguin Books, 1984.

3   Known colloquially as 'Ten Pound Poms', the British immigrants were required to pay a fee of just £10 prior to arriving in their new country. See A. James Hammerton and Alistair Thomson, *Ten Pound Poms: Australia's Invisible Migrants*, Manchester: Manchester University Press, 2005.

4   A full account of Hungarian refugees and Australia still awaits its historian. A solid outline of the story can be found in Klaus Neumann, *Across the Seas: Australia's Response to Refugees, a History*, Melbourne: Black Inc., 2015, pp. 150–8.

5   An interesting argument on the end of the White Australia policy can be found in Gwenda Tavan, *The Long, Slow Death of White Australia*, Melbourne: Scribe, 2005.

6   In what is now a huge literature, see Andrew Jakubowicz and Christina Ho (ed.), *'For Those Who've Come across the Seas …' Australian Multicultural Theory, Policy and Practice*, North Melbourne (Victoria): Australian Scholarly Publishing, 2013.

7   See, for example, Katharine Betts, *Ideology and Immigration: Australia 1976 to 1987*, Melbourne: Melbourne University Press, 1988.

BIBLIOGRAPHY

Scholarship on the Australian response to the Holocaust has been growing in recent years, most frequently manifested through journal articles and presentations at academic conferences. The Bibliography that follows is divided into three parts: unpublished archival sources (on which most of the research for this book rests), contemporary newspapers and a much longer list of secondary works that have been employed as the book was being written. Some works consulted as additional reading in the endnotes have been omitted from this list for reasons of space.

1 UNPUBLISHED ARCHIVAL SOURCES

National Archives of Australia, Canberra (NAA)

A1	Attorney-General
A367	Commonwealth Investigation Branch
A373	Security Service (Army)
A376	Security Service (Army)
A433	Interior
A434	Interior
A436	Interior
A445	Immigration
A457	Prime Minister
A458	Prime Minister
A461	Prime Minister
A659	Interior
A816	Defence Co-ordination
A981	External Affairs
A989	External Affairs
A1308	Treasury
A1608	Prime Minister
A1838/T116	External Affairs
A5954	Defence
A6119	Attorney-General

National Archives of Australia, Melbourne (NAA)

MP508 /1	Army
MP729/6	Defence (to 1939)
	Army (from 1939)
MP742/1	Army

The National Archives, London (TNA)

Dominions Office (DO 35)
705/M529/1
705/M529/20
705/M529/24
705/M529/47
716/M576/1
718/M582/2
Home Office (HO 213)
250
Foreign Office (FO 371)
21748
21749
22321
24101

Tasmanian State Archives, Hobart

TSA PD 1/607/55/1/39
TSA PD 1/624/55/10/40

Judaica Archive, University of Sydney

Max Laserson Collection, file 1.

National Library of Australia, Canberra, Manuscripts Section (Australian Reference)

NLA MS 4965   Papers of Brian Fitzpatrick
NLA MS 4851   Papers of J.A. Lyons

Australian Jewish Historical Society Archives, Sydney

File 832 Rabbi L.A. Falk Correspondence file
Miscellaneous Documents file (no number)

Australian Jewish Welfare Society Archives, Sydney

Minutes of ROTA Committee
Minutes of German Jewish Relief Fund
Minutes of Australian Jewish Welfare Society
History File

South Australian State Archives, Adelaide

Adelaide Hebrew Congregation files, SRG 162/2 vol. 6 (Committee Minutes).

Bibliography

Zionist Federation of Australia and New Zealand, Melbourne

Papers, Annual Conference minutes, miscellaneous.

Imperial War Museum, London

Department of Sound Records
004382/03   Interview with Julian David Layton OBE

Board of Deputies of British Jews Archives, London

E1/13/1
E3/238/9
E3/282/1

2 NEWSPAPERS

The Advertiser
The Age
The Argus
The Bulletin
Canberra Times
Courier-Mail
Hebrew Standard
Labor Call
The Mercury
Smith's Weekly
Sydney Morning Herald
West Australian

3 PUBLISHED WORKS

Aarons, Mark, *Sanctuary! Nazi Fugitives in Australia*, Melbourne: William Heinemann, 1989.
Aarons, Mark, *War Criminals Welcome: Australia, a Sanctuary for Fugitive War Criminals since 1945*, Melbourne: Black Inc., 2020.
Adler-Rudel, S., 'The Evian Conference on the Refugee Question', *Leo Baeck Institute Yearbook*, 13, 1968, pp. 235–73.
Amos, Keith, *The New Guard Movement, 1931–1935*, Melbourne: Melbourne University Press, 1976.
Andgel, Anne, *Fifty Years of Caring: The History of the Australian Jewish Welfare Society 1936–1986*, Sydney: Australian Jewish Welfare Society/Australian Jewish Historical Society, 1988.
Andrews, E.M., *Isolationism and Appeasement in Australia: Reactions to the European Crises, 1935–1939*, Canberra: Australian National University Press, 1970.
Ashman, Charles and Robert J. Wagman, *The Nazi Hunters*, New York: Pharos Books, 1988.

Bartrop, Paul R., '"Good Jews" and "Bad Jews:" Australian Perceptions of Jewish Migrants and Refugees, 1919–1939', in W.D. Rubinstein (ed.), *Jews in the Sixth Continent*, Sydney: Allen and Unwin, 1987, pp. 169–84.

Bartrop, Paul R., 'The Premier as Advocate: A.G. Ogilvie, Tasmania and the Refugee Crisis, 1938–39', *Tasmanian Historical Research Association Papers and Proceedings*, 35:2, June 1988, pp. 49–57.

Bartrop, Paul R., 'Enemy Aliens or Stateless Persons? The Legal Status of Refugees from Germany in Wartime Australia', *Journal of the Australian Jewish Historical Society*, X:4, November 1988, pp. 270–80.

Bartrop, Paul R., 'Incompatible with Security: Enemy Alien Internees from Singapore in Australia, 1940–45', *Journal of the Australian Jewish Historical Society*, VI:1, November 1993, pp. 149–69.

Bartrop, Paul R., 'The Nuremberg Trials and the Holocaust: Crimes against Humanity as Viewed from Australia (1945–46)', *Australian Jewish Historical Society Journal*, XII:3, November 1994, pp. 606–18.

Bartrop, Paul R., 'South Australia and the Nuremberg Trials: Perceptions of Inhumanity and Justice', *Journal of the Historical Society of South Australia*, 22, 1994, pp. 98–112.

Bartrop, Paul R., 'Foreign Immigration between the Wars: The Role of the Public Service', in J.J. Eddy and J.R. Nethercote (ed.), *Towards National Administration: Studies in Australian Administrative History*, Sydney: Hale and Iremonger, 1994, pp. 157–67.

Bartrop, Paul R., *The Evian Conference of 1938 and the Jewish Refugee Crisis*, London: Palgrave Macmillan, 2017.

Bartrop, Paul R., '"Enemy Aliens" and the Formation of Australia's 8th Employment Company', in Douglas E. Delaney, Mark Frost and Andrew L. Brown (ed.), *Manpower and the Armies of the British Empire in the Two World Wars*, Ithaca (NY): Cornell University Press, 2021, pp. 134–43.

Bartrop, Paul R., with Gabrielle Eisen (ed.) *The Dunera Affair: A Documentary Resource Book*, Melbourne: Jewish Museum of Australia/Schwartz and Wilkinson, 1990.

Benjamin, David J., 'Australia and the Evian Conference', *Australian Jewish Historical Society Journal and Proceedings*, 5:5, 1961, pp. 215–33.

Benjamin, Rodney, *A Serious Influx: A History of Jewish Welfare in Victoria*, St. Leonards (NSW): Allen and Unwin, 1998.

Bentwich, Norman, *The Refugees from Germany: April 1933 to December 1935*, London: Allen and Unwin, 1936.

Bentwich, Norman, 'The Evian Conference and after', *Fortnightly*, 144, September 1938, pp. 287–95.

Bentwich, Norman, *They Found Refuge: An Account of British Jewry's Work for Victims of Nazi Oppression*, London: Cresset Press, 1956.

Bentwich, Norman, *My 77 Years: An Account of My Life and Times, 1883–1960*, London: Routledge and Kegan Paul, 1962.

Betts, Katharine, *Ideology and Immigration: Australia 1976 to 1987*, Melbourne: Melbourne University Press, 1988.

Bevan, David, *A Case to Answer: The Story of Australia's First European War Crimes Prosecution*, Adelaide: Wakefield Press, 1994.

Bevege, Margaret, *Behind Barbed Wire: Internment in Australia during World War II*, St Lucia: University of Queensland Press, 1993.

Bird, David S., *J.A. Lyons – The 'Tame Tasmanian:' Appeasement and Rearmament in Australia, 1932–39*, Melbourne: Australian Scholarly Publishing, 2008.

Bird, David, *Nazi Dreamtime: Australian Enthusiasts for Hitler's Germany*, Melbourne: Australian Scholarly Publishing, 2012.

Bibliography

Blaikie, George, *Remember Smith's Weekly? A Biography of an Uninhibited National Australian Newspaper*, Adelaide: Rigby, 1966.

Blakeney, Michael, 'The Kimberleys Madness? Wartime Proposals for a Colony of Jewish Refugees in the Kimberleys', *Quadrant*, 27:7, July 1983, pp. 16–23.

Blakeney, Michael, 'Australia and the Jewish Refugees from Central Europe: Government Policy 1933–1939', *Leo Baeck Institute Yearbook*, 29, 1984, pp. 103–33.

Blakeney, Michael, *Australia and the Jewish Refugees, 1933–1948*, Sydney: Croom Helm Australia, 1985.

Bloomstein, Rex (producer), *Auschwitz and the Allies*, BBC-TV, 1982.

Boas, Harold, *Australian Jewry Book of Honour: The Great War, 1914–1918*, Perth: Lamson Paragon, 1923.

Borrie, W.D., 'The Role of Immigrants in Population Growth in Australia', *Australian Quarterly*, 16:2, June 1944, pp. 17–32.

Calwell, A.A., *How Many Australians Tomorrow?* Melbourne: Reed & Harris, 1945.

Calwell, A.A., *Be Just and Fear Not*, Adelaide: Rigby, 1978.

Campbell, Eric, *The Rallying Point: My Story of the New Guard*, Melbourne: Melbourne University Press, 1965.

Carr-Gregg, Charlotte, 'The Work of the German Emergency Fellowship Committee, 1938–1941', in W.D. Rubinstein (ed.), *Jews in the Sixth Continent*, Sydney: Allen and Unwin, 1987, pp. 185–200.

Carr-Gregg, Charlotte and Pam Maclean, '"A mouse nibbling at a mountain": The Problem of Australian Refugee Policy and the Work of Camilla Wedgwood', *Australian Journal of Politics and History*, 31:1, 1985, pp. 49–60.

Cochrane, Peter, *Best We Forget: The War for White Australia, 1914–18*, Melbourne: Text Publishing, 2018.

Commonwealth of Australia: Commonwealth Parliamentary Debates (Hansard), House of Representatives, vols 89, 116, 150, 153, 155–60, 185, 189.

Commonwealth of Australia: Commonwealth Parliamentary Debates (Hansard), Senate, vol. 157.

Commonwealth of Australia, *Review of Material Relating to the Entry of Suspected War Criminals into Australia* (Menzies Review), Parliamentary Paper No. 90/1987, Canberra: Australian Government Publishing Service, 1987.

Commonwealth of Australia, Attorney-General's Department, *Report of the Investigations of War Criminals in Australia*, 13 December 1993.

Crowley, F.K., *Modern Australia in Documents*, vol. 1, *1900–1939*, Melbourne: Wren, 1973.

Dapin, Mark, *Jewish ANZACS: Jews in the Australian Military*, Sydney: NewSouth Publishing, 2017.

Edwards, P.G., *Prime Ministers and Diplomats: The Making of Australian Foreign Policy 1901–1949*, Melbourne: Oxford University Press/Australian Institute of International Affairs, 1983.

Erbelding, Rebecca, *Rescue Board: The Untold Story of America's Efforts to Save the Jews of Europe*, New York: Doubleday, 2018.

Fitzpatrick, Georgina, Tim McCormack and Narrelle Morris (ed.), *Australia's War Crimes Trials 1945–51*, Leiden: Brill, 2016.

Fletcher, Frank, 'The Victorian Jewish Community, 1891–1901. Its Relationship with the Majority Gentile Society', *Australian Jewish Historical Society Journal and Proceedings*, 8:5, July 1978, pp. 221–71.

Fraser, David, *Daviborshch's Cart: Narrating the Holocaust in Australian War Crimes Trials*, Lincoln: University of Nebraska Press, 2010.

Gammage, Bill, *The Broken Years: Australian Soldiers in the Great War*, Ringwood (Victoria): Penguin Books, 1980.

Gettler, Leon, *An Unpromised Land*, South Fremantle (WA): Fremantle Arts Centre Press, 1993.

Gilbert, Martin, *Exile and Return: The Emergence of Jewish Statehood*, London: Weidenfeld and Nicolson, 1978.

Gilbert, Martin, *Auschwitz and the Allies*, London: Michael Joseph/Rainbird, 1981.

Gillman, Peter and Leni, *'Collar the Lot!' How Britain Interned and Expelled Its Wartime Refugees*, London: Quartet, 1980.

Gouttman, Rodney, 'First Principles: H.V. Evatt and the Jewish Homeland', in W.D. Rubinstein (ed.), *Jews in the Sixth Continent*, Sydney: Allen and Unwin, 1987, pp. 262–302.

Gouttman, Rodney, *In their Merit: Australian Jewry and WWI*, Melbourne: Xlibris Australia, 2015.

Hammerton, A. James and Alistair Thomson, *Ten Pound Poms: Australia's Invisible Migrants*, Manchester: Manchester University Press, 2005.

Holden, W. Sprague, *Australia Goes to Press*, Detroit: Wayne State University Press, 1961.

Jakubowicz, Andrew and Christina Ho (ed.), *'For those who've come across the seas … ' Australian Multicultural Theory, Policy and Practice*, North Melbourne (Victoria): Australian Scholarly Publishing, 2013.

Jupp, James, *From White Australia to Woomera: The Story of Australian Immigration*, Melbourne: Cambridge University Press, 2007.

Jobling, Ian, 'Australia at the 1936 Olympics: Issues and Attitudes', *Canadian Journal of History of Sport*, 13:1, May 1982, pp. 18–27.

Inglis, Ken, Seumas Spark and Jay Winter (ed.), *Dunera Lives: A Visual History*, Clayton (Victoria): Monash University Publishing, 2018.

Kinne, G., 'Nazi Stratagems and Their Effects on Germans in Australia up to 1945', *Royal Australian Historical Society Journal*, 66, June 1980, pp. 1–19.

Kohn, Rachael L.E., 'The Catholic and Anglican Church Press of New South Wales and the Jews, 1933–1945', in Paul R. Bartrop (ed.), *False Havens: The British Empire and the Holocaust*, Lanham (MD): University Press of America, 1995, pp. 159–85.

Kristianson, G.L., *The Politics of Patriotism: The Pressure Group Activities of the Returned Servicemen's League*, Canberra: Australian National University Press, 1966.

Kwiet, Konrad, '"Be patient and reasonable!" The Internment of German-Jewish Refugees in Australia', *Australian Journal of Politics and History*, 31:1, 1985, pp. 61–77.

Kwiet, Konrad, 'Die Integration Deutscher-Jüdischer Emigranten in Australien', in B. Bittner and J. Johe (ed.), *Das Unrechtsregime*, Hamburg: Christians, 1986, pp. 237–51.

Kwiet, Konrad, 'A Historian's View: The War Crimes Debate Down Under', *Dapim: Studies on the Holocaust*, 24:1, 2010, pp. 319–39.

Laqueur, Walter, *The Terrible Secret: Suppression of the Truth about Hitler's 'Final Solution'*, Harmondsworth (Middlesex): Penguin Books, pp. 223–8.

Lee, Godfrey S., 'Rescue or Rhetoric? Australian Jewry's Reactions during the Holocaust', *Journal of the Australian Jewish Historical Society*, X:4, November 1988, pp. 281–94.

Louis, L.J. and Ian Turner (ed.), *The Depression of the 1930s*, Melbourne: Cassell, 1968.

Lowenstein, Wendy, *Weevils in the Flour: An Oral Record of the 1930s Depression in Australia*, Melbourne: Scribe, 1981.

Lyng, Jens, *Non-Britishers in Australia: Influence on Population and Progress*, Melbourne: Macmillan/Melbourne University Press, 1927.

Machover, J.M., 'Towards Rescue – the Story of Australian Jewry's Stand for the Jewish Cause, 1940–1948', *Australian Jewish Historical Society Journal and Proceedings*, 7:1, 1971, pp. 1–61.

Markus, Andrew, 'Jewish Migration to Australia 1938–49', *Journal of Australian Studies*, 13, November 1983, pp. 18–31.

Bibliography

Markus, Andrew, *Australian Race Relations, 1788–1993*, St Leonards (NSW): Allen and Unwin Australia, 1994.

Marrus, Michael R., *The Unwanted: European Refugees in the Twentieth Century*, New York: Oxford University Press, 1985.

Matsdorf, Wolf Simon, 'A New Jerusalem in Australia – The Kimberley Plan', *Wiener Library Bulletin*, XXVII (new series, 30/31), 1973–1974, pp. 24–30.

Matthews, Tony, *Tragedy at Evian: How the World Allowed Hitler to Proceed with the Holocaust*, Newport (NSW): Big Sky Publishing, 2020.

Mayer, Henry, *The Press in Australia*, Melbourne: Lansdowne Press, 1964.

McKernan, Michael, *The Australian People and the Great War*, Melbourne: Nelson, 1980.

Medding, P.Y., *From Assimilation to Group Survival: A Political and Sociological Study of an Australian Jewish Community*, Melbourne: Cheshire, 1968.

Meyer, Winfried et al., *Geschlossene Grenzen: Die Internationale Flüchtlingskonferenz von Évian 1938*, Berlin: Zentrum für Antisemitismusforschung der Technischen Universität Berlin/ Gedenkstätte Deutscher Widerstand, 2018.

Miller, Barbara, *William Cooper, Gentle Warrior: Standing Up for Australian Aborigines and Persecuted Jews*, Bloomington: Xlibris, 2012.

Monteath, Peter, *Dear Dr. Janzow: Australia's Lutheran Churches and Refugees from Hitler's Germany*, Unley (SA): Australian Humanities Press, 2005.

Monteath, Peter, *P.O.W. Australian Prisoners of War in Hitler's Reich*, Sydney: Pan Macmillan, 2011.

Muirden, Bruce, *The Puzzled Patriots: The Story of the Australia First Movement*, Melbourne: Melbourne University Press, 1968.

Nasaw, Daniel, *The Last Million: Europe's Displaced Persons from World War to Cold War*, New York: Penguin Press, 2020.

Neumann, Klaus, *Across the Seas: Australia's Response to Refugees, a History*, Melbourne: Black Inc., 2015.

O'Donnell, Peggy, '"Gateway to Hell": A Nazi Mass Grave, Forensic Scientists, and an Australian War Crimes Trial', *Holocaust and Genocide Studies*, 32:3, Winter 2018, pp. 361–83.

Palfreeman, A.C., *The Administration of the White Australia Policy*, Melbourne: Melbourne University Press, 1967.

Palmer, Glen, *Reluctant Refuge: Unaccompanied Refugee and Evacuee Children in Australia, 1933–45*, East Roseville (NSW): Kangaroo Press, 1997.

Patkin, Benzion, *The Dunera Internees*, Sydney: Cassell, 1979.

Pearl, Cyril, *The Dunera Scandal: Deported by Mistake*, Sydney: Angus and Robertson, 1983.

Price, Charles A., *Jewish Settlers in Australia*, Canberra: Australian National University Press, 1964.

Rothwell, Nicholas, 'Bringing Nazis to Justice: The Menzies Report', *Quadrant*, 31:3, March 1987, pp. 21–5.

Rubinstein, Hilary L., 'Manifestations of Literary and Cultural Anti-Semitism in Australia, 1856–1946', *Melbourne Chronicle*, October-November 1983, pp. 2–4; February-March 1984, pp. 2–4.

Rubinstein, Hilary L., 'Australian Jewish Reactions to Russian Jewish Distress, 1891–1913', *Australian Jewish Historical Society Journal and Proceedings*, 9:6, 1984, pp. 444–56.

Rubinstein, Hilary L., 'Critchley Parker (1911–42): Australian Martyr for Jewish Refugees', *Journal of the Australian Jewish Historical Society*, XI:1, November 1990, pp. 56–68.

Rubinstein, Hilary L., *The Jews in Australia: A Thematic History*, vol. 1, *1788–1945*, Melbourne: William Heinemann Australia, 1991.

Rubinstein, W.D. (ed.), *Jews in the Sixth Continent*, Sydney: Allen and Unwin, 1987.

Rubinstein, W.D., 'Australia and the Refugee Jews of Europe 1933–1954: A Dissenting View', *Journal of the Australian Jewish Historical Society*, X:6, May 1989, pp. 500–23.

Rubinstein, W.D., Paul R. Bartrop and Suzanne D. Rutland, 'The Future of Australian Jewish Historiography: A Panel Discussion', *Menorah: Australian Journal of Jewish Studies*, 3:1, July 1989, pp 29–42.

Rutland, Suzanne D., *Edge of the Diaspora: Two Centuries of Jewish Settlement in Australia*, Sydney: Collins Australia, 1988.

Rutland, Suzanne D., 'Australia and Refugee Migration, 1933–1945: Consensus or Conflict', *Menorah: Australian Journal of Jewish Studies*, 2:2, December 1988, pp. 77–91.

Rutland, Suzanne D., '"Are you Jewish?" Postwar Jewish Immigration to Australia, 1945–1954', *Australian Journal of Jewish Studies*, V:2, 1991, pp. 35–58.

Shephard, Ben, *The Long Road Home: The Aftermath of the Second World War*, New York: Alfred A. Knopf, 2011.

Silberberg, Sue, *A Networked Community: Jewish Melbourne in the Nineteenth Century*, Melbourne: Melbourne University Publishing, 2020.

Stedman, S., 'Dr. Steinberg in Australia', *Australian Jewish Historical Society Journal and Proceedings*, 5:4, 1961, pp. 170–86.

Steinberg, J., [Isaac N. Steinberg], 'A Jewish Settlement in the Kimberleys', *Australian Quarterly*, 12:1, March 1940, pp. 24–30.

Steinberg, Isaac N., *Australia – the Unpromised Land: In Search of a Home*, London: Victor Gollancz, 1948.

Stirling, Alfred, *Lord Bruce: The London Years*, Melbourne: Hawthorn, 1974.

Stokes, H.J.W., 'The 1987 Eldershaw Memorial Lecture: Diplomats and War Criminals: Some Experiences of an Historian in the Service of the Commonwealth Government', *Tasmanian Historical Research Association Papers and Proceedings*, 35:1, March 1988, pp. 16–18.

Tavan, Gwenda, *The Long, Slow Death of White Australia*, Melbourne: Scribe, 2005.

Waters, Christopher, *Australia and Appeasement: Imperial Foreign Policy and the Origins of World War II*, London: I.B. Tauris, 2012.

Wilson, Sandra, Robert Cribb, Beatrice Trefalt and Dean Aszkielowicz, *Japanese War Criminals: The Politics of Justice after the Second World War*, New York: Columbia University Press, 2017.

Wilton, Janis and Richard Bosworth, 'Refugee Intellectuals of the 1930s', *Australia 1938*, 4, November 1981, pp. 31–9.

Wilton, Janis and Richard Bosworth, *Old Worlds and New Australia: The Post-War Migrant Experience*, Ringwood (Victoria): Penguin Books, 1984.

Writer, Larry, *Dangerous Games: Australia at the 1936 Nazi Olympics*, Sydney: Allen and Unwin, 2015.

Wyman, Mark, *DPs: Europe's Displaced Persons, 1945–51*, Ithaca: Cornell University Press, 1998.

Zuroff, Ephraim, *Operation Last Chance: One Man's Quest to Bring Nazi Criminals to Justice*, New York: St Martin's Press, 2009.

INDEX

Index

Index